The Intimate State

Critical Asian Studies

Series Editor: **Veena Das**

Kreiger-Eisenhower Professor in Anthropology, Johns Hopkins University

Critical Asian Studies is devoted to in depth studies of emergent social and cultural phenomena in the countries of the region. While recognising the important ways in which the specific and often violent histories of the nation-state have influenced the social formations in this region, the books in this series also examine the processes of translation, exchange, boundary crossings in the linked identities and histories of the countries of the region. The authors in this series engage with social theory through ethnographically grounded research and archival work.

Also in this Series

Living with Violence: The Anthropology of Events and Everyday Life
Roma Chatterji and Deepak Mehta
ISBN 978-0-415-43080-7

Enchantments of Modernity: Empire, Nation, Globalization
(Ed.) Saurabh Dube
ISBN 978-0-415-44552-8

The Intimate State

Love-Marriage and the Law in Delhi

Perveez Mody

Routledge
Taylor & Francis Group

LONDON AND NEW YORK

First published 2008 by Routledge

2 Park Square, Milton Park, Abingdon, Oxfordshire OX14 4RN
52 Vanderbilt Avenue, New York, NY 10017

Routledge is an imprint of the Taylor & Francis Group, an informa business

First issued in paperback 2019

Transferred to Digital Printing 2008

Typeset by
Star Compugraphics Private Limited
5-CSC, First Floor, Near City Apartments
Vasundhara Enclave
Delhi 110 096

British Library Cataloguing-in-Publication Data
A catalogue record of this book is available from the British Library

ISBN 978-0-415-44604-4 (hbk)
ISBN 978-0-367-17620-4 (pbk)

For my mother Ruby Mody
1944 – 1994

Contents

Note on Translation and Transliteration

1. Photograph of a pop-up card '*Love Tuzhe Main Karta Hoon*', ('I love you') purchased from a street vendor, Batla House, New Delhi. Such cards are available in the run-up to '*New Years*' (1st of January) and are used by young people to initiate their romances. By kind permission of Mr Ravinder Gupta, Times Cards, Chawri Bazaar.

In this book I have chosen to omit diacritical marks and transliterate Hindi or Urdu words after the simplified conventions of contemporary Indian-English. I use italics within quotations to indicate *transcription* of English words in spoken Hindustani, not translation from Hindi or Hindustani into English. Quotations that are not italicised are translations. (The only exception to this is transcription from archival documents in Chapter 1). This is one indication of the class or background of those I worked with because the language is represented as it is spoken. In Indian anthropology in general this issue of representing class is often overlooked and the use of English in speech is often misinterpreted as a sign of being 'westernised', which carries the pernicious implication that actors may be summarily dismissed as 'inauthentic Indians'. In fact, the use of English in Hindustani speech is often perfectly natural and is occasionally to add class aspirations or '*ishtyle*' (style). A small minority of my informants spoke with me only in English but the vast majority of my fieldwork was conducted in Hindi and Urdu. However, almost all my informants had attended some schooling (even in the *bustis* or shanties where I worked, it was an aberration if all the children didn't go to school)—and used some English in their conversation. English words are increasingly incorporated into the vernacular, so their usage is quite natural and unselfconscious. Thus, people often described a court as a *'court'* (not a *'kachery'*), a love-marriage as a *'love-marriage'* (not a *'prem-vivaha'*, or *'marzi ki shadi'*) and so on.

List of Photographs, Table and Figure

Photographs

Table

Figure

Acknowledgements

This book would not have been possible without the generous support of my Junior Research Fellowship at King's College, Cambridge. Through the years I have also benefited enormously from the support of scholarships from Trinity College, Cambridge, the prize of the Senior Rouse Ball Studentship, the Smuts Memorial Fund, the Dr Audrey Richards Fund, and the Cary Robertson Fund, all of which I gratefully acknowledge.

I must first thank all the love-marriage couples (who remain unnamed throughout this work) and the many people I spoke to and worked with in Delhi, who showed enormous trust in sharing their experiences and socially and emotionally intense and complicated lives with me. Most of all, I want to thank the person known throughout this book as 'Kamiyar', and Jyoti Verma for engaging with my work and extending me their friendship. They assisted this book in more ways than I could ever acknowledge.

Thanks are most especially due to James Laidlaw, who has been a truly extraordinary guide and friend, without whom this work would never have been possible. Susan Bayly threw herself into the fray with great gusto and successfully managed to steer me into the blue yonder where Indian history meets social anthropology. Thanks also to Barbara Bodenhorn for starting me off on one leg of this journey, and to Atlantic College, and Andy Kumalo, for starting me off on another.

On the ticket of sharing an interest in old and new forms of marriage in India, Jonathan Parry has allowed me to address endless anthropological questions to him. His patience and generosity have left their mark. I am also grateful to Veena Das whose work and writing inspires great respect, and without whose encouragement and drive this book would possibly still remain unfinished.

I am also indebted to the indefatigable Firdaus Ali, Reehana Raza, Ali Dayan Hasan, Silvy Pallit, Ali Cheema and Magnus Marsden, all of whom have in different times and places shared friendships that have inspired and entertained in equal measure.

In Delhi, I wish to thank my dear friend, the historian Umesh Jha, who came to my rescue as my research colleague in the final months of my work in the district court. I am grateful to him for having been such an excellent associate. Without his tremendous satirical wit and encouragement, my work in the court would have been trying indeed.

I was incredibly fortunate to have been able to conduct interviews with a whole group of love-marriage academic couples based in the various academic institutions around the city such as Delhi University, Jamia Millia Islamia University and Jawaharlal Nehru University. While I have chosen not to focus upon these interviews in this book, I nonetheless acknowledge my enormous gratitude to those who spoke with me about their personal and professional experiences and who lent me their time.

I also wish to especially thank Asha Lata, Kalindi Deshpande, Brinda Karat and all the women I worked with at *Janwadi Mahilla Samiti*, and AIDWA (the All Indian Democratic Women's Association), especially those at Dr Ambedkar Nagar, who encouraged and supported this research and allowed me to participate freely in their activities. Their legal aid cells allowed me a superb opportunity to come to grips with the many intimate aspects of domestic life in Delhi, as well as offering me a small opportunity to participate in the mediation of disputes.

Our stay in Delhi was made comfortable through the warmth with which Daman, Puja, Bobby and Varsha Bedi made us a second-floor appendage to their family. I am grateful to them and to Farrukh Dhondy and Danyal for sharing with us the delights of Old Delhi and particularly Karim's restaurant.

Permission from Cambridge University Press to use two published articles (Mody 2002; 2006) is gratefully acknowledged. I am also grateful to the following for copyright permissions:

Mr Ravinder Gupta of Times Cards, Chawri Bazaar, Old Delhi for the image of the greeting card '*Love Tuzhe Main Karta Hoon*'; The Times Group (*Times of India*), for permission to reproduce Arul Raj's cartoon 'To Cap-It-All' and Mr Maheshwari of Rajkamal Prakashan for permission to reproduce Alok Dhanva's poem '*Bhagi Huin Larkiyan*' from his book *Duniya Roz Banti Hai* (1998, Rajkamal Prakashan, Delhi). Thanks also to Esha Béteille, Nilanjan Sarkar and Pallavi Narayan at Routledge for the patience and care involved in the production of this book.

The gratitude that one wishes to express most expansively, to those who mean the most to us is clearly the toughest to articulate.

My family — Dady, Firoza, Jehangir, Jimmy and Mary, Jennie, and also Rob and Chrystalleni — have all helped keep this particular show on the road with their love and support.

To Ben, my thanks are of the most profound kind and they find expression in the sentiment that inspires and underlies this work. I dedicate this book to the memory of my mother Ruby, whose loss, even after all these years, is still hard to countenance.

Finally, to my little monkeys, R and Z, who seem to spend all their time trying to convince me that I could be doing many more exciting things than trying to write this book.

Foreword

It is a pleasure to present Perveez Mody's book on love marriages in Delhi, which contributes greatly to our understanding of how law, publicity and kinship/community norms in north India shape the lives of individuals in relation to what she calls 'not-communities'. The anthropological literature on the topic of love and desire and its intersection with law is growing, and this carefully researched study opens up new ways of thinking on these issues in the context of India. Its argument has much to say on the processes through which emotions of love and intimacy get shaped by ideas of liberal citizenship and also how, at the same time, emerging ideas of intimacy puncture given notions of community and the promises of citizenship. The concept of 'not-community' signals for Mody two specific conditions of the individual as revealed through the lens of love marriages: first that the individual, as a bearer of desire, is defined in law as if *subtracted* from the community rather than one who, as in the famous mushroom analogy of Hobbes, has sprung directly from the earth. The second way in which she uses the idea of 'not-community' is to allude to the fact that emergent publics come into being through the very act of a (defiant) love marriage—sometimes these publics are virtual (as in those who consume these news through newspaper accounts or television reporting) but there are other conditions under which they begin to function as actual communities.

One description of the subject matter of this book, then, is that of the relation between domesticity and publicity, since the contested nature of these marriages brings them into the domain of the public. Anthropological and literary work has previously highlighted forms of desire that are outside the normative structures of marriage, either contained through clandestine but tolerated relations or legitimised through compromises of various sorts. For instance, the distinction between primary marriage and secondary marriage allowed a variety of sexual and conjugal arrangements to be recognised while also demonstrating the adherence to caste-based norms of what are ritually 'correct' marriages. Mody's work brings out the points of rupture in the colonial period as in colonial legislative acts like the Special Marriage Act of 1872 (and subsequent revisions) which embodied all the contradictions of a promised liberal citizenship in that it provided legal protection for the individual's autonomous choices in relations of intimacy and yet constrained these choices by various other qualifications, especially relating to membership of religious communities. The relation between State and the domesticity continues to be a fraught one in India (as elsewhere)—Mody shows how laws underlying liberal citizenship continue to frame issues of intimacy and love even as the concepts of liberal citizenship are continuously punctured by them.

The second strand of the argument in the book worth thinking about is the constitution of publics, publicity and media on the question of love marriages. Agnes Heller, whose understanding of biopolitics is rather different from that of Giorgio Agamben, has reflected deeply on the issue of what kind of cultural politics are experienced as 'political' in a given context. In her diagnosis of the ills of American society is the present condition in which social questions are never properly politicised. Thus, she points out that while it is hard to mobilise the publics on the crisis of health insurance, 'sex scandals' can mobilise the press, television, universities and practically everyone. I suggest that underlying this fascination with sexual conduct in the United States is the notion that one's sexuality somehow represents the truth of one's being. In contrast, it seems to me that the newspaper reporting on love marriages and especially the violent aftermath that many couples face, draw upon a different range of affects. Most of the stories reported in the press and analysed in the book take up the failure of the State to provide protection to young couples. Interestingly, though, the relations of the loving couple are themselves mediated by these stories for they affect the manner in which they plan to confront the inevitable backlash they expect from relatives and also to find strategies to get legal protection against them. Even media and publicity become resources for some couples to create certain bonds with members of 'not-community'.

A striking aspect of the present book is that instead of using blanket concepts like 'modernity', Mody comes to these processes by tracking specific events such as the passing of the Special Marriages Act or using the case method to see how to render the emergence of novelty. Her careful rendering of what is new— given that the idea of love outside marriage or recognition of various kinds of conjugal arrangements was part of the socially accepted scenarios of male–female relations—is a contribution to anthropological method and theory. For example, Mody shows how ideas of conjugal compatibility travel between arranged marriage and self-arranged/love marriages—so that there is traffic of ideas between tradition and modernity in defining conjugality. Similarly, her demonstration of how kin-making as a practice is anchored upon certain ideas of caste and community even for those who are 'not-community' is specific in its questions about what would constitute the success or failure of a practice. She does not suffocate these subtle differences by covering them with the overarching blanket concepts of tradition or modernity.

There is no doubt that the very processes that made these marriages visible—the fact that they have come to the researcher's attention either in the space of the courtroom or through the media attention—accounts for the special characteristics of these marriages. The conflictual relations of these couples with their natal families, the allegations and counter-allegations of rape and abduction with which the husband is often charged, the failure of the law to offer protection to the couple is specific to those cases in which the family does not accept the marriage. Other kinds of arrangements of 'practical kinship' might work in cases in which the family opts to stand by the couple.

The experimentations with norms of kinship taking place in everyday life are beginning to be documented by other studies. Yet it is important to realise that the anxieties brought to the fore by these love marriages say something important about the relation between State and domesticity, citizenship and intimacy in the contemporary urban society in India. Some scholars have argued that what is at stake is a form of biological citizenship; others have argued that sexualisation of the social contract is at the heart of issues of the relation between law and domestic and/or sexual regulation.

I hope that *The Intimate State* will become part of the vibrant debates on the nature of law, regulation, familial norms and formation of desire in Indian urban society.

Veena Das
Krieger–Eisenhower
Professor of Anthropology
Johns Hopkins University

Preface

In the winter of 1998, Kamiyar,[1] a 24-year-old man from Kanpur, climbed a microwave tower outside New Delhi railway station for the second time in three months. His self-declared goal was to go on an indefinite hunger-strike and he demanded that the President of India intervene on his behalf and help him recover his wife from her family. He remained on a narrow ledge two-thirds of the way up the 210-foot tower and communicated to the press via a mobile phone and hand-written letters that he threw down or lowered on lengths of string. He could not have found a more central point in the city—the tower, located midway between Old and New Delhi, was clearly visible to the naked eye from most of the city's major landmarks, including Connaught Place, Rashtrapathi Bhawan, the Red Fort, and the crowded tenements and bazaars of Old Delhi. Thousands of people gathered below the tower in the freezing temperature of Delhi's coldest winter for the past thirty years; some to keep vigil, and others to be entertained by the media circus, the police presence and the filmy *'love-story'* unfolding before their eyes. Dialogues from one of the most popular Hindi films of all time—*Sholay*, a 'curry-western'—were jokingly enacted, with wolf-whistles and taunts to him to jump. *Sholay* had a similar scene in which the drunken hero climbed a water tower in the village square and demanded that despite his palpable ineligibility, he be allowed to marry the object of his desire, a village belle named Basanti. Inevitably, Kamiyar was cast by some in the mould of an attention-seeking madman, who was demanding the return of his 'Basanti', without whom he would not descend.[2] Kamiyar, however, fought back by steadfastly refusing food and by attending to the call of the *muezzin* from the nearby Jamma Masjid; saying *namaz* on the tiny metal ledge in the sky. These simple acts stirred both admiration and fear. As one woman in the crowd challenged another: 'How can you call him mad? Does a madman pray to God?' Others were horrified by the *'bad example'* Kamiyar was setting for the younger generation: "Even those who are trying to walk on the straight road will be led astray', a reference to the temptations of love which may lead them away from arranged marriages. Another day-tripper argued: 'If you say he isn't mad, and comes

from a good family; then why has he climbed a tower? Does he not
know better than to disgrace his family in this way. God, have pity
on his parents. Imagine what they are living through!' The crowd
was seething with speculation, condemnation and the occasional
adulation for this latter-day hero.[3] One boy from Delhi University
tried to hustle a crowd to march to the President's residence, and
block the phone lines by protests against the lack of government
support to Kamiyar and his wife.[4] Others came to the tower merely
to 'time-pass', and to see the *tamasha* (entertainment). A surprising
number of people came to unburden their own tragic love-stories
in solidarity with Kamiyar at the bottom of the tower.[5] The press,
Hindi and English, carried his story on their front pages during the
entire saga, and the *Times of India* claimed that they were receiving
an unprecedented fifty-odd telephone calls everyday from members
of a concerned public who enquired after the boy's well being.[6]
Additionally, Doordarshan and the satellite channel's Star TV News
carried daily updates from the tower in their national broadcasts.
In the meanwhile, senior Delhi police officials, embarrassed by the
repeated security breach on a tower so vital to 'National Security'
(the microwave tower apparently controlled railway traffic signals
for tracks across northern I ndia), and irritated by the 'madman',
repeatedly refused to do anything other than wait for Kamiyar to
jump (or die on the tower itself): '… at least that way he would
achieve something by becoming a martyr'.[7] For his part Kamiyar,
wrote prolific long letters in English to the President of India, the
Supreme Court and the media assembled below.

This is a transcript of one of his letters:

[Date witheld]

Dear Sir,

*I would like to tell the reason of climbing this tower for the second
time. The first time did was* [date witheld].

*Me and Priya (my wife) were in love since 1993. Unlike in the
cares of love we are the inspiration for survival for each other. She
is respectable to me after my Mummy. She gave me reason to live.
Anyway we married on the 4 Nov. 97 and I let her go back to her*

parental house and I tried my best to make reason our parents and family but failed. It was an effort which was a five years period. I think enough time to make reason God for any purpose. When I saw nothing is going to happen I called finally PRIYA on 18 Nov. 97 morning 8.00 and we went to Akbarpur to my uncle place.

The family of PRIYA came to know about our stay through someone and with 24 hours they make such a terror on my family at Kanpur that they have handed over my marriage papers as well as [marriage] photographs. They forcefully took my PRIYA my life away from me. They warned me not to take any legal action.

After 4 days of this acident [accident] I ran towards Delhi in search for help and for this I went to Hon'ble President, Primeminster, and somany else but it was no matter for any one 12 or 14 lives does'nt count for them and [date] event took place of climbing tower for first time. This helped us to make safe upto some extent. My brothers open their readymade shop and Daddy start going to [work], kids to their school. But I got shocked terribly when Hon'ble Supreme Court of [India] didn't accept my reit [writ] petition of Habeus Corpus and it was a shock not less than lossing [losing] PRIYA forever.

Anyway time was passing and I was going door to door for help and a little support of someone makes me able to walk. But when somehow on [date] I dialed .... [telephone number] the phone of my in laws and PRIYA was on line I can't tell you in words the exact condition of that time but [both] of us were soundly cry we talk for 30min. at least in between 5.00 p.m.–5.30 p.m. It stir my soul I was confused what to do. To snatch out her forcefully or to go court once again or what to do because she was very afraid, seem no hope I decided to seek help from Hon'ble President of India to order concerning authorities to bring back my wife PRIYA once again. It is really sad that no one has even come from President House to ask even that you are on [in Hindi] Aamaran Anshan [fast-unto-death] (86 hours so far) what sort of help you want from Mr. President.[8]

I just want that Mr President recommend my case to reconsider to Supreme Court or to accept Allahabad High Court (Habeus Corpus) and till my wife come to spot I stay here dead or alive.

One more thing Mr Mulayam Singh Yadav [leader of the ruling
Samajwadi Party in Uttar Pradesh] *can help me in a big way as
well. He can solve my problem in no time.*

[signed] *Kamiyar*

Kamiyar was convinced to descend from the tower, not through
the intervention of the President, the police, or Mulayam Singh
Yadav, but rather through the good offices of the National Human
Rights Commission (or NHRC). As a Muslim who had married a
Hindu, Kamiyar trusted the NHRC and believed that they would
be impartial to his case and would indeed help him and his wife.
He was promised their assistance but it was soon evident that it
was not forthcoming. I got to know Kamiyar when he descended
from the tower after six days in near-freezing temperatures, and
much of my time in the next few months was spent with him.
Unfortunately, however, Kamiyar and Priya were unable to see
each other again. Both have had arranged-marriages, and Kamiyar
(whose subsequent life I have been able to follow) has moved to
another city and has built a new life with the loving support of his
kin and his wife and child.

Notes

1. In keeping with anthropological convention, all proper nouns except
   those of figures holding public office have been changed. Additionally,
   some details such as dates and place names have been changed or withheld as these would compromise the confidentiality of those I worked
   with. Exceptions to this are names and details that appear in the print
   press, especially of cases I have not worked with. This is because I am
   referring to information already in the public domain, and am not
   providing any new information with details reported as they appear.
2. The press in particular played on the film metaphor with newspapers
   adapting dialogues from films like *Sholay* as headlines, and with Star
   TV News actually juxtaposing a clip from the film with news footage
   from the tower. For instance, the *Pioneer*, 'Gaon walon, President ko
   Bulao', ('People of the Village, Call the President') (date withheld), New
   Delhi; or *Vanita*, '1998: A Love Story' (an allusion to the hit film '1942:
   A Love Story'), by Meena Pandey (date withheld), New Delhi.

3. Of all the unusual rumours that went around the crowd at the tower was the intriguing one that Kamiyar had on his person one-and-a-half lakh (million) rupees. Clearly, the fact that he had a mobile phone and wrote his letters in English played an enormous role in the perception on the ground that he was a 'handsome, high-class' man, of a 'good' family, whose unusual circumstance lent itself more to a film plot than a domestic saga.

4. In fact, on the day of his descent, I heard that some students from the University had indeed mobilised support for a vigil at the tower.

5. Some of these I was able to follow up and interview at greater length, and they appear in the text of this book.

6. Personal communication from the *Times of India* crime reporter, New Delhi Crime Desk.

7. Off-the-record interviews with police officers of various ranks belonging to the area under whose jurisdiction fell the microwave tower. However, similar statements were also made to the press. For instance, see *Navbharat Times*, 'Badi Be-dil Ho Gayi Hain Dilwalo ki Dilli' (date withheld), New Delhi.

8. Incidentally, the then President Mr K.R. Narayanan's Press Secretary told the Press: 'It is a personal drama of an individual. The President is aware of it. But we are not likely to intervene.' In the *Pioneer*, 'For Kamiyar, There's No High Life Without Wife' (date withheld), New Delhi.

2. Kamiyar spent six days and seven nights on this tower protesting against the abduction of his Hindu wife by her family. In this photo, he is barely discernible (in the foreground of the platform just above the middle of the photograph) lying down, sheltering from the freezing winds.

3. Gathering crowds on day 3 of Kamiyar's vigil. The large number of people that came to the tower caused the Delhi police to allege that the media was encouraging Kamiyar and triggering 'communal tensions'.

4. The dangerous descent on day 6 to the cheering of the thousands of people gathered at the base of the tower.

5. In the *Times of India*, Delhi Times, New Delhi. Reproduced courtesy the *Times of India*, Delhi.

Introduction

'Yeh hamari bahu nahin   'She is not our daughter-in-law
   Tumhari gunah hai'   She is your sin!'

from the film *Pakeezah* (1971), Director, Kamal Amrohi

Anthropological work on India has been predominantly community-specific. By this I mean that the point of departure is more often than not a particular caste or a particular community, often the classic community of the Indian village. Looking in particular at the study of family and kinship and the work done on marriages, some trends can be identified. Firstly, the study of marriage forms has been largely confined to the study of particular castes or ethno-religious 'communities' and the ways in which their rituals and ceremonies fit into their larger cosmologies (for instance Dumont 1998; Fruzzetti 1982; Srinivas 1952). Secondly, and in relation to this work, many anthropologists have encountered the practice of intermarriage between castes and 'communities' (Béteille 1997: 150–77; Dube 1996; Dumont 1998: 126–29; Fruzzetti 1982: xxii–iii; Fuller 1992: 14). Invariably some mention is made of the fact that a study of such marriages could reveal important dynamics of social change; but the task of actually researching such marriages has been left relatively untouched.[1] One salient point emerges from this: that the lens through which so-called *'love-marriages'*[2] are viewed is always that of the *community as monolith* which marks as renegades those who have violated its boundaries. Hence the subjective, lived experience of being marginal or even excommunicated from one's caste or community is never addressed. Instead we find that the widespread prominence of the dominant view that such marriages are necessarily illegitimate, unusual and the westernised practice of an urban deracinated elite, has led anthropologists to ignore the potential for ethnography of changing marital forms. As Susan Bayly (1999: 54) has pointed out, the marital aspect of caste has been a key concept in twentieth century anthropology. By defining the marriage bond as an index of caste status ('who will take one's kin as brides or grooms'), and 'caste' in turn as an overarching principle of Indian social relations, the post-Dumontian ethnographic record has been reluctant even to register the modern phenomenon of love-marriages, or what Singh and Uberoi coin as 'self-arranged' marriages (1994: 101). This book attempts to correct this imbalance by demonstrating the importance of such marriages for our understanding of changing marriage forms, kinship structures, gender relations, and communal and caste politics in urban India.

One strategy of apprehending this phenomenon without having to go through networks of family and kin who were disapproving of such marriages was to do a non-community-specific ethnography of love-marriage couples in Delhi. These formed a disparate constituency, a *not-community* that nonetheless exists, mainly in urban and semi-urban settings, and who, by their mere existence, exert a powerful influence on the imagination of modern India by seemingly subverting the essentialised ideas about 'Indian marriage', 'Indian wives', and 'Indian love'.[3] So, for instance, one of the many auto-rickshaw drivers I interviewed described the perils of such a relationship: 'A slap would evince anger from the woman'. The implication is that women who had love-marriages would dare to consider themselves equal, or would express offence if the husband tried to impress his will upon her. Another argued that, abroad, love meant *'open sex'*, whereas in India, '... at least we have *purdah'*. Then, as if to contradict himself, he added as an afterthought: '... but these days it is difficult to concentrate on the road. Sometimes my clients turn my three-wheeler [auto-rickshaw] into their bedroom'. His reference to the amorous embraces he has seen in his rear-view mirror shows that not *all* Indians are willing to hide their love behind *purdah*.

In this book, then, I seek to study love-marriages in the first instance through the *creation* of a *not-community* of people who are so defined by their assertion of 'choice' in marriage: 'not-community' because love-marriage couples neither did nor do constitute a community in the conventional sense of the word. By using this neologism, I hope to draw attention to their unique relationship with the social groups they are often forced to leave. They are deemed not to belong because of their transgressions, and yet, their identity is firmly that with which they are born.[4] I use the word 'creation' for two reasons: firstly because these couples form a constituency only as a result of their being a category that people talk about and identify. They rarely identify themselves with other couples who have married under similar circumstances, and do not take pride in or even necessarily admit to this identity. Rather, they seek to merge into the urban milieu and disguise their 'difference' through affected sameness (such as, say, a change of one or the other spouse's name if their names are indicative of different castes or ethno-religious communities). Secondly, it is not just their lives after marriage that I try to understand, but also the process of rupture and of reconfiguration. The gradual or dramatic events that lead to the marriage and the often inevitable 'excommunication'—out of community and into 'not-community'—allow us to explore the transformations effected through the aegis of the state, politicised communities and the agency of the loving-couple.

In *Critical Events* (1995), Veena Das makes the argument that theories which define communities as based on the notion of face-to-face interaction tend to romanticise communities as enabling spaces that serve to resist the homogenising pressures of modernity and the excesses and intrusions of the state. She challenges this definition with the observation that a community can 'colonize the life-world of the individual' in the same way in which the state 'colonizes the life-world of the community' (1995: 15). This leads her to redefine communities-as-political-actors by their 'rights to define a collective past', to 'regulate the body and sexuality through the codification of custom', and the ability to 'make consubstantial acts of violence and acts of moral solidarity' (ibid.). The individual, then, is provided with a collective existence (for instance, lineage/clan/caste/ethno-religious community) that makes available collective traditions through which to make sense of the world. Das's contribution is to write into this definition the threats to 'selfhood' that such communities can pose, making selfhood conditional upon an individual's ability to 'break through these traditions and live on their limits' (ibid.: 17). It is this reworked definition of 'community' (most commonly configured in Delhi as castes, ethno-religious or linguistic groups) that I use in this book. It refers to the *politicised* groups that provide the individual with a collective existence while simultaneously regulating the lives of their constituent members and thus defining the limits of their selfhood.

By using the term not-community I am trying to explore the limits of both community and the 'selfhood' of individual members of communities. Not-community (for the purposes of this study) is defined by the criteria of choice in love-marriages. For the majority of couples, this state of 'undoing' (not-ness) is but a brief interlude before they manage to be re-socialised into their communities and families. In this majority of cases, communities-as-political-actors prove themselves capable of extending their limits by making themselves heterogeneous and complex. This does not mean that they *redefine* their identities as either heterogeneous or complex, but that they see themselves as able and willing to absorb outsiders into their fold, and so transform them by varying degrees into 'insiders'. For others, the limits of community have already been tested and found to have been inflexible. Under such circumstances, freedom from the stranglehold of the community becomes the prerequisite of choice. It is in instances such as these, when freedom is obstructed and norms enforced, that we sometimes see couples paying the price as victims of grisly violence. In Das's words, this is when communities make '"consubstantial" acts of violence with acts of moral solidarity'.

We might pause to consider two possible problems with this formulation by asking firstly, to what extent the violence directed at love-marriage couples is purely the outcome of corporate or community action and to what extent the state participates or bears silent witness to such acts of violence? The second question is related and asks why some cases of violent death or even murder of one or the other of a love-marriage couple shortly after their wedding gets recorded as 'suicide'? I will do this by looking briefly at the patterns that emerge from two cases reported in the media, one that I know first hand and the other that has received nationwide coverage in the Indian press.

The only case of a love-marriage death that I did encounter during my fieldwork in Delhi was the alleged outcome of violence directed by the family of the in-laws, in mysterious circumstances (it seemed to be a case of poisoning by the in-laws) and in a domestic setting with no outside witnesses. The death happened soon after the wedding at a temple in the city. The girl's parents had vehemently opposed the marriage, and had called the boy over to their house in a surprising gesture of reconciliation. A short while later he was found outside their house vomiting and barely conscious. The lack of any investigation by the local police into the circumstances behind the death and the unsubstantiated insistence of the police that it was a suicide led the victim's family to argue that there was police connivance in protecting the perpetrators of their son's murder. Furthermore, the temple priest who solemnised the wedding was approached by the girl's family and urged to destroy the record of the marriage in their register, thus making it harder for the boy's family to even prove that the wedding had taken place and that there was a clear motive for the murder. Many people I spoke to in the locality where the girl lived commented upon the case by pointing out that the girl's family were jewellers and had wealth and resources that would keep inconvenient investigations at bay.

Another instance of a death in suspicious circumstances is the death of one Rizwanur Rahman on the 21 September 2007, the details of which have been all over the Indian news. Rizwanur, a Muslim graphic designer and teacher who grew up in a slum in Calcutta married the incredibly wealthy Priyanka, a Hindu and the daughter of the owners of a corporate powerhouse in India. The inter-community love-marriage was solemnised in court under the Special Marriages Act, an indication that neither party intended to convert to the religion of the other. It has been reported in the press that despite their legally sanctioned court marriage, and an appeal to various police officers (in writing) for protection due to harassment from Priyanka's family, they were summoned thrice to the local police station and Priyanka pressured to return home with the threat that if she didn't, the police allegedly said that they would arrest Rizwanur for abduction and theft. When she finally relented and returned home she was apparently discouraged from returning to her husband. Rizwanur approached a Human Right's organisation: The Association for Protection of Democratic Rights, for help to get his wife back. A few minutes after he phoned them, his dead body was found on the railway tracks and the Calcutta police (prior to a post-mortem) declared that he had committed suicide.

In a subsequent press conference, it is reported that the Chief of the Calcutta police justified the family's opposition to their daughter's marriage as 'natural' and wondered about the desirability of marriages in which there were disparities of financial background and social status. The Chairperson of the Scheduled caste/Scheduled Tribe Commission in Uttar Pradesh said ruefully in the context of this case: 'For inter-caste and religious love affairs to crystallise into marriage and then for the couple to survive, they require three M's: Money, Muscle Power and Man Power'. The case has provoked public outrage in the Leftist state of West

Bengal and the Calcutta High Court has directed the Central
Bureau of Investigation to probe the allegations of apparent police
involvement in Rizwanur's death.[5]

It has been reported in the press that Rizwanur and Priyanka
sent written letters to many of the top police officers in the state
to alert them to the fact that they feared for their lives after their
marriage, and it is reported that they alleged that if either of them
was to be killed then the finger of blame should point to Priyanka's
father.[6] However, the Chief of Police's comments in the press conference can be seen to be part of a pattern: the police rely upon the
widespread dislike of love-marriages, especially those between
Hindus and Muslim's. By declaring this to be a case of suicide
and by focussing on the 'natural' objections of the girl's father, the
public is left with the popular image of love-marriage couples as
no-hope renegades who would rather kill themselves than face up
to the social consequences of their actions. In this way, justice can be
deferred and the media soon move on to whatever is the next big
story. In many instances, the real perpetrators of outrages against
love-marriage couples often get away scot-free, and the death gets
counted as yet another 'suicide'.

While the violence that meets such marriages is something that
Delhi has become inured to, the savagery of some of the attempted
murders of love-marriage couples is truly shocking and most of
them never make it to the press. One such instance took place in the
early 1990s when a woman from Madangiri, a working-class area
in Delhi, resisted her family's attempt to arrange her marriage and,
when she was forced into it, managed to escape from her in-laws'
home with her lover. The two of them were caught by her family
on the outskirts of the city. The boy was let off with a severe beating
but the family tried to kill the girl. Her skull was split open with a
sharp implement and chilly powder was poured into her wounds.
Miraculously, she survived after medical attention and managed
to escape yet again with her lover. Because of the extreme violence
she had been subjected to, some of the city's women's groups were
able to warn the family against any further reprisals.[7] The couple
now live incognito in the city. There were a number of similar cases
reported in the press during my research in Delhi, in which women
were either raped or the couple killed for their transgressions.[8]
As a theoretical device then, the notion of not-community serves

to delineate a hypothetical social space of moral ambivalence. It is the testing ground of the limits of community. Will the couple be obstructed in their attempt to marry? Will they be pursued by the police and their families? Will the parents and families force a capitulation and welcome them back into the fold?

The Metropolitan View of Marriage[9]

In north India, marriage amongst Hindus is seen as a religious union. Among Muslims it is viewed as a contract. In both cases, however, the gift of a virgin girl[10] is made by her parents to the family of a boy with whom they have engaged to arrange a marriage. For all communities, it is a celebrated and emphatically public event and the occasion for lengthy ceremonies and lavish presentations. A proper marriage is often described as a *'band-baja shadi'*, i.e. a marriage with a band playing, or a *'dhoom-dham ki shadi'* (*'dhoom-dham'* being the loud celebratory noises of drums). The act of drumming is ethnographically significant as it puts an unambiguously public face to the event. Thus marriage is an occasion wherein religious ritual (in the case of Hindus) and community celebration (in the case of Hindus and Muslims) sanctify and acknowledge the relationship of the boy and girl as man and wife.[11] Marriage, then, is not concerned with whether or not the couple are 'in love'—in fact, in the case of Hindus it is geared around the assumption that ideally the girl and the boy are strangers to each other and that it is their obligation to their parents that makes them sometimes reluctant, though consenting, parties to the marriage. For Muslims, where marriage can be between close kin such as first cousins, the kinship proximity does not translate into social familiarity, and the boy and girl nonetheless behave as strangers on the day of the marriage. Hence, the construction of the relationship between love and marriage is that love should never precede marriage; but equally, marriage does not preclude the possibility of a loving and intimate relationship. In the words of a Brahman I spoke to in my public interviews:

> Love is a gift from God, gifted to two people on the day of their marriage. Love isn't something that one does, that is lust. Love is given, only by God.[12]

An arranged-marriage is rhetorically described as a religious ritual, sanctified and validated by kin and community and blessed by God with the gift of love from that day onwards.[13] Love between husband and wife is expected to grow as the relationship develops, and it is predicated on the notion of devotion, both to God and to each other. In practice, this is arguably much more asymmetrical, with the wife assigned the task of devoting herself to God and to her husband who must (in the case of Hindus) be worshipped as if he were her God.

Love-marriages, on the other hand, are widely viewed as a most unholy union. They challenge 'natural' (that which *kudrath* or nature has created) caste hierarchy and social considerations of class, status and standing. Based on *vasna*, lust, and far from being social events, they are considered to be anti-social and *kharab*, bad. Simply put, arranged-marriages are seen to consolidate the community through what Dumont describes as 'endo-recruiting' (1998: 112). Love-marriages represent the exact opposite—the deconstruction of the group or community through the two-fold rebellion of (*a*) choosing one's own spouse and thus exercising autonomy (i.e. ignoring the obligation to marry the person of your parent's selection), and/or (*b*) contravening the strict caste and community injunctions against out-marriage. The fact is that one of the most important defining features of caste (for Hindus and Muslims[14]) is the obligation to marry within the group (Dumont 1998: 109; Fuller 1992: 14); and for this reason alone, love-marriages do involve a substantial departure from the norm.

One could argue that the narratives and characters of popular Hindi films also consist of a 'metropolitan' view, in that these representations provide an important sounding board from which people can both draw inspiration and sustenance or model their moral opinions and condemnation. Whilst I am clear that my love-marriage informants were eager to distance themselves from the films they often described as trivial and *bakwas* ('rubbish'), I am also certain that popular Hindi films do much to traverse an imaginative terrain that many viewers find entertaining, exciting and challenging. By stomping away in this celluloid dreamscape, popular films greatly enlarge the realm of the possible, and since love-marriages are largely characterised as inhabiting precisely this world of possibility and personal fulfillment, it is difficult to ignore the influence of Hindi movies upon the dreams and aspirations of ordinary people. Whilst a study of love in Hindi movies is beyond the scope of this work, we will see the uncanny way in which real and reel life seem to get an echo off each other. What we will see in this study of everyday love-marriages is how the tribulations and triumphs of couples in Delhi seem to often bear the insignia of cinematic drama. This can be most clearly demonstrated in the case of Kamiyar on the microwave tower and the numerous discussions in the crowds below that we were witnessing the first performance of a true Hindi movie star in the making. His attempt to convince his wife's kin that they should release her ultimately failed, and ironically, the publicity of his tower episode, while keeping him safe from harm, also made it impossible in the long-run for reconciliation with his wife's kin.

As will be seen in Chapters 3 and 4 of this book, love-marriages have particularly salient implications for the ways in which people view the making of kin. This is because arranged-marriages are perceived as marriages between families who ritualise their affinal bonds and recognise each other as honour-bound partners in an exchange, while love-marriages are seen to thrust an unnatural and disorderly 'kinship' on *incomparable* groups.[15] Instead of acknowledging their newly shared kinship, such forced affinity means that groups must delicately negotiate their relationships despite possible antagonisms over their differences. The mother of Lata, a Brahman school girl who eloped with her low-caste Harijan *'tuition-master'* Gopal, consistently refused to call him by his name, and instead used the rather cumbersome title of 'The-One-Who-Has-Made-Himself-My-Son-in-Law'.[16] In using this rhetoric, she alerted everyone to the fact that for her, kin are made through properly arranged marriages by elders—not through the actions of one's own under-age daughter. The implications are clear—the act of making kin can only be done by 'adults' who legitimately represent the family. Kin-making is not something open to individual acts of agency (other than the agency of individual elders acting as representatives of the group), even if these derive from a legally sanctioned court-marriage. However, in saying this I do not wish to imply that this is a foregone conclusion, or that I am assuming answers to the anthropological questions of what qualifies one to be an 'adult' and to 'legitimately represent the family'. Chapters 3 and 4 explore the issue of love-marriage agency by examining the making *and* breaking of kin. This is found to be an integral part of the love-marriage enterprise, which explains something of the power and threat that such individuals can exercise despite the corporate might of their kinship groups. Referring to actual cases of 'out-casteing' amongst his informants in Bhilai, Parry has put it rather vividly: 'The caste panchayat may huff and puff, but can no longer blow down houses' (2001: 805).

However, we must be clear that the making and breaking of kin, threatening and dangerous as it is, is an inadvertent effect of love-marriages. Many of the couples I worked with reserved their enthusiasm to talk of their marital bond rather than their newly made affinal relations. This is partly because they themselves recognise that kin-making is a two-way process that must be reciprocated, and that the affinal relations they have made are often openly scornful of their creative enterprise. This is what animates my discussion of the historical background and the current context of laws that support love-marriage, because in looking at the enabling and transforming effect of the state and its laws and practices, we see how law becomes integrated into social relations. There is also an undercurrent of resistance encountered when newly-made relatives insist that they cannot just be 'made', but that the process of *making* with appropriate kinship authority is what is really at stake. In this way, we can think about the intimacies of the law with society, of the new possibilities for protection the law offers members of not-community, and of the difficulties encountered in the processes of making kin.

The couples I worked with in this book all make use of the law in ways that they themselves describe as more strategic and deliberate than their contemporaries having more conventional marriages. This book is about those intimate relations that are visible to an ethnographer because of the particular circumstances that cause them to call upon the law. In turn, it is not about forms of romance that might develop and be either circumscribed through clandestine but tolerated relations, or those that may be legitimised by compromises of various sorts. What we need to note here are the ways in which the law (I use this in the widest sense of the word to mean the legislation, as well as the practice and constellation of ideas surrounding love-marriages, court-marriages, and what constitutes a conjugal bond) has had a significant effect on enlarging the sphere of legitimacy for certain relationships, with the outcome that most of my informants would take great pains to emphasise the legal validity of their conjugality and the substantial nature of their relationship rather than digressing to talk about the alleged social illegitimacy of their union; a subject that often evinced painful memories.[17] For instance, many of my female informants told me that they had been willing to flout social norms and incur the almost certain wrath of their families by embarking upon a socially inappropriate love-relationship, because they felt utterly confident that the relationship would end in a legal and binding marriage and that the husband would never abandon them.

For an ever-increasing number of my informants, the greater emphasis on intimacy within marriage is accompanied by another important preoccupation—what Parry has described in his work as the 'indissolubility of their relationship' (2001: 817).[18] Here, Parry refers to the greater emphasis amongst some of his informants on the stability of marriage and the primary marital bond. I would like to argue that for my love-marriage couples this also holds true, but what is interesting is that they are also heavily preoccupied (for good reason) with the indissolubility of the *pre-marital* romantic relationship. This is because their actions of taking an interest in each other can, upon discovery, create mayhem and bring on retribution. It becomes a matter of some importance then, to gauge whether the risks are worth taking and whether both parties feel equally up to the challenge. This often means that a typical love-trajectory would look something like this: the first signs of romantic interest, exchange of information and flirtatious encounter are usually followed by quite serious, almost business-like discussions and negotiations between the couple about what they expect, and where they think the relationship would end up, with vows that the love being exposed is *sacha* (true) and for keeps (i.e. culminating in marriage). In Delhi, such meetings would often happen in the everyday unromantic settings of bus-stops, canteens, bazaars and temples so that no suspicions would be aroused by a sighting in such public places. However, for many of my female informants who were strictly chaperoned or who were too scared to meet in person, these love-relations flourished via discretely transacted notes, signed cards and letters, or more commonly, by 'PCO'[19] or telephone and increasingly, through mobile phones. So, we can see a two-fold shift in the values of young people: on the one hand, they are willing to embark upon romantic trysts and relations of intimacy, but this is accompanied by an equal determination to see their 'first love' culminate in marriage. People described their early courtship conversations in Hindi: *'Ek bar tu ne meri hath pakad li, tho kabhi chhodna nahin!'* (Once you have held my hand, you must never let it go!) or, *'Ek ke sath pyar kiya, tho usi ke sath shadi'* (If you start to love someone, then you must marry them). This sort of love, which is a once-in-a-lifetime experience, and which closely follows ideas about female sexuality being given to just one man, sets up truly 'Indian' love as that which culminates in a marriage to the object of their desire.[20] It is important, then, to see how the research of this book weighs heavily in the direction of forms of intimacy that seek out legitimation through conjugality and marriage in one way or another. In doing so, we can see how young men and especially women minimise the risks to their reputations by insisting that romance is only permissible if it is to be followed by legitimate marriage.

Since love-marriages are defined by the criteria of personal choice, it could be argued that arranged-marriages are about *'social'* choice.[21] That is to say, in the words of my informants, if love-marriages are about individual compatibility, arranged-marriages are about *'social* compatibility'. This does not mean that the two categories are mutually exclusive. In fact, many love-marriage couples I worked with sought to defend their choice in terms of *'social'* rather than individual compatibility, that is, that their choice was for the good of society or the group. For instance, one man defended his choice by saying that he 'selected' his wife because she was a 'traditional Indian girl' and would consequently respect his mother in his joint family. Another Hindu–Muslim couple subverted the discourse about Hinduism and Islam being antithetical to each other by arguing that they were actually having a *'same-caste'* marriage. The boy's Muslim caste ('Khan') was argued to be equivalent to the girl's Hindu caste ('Thakur') as both castes were 'originally Rajputs'. Similarly, and much more commonly, equivalences of education or wealth (in terms of class) were cited as making love-marriage couples eminently 'socially compatible'. The increasing use of more 'secular' criteria to define and inscribe homogamy ('culture', class, education, career prospects, 'thinking') for love-marriages implies their importance in urban life in India today, but equally points to the continued ambivalence towards love as a basis for marriage. These attempts to confer some of the legitimacy associated with arranged-marriages on love-marriages must be seen as an important indication of the ways in which couples in Delhi are negotiating spaces for marriages of choice. However, as we shall see later in the book, representing and transforming personal choice into 'social choice' is both an important driving force, and a problematic contradiction in the personhood of love-marriage individuals.

Equally, it is a sign of the times that families arranging marriages are increasingly careful to select not just 'socially', but also temperamentally suitable spouses. Sometimes these could consist of brutally honest assessments: such as a matrimonial advertisement on behalf of an 'impotent' man seeking a woman who wasn't interested in sex. In most cases, however, equivalence of educational qualifications, 'looks', wealth, job and 'cultured', 'traditional', 'modern' or even 'cosmopolitan' background are viewed as sufficient indicators of temperamental compatibility. Other than the commonplace preoccupation with matching horoscopes and skin-colour, 'individual compatibility' in an arranged marriage also takes into consideration the aesthetics of how a couple (*jodi*) would look side-by-side. So, short women are considered suitable only for short men, and a fat woman would be loath to marry a skinny man.[22] The appearance of the couple had to be pleasing, not awkward or disjunctive. We must note that this is in sharp distinction to the repeated rhetoric (amongst anthropologists and informants alike) that love-marriages are based on emotion and 'physical attraction' and that arranged-marriages are based on bio-moral considerations guided by historically stable kinship. As we can see, there are similar aesthetic judgements at play; the difference being whose judgement (the young lover or the experienced elder) is considered a valid basis to initiate a marriage.

Further, in cities like Delhi, the emphasis in arranged-marriages on social compatibility does not preclude the offspring from taking an active role (often by veto, but equally by subtle direction)[23] in the parent's selection of the spouse. Increasingly, amongst both the rich and the poor, couples are made to meet, and the process of selection and approval is arguably much more open-ended than the stereotypes about 'arranged marriages' make them out to be. For instance, while it is virtually a truism that in primary arranged marriages 'husbands expect to get virgins' (Parry 2001: 797), women in Indian cities are also increasingly asserting the need for sexual equivalence. Responding in a recent survey by an English language magazine, 60 per cent of the respondents in Delhi said that they too would like their husbands to be sexually celibate before marriage.[24] It is also clear that increasingly, upwardly mobile young people in cities are *choosing* to have arranged-marriages because they believe that in the fast-paced urban world in which divorce is becoming increasingly commonplace, the idealised arranged-marriage can create stable social relations and ensure the continuity of ritual practices, kinship and gender hierarchies, religious traditions, culinary styles and moral values to the next generation.

However, we note that it isn't just the issue of compatibility (individual or *social*) that distinguishes love-marriages from those arranged by the families. The exercising of choice in a love-marriage sometimes can be enough reason to cause outrage in the family, even if that choice happens to be the person with whom one's parents sought to arrange a marriage. Amit,[25] a Bihari student at Delhi University fell in love with the girl his parents had always urged him to agree to marry. After a few years of corresponding with each other, they decided to get married and confidently told their parents. To Amit's surprise, while his girlfriend's parents were happy with their decision, his own parents were categorically opposed to the marriage, despite the girl having hitherto been the perfect match for their son. The reasons were that the revelation of the affair and the disclosure that the son had 'chosen' the girl for himself undermined the very nature of an arranged marriage. A boy who brings into his joint family a woman for whom he openly declares 'love'[26] upsets the hierarchy of mother-in-law over daughter-in-law, and would be seen to prioritise conjugal relations over more enduring kinship bonds. As Raheja points out, a common north Indian proverb warns that:

> Whoever kicks … his mother and father to strengthen his relationship with his wife
>
> His sins will not go away even if he wanders through all the pilgrimage places … (1994: 121).

Even when the spouse is perfectly compatible in social terms, as was the case for Amit and his wife, the declaration of 'love' between the conjugal couple is seen to upset the ties of duty and obligation that govern the extended family.[27]

As an adjunct to Amit's marital dilemma, a brief note is called for on the categories of 'love' and 'arranged' marriages. It should be clear by this point that I am using these two categories in the definitive *and* ambiguous ways that came to qualify their use by my informants, thus leaving it up to the analysis of the ethnography to detail their specific and complex configurations. So for instance in Chapter 3 of this book I introduce the notion of *'love-cum-arranged'* marriages where the initial choice of the loving couple is suitably domesticated by one or both their parents through an 'arranged-marriage'.[28] Sometimes this is done so as to erase or negate the love that is seen as shameful; in other instances the families arrange the ceremonies socially and publicly so as to endorse the choice of their offspring. Amit's situation in which arrangement gave way to love, which again gave way to grudging arrangement, amply illustrates the fact that 'love' and 'arranged' aren't the polar opposites that they are usually made out to be, but are really best seen as part of a continuum (Prinjha 1999).

Reflections on Marriage Forms and 'Indian' Intimacies

The marriage phenomena I go on to describe in this book have ancient and recognisable cultural antecedents with marked similarities between the utterly modern phenomena and categories and archetypical stories derived from a shared 'Indian' cultural repertoire. Indeed, far from being esoteric or specialist knowledge, many of my informants in the district court and members of the public such as rickshaw drivers would mention these forms of marriage to signal just how ancient is the whole phenomenon of self-arrangement[29] (in one form or another) in the Indian context. The fact that these concepts had fairly common currency amongst my informants did not mean that these informants were conferring upon modern love-unions any legitimacy. Indeed, love-marriage couples were alert to these ambivalences and were keen to rebuff any attempt to link their actions to such archaic pre-modern social forms.

However, due to the widespread references to such ancient categories of marriage, and because we can use them to get an echo off current marriage practices, it seems worthwhile to briefly describe four such marriage forms found in the *Dharmasastras*.[30] These texts recognise but notably withhold approval[31] of marriages described as: marriage by capture (*raksasa vivaha*), marriage by persuasion (*paisaca*) and two forms of elopement (*svayamvara* and *gandharva*). Marriage by capture consists in the forcible abduction of an unwilling woman whose relatives put up a valiant defence.[32] In marriage by persuasion the woman is tricked by the man and forced into marriage after having been ravished in her sleep or while intoxicated. In the third type of marriage a woman selects her husband in an open assembly after an exhibition of skill and strength from a crowd of eligible contenders. In the *Mahabharata*, the great hero Arjuna wins the hand of Draupadi in such a union, and so does Ram with Sita in the *Ramayana*.[33] Finally, the *Kamasutra* provides ample descriptions of the last form of marriage: the *gandharva* rite is described as the result of the mutual attraction between a man and a woman without the prior sanction of the respective families. The woman is enticed with gifts and lured into a marriage that the man himself performs before a sacred fire. The families are then informed of the marriage and asked to give the daughter away more formally in a socially sanctioned *kanya daan*. The importance of the two categories of marriage in the *Dharmasastras* (*dharmiya* and *adharmiya*) are that marriage is seen as an 'instrument for the pursuance of higher goals in life [*dharma*], rather than as a means for personal gratification' (Basu 2001: 24), and this is the defining feature as to whether a marriage is classed in the first *dharmiya* (approved) or *adharmiya* (disapproved) category.

While conjugal love in marriage ('*rati*') was recognised in the *shastras*, it was considered less important than duty (*dharma*) and the production of progeny (*praja*).[34] Furthermore, in traditions such as Vaishnava devotional practice (and also in *Shakta tantra*), there is a recognition of the importance of desire as essential to certain kinds of devotion but not as a means of making marriage—at least not worldly marriage.[35] So, the relationship between Radha and Krishna (interestingly, an inter-caste romance[36]) that through the ages has been viewed either as erotic or as truly mystical, is never consumated in marriage as that would corrupt and transform their egalitarian love.

There are many other instances where Hindu textual sources describe forms of coupling for the procreation of children, and social practices that differentiate between various kinds of permissible sexual and conjugal unions. One such practice known as *Niyoga*, consisted of a widow or a woman whose husband was incapable of giving her a child being allowed to have sex with a man (or a widower) out of the desire for *praja* or progeny. In poetic conventions, for example, there are three sorts of woman described: the courtesan (*'veshya'*), the wife (*'svakiya'*) and the 'other woman' (*'parakiya'*). In this last category, we have two types: the unmarried nubile young girl (*'kanyaka'*) or the married woman (*'parodha'*). So, for instance, Kakar and Ross (1995) quote a Sanskrit courtly poem extolling the subtly different joys of sexual encounters with a loose woman, 'the deep shyness of one's own wife', but best of all...

> [...] who in this world can
> fill one with joy
> like another man's wife
> loving with naked breast (Kakar and Ross 1995: 94).[37]

In modern-day Delhi, cheap Hindi self-help manuals that are sold everywhere on the footpaths, bus-stands and railway stations have detailed descriptions of the transgressive sexual peccadilloes of Indian men and women, all under the serious pretext of providing intimate descriptions and details to help solve complex emotional and sexual dilemmas. Anyone who reads one of these would be in no doubt that the loud protestations of public morality that Delhi's denizens are keen to make are like similar protests anywhere, too loud to ring true. Vanita and Kidwai cite various ancient, medieval and modern sources and literary texts depicting same-sex love to show how, over time and geographical space, heterosexual marital arrangements have not necessarily precluded extra-marital love and sex with someone of the same gender (2001).[38]

The ethnographic evidence about non-Hindu marriages that none the less bear a resemblance to the *Dharmashastra* categories is relevant here. In the first instance, it is clear that the *gandharva* mode most closely resembles the stereotype of self-arranged 'love-marriage' in Delhi. While the bulk of anthropological writing largely ignores inter-caste and inter-religious love-marriage, there is some evidence that features of self-selection as a motive for marriage and romantic love are more prevalent in *adivasi* (tribal) India. Marriages bearing a resemblance to these broad categories (for instance, 'thieving or capture' marriage (known as *'dongatanam'*) amongst the Koya in central India, *paitu* marriages amongst the Bison Horn Maria)[39] are prevalent, but nonetheless described as non-ideal both within these societies (undoubtedly due to the extensive nature of the process known as *Sanskritisation*[40]) and from without. Non-ideal, however, is not the same as subject to interdiction, and in Koya ideology 'abduction and elopement have always been acceptable, even valued, as the expression of strong-willed individuals, men and women alike, who do what they wish' (Brukman 1974: 308). Brukman also makes the point that 'collusion at some level is practically a requirement in cases of abduction',[41] a phenomenon I will explore in some depth in Chapter 3.

Within the wider context of mainstream non-*adivasi* society, however, these a-typical marriages become a feature of such groups' lower ritual (and consequently, lower cultural) status in caste-Hindu eyes (Brukman 1974). However, we must be cautious about overly simplifying or generalising matters as there is a vast heterogeneity of marital arrangements amongst (and even within) different *adivasi* groups, as indeed there is in caste-society, where there are ideal, high-status, high-stakes marriages and others which involve considerably more personal choice while being recognised as non-ideal, and particularly suited to those who have little political influence or status to lose.

Even a cursory look at the ethnographic evidence on forms of marriage amongst *adivasis* points to a complex situation when it comes to identifying what constitutes a 'marriage'. Vitebsky describes the Sora of Orissa and Andhra Pradesh by noting that most people had several affairs before they settled down and raised a family:

> Setting up house together is recognised as a declaration of intended permanency but in the early years there are many breakups. Most marriages originate in this free-choice way. *Dari* [affairs/love-marriage] marriage is not marked by any ceremony and need involve no dowry and bride-price. But the desire of a girl's parents or brothers to interfere or hold onto her can be intense, especially if the family is wealthy. This tendency is compounded by the simultaneous availability of a pattern of arranged marriage (*pang-sal*, 'taking wine'), involving bride-price and favoured by the better-off. There is no word meaning 'marriage' as such, covering both these ways in which a man and a woman may come to live together (1993: 48).

Furthermore, what might appear on the surface to be a social system that encourages premarital romantic and sexual liaisons (for instance, Verrier Elwin's famous description of the Muria *ghotul* or dormitory, 1948) may subsequently be shown to function as the 'antithesis of marriage', with sleeping relationships (*jor*) often being between people who are classificatory siblings and thus prohibited from marriage altogether (S. Man Singh Gell 1993). From all this we must take away the rejoinder that while romantic love, abduction and elopement are a far more obvious feature of *adivasi* life, they coexist with more formal marriages which are most commonly associated with alliances based on kinship arrangements. Consequently, there is no necessary linear progression of romantic liaisons leading to more permanent marriages of choice.

Indeed, Parry makes this point forcefully in his comprehensive work on sex, marriage and industry amongst Satnamis in Chhatisgarh, Madhya Pradesh (2001), where he shows that *primary* marriages are in effect often 'forced' and are the outcome of pressures to marry appropriate spouses, while secondary marriages are much more likely to involve significant elements of freedom in terms of the choice of partner, and are more than likely to cross caste boundaries.[42] For instance, in his work in the periphery of Bhilai Township (the erstwhile villages of Girvi and Patripar), he found 116 inter-caste marriages, of which a stupendous 90 per cent were secondary marriages. As a proportion of all current marriages (and including in his count all wives, sisters and daughters who married outside the caste and now resided elsewhere), he found that 10 to 15 per cent of all households had present or previous members who had had an inter-caste marriage of choice (2001: 803). In sum, he shows very convincingly that the coercions of affinity fall unequally upon primary and secondary unions, a reminder of the need to qualify the scope of this work. In this book all the couples I worked with were having (or had already had) a primary love-marriage, which explains to some extent why we see the idiom of affinity and kinship so forcefully dramatised.

The ground covered in this book by no means exhausts the range of forms of self-arranged marriage with political significance in contemporary India. Thadani (1996) in her work on lesbian desire in India draws attention to attempts by women to marry each other, which, as we shall see in Chapter 2 of this book, are strikingly reminiscent of Delhi's heterosexual love-marriage couples' thwarted attempts to bend the will of the state in their favour. In one instance, two girlfriends in a small town called Chandrapur in Maharashtra tried to obtain consent from their parents and, failing in their attempts, presented themselves before the civil marriage Registrar who, along with the Police Superintendent, managed to 'dissuade' the women from solemnising their marriage (ibid.: 109). A similar incident of a love-marriage between Shumail Raj and Shehzina Tariq who fled from Faisalabad to Lahore in Pakistan to seek legal protection of their marriage has attracted intense media attention. In this case, the judge of the Lahore High Court accused them instead of perjuring themselves when they sought protection, on the grounds that Shumail Raj, the transgender husband (who, it emerged, had undergone two surgeries to change his sex), had claimed to the court to be a man.[43] Thus, heterosexual and homosexual couples that seek to legitimise their relationships in marriage may face similar forms of opposition and dissuasion, both being viewed as essentially 'unnatural' and beyond the boundaries (*maryada*) of morally acceptable behaviour.

The numerous 'Party Marriages' I heard of in Delhi were equally difficult to research once I had begun my fieldwork looking at more mundane love-marriages, because they involved a very different network of people in Delhi. In these unions, members of the Communist Party of India (especially amongst the youth members of the Student Federation of India) solemnised their marriages through declarations taken in the presence of their Party leaders and comrades: a means of unifying and consolidating the personal with the political, while simultaneously rejecting the 'patriarchy' and 'oppression' of the bourgeois state. Such marriages, based largely on political ideology, are found in other parts of India too. In the central Bihar plains, Gandhian socialists of the Chhattra Yuva Sangharsh Vahini (established in 1978) have been performing inter-caste love-marriages amongst their activists as a response to Jayaprakash Narayan's call for 'total revolution'.[44] In Gaya district, activists of the radical Maoist Communist Centre (MCC) and of the Communist Party of India, Marxist—Leninist Liberation front ('CPI-ML Liberation') conduct 'mass marriages', which are often marriages of choice, amongst their supporters in the eminent grace of a duly erected photograph of Mao, whose aura, no doubt, is meant to bear witness to the absence of even the slightest whiff of dowry. I was told that further afield, ULFA (the United Liberation Front of Assam, a secessionist group in the troubled north-east of India) also recognised same-sex marriages within their ranks.[45] Such radical positions on marriage reflect the enormous differences in what may be called the 'gender geography' and social politics in modern India. While these examples may be so few and far between as to be largely irrelevant, they nonetheless indicate the extent to which marriage in India continues to be an arena of intense political and social contestation. Indeed, one could safely conclude that the way one marries is usually 'read' (I would argue, misleadingly) by other people as a good indication of one's politics—and it is this symbolically and politically overlaid arena of marriage that anthropology needs to re-examine. Put another way, the paradigm of the 'marital dimension of caste' (Bayly 1999: 54) should perhaps give way to new models that can better apprehend the political significance of marriage in the India of today. The material that I present in this book is different precisely because most of the informants I cite do *not* see themselves as making a political 'point' in their marriage. The political significance of what they do isn't the same as their conscious intention and it is this that makes them even more interesting to a study of marriage, politicised community and individuality in India today.

Abduction Politics:
Gender and Inter-community Relations

In a recent workshop,[46] Uma Chakravarti pointed out that the largest number of *Habeas Corpus* petitions in the courts in Delhi are not about state or police custody but rather concern the retrieval of women from domestic settings.[47] These consist of parent's filing cases to aid retrieval of their off-spring who may have married against their wishes, or the man of a love-marriage couple—(the process of retrieval is quite gendered)—filing a *Habeas Corpus* petition to retrieve his legally constituted wife from the custody of her parents. This has led Chakravarti to argue that we should be thinking about matters of 'sexual governance', so that, as with current debates about custodial killings, we might contemplate the ways in which women are held hostage and killed in their homes by their own kin. For Chakravarti, the question of marriage is a deeply political issue and the heart of it is 'sexual governance'. Thus rhetoric about appropriate forms of marriage (or about preventing inappropriate, 'immoral' unions) strengthens the discourse about appropriate forms of kinship, community and state governance and control over the young, over their morality and most especially, over women and the female body. As I will show in the concluding part of this section, for a Hindu zealot like Babu Bajrangi, the nation of his imagination can only be kept pure by guarding the purity of the female Hindu body. It is in this context, and keeping in mind what Chakravarti describes as 'sexual governance' that I would introduce the concept of an abduction discourse that is key to the creation of a particularly problematic imagining of the Indian nation.

What follows is a brief analysis of Sita's abduction as it appears in narratives about her righteousness and about wifely devotion. This important archetypal narrative forms the thematic ground to a survey of abduction between 1901 and 2007 as described in three academic works: Viswanathan's *Outside the Fold* (1998), Gupta's article '(Im)possible Love and Sexual Pleasure in Late-Colonial North India' (2002) and Menon and Bhasin's *Borders and Boundaries: Women in India's Partition* (1998). Lastly I examine a contemporary embodiment of the notion of 'sexual governance' informed by the abduction narrative in the person of Babu Bajrangi, a Hindu nationalist extremist. It is an eclectic selection of ethnographic evidence and as such, it certainly isn't a comprehensive review of either a historical period, a people or even an existing subject of enquiry. It is an ethnographic observation of public discourses of abduction—if you will, a brief history of abduction as fact or as rhetoric or as a resonance in the mind of north India's collective consciousness. In marshalling disparate sets of evidence and drawing them together to delineate the contours of a wider 'abduction narrative' we can see how the reportage of love and marriage functions to engender the 'sexual governance' of the Indian state as well as animating the controls extended by kinship groups and families upon individuals and couples. In this account, I will argue that love-marriages appear to explode the certainties of Indian kinship and abduction narratives reveal that the construction of a monolithic idea of an authentic 'Indian marriage' (i.e. 'arranged marriage'), far from being a mere ethnographic nicety is in fact a fiercely political construct with significant legal and moral effects.

Such constructions, ostensibly in the domain of family and kinship, are central to the reproduction of ideas about the modern, virile and globally successful Indian nation and serve to justify an even greater vigilance by the state, communities and families towards 'sexual governance'.

In assessing how everyday kidnap or abduction stories in the press 'play' to an Indian audience we should recognise that the most widely recognised abduction story in north India is that of the wife of the Hindu God-king and 'ideal man' Ram, whose wife Sita is captured by the evil Ravan and taken against her wishes to Lanka. The ancient and venerated Ramayan contains the story about the violent abduction of a married woman. However, despite Sita being the epitome of wifely devotion and chastity, her fate after abduction is by all accounts tragic. She is the ideal wife, chaste and true to her Ram, but when she is reunited with him he spurns her because of the taint of having been abducted and held hostage under another man's roof and thus open to the suspicion of infidelity and inappropriate union. Even though Sita agrees to and successfully undergoes a test of trial-by-fire ('agni pariksha'), Ram is unswerving in his resolve that she is impure and, despite her being pregnant, he refuses to take her back.[48] Crudely speaking then, the meta-narrative of abduction in this tradition is that of the male's attempt to safeguard female sexuality from the lust and aggression of non-kin and inappropriate males—an attempt that fails because Sita is already sullied by association with Ravan.

The *Ramayana* is not just any mythological story, but a particularly immediate narrative[49] that is annually re-enacted and recited for a whole month in virtually every village, town and city across most of north India at *Dusshera*.[50] It is watched and participated in by men, women and children in a cultural context in which Ram and Sita are widely believed to be 'real' personalities in history, as well as being potent forces in the here and now of domestic ritual worship. It contains important models for husband-wife relations,[51] as well as ideas about the ideal nation. For instance, *Ramrajya*—the reign of Ram—is used to describe a utopian state associated with abundance of wealth and justice, and is frequently evoked by Hindu religious nationalists as their ultimate goal for the modern Indian nation.[52] While much academic attention has focused on the ways in which Ram rejects Sita after her rescue (described appropriately by feminist writers as the 'raw deal' meted out to Sita by Ram consisting of her trial by fire, her abandonment, and her banishment to the forest to raise her children alone),[53] the abduction of Sita has received less attention. I would like to propose that just as the idealised Sita is central to understanding the cultural norms that adhere to north Indian women's aspirations, morality and ethics, it is her abduction that gets used as a reminder of women's inherent vulnerability.[54] While Sita herself is a figure of wifely devotion, her abduction compromises Ram, so that it becomes a dramatisation of an idiom: that of hurting the male community and nation through the forcible abduction of chaste and good women. As we shall see later, it is no small coincidence that as Hindu publicists in the early part of the twentieth century reinstated Ram as the principal god of the Hindu nation, they have simultaneously focused their energies on identifying the 'abduction of Hindu girls' by 'foreign' men (in this construct, Muslims) as a significant mobilising platform for their political activism.

Gauri Viswanathan's book *Outside the Fold* (1998) examines the juncture between religious conversions, the law, communities and the state. It is a historical account of conversion, and in it Viswanathan draws attention to a remarkable source of inadvertent documentation concerning love-marriages: in the 1901 census of East and North Bengal, the principal 'Cause of Conversion' documented by the returning officers is *not* proselytising, or religious revelation but rather is listed in the census records as the outcome of romantic love between Hindus and Muslims. Furthermore, the returning officers who were bound to declare their own religious affiliation[55] were inclined if Hindu, to characterise the conversion as forcible (using words such as 'enticed', 'paramour' and 'elope', thus coding 'love' as 'seduction'), and if Muslim, to describe it as precipitated by 'love', and 'embracing the religion of Muhammad' of his or her 'own accord', thus coding it as an act of self-will (1998: 167–68). Equally interesting are the results recorded by British officials who tread a careful line between the two positions of love and conversion by viewing the latter through the lens of caste, and describing the conversions as the result of the excommunication of the Hindu partner by the caste rather than the result of either force, or unfettered choice or agency (the conversion thus happens because the love-relationship causes them to be outcaste). Already we can see how love-marriages are represented to the public in bureaucratic census records and the ways in which the identities of colonial or Indian officials leave a hefty footprint upon the interpretations they supplied to provide exegesis on individual cases of love-marriages.

If we compare this work with Charu Gupta's (2002) essay that examines the rhetoric and activities of Hindi language publicists in the 1920s and 1930s in the Hindi heartland of the then United Provinces (now Uttar Pradesh), we see an even greater polarisation of accounts of female agency through the work of Hindu religious nationalists who, interestingly, use the new media of the newspapers to publicise their dramatic encounters with the law and the legal machinery of the colonial state. Gupta describes the orthodox Arya Samaj's[56] call for Hindus to capture Muslim women 'for *shuddhi*' (or re-conversion).[57] Elsewhere, she tells us of a 1923 speech delivered by the President of the Hindu Mahasabha[58] at Banaras who described the abduction of Hindu girls (for marriage) not just by Muslim '*badmashes*' (rogues) and '*goondas*' (thugs), but also by Muslims of standing and significance; so for instance, a campaign was launched in 1924 in the Hindi press and in public meetings to smear a Muslim Deputy Collector of Kanpur for having married a Hindu girl and allegedly, 'forcibly converting' her to Islam (2002: 208–209).

Gupta's work allows us to see a demonstrable shift from the innocuous census data where love-marriages appear to remain the property of the individuals (and the reporting state) to a situation where such marriages are immediately the subject of politics and activism. She traces the development of a full-blown polemic about the abduction of women, conducted in community halls full of caste and community members, and witnessed and reported by the vernacular press that begins to sit in judgement on these stories and allegations, and finally, acted upon in some instances that lead to violence. The private love-choices of couples no longer remained the domain of local gossip; by 1923 such instances were grist to the Hindu nationalist mill and came to constitute the full-blown political rhetoric of 'abduction-campaigns' (Gupta 2002: 209) that formulated action plans to condemn Muslims who married Hindus and demanded the 'recovery' of the Hindu woman. For instance, the setting up of a Hindu group called the 'Mahabir Dal' (Group of the Brave) to prevent Muslims from allegedly kidnapping Hindu women in the United Provinces was explained by Hindu publicists in the following manner: 'It has its own attractions as it reminds one of Hanuman and the way he aided in Sita's release who was abducted by Ravan. Same way [sic] we have to aid in the release of our women from the present day abductors' (2002: 211).[59] Such emotive descriptions of events took local, domestic love-affairs and turned them into metaphors (if not direct motivation) for tense inter-communal relations and conflagrations. Thus, Gupta found a number of public order disturbances and even a communal riot reported during this time.

This trend is taken to an altogether different plane of significance when the abduction of Hindu women is discussed and debated in Parliament in post-Partition India (1947–48). Looking at the forced abductions and recoveries of women in the immediate aftermath of Partition, Veena Das, in 1995, followed by Butalia (1998) and Menon and Bhasin (1998) provide a sophisticated discussion about the abductions, the recovery programme of the Indian state, and the laws enacted to cope with the human tragedy of Partition. So, the Indian National Congress at Meerut passed a resolution that said that 'Women who have been abducted and forcibly married must be restored to their houses; mass conversions have no significance or validity and people must be given every opportunity to return to the life of their choice' (Menon and Bhasin 1998: 69). In the aftermath of the large exchanges of Hindu and Muslim populations that characterised the later months of 1947, the two governments of the new nations were swamped with petitions and requests from families to locate their missing women and children. As a result of the enormity of the task, India and Pakistan signed the 'Inter-Dominion Agreement' to recover as many women, as quickly as possible and restore them to their families (ibid. 1998: 68). Passions ran high as it was widely acknowledged that nothing fuelled the flames of violence more than accounts of female abduction, rape and mutilation. As one leader pronounced in the Indian Parliament,

If there is any sore point or distressful fact to which we cannot be reconciled under any circumstances, it is the question of abduction and non-restoration of Hindu women. We all know our history, of what happened in the time of Shri Ram when Sita was abducted. Here, where thousands of girls are concerned, we cannot forget this. We can forget all the properties, we can forget every other thing but this cannot be forgotten (in Menon and Bhasin 1998: 68).

Sadly, a common plea amongst women who resisted state 'recovery' was that they had chosen to take advantage of the social turmoil and marry men of their own choice, with the full knowledge that such liaisons would have been heavily opposed by their kin, and would have almost certainly been prevented at any other time (ibid.: 118). The tragedy was that the Indian and the Pakistani states had decided that 'forced marriage' and 'forced conversions' were not to be recognised, and because of the nature of the heinous crimes that *were* committed at the time, many inter-community marriages of choice (being in any case the subject of great unease and social disdain) fell almost by definition under the all-encompassing rubric of 'force'—so that 'forced marriages' could only be somehow undone by the 'forcible recovery' of the woman by the state. Das sums up the paradoxes of the state response by showing how the heterogeneity of practices in the domain of kinship allowed communities and families to cope in the aftermath of extreme violence, but that these were soon replaced by the blinkered state-defined idea of a woman: as either a Hindu or a Muslim. So while the kinship practices within families were geared towards absorbing such women and their children via practical measures such as marriage and conversion, the state's programme of recovery gave them a new visibility (ibid.: 81–82). This leads her to conclude that the violence to which they were subjected must be 'understood as doubly articulated in the domains of kinship and politics' (ibid.: 56). It is this double articulation that explains, for my purposes, the power of such abduction narratives (above and beyond their descriptive or communicative purposes) because they work as a kind of rhetoric that tries to consume individuals and their rights and engulf these within the overarching claims of kinship, community and the politics of the state.

The fact that abduction narratives appeal to the values of kinship and honour makes them an essential component in the politics of nationalism. This is exemplified in the case with Babubhai Patel (alias 'Babu Bajrangi'), a Hindu nationalist and a Bajrang Dal leader[60] of an area called Naroda-Patiya in Gujarat. Babu Bajrangi is infamous in his own right—he has pledged to rescue all 'Patel' girls who marry outside their community or who have love-marriages. In a leaflet issued in his name by the Navchetan (New Awakening) Trust he says:

In every home there is a live bomb that can erupt at any time. Do you know who that is? Daughters are the honour of the family and the community, and to protect that is our Hindu duty and Hindu culture ... Come, lets unite to save bombs ... Jai Shree Ram.

Bajrangi, also known as the 'serial kidnapper of Gujarat' has claimed to have distributed 100,000 such leaflets across Gujarat and to have 'rescued' 918 women from his Kadwa Patel community.[61] Of these, 70 per cent are apparently marriages to Muslims or Christians and the rest to other Hindu sub-castes.

Rather unsurprisingly, Bajrangi has also made public his views on love-marriages:

I don't believe in love marriage. We have to marry within our own community. These girls go to college, make friends with some *lafanga* [loafer], roam with them on their bikes, fall in love, and then run off and get married.... We bring them back and convince them that they are ruining their future. They stay with me for a while and then return to their parents (Bunsha 2006).

Considering the recent political history of Gujarat, Bajrangi's views may well be representative of certain people in the state, but what is truly significant is that he is able to undertake his vigilante operation publicly and with impunity. For instance, Dionne Bunsha, a journalist with the English language magazine *Frontline*, has reported on a case that has been filed in the Supreme Court of India by four Hindu boys living in Maharashtra who claim that Bajrangi kidnapped their wives (ibid.). Ajay Nikam, whose wife Geeta was allegedly number 561 on Bajrangi's list, was picked up by Bajrangi and taken to Naroda in Gujarat. When Ajay traced a mobile call from her phone and tried to find her he claims he was accosted by armed men with sten guns, pushed into a vehicle and taken to a deserted construction site where his wife was present. 'She told me', he says, 'If you love me, then sign the papers'. I realised the danger, and so I listened to her and signed'. When he returned to Bombay he filed a case with the police. Finally, when Geeta was produced in court she was escorted by a huge crowd. The judge called both of them into his chamber where she told her husband that both their lives were under threat. She was too scared to speak the truth in court.[62] Apparently, when Ajay's case became public he was contacted by the other three boys who had similar stories to tell.

Bunsha has described Bajrangi's activities as an 'abduction crusade'.[63] His charismatic metaphor of daughters as bombs shows that he has a keen awareness of the power of the modern media to hook a story and to represent his views about female sexuality and its destructive potential for kin and community.[64] A pamphlet distributed by the Navchetan Trust likens the rescue of girls to the Cow Protection Movement and says: 'If you rescue one girl, it is the same as saving 100 cows. One daughter equals 100 holy cows'. From this formulation we can see how Hindu nationalism comes to link matters that affect the honour of families and communities, and to make it a concern of the nation. Calls to protect *gau mata* (mother cow) in the form of the Cow Protection Movement at the end of the nineteenth and early twentieth century were central to defining the boundaries of Hinduism from colonial and Muslim incursions (Van der Veer 1994: 83–99). In the current scenario, it is control over the body of the Hindu woman, her desire and sexuality that must be protected, managed and 'recovered' from the predatory and corrupting influence of Muslim boys (*lafange* or loafers), crashing through the political landscape on their motorbikes.

Van der Veer has said: '[T]he sense that the nation is one's own family writ large appears to be exactly what nationalism attempts to foster' (ibid.: 85). Love-marriages declare the boundaries of caste and community to be negotiable and porous. In insisting on treating all such marriages as abductions, and forcing upon these unions 'rescues' followed by divorces, separations and abortions, vigilantes such as Bajrangi declare themselves as the new moral watchdogs of the Hindu female body; and, in so doing they reiterate the message that the nation is the family writ large. It is also telling that Bajrangi is from Naroda-Patiya, a place 15 km outside Ahmedabad (Gujarat), whose very name is now synonymous with religious intolerance and the most grisly massacre in 2002 of eighty-nine men, women and children by Hindu mobs dressed in khaki half-pants, saffron vests and black bandanas, bearing spears, swords, iron rods, acid and petrol bombs.[65]

Menon and Bhasin have quite properly argued in the context of the state-sponsored 'rescue' of abducted women post-Partition that 'recovery' itself becomes a 'symbolic activity', and they draw parallels with the rhetoric about 'recovering' Hindu women post-Partition and 'recovering' the sacred Hindu sites such as the Ram temple in Ayodhya from Muslim control (1998: 123). In a similar fashion, Bajrangi likens the 'rescue' of one girl to a hundred cows. This mathematics of scale (1: 100) is used to emphasise both the significance of the threat and the achievement of each recovery. Hindu girls, Hindu temples, and Hindu cows all need recovering from Muslim aggressors. Bajrangi makes this explicit when he says to Bunsha, 'If it's a Musalman [Muslim], we definitely use force even if the girl doesn't want to leave. Musalmans don't have a right to live in our country. How dare they marry our girls?' (Bunsha 2006).[66]

Love Bombs and the Intimate State

Thomas Hansen has proposed that Hindu nationalism has 'emerged and taken shape not in the political system as such nor in the religious field, but in the broader realm of what we may call public culture—the public space in which a society and its constituent individuals and communities imagine, represent, and recognise themselves ...' (1999: 4).[67] I have tried to show in the previous section four instances in which private love-marriages are dragged into public discourse to score political points and to serve as rhetoric. This bears very heavily upon their reception in the here and now of social relations. Abduction narratives thus work to erase all traces of choice, agency and sexuality, while at the same time proffering personal and communal redemption through the aegis of politicised male communities that are willing to defend women and bring them back into the fold of community and the nation. In this way the narratives serve to reconstitute the making of publics, politics and indeed, the nation.

As we will see later in this book, the ground reality (viewed from the perspective of non-political players and of love-marriage couples themselves) is rather different. During my fieldwork, when I had the opportunity to speak with police officers, lawyers and journalists, there was a knowing consensus that whenever they heard abduction reports the first thought that would occur to them was that the girl had had a love-marriage or had eloped. On the other hand, people in the general public, such as my rickshaw-driver informants (more about these soon) or women in the south

Delhi shanty, were much more likely to interpret such news as though the girl had in fact been violently abducted or assaulted, and explained that such incidents were commonplace and were regularly in the news. This mismatch in perception stems from an obvious phenomenon, which is that the more media space and coverage given to such sensational narratives the more widespread they appear and the more easily they get incorporated into a repertoire of reality. From this perspective, stories about college girls running off or being abducted by predatory Muslim boys on motorbikes become a code for thinking about the values of caste, community, gender and sexuality. I am not suggesting any simple unilinear model here—nothing so naïve as love-marriage reportage furthering the cause of Hindu religious nationalists (though in many instances such as the Hindi publicists of the 1920s and 1930s this may well be true), or indeed, of representing the cause of secularists like Nehru and Gandhi who supported such unions (see Hingorani 1966: 127–31). What I am trying to propose is that these stories about marriages, abductions, elopements, violent double suicides, or even double murders expose a play between representation and representativeness which we would do well to take notice of. They tell readers about matters that they can relate to in an intimate way. At the same time, we must make note of the way they work to normalise the rhetoric that often accompanies such stories. This explains how people who are sensitive to the 'representation' of events and who know to look for a story behind a story (people whose professional training involves unearthing matters that are often concealed, such as police officers, lawyers or journalists) may detect the interests and political motivations of publicists in press reporting about abductions, whereas members of the public who perceive themselves to be bombarded by stories, pamphlets and reports of countless random violent acts are more prone to just take the story at face value and accept that these things happen. As Asad reminds us, '[T]he media are not simply the means through which individuals simultaneously imagine their national community; they *mediate* that imagination, construct the sensibilities that underpin it' (2003: 5).

Mani (1989) has described the ways in which colonial discourse about incidences of female immolation or *sati* cast the women as victims but not as subjects acting with agency. In this way, both the colonial state and the indigenous male elite see women as representing 'tradition': for the colonials, women who climbed a burning pyre and became *sati* were represented as fragile and in need of legislative protection from the retrogressive native male, whereas for the male leaders of 'community' these same women represented the true tradition and allowed them to justify the need to keep them pure of corrupting influences. If we look at these debates and juxtapose them with the debates I have just drawn upon concerning abduction and love-marriage, we will see that while the colonial debates were about the grounds upon which tradition was debated, abduction debates are about redefining the grounds (if I may) upon which modernity is being projected and achieved. As we shall see, love-marriages bear the distinctive insignia of being matters that concern bigger things, matters in fact, that concern the way we think about the Indian family and project these onto our ideas about the Indian nation.

The question now is, what of the love-marriage family? Partha Chatterjee (1989) has famously argued that during the colonial era, social reformers 'resolved' the 'women's question' by devising a model in which the domain of the home (*ghar*)—associated closely with the respectable and chaste wife—was viewed as the locus of Indian tradition and superior morality, as opposed to the domain of the world (*bahir*) in which Indians had been subjugated by the superiority of the colonising Europeans. In this construction, Indian women (suitably domesticated by their men) are the caretakers of a 'reworked Indian tradition'. My work on love-marriages tells a quite different story. In fact, what we see is that the penetrative power of the new legislation for love-marriage is inflicted precisely upon those intimate spaces of family and home that feel themselves unable to repel the attack. What is also surprising is that the invitation for such meddling legislation comes from those who seek the help of the colonial state in order to reform Hinduism from within (in Chapter 1 I deal more with the Brahmo Samaj's fervour to reform idolatrous Hindu marriage rites). And furthermore, the sacred space of *ghar* (home) is precisely the location in which young idealists declaring the desire to marry out of choice and love make their most devastating assault. Far from remaining pure and superior, the space of the family and the *ghar* is a vessel bursting with the potential to heap dishonour upon communities (in the language of Bajrangi, the family contains a ticking bomb); unless of course, it can be contained and controlled.

What is it about love-marriages that Bajrangi finds so threatening? The bomb, traditionally regarded as a site of 'masculine accumulation'[68] is reconfigured in modern times as modern girls who through their loving actions actually threaten to explode the certainties of Hindu kinship. If we were to pause and think about this ethnographically, we would do well to think about one of Parry's informants in Patripar, Bihar. His father was a Sindhi refugee, his mother a local Satnami. He had married a neighbour whose father was Maharashtrian and whose mother was a Chhatisgarhi Mahar. Parry says: 'With grandparents of four different castes from three different regions, it is not easy to imagine what sense caste will make to their children. And though the numbers of such children is limited, it is certainly growing' (2001: 814). Indeed, it is precisely the mixing represented by love-marriages and the abundant opportunities available in urban life that have led the activist-academic Gail Omveldt to call for more inter-caste and inter-community marriages to break down centuries of religious-based exclusion and separation. The 'motto' of the Indian nation, as any school-going child can tell us, is 'Unity in Diversity'. It used to be the case that the rhetoric of unity was provided by the principle of secularism that served as a kind of overarching model transcending the particularities of religion, caste, ethno-religious community, gender and class. Disillusionment with the paucity of models for 'Unity in Diversity' has led people to look elsewhere, and one very obvious place is to view love-marriages as emblematic of *secularism as practice*. However, this has often meant that people have interpreted such marriages as representing a particular *politics* of secularism. Take this ethnographic case: one of my informants, a relatively high-caste girl, had married a landowning Muslim from Uttar Pradesh. Despite their love-marriage, she had deep reservations about Muslims and much of her conversation was about how Hindu nationalism is correct in its assessment of Islam. Her political views are diametrically different to those that one could read into her actions (marriage to a Muslim). This leads me to argue that while Hindu religious nationalism might have emerged in the public sphere (per Hansen), it is inadvertently both challenged and cemented in the intimate domestic realms of marriage, gender and kinship.

Talal Asad makes the point that we should not 'pursue modernity' (or indeed in this instance 'secularism') by 'aim[ing] at it', but instead by looking in its shadows (2003: 16). I would like to propose that a study of love-marriage and the law does precisely this. By looking at the enabling circumstances in which change occurs, and by examining ethnographically the ways in which people who legitimate their love through marriage describe and think about their actions, transgressions and intimacies, we have a real basis for thinking about how these couples and families intentionally *or* inadvertently transform or transcend boundaries through their practices and how they negotiate the 'conceptual binaries' that otherwise appear to keep people apart (Hindu and Muslim, Brahmin and Shudra, traditional and modern, secular and religious, individual and community). This, then, is my project in this book. It is not a study about the state or its grand imaginings and ideas of 'secularism' or 'modernity'—it is a study about the detritus of these ideas that comes with the mess of life: an ethnography of the often contrary and complicated circumstances in which Indian individuals in Delhi pursue intimacy and marriage in the shadow (and occasionally in the full glare) of their religious groups, the law and the state.

Theoretical Foreground

There were three related problems that confronted me in this study of love-marriage. The first, which I have already described, was how to get an anthropological handle on the phenomena of love-marriages when the couples I spoke to came from such a diverse range of backgrounds and circumstances. This was resolved by my decision to view love-marriage from the perspective of the couples rather than their families or 'communities', and to capture their liminality through the notion of not-community. The event-specific nature of my research, where I would meet love-marriage couples on the day of their wedding and then they would disappear until they could meet me again, nonetheless raised problems for the writing of this book. The second problem, which I will explore later, concerned the way in which I could conceptualise the enormous complexity of an urban space like Delhi. Thirdly, I needed some anthropological work which would help me think through the relevance of my archival material on the history of changing marriage forms in India. There were three anthropological works that helped me with these methodological and theoretical issues, and I would like to touch upon the relevance they have for this book.

Much of Veena Das's recent writing works against the grain of the sort of anthropology that she describes as producing 'totalizing visions' in which every individual is seen as a microcosmic template of the whole culture. Her theory of 'community' is one of communities-as-political-actors which have rights to define the collective past, regulate sexuality and custom, and transform acts of violence into acts of moral solidarity. In this book, I discuss a city of enormous diversity, and when I speak of 'communities' (or castes/ethno-religious groups) I do so keeping in mind Das's definition of these political configurations (see Das 1995).

Similarly, Bauman (1996) in his ethnography of Southall discards the epithet of 'ethnic minority' for non-white migrants to the UK and challenges the 'neat cultural holism' propounded by the literature on South Asian diasporic communities. He rejects the *a priori* significance of categories such as 'Hindu' or 'Muslim' and instead sets out to examine Southall as a 'social field' in which various castes, communities, nationalities, 'cultures', language groups, age cohorts and party–political groups summon differing and often contradictory alliances upon the residents of this multiethnic milieu. He is thus able to map the ways in which the Maussian notion of cultural totalities are shown to be important 'social categories' employed by his informants rather than anthropological 'fact'. For instance, Bauman shows the ways in which young Sikh, Hindu, Muslim South Asians as well as Afro-Caribbeans and some 'white' Southallians converge upon cousin-bonds and cousin claims (1995: 725). Such work that studies an urban space as a 'social field' challenges 'ethnic' or 'ethnoreligious' boundaries to anthropological study and provides important guidelines for my own examination of marriages that cross boundaries in Delhi.

Finally, Simeran Man Singh Gell's examination of British South Asian marriages in Bedford has challenged the unremitting stereotype in anthropological writing about arranged marriages as if they are 'touchstones of cultural integrity, resistance and resurgence' to 'western values' and 'individualistic ways of life' (1994: 346). Gell provides a detailed ethnographic account of Town Hall and Registry marriages that regularly precede religious and ritual marriages amongst South Asians of various communities in Bedford, and have done for many years. Such marriages affirm the historical nexus between migration and the law, and ritualise the migrant's relationship with the British state.

By contextualising her own work within the history of migration to Britain and by exploring the surveillance role of the British state in its assessments of what constituted 'genuine' marriages, Gell is able to show how contemporary South Asian marriage forms do not somehow overcome the 'historical facts of migration', but are severely conditioned by the same. This work on love-marriages, in a similar vein, examines the historical background to civil marriages in India, and uses it to help explain the peculiar ways in which the state, communities and individuals contest and subvert the issue of choice in marriage. In so doing, what I hope to show is that the 'newness' of such marriages need not be summarily dismissed through ready-made concepts such as 'individualism' or 'modernity', but rather through a study of the ways in which we can unpack the newness but still require an address to so-called traditional concerns of kinship.

Fieldwork in Delhi

The research for this book was conducted in Delhi between March 1997 and July 1998, with three month-long follow-up trips between 2001 and 2007. Much of the first twelve months of intensive fieldwork was spent working with touts, lawyers and minor court functionaries outside the 'Marriage Room' in the district court of Tis Hazari[69] and in Hindu temples around the city where most love-marriage couples came to get married. One of the reasons I worked in the courts and temples was to meet a cross-section of love-marriage couples of diverse social classes, as all except the very rich or powerful would have to come to the Registrar in the marriage room or the priests in the temple to obtain a legally valid marriage certificate. As I was aware that love-marriage couples can be particularly vulnerable to social disdain, I decided to work with the touts, marriage-room lawyers and minor court functionaries so that I was able to observe the ways in which ordinary couples encountered the judicial apparatus for marriage—that is, to see the legal system from the 'bottom-up'.

Additionally, I conducted numerous and extensive 'public interviews' (a stop-and-research method!) with people on the streets of the city in order to elicit what members of the public made of such marriages. Unlike the work with love-marriage couples, my public interviews were always structured (inasmuch as I worked with a questionnaire), but they were often quite literally 'public' as crowds gathered around and joined in with their own 'running commentary' on both my questions and on the interviewee's answers. Such occasionally raucous settings were extremely interesting because they triggered debates which were far more helpful than the stock-in-trade answers that people often feel compelled to provide to 'interviewers'. Descriptions of these public conversations and responses about the love-marriage stories that people had heard of make regular appearances throughout this book.

Many of the informants in my 'public interviews' were working class, notably auto-rickshaw drivers at railway stations,[70] women from the bustis[71] of Madangiri and Ambedkar Nagar, and couples in Delhi's many parks and gardens. A second series of interviews were conducted amongst those working or studying at Delhi University—which serves (quite literally) as a hot-bed of love and romance. These interviews (which were also structured) allowed me to settle upon the issues I wished to pursue in greater depth during the rest of my fieldwork, and I am indebted to those academics who both embraced and challenged the agenda and paradigms of this research.

The love-marriage couples, their families and friends who principally inform this book are a group of individuals whom I met and worked with through the networks of the city—the court and its touts, members of the public who mentioned that they knew someone I might be able to speak to, and the newspapers and police stations where many love-marriage cases landed up. The couples, their families and friends lived in every corner of the city and most of my time was spent following their progress on a day-to-day basis—from marriage through to confrontations with their families and, often, to reconciliation.

I was also able to work with a few people whose marriages had been broken up by dissenting families and it was through such cases that I got involved with the workings of the Delhi police, the National Human Rights Commission and the National Commission for Women.[72] During the last six months of my fieldwork I worked with a number of women's organisations, primarily Janvadi Mahila Samiti (or JMS),[73] which runs legal advice centres across the city that seek to provide arbitration and legal help for marital and family disputes. The large number of instances involving conjugal and domestic matters of the most intimate kind aired in the conviviality of a women's support group provided an ethnographic richness which grounds many of my observations about north Indian conjugality and kinship.

Socio-political 'Fields'

As the national capital, Delhi used to be a 'Union Territory' (directly under central rule), but in 1994 it was awarded the status of a state, having its own locally elected government. In the first Delhi state elections in 1994, the Hindu revivalist Bharatiya Janata Party (BJP)[74] was brought to power—four years before the same party was able to win a majority of seats at the national level in a coalition alliance in 1998. The period of my fieldwork was one of enormous uncertainty in the national government. Two ruling coalitions were brought down through votes of no-confidence, leaving the nation ungoverned for nearly a month in 1998, prior to the general elections. In this period, Delhi was gripped by fear, with hushed talk of imminent riots should the BJP fail to get a majority. The fear manifested itself in a spate of grisly urban myths resulting in the area in which I was based being guarded by vigilante groups who set up all-night vigils to protect their women and children against strikes from men who allegedly greased their bodies black (so they couldn't be caught), and who made wailing baby sounds outside homes in the *bustis* until they were let in and thus able to murder the guileless inhabitants. Across the city rumours circulated about decapitated bodies being found—interestingly they were always Muslim men—[75] and it was only once the election results were declared that the tension subsided and the local men stopped gathering together in gangs to keep watch at night.

The BJP's bellicose nationalism was celebrated in the nuclear blasts in May 1998, towards the end of my fieldwork, at a time when the effect of the rising tide of their brand of *Hindutva* (lit. 'Hinduness', but more generally, their brand of Hindu cultural nationalism) populism was being flaunted in local state governance. In the following days, while the BJP-supporting middle classes of the entire nation seemed to be celebrating India's regeneration through its 'Hindu bomb', the majority of people in the *busti* where I was working hadn't even heard the news. Not only were *busti* dwellers seemingly indifferent to the nation's 'triumphs', they were also seemingly reluctant to brandish much of the racist propaganda of the Hindu-right. Even during the vigilante period, women I spoke to believed that the decapitated bodies of men found near a few large clusters of *bustis* in the city were only coincidentally Muslim.

Unlike in the court, and the Hindu temples, where my Persian name always brought forth a particularly self-conscious Hindu discourse about Muslims (because it was assumed that I was Muslim), in the *bustis* of Ambedkar Nagar and Madangiri this was a matter of no consequence, and instead the significant marker of difference was my class status. I mention this not simply as ethnographic scene-setting: these factors had a strong bearing upon the ways in which people interacted with me, and they allowed me an unexpected insight into Hindu–Muslim interactions and Delhi's class relations—both of which were significant factors for many of the love-marriage couples I worked with. Furthermore, the unique political scenario that I was to witness during my fieldwork (the rise of Hindu revivalists to legitimated, electorally-sanctioned parliamentary power with a mandate that few believed was possible), placed inter-caste and inter-community love-marriages in an altogether more hostile political environment, as the Hindu parties are markedly partial to parentally-sanctioned and caste-based arranged alliances.

Urban Collectivities and Identities

Delhi, or *Dilli* to those who prefer its Hindi name, also contains the kernel of the Persian word *'dil'*, meaning heart, or soul or spirit (McGregor 1997: 496–97). It is a derivation that *Dilliwale* (Dehli-ites) pun with to remind themselves that *this* is a city with a heart.[76] In equal measure, however, people I spoke to described the city as heartless and cruel: a place of loneliness and misery. In a city that now officially racks up 14 million on the population count (the two last census enumerations which are believed to be underestimates were 9.4 million in 1991 (Singh 1996: xix), and 13.7 million in 2001),[77] this is an unsurprising state of affairs. The city is swelling at a remarkable rate, and its civic machinery is being pushed beyond its natural limit. Between 1991 and 2001, the population of Delhi increased by an astonishing 46 per cent.[78] Another million people are known to commute daily to Delhi from its satellite towns ('bedroom towns' as they are popularly known—places where people return only to sleep). The current rate of migration means that over 60 per cent of Delhi-ites aren't Delhi-born (even in the 1981 census, 48.05 per cent of Delhi people were not Delhi-born [Singh 1996: xx]). Consequently, few people claim their identity as exclusively '*Dilliwale*'. Migrants continue to pour in, stretching the limits of the national capital into the adjoining states of Rajasthan, Uttar Pradesh and Haryana. The sex-ratio for the city (the number of females per thousand males) is depressingly female-adverse at 821.[79] Many recent migrants find themselves living in *jhuggi-jhopdis* or illegal colonies; shanties of squatters who face the imminent threat of displacement at the hands of the Municipal Corporation of Delhi.[80]

Delhi is situated on the west bank of the river Jamuna, on the periphery of the Gangetic plains, and its urban and industrial complexes sprawl across an area of nearly 1,500 square kilometres, engulfing many of the older villages after which much of the city is named. With a long overdue underground Metro that is the new wonder of Delhi, and privatised buses that many of the elite proudly profess never to have embarked during their entire lives,[81] Delhi's roads are nonetheless clogged with four million vehicles: more than those of Bombay, Chennai and Calcutta put together.[82] The chronic state of disrepair of many of these make the city one of the most polluted in the world, and in the dark, smog-filled winter nights one can imagine oneself witness to an apocalyptic vision where human silhouettes and the faint outlines of chaotically manoeuvred vehicles jostle for room on the roads as each clamours past the other to make their way home. The struggles and trials of urban life and the very real fear of violence are palpable—Delhi people have animated discussions about the increase in road accident fatalities, murders and rapes, with the popular press dubbing the city as India's 'Crime Capital'.[83]

To understand everyday social interactions in Delhi, one needs to first recognise that this is an intensely hierarchical society, with strong emphasis on the *forms* of social interaction that often hark back to its Mughal past. '*Tehzeeb*', manners, and '*tameez*', cultured conduct, are still highly regarded in this city, and are signs of descent from a 'good family'. As someone from Bombay,[84] I was marked as sorely lacking in both, in part because *Bombaiya* (Bombay speech) replaces the plural pronoun with the personal—thus introducing a familiarity and informality that Delhi people consider rude, particularly when coming from a young Indian woman. A good example of this was when a rickshaw hit the side of my Fiat car at Connaught Place. Angered by the driver's attempt to flee without so much as an apology, I pursued him to a signal and, jumping out of the car, went up to him and said in Hindi, 'What do you think you were doing there?' adding the appendage *'yaar'* or 'friend'—a common way of indicating in Bombay that you aren't trying to pull class on someone. He was outraged, and interpreting the familiarity of the first-person pronoun and the added *'yaar'*, shouted back in Hindi: 'Am I your *YAAR* (lover)?' Typically, a term which has no sexual overtones in Bombay was interpreted as far too familiar a form of address for a stranger (woman) to use to any man, thus instantly giving him the moral high-ground in the exchange. As I was to discover, the contextual use of words is complex and difficult to master. In another instance, an informant, a Hindu girl in the *busti* who had had a secondary marriage to a Muslim boy, narrated the entire story of their courtship and romance without once using a word for 'love'. When I pointed this out to her and asked her whether she had 'loved' *(pyar karna)* her husband, she rebuked me with the response: 'Love means an immoral relationship. I said, "Marriage first. After that, love or whatever"'.[85] Her earlier description of their romance made it evident that she was now equating *'pyar'* with moral impropriety; as I was to discover, a common enough interpretation of the word. Many of my informants described their romances with the English words *'friendship'* and *'affair'*, because to be a *'friend'* of a person of the opposite sex was in most instances meant to tactfully imply an *'affair'*.[86]

Delhi has attracted Partition migrants from the Punjab, civil servants from across the many states of India, the young, intelligent and politically ambitious, business people and non-governmental organisations seeking to lobby parliament and bureaucrats, and rural migrants, in equal measure—making it one of the most ethnically and socially diverse of India's cities, a 'mini-India' as school textbooks say. The People of India survey helpfully lists the populations of Delhi's 'major communities': 83.60 per cent Hindus, 7.75 per cent Muslims, 6.33 per cent Sikhs, 1.19 per cent Jains, 0.99

per cent Christians, and 0.11 per cent Buddhists (K.S. Singh 1996: xx). However, as I have already explained, there is no 'ethnos' to this ethnography as it seeks to capture love-marriage as an aspect of urban life, rather than as an aspect of endogamously defined ethno-religious communities. Consequently, my 'field' was the city as a whole, and I included as subjects those love-marriage couples who came to Delhi to seek refuge or to start their new life.

The rich can afford to live in colonies with members of their own ethno-religious communities, though increasingly, newer accommodation (for example, across the river Jamuna) is markedly cosmopolitan. The professional, educated middle classes have Group Housing Societies where members pool their finances to form societies that build flats for the group.[87] These can take the form of large associations—such as those of the Armed Services or the Railway, but often they are more specific, profession (and class) based—for instance, a colony of journalists at *The Times of India*, or of media persons working in one or the other satellite TV channels; even a society for those professionals who work at Oxford University Press. Other forms of associations are ethno-linguistic, such as a south Indian (Tamil) society, or the Malyali (Keralite) housing society in West Delhi.

The *bustis*, on the other hand, have always had a mish-mash of people from across north India. Sometimes one finds that a *gully* (a row of houses) is taken over by members with ethno-religious ties (a *'buniya gully'*, or a *'pandit gully'*), and this can extend to more than a cluster of homes,[88] but the predominant pattern is that of a heterogeneous community of owners and poorer (usually younger) tenants, castes and religious groups, and migrant and more permanent settlers. In any case, the urban experience of co-education, work in factories, homes (the usual retinue of the rich: servants, drivers, cooks, watchmen) and offices implies that people frequently encounter all manner of interesting 'others' and that the public spaces such as Delhi's notoriously enchanting parks and gardens all serve up an inviting brew of desire and opportunity to which many of the denizens of this city inevitably fall prey. These spaces are regularly frequented by office-goers in their lunch-breaks, religious devotees listening to sermons, florets of card-playing civil servants sprinkled across the grass, and anybody seeking refuge from the searing heat of the summer under the shade of a tree. The parks are viewed by many couples as safe places to venture on romantic dates during the day and in the early evenings. They are also relatively vast; as a result they have the added advantage of providing a reasonable amount of privacy from prying eyes. *Dilliwale* know that they are privileged—they have at their disposal the most beautiful ancient gardens, now in graceful ruins, built by generations of Moghul aesthetes who believed, quite literally, that their royal gardens should provide a glimpse of paradise.

The Successes and Failures of Love in Delhi

An Indian magazine conducted a survey on marriage in the 1990s, interviewing couples from Bombay, Calcutta, Hyderabad and Lucknow. The poll covered 616 people in the age group 20 to 35 years, earning monthly salaries of Rs 3,000 and above, i.e. the middle and upper middle class, and the elite. Eighty-one per cent responded that theirs was an arranged marriage; 19 per cent said that theirs was a love-marriage.[89] Another 'poll of Indian youth' with 3,208 respondents between the ages of 18 to 21 years 'carefully chosen to guard against urban/rural, gender or socio-economic bias', found that 19 per cent replied that they would want to have a love-marriage while 81 per cent said that they would want to have an arranged marriage (the question they were asked was, 'What sort of marriage would you want?'). When separate calculations were made of urban and rural populations, 27 per cent of urban youth and a lower 16 per cent of rural youth said they wanted to have a love-marriage.[90] If these figures are in any way representative of Delhi, they show that a significant number of people believe that the way one marries isn't a foregone conclusion, and that the relevant issue of choice may lie both in choosing one's own spouse in a love-marriage *and* in actively *choosing* to have an arranged marriage. The question that must be addressed is, how frequent are such love-marriages and who is having them? On this matter, there are many who feel utterly confident to provide commentaries on 'rates' (without specifying what they might be) and increases or decreases in love/arranged marriages (again, without any indication of what they were, and what they now are).[91]

One possible source of data about the frequency of such marriages in Delhi is the numbers of registered civil or Hindu marriages as counted and calculated from the hundreds of ledgers in the record room in the court. This cumbersome work is presented in

Chapter 2. Its reliability as an indicator of love-marriages is suspect not least because there is no direct equivalence between numbers of civil marriages and numbers of love-marriages. Furthermore, it doesn't reflect the many Muslim *nikkahs* (or marriage contracts) in Delhi, but also because a vast majority of couples have religious marriages that they see no need to register. Furthermore, my data are not consonant with other claims. For instance, the President of the All-India Lawyer's Forum for Civil Liberties claims that more than 200 civil marriages are being solemnised *each day* (a '30% increase in the past 5 years') at the Tis Hazari courts and the offices of the Deputy Commissioners in the nine districts of Delhi.[92] My own work in the archive presents a much more modest picture (see Table 2.1), with centralised annual records up to 1996 (the year prior to zonalisation when the current registers were found in the zonal offices and not at Tis Hazari) amounting to a mere 285 civil marriage registrations and 3,407 Hindu marriage registrations for all of Delhi in the year 1996. However, it is highly likely that my data refer to the smaller area of Old and New Delhi, while the data of the All-India Lawyer's Forum for Civil Liberties is for the entire state of Delhi, which represents not just the nine zones that I covered, but the nine districts that comprise the National Capital Region (NCR) with generous boundaries (30,242 square kilometres) that extend into the states of Uttar Pradesh, Haryana and Rajasthan, and which would quite properly include Delhi's populous suburbs like Ghaziabad, Noida, Faridabad and Gurgaon.

While there simply aren't any sufficiently reliable data for Delhi on these matters, one can also come to the question 'ethnographically', that is to say, we can examine the pronouncements of *Dilliwale* on the matter. It must be emphasised that I wasn't looking for statistics; but the mere discussion of love-marriage brought forward these bold assessments. They indicate the strong sense amongst the Delhi public that love-marriages must be condemned as shameful and illegitimate, and that while corrupt Bombay with its raunchy films may find such things glamorous, Delhi isn't such an '*open*' or even '*social*' society. Here is a modest sample of my findings, taken from a selection of my public interviews:

'90% love-marriages don't last—only 10% last'.

'99% love-marriages end in divorce. The women become prostitutes'.

'If boys in this city are 40%—then the girls today are 60%! This is the effect of Hindi films' [This is with reference to their alleged sexual precociousness].

'Today, 80% of boys and girls [lovers] don't marry. They only use each other in *body-business*'.

I would like to suggest that the overwhelming obsession with success rates of love-marriages, and with who is 'winning out'— 'love' or 'arranged', indicates what others have noted before me: that marriage and its forms have come to be viewed in Delhi as a 'touchstone of cultural integrity' (Simeran Man Singh Gell 1994: 346), as well as a domain from which opinions about gender and sexuality can be drawn. This was brought home quite sharply when numerous men in my public interviews (including one police inspector) insisted on equating girls who had had love-marriages with prostitutes. As one informant helpfully explained in English: *'To go with a pross* [prostitute] *or to marry another caste is considered as heinous a crime.'*

The need to express such views is influenced by a larger sense that arranged marriages must be valourised because they indicate a resistance to the moral values depicted by the wealth and bodily-bedazzling images of the Western world that both tantalise and bewilder urban Indians. Uberoi makes this argument by showing how Indians believe they must modernise, but never lose their 'culture'. A 'traditional Indian woman' must always have a 'traditional Indian marriage', which safeguards her honour and in so doing celebrates the timelessness and conjugal bliss of the non-divorcing 'Indian family'; it is this firm domestic base that underlines the financial prowess of Indians the world over (1998: 306). The pleasures of the 'joint-family' lifestyle and of being 'respected and respectful members' of society (ibid.) derive inexorably from the critical point of departure—the arranged marriage—such that the way one marries continues to define the moral essence of one's personhood and provides the strata on which one builds all relationships, including that with the modern nation and the globalised world. Thus rhetoric about arranged marriages and the Indian family are important ingredients of the modern urban Indian's cosmology and, as we shall see, rather ironically, it is this same ideal that also motivates the actions and ambitions of many of Delhi's love-marriage couples.

Aims of the Book

While most of my research focused on anthropological fieldwork with love-marriage couples, I also sought to explore the historical antecedents of the Special Marriage Act, 1954, the law of civil marriage that was currently in use in the court in Delhi. The first chapter of this book concerns the contestations through which the first law of civil marriage came into existence in 1872. This legislation for civil marriage is suffused with contradictions and paradoxes about the extent of individual and community 'rights' and the significance of caste and religion in marriage, and it is this confusing inheritance that is carried over into the modern day court and its legal practice. I then turn to the district court of Tis Hazari in Delhi where many couples go to get married. Here, I explore the continuing tensions between those who seek to legitimate their love as a basis of marriage, and those who take issue with the right of the state to intervene in matters such as religion and marriage. The subject of Chapter 3 is the manipulation of the stereotype that love-marriages necessarily take place under a veil of deceit. Using a number of very unusual stories that appeared in the press during my fieldwork, I shift the emphasis away from the public perceptions of such marriages towards the domestic lives of eloping couples and their families. The issue of agency is central to this study, and in Chapter 4, I provide an analysis of agency and personhood in love-marriages. I explore the ways in which agency is a double-edged sword: it makes itself known to individuals through their acts of freedom and efficacy, but it also constrains and makes them accountable to their groups. I propose a model that sees love-marriage couples as caught between a dialectic of self-agency *and* self-as-agent-of-groups. In using this model, I am able to explore my ethnography in the context of the anthropological literature on the moral meanings of marriage, legal 'rights', sexuality, consent and 'love'. It is hoped that this book isn't merely about politicised marriage between 'communities' or endogamous castes in Delhi, but also provides an anthropological analysis of the small divisions and points of contact of individual human beings seeking to marry and striving to live with people they love.

Notes

1. The notable exceptions to this are C.T. Kannan's work on inter-caste and inter-community marriages (1963), Corwin's paper on love-marriage in a small town, Mahishadal, in West Bengal (1977), more recently, Prem Chowdhary's paper (1997) on community violence directed at those who violate caste and gender codes through inter- and intra-caste marriages, and Jonathan Parry's important work on the fascinating correlations between primary and secondary marriages, inter-caste liaisons and the changing nature of the stability of marriage amongst workers and managers at the Bhilai Steel plant in Chhattisgarh, Madhya Pradesh (2001). Dwyer (2000) has written on love and romance in Hindi films, but perhaps too ambitiously claimed her work (which is about cultural products such as film, film magazines and popular texts) to be simultaneously something of an ethnography of 'love' and romance for the new middle classes of Mumbai. Jauregui and McGuiness's paper discusses twelve inter-married families of urban elites from the perspective of hybridisation and social change (2003). Patricia Uberoi has written some seminal papers on romantic love and the family in Hindi films in popular women's magazines (1997, 1998, and 2006 jointly with Amita Tyagi Singh), and her most recent collection of essays (2006) gives a comprehensive overview of her pioneering work in thinking about the family, marriage and sexuality in India today. Béteille (1997) has also worked on urban middle-class trends regarding inter-caste marriages, but as far as ethnographic evidence is concerned on 'love-as-observed' as opposed to 'love-as-represented', most of what academics have written on love-marriages is based on what Béteille has called 'casual empiricism' (1997: 163). In saying this I do not wish to imply that their findings are invalid—merely to draw attention to the infancy of this specific anthropological field. Although located in Nepal, Ahearn's work on love letters and courtship is a wonderfully refreshing ethnography about love-marriage (2001a). She prefaces it with an outline description of a royal domestic tragedy that demonstrates just how widespread (in both geographical place and class) the dilemmas of love-marriage actually are. In 2001, the Crown Prince of Nepal, Dipendra, gunned down his parents, siblings and royal relatives (and then shot himself) because they didn't support his choice of spouse.

2. The untranslated English words 'love' and 'love-marriage' are frequently used in Delhi Hindi and Delhi Urdu to talk about marriages of choice. They are also used in the context of declarations of love such as 'I love you'. The words pyar and muhobbat both mean love or affection. Ishq also means love, but it carries the meaning of excessive passion, as well as divine love and is often used to describe an illicit love affair. Equally, ishq

is used ironically (and often in the context of humorous anecdotes) to describe the alleged love of others or the suspicions that the declarations of *sacha pyar* (true love) may be riven with contradictions, such as the desire for sexual gratification. For the purpose of this book, I am defining *love-marriages* as those marriages in which the couple fall in love and choose for themselves their own marriage partner. I have hyphenated the words *love-marriage* to emphasise that the idiom is used generically in India to mean a completely distinct phenomenon from marriage understood as arranged marriage, and is not merely viewed as marriage for love, as is implied by the use of the two separate words, love and marriage.

3. Indeed, Uberoi in her examination of two blockbuster Hindi films of the 1990s has gone so far as to conclude that the conflict between individual desire and social norms with regard to marriage constitutes the 'animating logic of South Asian romance' (1998: 306).

4. Tellingly, this gave rise to an untenable contradiction in the colonial attempt to legislate for civil marriage in the 1860s and 1870s—the subject of Chapter 1 of this book.

5. See leader article in the *Times of India*, by R. Dasgupta, 'Hide Your Love Away', 4-10-2007, *http://timesofindia.indiatimes.com/articleshow/msid-2426738,prtpage-1.cms*

6. See M. Banerjie, 'Letters Add New Twist To Rizwan Case', 26-10-2007, *http://www.ndtv.com/convergence/ndtv/story.aspx?id=NEWEN200700309 37&ch=10/29/2007%2011:22:00%20PM*

7. I am grateful to Asha Lata for recounting the details of this incident. This was one of the couples I was dissuaded from meeting because it was felt that it would be too traumatic for them to have to discuss the past.

8. For instance, 'Relatives Sentence Two Lovers to Death' in the *Times of India*, by Lalit Kumar, 12-4-1997, p. 3, New Delhi, or 'Sudaka, the Heart of Darkness' in the *Times of India*, by S. Hameed, 18-8-1997, p. 13, New Delhi. In Pakistan, this phenomenon is much more widespread, particularly in the province of Sind where they are known as '*karo kiri*'. To give a sense of the scale of such violence, during my fieldwork in 1997, in a single month the Pakistani newspaper *Dawn* reported fifty such homicides. See *Times of India*, 'Current Topics: Murderous Custom', 1-10-1997, p. 12, New Delhi.

9. I use the term 'metropolitan' to suggest the dominant status of such a view despite the evident historical and cultural diversity of 'north India'.

10. Though Muslims do not use the term '*kanya daan*' ('gift of a virgin'), a daughter is nonetheless 'given' by her father in marriage to the family of the groom. Here I am not interested in emphasising the meanings of the gift (I am aware that doctrinally, Islam is accepting

of remarriage and, consequently, the emphasis in marriage is not on virginity but on the consent of the girl), other than to draw attention to the fact that in these forms a girl never gifts herself in marriage to a boy of her own choosing, but that the gifting and receiving is done by the two families.

11. Throughout this book my use of the English words 'boy' and 'girl' for legally adult couples stems from a direct translation of the Hindi terms that are almost always used: *'larka'* and *'larki'*. There is a reason for this diminutive usage. Unmarried people, even those between the ages of 20–30 years, are still considered to be dependents on their families and as such, do not qualify for the more exalted *'admi'* (man) or *'aurath'* (woman) which is usually conferred after marriage, usually upon the birth of a child.

12. Translated from interview in Hindi, *'Pyar bhagvan ka dan hai. Shadi ke din, yeh dan diya jata hain. Yeh* kiya *nahin,* diya *jata hai'.* Ironically, my informant's favourite Hindi film is about lust—entitled *Aao Pyar Karen* (Come Let's Fall in Love).

13. I use the term rhetoric to signify the way in which people *represent* the ideal types of 'love' versus 'arranged' marriage. It goes without saying that the reality is often far removed from these types, with arranged marriages capable of generating dissonance, discord and strife in equal measure. For instance, many of my informants would often discuss the serious difficulties of marriage from the positional perspective of daughters-in-law, mothers-in-law and so on. We would often use these observations to talk about the difficulties encountered in marriage *per se* in order to draw out quite different conclusions about what makes a successful marriage. In thinking about the rhetoric used I am able to distinguish how some representations are important for my informants even though the reality that both informants and anthropologists discern is rather more subtle and nuanced than these descriptions suggest.

14. I speak of 'caste' for north-Indian Muslims as both an analytic category and ethnographic fact evidenced in my fieldwork.

15. Love-marriages are often assumed to join two incompatible groups, though this was not how my informants chose to describe such unions. More frequently objections raised concerned the 'incomparable' nature of the two groups. The Hindi word used by my informants to describe the motivating factor behind arranged-marriages was the principal of *'barabari'*, which means equality, but also very significantly means 'comparability'. People said that every family was different, so one expected that one's daughter may find herself in an 'incompatible' household after marriage, to which the girl would then have to *'adjust'*. However, the objection to love-marriages was that they often *forced*

comparisons between groups that were so different that they were considered beyond reasonable comparability.

16. In Hindi, *'jisne-apne-aap-ko-mera-damad-banaya'*. Often she would add to this another honorific: *'vo-jo-aurat-aur-daru-ke-bina-nahin-reh-sakta'* (The-One-Who-Cannot-Live-Without-Women-And-Liqour), thus playing on Brahmanical high-caste stereotypes about the degenerate nature of low castes.

17. We will see this distinction most sharply in Chapter 1, where debates about the law's ability to legitimate inter-caste and inter-religious marriages are framed in terms of the forms of intimacy that are tolerated but kept outside the bounds of legitimate kinship, and are described (often with the derogatory tone of virtuous Victorian morality) as 'prostitution', 'concubinage' and 'polygamy'.

18. While Parry's finding is ethnographically particular and relates to his work on forms of labour and correlations with marriage amongst Bhilai Satnamis, I think it has salience for understanding the nature of primary love-marriage across urban north India.

19. PCO is the English acronym for 'Public Call Office' or payphones.

20. This is also reiterated in Hindi movie elaborations of romantic love, which are more gendered in that they tend to emphasise that an Indian girl only loves once and must always marry the object of her desire. See Parry on *Taal* (2001: 817).

21. Here I am not alluding to the area of economic and social theory concerned with 'social choice', but rather with what my informants considered to be society's choice of partner for themselves. The English word *'social'* is often used in Delhi to narrowly mean 'for the good of other people', which squares well with the notion that one marries for the good of one's people, not just for oneself. It also can be used as an adjective to mean 'of loose morals' if, for instance, it is used to describe the character of a girl who is seen to mix and move freely in the company of men: *'ladki badi social hain!'* (the girl is very *'social'*!)

22. Having said this, and putting aside the aesthetics of how a *jodi* should appear, Uberoi reminds us that in all the defining characteristics relating to gender relations in an arranged-marriage, asymmetry is a planned prerequisite so that husbands must be older, taller, have more prestigious jobs and earn better wages than their wives (2006: 35). Take the following anxious query to an Indian 'agony aunty' in a daily newspaper from 'S': 'I am a 24-year-old male 5'8" in height. I am in love with a girl who is one-and-a-half inches taller than me. We are both deeply in love and would like to marry. Our parents may object on grounds of my height. Can I increase my height by about two inches or so? (*a*) By any medicine or treatment? (*b*) If so, does this have any side effects? (*c*) Can exercise help in increasing one's height? (*d*) I have heard that treatment for increase in height can adversely

affect the sex organs. Is that so?' In *Hindustan Times*, 22 April 1998, Metropolitan, New Delhi, p. 5.

23. Chekki, writing in the late 1960s about modern values concerning personal choice in marriage among the Lingayats of southern India says: '[…] [I]n matters of marital alliance, the parents should approve the family and the boy should approve the girl. This idea itself seems to be a radical one. More radical would be the idea of a girl's need to approve the boy' (1968: 709). This scenario is more prevalent in Delhi too, though it is arguably changing, with girls increasingly able (and willing) to use arguments about continuing education and careers to bolster their requests to delay or veto impending marriages with boys they consider unsuitable.

24. 'What Women Want', cover story in *Outlook*, 28 October 2002, New Delhi.

25. While I was acquainted with Amit, his circumstances were revealed to me by a common friend. When I sought to broach the subject with him, he was embarrassed and uneasy, and I had to abandon the attempt. The discussion above is as reported to me by the common friend.

26. Although Amit's parents did finally agree to the marriage, I was told that his wife was taunted at her *sasural* (in-law's) by women in the neighbourhood about her alleged sexual licentiousness.

27. Unsurprisingly, I encountered a case of a love-marriage couple in their 50s whose subsequent actions dramatised some of the long-term effects of self-arrangement and social exclusion. The husband, who described his marriage as one in which 'not one *cowrie* was exchanged' (no dowry was received) said that his wife and he were now against love-marriages and had insisted that all their daughters had appropriately arranged and highly ritualised marriages with huge dowries worth many thousands of rupees given as prestations. He argued that he had lost so much prestige and status through his own love-marriage, that he was determined to regain lost ground through these arranged-marriages, to the enormous satisfaction of his kin group. Jauregui and McGuiness also report one such case (2003: 81–82).

28. This phenomenon has been variously described as 'boy-arranged or self-arranged marriage' (Kanan 1963) or 'semi-arranged marriage' (Corwin 1977: 827). Corwin observes that in Bengal, these sorts of marriages usually involved people from closely related caste groups or related sub-castes where only the immediate family knew that the marriage was in the first instance a love-match.

29. I use the term loosely here to refer to a whole spectrum of behaviour ranging from self-arranged love-marriages, elopements to 'abduction'. I do this only for the purpose of examining the cultural terrain we encounter. I am careful to tease out the implications of force, the

appearance of force and actual coercion in the reckoning of love-marriage phenomena later in this Introduction, and more specifically in Chapter 3.

30. The *Dharmasastras*, composed roughly between 500 BC and AD 500, are a collection of religio-legal texts written in large part by Brahmans. Since they were seen to be the basis of Hindu religious law the *Dharmasastras* were used by colonial authorities to form the basis of their understanding of Hinduism and laws that they subsequently enacted for Hindus.

31. These four types are described as '*adharmiya*'—or 'disapproved by religion' and are contrasted by the four '*dharmiya*' types (sanctioned by religion): *brahma*, *daiva*, *arsa* and *prajapatya* (see Basu 2001: 23).

32. Indeed, *raksasa vivaha* was enjoined upon the entire caste of Kshatriyas or warriors as a means of enabling them to obtain wives during their campaigns and wars.

33. The *Ramayana* is the Sanskrit epic poem composed about 900 BC, recounting the feats of Ram, King of Ayodhya (Thapar 1969: 33).

34. See Basu (2001: 24).

35. Personal communication from Veena Das.

36. Radha came from a family of cowherds while Krishna, though brought up by cowherds, was in fact the son of a Kshatriya prince (see Fuller 1992: 156).

37. This brings to mind the insightful observation by Gell (1996) in the context of Melanesian Umeda sexual relations between unmarried boys and married women in Melanesia: 'If cross-cousin marriage is the 'elementary form' of kinship alliance, then the elementary form of love is adultery'. That said, while the conventions of *Bhakti* poetry celebrated the illicit and the transgressive, the Sanskrit epics considered adultery as one of the five sins for which there is no atonement, causing one to be endlessly reborn as vile animals such as wolves, dogs and snakes (Kakar and Ross 1995: 92).

38. The sources they use range from the *Mahabharata*, *Panchatantra* and *Kamasutra* to medieval Sanskritic and Perso-Urdu texts, and more recent sources from the late 18th century to the present.

39. The Koya of Madhya and Andhra Pradesh prefer symmetrical cross-cousin marriage (MBS/FZD) but also accept 'improper' or thieving marriages—in the case of Brukman's work, all the men under the age of 35 in one hamlet had had such marriages in which abduction or elopement had taken place. The families often relented in the face of such actions, resigning themselves to a Koya aphorism: 'If a dog bites something you value, then you have to give it to him' (1974: 310). A *paitu*, amongst the Maria as described by Elwin (1950), is a young woman who comes of her own accord to cohabit with a man, thus forcing him to marry her.

40. *Sanskritisation* is the term coined by the Indian anthropologist M. N. Srinivas to refer to a process whereby lower castes took on the language, social practices and rituals of upper-caste groups in order to claim a higher position in the caste hierarchy. One could add to this vocabulary the equally dynamic and interesting process in the other direction—what I call *'Mandalisation'*, whereby intermediate ranking castes that are often economically poor seek to lower their status through bureaucratic and state recognition in order to avail of positive discrimination in the form of jobs and educational privileges.

41. Of course, it is important to add a caveat at this stage too, that this is not always and necessarily so. For instance, Nivedita Menon describes a case in which three men accused of abducting a 14 year-old girl (one of them subsequently raping her) appealed on the grounds that as Bhils of Jhabua in Madhya Pradesh, they had merely followed the tribal custom of *Bhagoriya* marriage in which a woman is abducted, the couple have sexual intercourse and the man settles the matter by paying the girl's father an agreed sum of money. The court established that a rape had indeed been committed, and ruled that the law (ironically, the Hindu Marriage Act which due to its colonial conceptions completely overlooked the distinctiveness of *adivasi* communities and tribal culture) superseded 'tribal custom', though the punishment was reduced due to an out-of-court settlement between the girl's father and the accused. Such are the legal ambiguities that exist in India (N. Menon 2000: 79–80). Menon argues convincingly that many tribes have marriage customs that allow women more independence in marriage than the provisions of the Hindu Marriage Act; the judgement thus serving to curtail (rather than empower) women's rights in tribal communities.

42. Parry (2001: 787) shows that the basic argument about primary and secondary marriages can be found in Dumont, who describes primary marriage as the marriage form that is more strictly regulated, more expensive and prestigious; where the marriage bond is dissoluble, the secondary marriages are inferior, less expensive and less elaborately ritualised. While this explains the high frequency of secondary inter-caste marriages, it also points to a very important dimension of these which we might describe as the seeming sexual liberation of women, and the fact that the rigid controls over female sexuality that exist prior to her primary marriage are much more loosely interpreted when that marriage breaks down. Parry's theory is that there is a correlation between the instability of marriage and inter-caste relationships. This goes some way towards explaining why the marriages I look at are so problematic because they flout the appropriate norms of an *unmarried* girl's chastity and good conduct.

43. The couple were given a 'lenient' sentence of three years rigorous imprisonment and a monetary fine of Rs 10,000. See Jessica Stern's report for Human Right's Watch on *http://hrw.org/english/docs/2007/06/21/pakist16231.htm*
44. The enormously popular Bihari leader Jayaprakash (known as 'JP') was a member of the Janata Party coalition which displaced Indira Gandhi's Congress Party in 1977, after the latter's infamous period of rule through resort to the state's emergency powers.
45. I am grateful to Bela Bhatia and Tarun Bharati for information about Bihar and ULFA respectively.
46. Gender Politics in South Asia, 6/11/2007, Institute of Commonwealth Studies, London; organised by Prof. S. Rai and Prof. S. Sardar Ali of the University of Warwick, U.K.
47. I should add a caveat here. It has also been noted that lovers who are retrieved by the police on behalf of their families are particularly vulnerable to torture and indeed, there have been cases of alleged 'suicide' in police custody. Take for instance the table of 3 cases of 'suicides' in Police stations in Delhi in a People's Union for Democratic Rights (PUDR) report entitled 'Courting Disaster', 28/08/2003 (*http://www.pudr.org*). In the first case of suicide in Azadpur Sabzi Mandi Police Station, a Muslim man who had eloped with a married Kashmiri woman 'committed suicide by taking poison in the presence of police and brother-in-law'. The second case concerned a 20-year-old vegetable seller and his allegedly 15-year-old lover at the ISBT (Inter-State Bus Terminus) police post in Delhi. It isn't clear from the PUDR report if the man alone or both he and his lover 'committed suicide'. In the third case registered at Mangolpuri Police Station, Bijender, a 25 year-old-Sikh man and Reena, a low-caste Jatav (or *chamar*) married and returned home at the advice of his family and surrendered to the police. He allegedly 'committed suicide' by consuming poison in the police station. Four hours later, his wife 'committed suicide' by swallowing poison in the police station toilet. In these three cases of death in custody, only one resulted in any action being taken against the police. In the last 'double suicide' case, the SHO or Station House Officer was transferred.
48. For a full description of Sita's rejection see Hess (1999). It is important to remember that the Sanskrit epics are not unified texts but are the result of accretions and diverse oral and literary traditions. As Van der Veer makes clear, 'The entire notion of a homogenous literary tradition is the result of hard, Orientalist labour in the production of "critical editions"' (1994: 145). One should add that the hugely popular televised serial of the *Ramayana* in 1987 disseminated the standard version of the epic across India and especially amongst the middle class. For a historical analysis of the different ways in which

Ram and Sita are represented through history, including the earliest documentation of the Ram legend, the *Dasratha Jataka* in which Sita is described both as Ram's sister and his wife, see Jaiswal (1993).

49. A suitable analogy would be that of the Christian Nativity play in England.

50. Dussehra is a ten-day festival of fasts, ritual observances and festivity, culminating in a celebration of Ram's killing of Ravan. The Hindu religious nationalists such as the VHP (Vishwa Hindu Parishad, literally, 'World Hindu Organisation; an organisation of Hindu religious leaders, also regarded as the 'cultural wing' of the BJP) use the occasion to organise marches in Indian cities and towns bearing uniforms and accompanied by music. They also worship weapons on the occasion of *Dusshera* (Hansen 1999: 251). The month-long dramatic *Ramlila* can be traced back to Tulsidas' epic *Ramcharitmanas* written in devotional Hindi in the 1570s, and still recited verse by verse during *Ramlila* performances.

51. See Derné for middle-class men in Banaras and their reactions to the televised Ramayana serial. For instance, he describes one of his informants: 'Nathuram Mishra quotes a verse from the epic to suggest that chaos is the result of granting women freedom' (1995: 129).

52. Van der Veer points out that it was Mahatma Gandhi who first began to publicly quote Tulsidas and refer to *Ramrajya* as an ideal social order, but this was soon hijacked by Hindu religious nationalists who were quick to seize the potential for such an articulation to alienate Muslims and to define the new nation of India in the language of Hindu religious nationalism (1994: 174). See also Hansen (1999).

53. See for instance Hess (1999) and Kishwar (1997).

54. Partha Chatterjee has described the *Sita-Sati-Savitri* construct as emerging out of a middle-class culture in the era of Indian nationalism. He argues that by characterising women as goddesses, the nationalists liberated women from their sexuality and facilitated their safe movement into the outside world (1989: 248–49). I would disagree with this simple characterisation of how women emerged into the public sphere on the grounds that part of Sita's story is the account of her abduction for which she suffers a great deal. If women did emerge into the public sphere, it was with the full awareness that this was fraught with danger because even chaste and pious women risked the consequences of hurt male honour and pride.

55. Presumably in an attempt to provide transparency.

56. The first branch of the Arya Samaj in Delhi was founded in 1878. Jones has pointed out how organisations such as the Arya Samaj were integral to the growth of Hindu religious nationalism in north India, and how Delhi became the centre of these movements from the 1890s onwards. While the Arya Samaj was initially a reformist

Hindu organisation seeking to transform orthodox Hinduism, the tensions between Hindus and Muslims meant that the Aryas often aligned themselves with the orthodox, against Muslims and Christians (Jones 1986: 336). In 1911, the Arya Samajis began their campaign to 're-convert' Muslims in Delhi through the *shuddhi* ('purificatory' or 'reconversion') ceremony. This led to wide-scale communal tensions in the city. The reconversion movements of the Arya Samaj have sought to reverse the total excommunication of apostates from Hinduism, thus serving as what Viswanathan has called a 'handmaiden of memory', reclaiming Muslims as Hindus, and in so doing, reminding them that their claims to 'difference' and 'otherness' are false (Viswanathan 1996). See Mayaram for a chilling account of reconversion activities of the Arya Samaj amongst the Meo's in north India at the time of Partition (1996).

57. See Gupta (2002: 207).
58. The Hindu Mahasabha subscribe to the view that the nation should consist of a unified community of Hindus only (See Hansen, 1999: 45).
59. Stories such as these were blatantly provocative (with headlines such as '*Miyaji ki Kartut*' or 'Sinful Act of a Muslim'; '*Musalman Utha Le Gaya Hindu Yuvaki Ko*' or 'Muslim Abducted a Hindu Woman') presenting themselves as 'fact' (2002: 212–13).
60. The Bajrang Dal is the youth branch of the Vishwa Hindu Parishad.
61. This claim was made in April 2007. Earlier, in Dec. 2006 another journalist reported his boast that he had 'rescued' 706 girls (Refs. below). A crude count of how many girls he has 'rescued' in this short period of time from December 2006 to April 2007 (even counting both months) would equal 212. In five months that would average 42.4 rescues a month, i.e. an average of 1.4 so-called 'rescues' a day! Surely we would have to conclude that he overstates his numbers or that there are an enormous amount of love-marriages taking place all over Gujarat (and indeed western India) and that he and his Bajrang Dal activists are exceptionally effective in finding out about them and locating the couple's whereabouts. See Countercurrents.org; Krishnan, Kavita, 12 April 2007, 'Betis as Bombs—Exploding the Borders of Caste and Community'; *http://www.countercurrents.org/kavita120407.htm*. Dionne Bunsha 16–29 December 2006, 'A Serial Kidnapper and his 'Mission'', in *Frontline*, vol. 23, Issue 25, *http://www.hinduonnet.com/fline/fl2325/stories/20061229001810100.htm*
62. The High Court apparently ordered a police enquiry into the case. The police report verified that Bajrangi had beaten and abused girls and made them ask for divorces under duress. Pregnant girls had been forced into abortions. They suggested that Bajrangi be arrested and that further investigations be made into all cases of female

kidnappings. However, the High Court ruled that since the allegedly abducted wives hadn't substantiated their claims under oath in court, no action could be taken other than to refer the cases to the matrimonial courts (Bunsha ibid.).

63. Babu Bajrangi and his ilk could easily be described after the anthropological convention (after Strathern and Godelier) as 'big men'. Das and Poole characterize such 'big men' not as embodying traditional authority, but rather as bearers of the mutation of 'traditional authority made possible by the intermittent power of the state', and its ability to dispense private justice and violence (2004: 14).

64. Indeed, Bunsha begins her article with the following: '"I have some *masala* [something spicy] for you", Babubhai Patel (alias Babu Bajrangi) told me excitedly when I called to arrange an interview with him. "There are three new girls with me". [...] Every time I meet him, he brags about the girls he has "rescued", almost as if each one were a new conquest"'.

65. The violence was both literally and metaphorically pornographic, with unthinkable atrocities committed and known perpetrators escaping without charge. See the report of the Concerned Citizen's Tribunal which was headed by Justice V.R. Krishna Iyer (Retired Judge of the Supreme Court) and consisted of two retired Supreme Court judges, one retired judge from the Mumbai High Court, and two Professors from Jawaharlal Nehru University, Delhi. Concerned Citizens Tribunal—Gujarat, 2002, *Crime Against Humanity: Volume I: An Inquiry into the Carnage in Gujarat, List of Incidents and Events*, p. 39. (See pp. 36–43 for details of Naroda Gaon and Naroda-Patiya.)

66. During the final edit of this book in November 2007, an expose by the Indian internet news group Tehelka.com came to my attention, featuring the organisation and role of the Hindu right in the 2002 Gujarat killings. Centre stage in this was a lengthy and detailed secretly filmed statement of Babubhai Bajrangi for his leading role in the events at Naroda Patiya (*http://www.tehelka.com/story_main35. asp?filename=Ne031107After_killing.asp*).

67. There has been much recent writing on the formation of publics: See for instance Michael Warner on publics and counterpublics (2002), Dale Eickelman and Armando Salvatore on Islamic publics (2004), and Francesca Orsini on Hindu publics (2002).

68. Cohen's term (1997: 302).

69. The name, Tis Hazari possibly comes from the rank of *Mansabdar* in the Mughal period. They maintained private armies for the rulers—in this case, of *tis hazaar* or 30,000 men. In the more recent past, the name refers to the '*Tees Hazari Maidan*' (grounds) on which the court complex was built, and which was situated to the west of Rajpur road

and flanked by Boulevard road (Bastavala 1922: 10). More recently, Tis Hazari has entered the geographical imagination of the city as an important stop on the new underground Metro service.

70. Rickshaw drivers were important informants because they came from a wide variety of backgrounds, and due to their evident mobility, had an intimate sense of the diversity of the city and its complex politics and social relations. Further, I was able to conduct lengthy and intensive 'public' interviews (often in groups) while they queued-up and awaited the arrival of long-distance trains at railway stations.

71. A *busti* literally means a settlement, but is commonly translated as a slum. However, the *bustis* I worked in consisted of solid structures, with water, electricity and some sanitation, for working class families who comprise the vast pool of labour for the city. The lifestyle in these *bustis* was relatively more prosperous than those in 'J-J Colonies' or *jhuggi-jhopdi* colonies, meaning non-permanent structures without any security or safety). These *bustis* are what are called 'resettlement colonies' set up by Delhi's municipal government in the 1960s to push slum dwellers outside the limits of what was then the city. Each home consists of a square plot upon which precarious structures are built to optimise the available space. Cramped and crowded as they are, they are nonetheless symbols of a relatively settled urban existence.

72. The National Human Rights Commission (NHRC) was established in India along with the State Human Rights Commissions in states and the Human Rights Courts in 1994. It includes the National Commission for Minorities, the National Commission for Scheduled Castes and Scheduled Tribes, and the National Commission for Women.

73. JMS is a grassroots women's organisation that has a presence in the shanty I worked in. Many of the women I worked with had originally brought their cases to the meeting of the legal disputes cell of JMS, where local women met to arbitrate disputes. JMS is a member of AIDWA—the All India Democratic Women's Association, and is politically affiliated to the Communist Party of India (Marxist).

74. The Bharatiya Janata Party (Indian People's Party) was founded in 1980, and since the late 1980s has been at the forefront of the rising tide of Hindu nationalism in Indian politics.

75. Indeed, local gossip had it that one such body had surfaced in a public latrine down the road from where we lived. Interestingly, most of the national papers failed to publish any of these details so as not to further incite religious tension (personal communication from a *Times of India* reporter).

76. For instance, *Navbharat Times*, '*Badi Be-dil Ho Gayi Hai Dilwalo ki Dilli*' (rather crudely, 'The City of the People with Heart has Lost its Heart' (date withheld), p. 1, New Delhi.

77. *http://www.censusindia.net*

78. In *India Today*, 'The New Delhi', 6-12-1999, *http://www.india-today. com/itoday/19991206/cover/html.*
79. *http://www.censusindia.net.*
80. There are over 1,600 'unauthorised colonies' and settlements in Delhi with an estimated 3 million people. Unauthorised colonies are built by squatters, usually on government land, and they lack basic infrastructure such as sewage systems, electric and water supply or roads. In *The Hindu*, 'The Delhi That Is Unauthorised', by Ashok Kalkur, 11-5-1998, p. I, New Delhi. See Tarlo (2000) for a history of resettlement colonies and forced sterilisation programmes for dwellers of *jhuggi-jhopdi's* in Delhi.
81. The notorious Blueline buses that rattle around at break-neck speed are considered dangerous and unreliable, particularly for unaccompanied girls and women. The result is that private vehicles, especially the more affordable 'two-wheelers' (scooters), are greatly valued and seen as an essential facility for urban life.
82. This situation has been somewhat ameliorated by the expanding network of the underground Metro, which incidently has a station at the district court, the land for which was acquired from some lawyers' chambers in Tis Hazari.
83. See, for instance, *Times of India*, 'Delhi's Rape Rate is Double Country's Average', 11-12-1997, p. 4, New Delhi, or *Times of India*, '60% Drivers have no Knowledge of Rules: Study', 24-11-1997, p. 4, New Delhi.
84. Throughout this book, I refer to India's commercial capital as Bombay rather than Mumbai. This is not because of ignorance or rebellion—I am well aware of the name-change effected by an Act of the Indian Parliament in 1997 that made the city officially 'Mumbai'. However, in using the name 'Bombay' I am conforming to local styles of speech that continue to refer to the city as *'Bombay'* in English, *'Mumbai'* in Marathi and Gujarati and *'Bumbai'* when speaking Hindi. It is the same convention I adopt when referring to Calcutta rather than Kolkata.
85. In Hindi, *'Pyar ko kehte hai najaish rishta. Hamne kaha, "shadi pehle, uske bad, jo bhi pyar".'*
86. Dwyer notes that in Hindi there is no word for a friend of the opposite gender: 'The term "male friend" (*dost, mitra*) if used by a woman would mean "boyfriend", and similarly for "female friend" (saheli, *bahenpani*) ...' (2000: 51). It is in this context that one needs to recognise that even 'professional' relations in Delhi between women and men are invariably strained and often imbued with quite overt sexual or romantic overtones.
87. I am grateful to Maya Warrier for information about 'Group Housing' in Delhi.
88. See Das in Das and Poole (2004: 231) for a similar observation for *jhuggi-jhopdi* clusters in Delhi.

89. In *India Today*, 'A Search for Intimacy', by Madhu Jain, 31-12-1996, pp. 78–86, New Delhi.
90. In *India Today*, 'Youth Poll', 27-9-1999, *http://www.india-today.com/itoday/19990927/cover12.html*.
91. So, for instance, one article in the newspaper says 'More and more modern Indians today are opting for traditional, arranged marriages where parents guide or even decide who they should settle for. If the '70's and '80's saw an explosion of love marriages by young Indians, in the new millennium, the trend has reversed. "Arranged marriages are making a comeback now", says [Sociologist] Singh.' In *Times of India*, 'Arranged Marriages Bounce Back', by Malvika Kaul, *http://www.timesofindia.com/today/03revw1.htm*; 3-9-2000.
92. In *The Hindu*, Metro Supplement, 'Court Marriages Catching On', by Debasree Banerjee, 15-9-1997, p. 1, New Delhi (Ref. I/186).

ॐ

1

'A Form of Marriage in Certain Cases'

In March 1872, as a result of a petition from Keshub Chandra Sen and the Brahmo Samaj (the 'Keshubites'),[1] the Governor General of India assented to 'an Act to Provide a Form of Marriage in Certain Cases', otherwise known as Act III of 1872. This Act provided for the first time in India a law for civil marriage. It was not a civil marriage law that made no distinctions on the grounds of religion, but rather was conditional on certain declarations that the bride and groom had to make before the Registrar could marry them. The Legislative Council, responding to the call by social reformers for the legalisation of inter-caste and inter-community marriages, managed to make the ability to contract such marriages conditional on a repudiation of faith in the form of a written declaration. The declaration said: 'I do not profess the Christian, Jewish, Hindu, Muhammadan, Parsi, Buddhist, Sikh or Jaina religion'.[2] While it did not demand a renunciation of 'religion' altogether (one could profess other beliefs such as the creed of the Keshubite Brahmo Samaj, which were not Christian, Jewish, Hindu etc.), it did imply that any persons choosing to avail of the law would have to place themselves outside the professed faiths of these eight religious groups. The law thus sought to create an open-ended category of those who, quite literally, belonged to 'not-community', or at least none of the communities mentioned here.

The remaining conditions for the applicability of the law began with a declaration of being 'unmarried'. The second was a declaration of being above the age of 18 for men, and 14 for women. This was an extremely sensitive issue, as proved by the Age of Consent debate nineteen years later (Chakravarti 1998; Chandra 1998; R. Kumar 1993; Sen 1980). In 1891, opposition to the Age of Consent Bill came from orthodox Hindus who sought to prevent reformers from raising the age of consent for girls from 10 to 14 years. Act III of 1872, on the other hand, managed to set a higher age for civil marriage because the Keshubites were willing to submit to its provisions. However, a concession to the orthodox opponents of Act III pushed the age at which a person could independently contract a marriage even higher. A clause in the Act raised the age of individual consent (from 18 for boys and 14 for girls) to 21 years of age, unless there was written consent of the parent or guardian. The third provision of Act III of 1872 concerned a disavowal of being related by the laws of consanguinity or affinity to which either of the parties was subject, which would render a marriage illegal under their own respective 'personal laws'. The law regarding 'prohibited degrees of marriage' (who one could or could not marry) was to be the custom or religious law of the two contracting parties. Thus, in one breath there was a renunciation of religion, and in the other, the acknowledgement of religious injunctions regarding kinship relations between marital partners. We must note here the disconnecting of certain aspects of religion from others; in this case, faith from marriage rules on kinship distance.

By 1872, three bills had been debated; the Council had wrestled with them for three-and-a-half years, and the result was a muted civil law for marriage. In all its forms, it was bitterly contested and opposed by most 'natives' whose opinion had been solicited. Other than the members of the Brahmo Samaj who had originally sought the enactment, it was viewed with outright hostility as a measure that was unnecessary, a violation of the religious rights of communities, and an invitation to the destruction of castes and communities. It was felt that it would ruin 'public morality' through licentiousness and rebellion, an invitation to 'make Europeans out of Indians'. If the Act met with anything other than hostility, it was extreme ambivalence. As one commentator of the time warned, people would merely view such marriages as 'a sort of authorised concubinage'.[3]

The anthropological relevance of this act is three-fold. Firstly, it allows us an insight into the historical circumstances in which colonial marriage legislation was framed. This provides valuable details about the ways in which Indians viewed the relationship between the legal system and 'social reform' which was beginning to gather momentum around this time. It also allows us to examine the process by which the law opened up a space, albeit half-heartedly, between the letter and practice of the law, indicating that the law is only partly willing to support the individual right to marriage. Secondly, the debates surrounding the legislation of this act illustrate the ways in which the location of love and desire within marriage were seen to be problematic and to threaten reputations within the *biradari*, caste or community. It raises pertinent questions about the ways in which educated Indians and British colonial legislators viewed marriage as an arrangement between groups rather than individuals, and morality as a domain outside the legitimate bounds of intervention by the colonial state. Finally, it provides a range of discussions about public morality in the specific context of various groups and communities raising objections to the introduction of civil marriage and 'marriages of love' to India. Such reactions over the legalising of 'love' liaisons show the apprehensions over the possibility of social 'mixing' between castes and ethno-religious communities, and the perception that anyone having a civil marriage is shameless and profligate. The salience of 1872 to an ethnography of love-marriage in Delhi in the 1990s is that this debate and the subsequent enactment created a theoretical, and subsequently legal space for not-community. In modern-day Delhi, its relevance is even more immediate because love-marriage couples must negotiate legislation inherited from the colonial era which is suffused with paradoxes and prejudices about the meanings and extents of community 'rights', the importance of 'caste' and religion, and the gendered nature of desire.

In examining this legislation I also want to draw attention to the anthropological implications of this particular attempt to regulate Indian marriage. Mendelsohn (1981) in the context of Cohn's assertions about the alleged 'litigious disposition of Indians' has argued convincingly that the British drew land relations 'more tightly into the web of government than any other facet of social life', and this is the reason why land disputes rather than say, marital conflicts, find their way to the Anglo-Indian courts (1981: 843). Even though both marital disputes and conflicts over land are endemic to village India, he argues that 'land disputes have been shown to account for the great bulk of litigation' in the colonial era. He compares this situation to Africa, where British intervention into domestic matters they regarded as 'uncivilised' prompted a much greater preoccupation with matrimonial law than in India, where there prevailed a 'general policy of non-intervention' (ibid.: 843). Mendelsohn's argument rests upon the notion that land was a major factor in litigation because there existed clear *material* causes to litigate. I am going to suggest that this early attempt to make incursions into the most contentious aspect of marriage was so eagerly repulsed by urban educated Indians because it had both moral *and* material implications in the crucial matters of inheritance and succession.

Mendelsohn points out that disputes in matters concerning marriage had hitherto been adjudicated by a range of authorities including heads of clans and lineages, village headmen and *panchayats* (loosely, an 'assembly'), dominant castes and caste *panchayats*. Such authority allowed these various assemblies to decide matters of custom, for example, the toleration of widow remarriage or the modification of rules pertaining to intermarriage (Dumont 1998: 173). One would expect that the introduction of a new authority willing to recognise and authorise inter-caste and inter-community marriages would provide a fresh opportunity structure in matrimonial affairs and, over time, this would lead to an increasing dependence on Anglo-Indian courts. However, this was never the case, and in this chapter I try and explain why civil marriage never became popular amongst Indians until well into the post-Independence period.

The Native Marriage Bill, the Brahmo Marriage Bill, and the Final 'Act III of 1872'

In their petition of 1868, the Keshubites submitted a draft to indicate the lines along which they hoped to obtain legislative relief. It proposed that a 'Brahmo' in any of the provinces be appointed by the local government or Chief Commissioner who would authorise him to grant certificates of marriage between 'Brahmos'. The main conditions for such marriages were a minimum age of 18 for a boy and 14 for a girl, substantially higher than that set as the age of consent in 1860. If the girl was a minor, the consent of her father or guardian was to be obtained.[4] Neither party should have a husband or wife still living, thus enshrining the principles of widow remarriage and monogamy. Finally, the vows taken before the Brahmo Registrar declared: 'I, A.B., am a Brahmo, and I do declare in the presence of the Almighty God that I take thee C.D., to be my lawful wedded wife (or husband)...'[5] The condition of marriage then, was a profession of faith to the Brahmo religion. The Keshubites effectively requested the government to pass a law which would recognise them as a distinct 'community' whose members could intermarry freely according to their own rites.

A little over two months later, Henry Maine, then Law Member of the Governor General's Legislative Council, responded to the Keshubite petition by presenting the Council with a draft Bill entitled 'A Bill to Legalise Marriages Between Certain Natives of India Not Professing the Christian Religion'.[6] This was the first of the three drafts and it was more commonly referred to by its shorter name: the Native Marriage Bill. The main significance of this Bill was that it was not restricted to the Brahmos, and that it introduced civil marriage to India. Any two 'natives' (crucially, 'not professing the Christian religion') who 'objected to be married in accordance with the rites of the Hindu, Muhammadan, Buddhist, Parsi or Jewish religion' could legalise their marriages under this law. The caveat regarding Christians was explained by Maine as necessary since civil marriages of Christians in India, i.e. marriage by a Registrar, had already been legalised by an Act of Parliament.[7] Maine's justification for extending the applicability of the Bill to non-Brahmos was two-fold. Firstly, the Brahmos were an ill-defined group, whose formation as a sect was undergoing constant changes. This made it difficult to define a Brahmo for legal purposes.[8] Secondly, young educated Hindus who were approaching marriageable age were, he noted, increasingly 'abandoning Hinduism and Hindu rites'. However, not all of these people enrolled in sects such as the Brahmo Samaj. If the Council were to limit the measure to the 'Brahmo Creed', then those who were not conscientiously Brahmos but who wished to discard their religions would make applications for a fresh measure. Despite the principle that measures concerning Native religion should be confined to those seeking them, which he entirely agreed with, Maine argued that it was more prudent to legislate once and for all on the matter of marriage.[9] Maine's justification for introducing a 'civil marriage' registration was the idea that, as in several European countries, there would first be a civil and afterwards a religious marriage. This would allow groups like the Brahmos to add whatever ritual they desired.

However, sufficient objections to the measure were received by the Council that there was considerable unease at not knowing the depths of 'Native opinion'. The most significant objection was that although Maine claimed it was a 'permissive act' (it did not affect the rights of those to whom the Bill did *not* apply), the application of the Act was not restricted to the Brahmos; instead, it provided a much wider ambit for those who wished to avail of its provisions. In the light of this it was finally agreed that the Bill should be introduced to a Select Committee and, under a suspension of rules, it should be published so that 'public opinion might pronounce on it'.[10] The Council also sent out a circular letter to request information from all local governments and administrators as to how the application of the principle of civil marriage was likely to be received by 'natives'.

The responses poured in over the next year and were assessed to be unanimously opposed to Maine's Bill. It was agreed that the Native Marriage Bill as introduced should not be passed. However, the Council felt that 'all' the local governments agreed that the Bill would be unobjectionable if confined to the Brahmo Samaj. James Fitzjames Stephen, who by this point had taken over from Maine as Law Member, drafted a second Bill called the 'Brahma Marriage Bill, 1871' which was introduced and published in the *Gazette*. The substance of the Bill was almost exactly what the Keshubites had originally petitioned for. It included a declaration prior to the solemnisation of the marriage to the effect that both parties were members of the Brahmo Samaj, that they were unmarried, and that the minimum age of marriage was to be 18 for the boy and 14 for the girl. Furthermore, as the Brahmos had wanted, the Registrar was to be known as the 'Registrar for Brahma Marriages', though it was unclear whether he would necessarily be a Brahmo.[11]

The second Bill brought forth an even more vitriolic outpouring than the first; this time from those members of the Brahmo Samaj who were not Keshubites. In particular, the Adi-Brahmo Samaj ('Original Brahmo Samaj') petitioned the Council in 1868 following Maine's Bill, and objected to the Keshubite reforms and the government's interventions to validate the practices of the breakaway sect as if they constituted the entire Brahmo Samaj. On 27 June 1871, the Council received a petition signed by 2,050 Adi-Brahmo Samajis who alleged that their 1868 memorial discrediting Keshub Chandra Sen had been wholly ignored. Stephen, who had taken over from Maine in 1869, defended himself by saying that even though he had signed a document declaring that amongst many others the Adi-Brahmo petition had been given due consideration, he had never actually seen the document. Incredibly, he also claimed not to have even known that there had been a split in the Brahmo Samaj or that the Keshubites were a breakaway group.[12]

The third Bill that emerged was passed into the Act III of 1872 with only a few minor changes. It was in many respects the same as Maine's first Bill, but with a few significant modifications that made concessions to earlier opposition. To begin with, it permitted dissenters from Christianity to avail of its provisions. Despite Maine's legal justifications for the exclusion of Christians, the perceived inequity of the first Bill had been a particular cause of irritation because it was interpreted as meaning that marriages between Christians and non-Christians would still involve conversion in a church. Further, the wording of the Preamble of the third Bill made it clear that those who availed of the Act were no longer to be considered members of their respective religious communities.

The emphasis on parties to such marriages being outside communities and claiming no religion, through the words 'do not profess', 'have renounced or been excluded from the communion of...' was a major triumph for the orthodox opponents of the measure. However, the tone was tempered in the final Act (III of 1872), so that it merely declared that it was a form of marriage for those 'who do not profess the Christian, Jewish, Hindu, Muhammadan, Parsi, Buddhist, Sikh or Jaina religion.' The declaration that Maine had proposed in the first Bill ('...I object to be married in accordance with the rites of the Hindu, Muhammadan, Buddhist, Parsi or Jewish religion') was replaced in the final Act with the declaration, 'I do not profess the Christian, Jewish, Hindu, Muhammadan, Parsi, Buddhist, Sikh or Jaina religion.' It also stated a minimum age of 18 for boys and 14 for girls. Further, boys and girls below the age of 21 years of age had to obtain the consent of their father or guardian before a marriage could be solemnised. [13] This was clearly directed at impetuous youth who could, it was alleged, avail of the Act themselves without considering its consequences. This concern was to some extent retained in the amendment of Act III of 1872 in 1954, when Nehru's government legislated the Special Marriage Act.[14] In this, the legal age of civil marriage was 21 for men and 18 for women. Interestingly, Act III of 1872 made the case that a widow of any age was *not* deemed to require the consent of her father or guardian, whereas widowers, unless over the age of 21, still required consent to marry according to their own conscience.

As Kopf has shown, 1872 was a major victory for the reformist Keshubites. Lord Lawrence had signed into law a 'virtual social reform act' which allowed for inter-caste and widow remarriage, and prohibited 'social evils' such as child marriage and polygamy (1979: 104).[15]

Other additions were that it held bigamy to be punishable under the Indian Penal Code, and made the provisions of the Indian Divorce Act applicable if any of the conditions of the Act were shown to be contravened. These conditions were that neither partner should have a living spouse; that neither be related to each other 'in a nearer relationship than that of great-great-grandfather, or great-great-grandmother', and residence of fourteen-days (in the district in which the marriage was to be registered) prior to the submission of notice. The submission of notice would be entered into the Registrar's Marriage Notice Book, which would be open to public inspection.[16] Another fourteen-day period was required after the submission of intended notice before a marriage could be solemnised in the presence of the Registrar and three witnesses. Once again, Stephen's Bill prior to Act III had suggested a much shorter five-day period of residence prior to notification, and five days following entry of notice in the Registrar's Notice Book, after which the marriage could be solemnised.[17] The extension of this period to two weeks prior and post-registration (in Act III of 1872) was another concession to the orthodox who felt that sufficient time should be allowed for families to travel to the relevant district and put forth their objections against the marriages of their children. Interestingly, the Special Marriage Act of 1954 extended the period from two weeks to thirty days prior to and post-registration. Clearly this was a concession to the notion that parents should be given ample opportunity to marshal their forces and raise whatever objections they might have against such marriages. Such measures made marriage a serious problem for eloping couples, who would have to escape their families for twenty-eight days in the period following 1872, and two months in post-Independence India.

On 22 March 1872, the first civil marriage law for Indians was enacted. It was a civil law on the basis that it was a form of marriage that was to be solemnised not by a religiously appointed 'clergyman', but rather by a state-appointed Registrar. However, the primary requisite of Act III of 1872 was a statement to the effect of a surrender of religious community through admitting not-community. In an ironic twist, an Act born out of a petition that pleaded for legal recognition of marriages that could be solemnised in accordance with the 'rights of conscience', made marriages under its provisions dependent on a denial of precisely some of those rights of conscience. By upholding the right *not* to be 'religious' (arguably, one element to the bundle of rights of conscience that was being upheld by the declaration: 'I do not profess the Christian, Jewish, Hindu…religion'), the law denied individuals availing of the Act of another: the right to retain belief, despite marriage.

Reassessing the Terrain: Native Collectivities

The declaration in Act III of 1872 served to limit civil marriage to those individuals willing to declare themselves not belonging to any of the specified religions and thus hypothetically constituted as a not-community of people. However, it was born out of a petition to the Governor General's Council for making Laws and Regulations to legitimate the marriages, not of free-willed individuals or atheists, but rather a 'community' of modern Hindus: the Brahmo Samaj of Keshub Chandra Sen. In its enactment, the law defined the limits of religious authority and sought to make provisions for those who moved away from their castes and ethnoreligious communities. It involved a substantial shift in emphasis in defining religious groups as being constituted not of birth but rather by 'choice' and 'individual conscience'. The two categories of communities of 'birth' and 'choice' were by no means exclusive, nor were they used by the British alone. Indeed, Sen's petition used both definitions to plead his case for a new marriage law.[18] In it the Brahmos, while 'enjoying social communion with the Hindus, assumed the position of a separate religious sect amongst them' and, in the course of the development of the sect had come to abhor from 'motives of conscience' the 'idolatrous, superstitious' and 'immoral' customs and rites in the marriages of Hindus. Their intentions were to 'restore the primitive monotheism of Hinduism' and solemnise marriages between those who may be of different castes through rites that were not idolatrous. His petition goes on to argue:

> Your memorialists have been advised that although it has been a matter of conscience with them to effect such innovations in the institution and

rite of marriage, yet that, as the *Brahmos are by birth Hindus to whom the Hindu law of marriage applies* in the absence of any special legislative enactment sanctioning Brahmo marriages, such marriages are illegal and their issues are illegitimate, and as such subject to many grave civil disabilities and to social reproach.[19]

He concludes that such an enactment, although not 'prejudicial to the community at large', would leave them 'unfettered to act according to the dictates of their religion and conscience' and would materially further the cause of 'Indian social reformation'. The argument they propounded is that being so disabled by the law of their birth, they require the law of the land to legitimate their 'individual consciences'. So the Brahmos argued that they are by birth Hindus, they enjoy social communion with Hindus, but for reasons of conscience, and in a bid to reform Hinduism and revert to its primitive monotheism, they have formed a separate sect.

One of the first problems for Sen was that his representation to the Council claimed to be on behalf of 'the Brahmo Samaj'. There is no indication in it that prior to this he had initiated a split with another faction within the Samaj, and thus could only claim to represent one of the groups. The Council received a petition from the Adi-Brahmo Samaj which vociferously rejected Sen's suggestion that all 'Brahmo Samajis' had broken away from the 'Hindu community'. They argued:

> The Brahmos, notwithstanding that they have renounced certain opinions and practices which they look upon as superstitious, and which are in no way essential portions of the Hindu religion, have always been recognised and treated even by the most orthodox Hindus as undoubted members of the Hindu community. [...] The reformed Hindu marriage ritual has in it all the essential elements which constitute a valid Hindu marriage.[20]

The Adi-Brahmo Samaj petition contested Sen's justification for legislation with the argument that Brahmo marriages were already legal Hindu marriages, and further, that Brahmos already belonged to what was being defined as an ethno-religious community: the 'Hindu community'. The attempt by the Keshubites to establish a 'Brahmo community' outside of Hinduism raised the spectre of total estrangement with the larger Hindu community, something that the Adi-Brahmo Samaj wished to avoid at all costs.

A brief look at the background of the Keshubites indicates that, indeed, they were increasingly straying from Hinduism, if by that was meant Hindu orthodoxy. In 1866 Sen led a group of liberal Brahmos to break away from the conservative elders of the Samaj to form the 'Brahmo Samaj of India' under his leadership. High-caste Brahmos removed their sacred threads as symbols of a renunciation of caste. Increasingly however, young Brahmos were being excommunicated by their castes and thrown out of their families for their pains at reforming Hinduism. The orthodox backlash against Brahmoism was formidable. For instance, Kopf cites an incident in the 1860s in which a Brahmo youth, Durga Mohun Das, 'fired up by the ideal of female emancipation, married off his widowed stepmother to a local medical practitioner. It was a love marriage.' The result was social excommunication. 'The doctor's clients deserted him, and he had to give up his practice' (Kopf 1979: 101) Kopf also argues that by the time Sen submitted the petition regarding the marriage Bill, he was increasingly aware that while the Brahmo Samaj was viewed as a 'religion' and an ideology, he had to make it a full-fledged 'community' in order to strengthen its ranks. The Brahmo Samaj offered refuge to young people: 'one of the most effective and practical ways early Brahmo leaders offered protection was to organise, institutionalise and legalise community solidarity' (ibid.: 102).

The split in the Brahmo Samaj into two groups—the Hinduised Brahmos (the Adi-Brahmo Samaj) and radical Keshubites—over the marriage laws meant that the Council could not legislate for the group 'Brahmo Samaj marriages'. Further, the Council felt it prudent to protect not just Sen's faction of the Brahmo Samaj but *all* those who dissented against marrying in conformity to the religious laws of any of the 'native' communities. This relief for dissenters was one of the reasons for extending an enactment which was initiated by a legal petition for relief covering a few thousand Hindus, to one that encompassed all dissenters (other than Christians) in India.[21]

In defence of his argument that increasingly, young educated Hindu men were abandoning 'Hindu rites' but were reluctant to 'enrol themselves in any one sect, or to proffer any definite creed', Maine cited the register of Calcutta University in which, under the records of the religions of students, 'Theist, Vedaist, Pantheist and Spiritualist are among the commonest...'[22] Stephen later expressed a similar concern with the ambiguities of the new religious movements:

> Be a Hindu or not as you please; but be one thing or the other; and do not ask us to undertake the impossible task of constructing some compromise between Hinduism and not-Hinduism, which will enable you to evade the necessity of knowing your own minds.[23]

The legislation that was framed (Act III of 1872) described the 'major' religions of India and created a category of 'none of the above' (i.e. not-community). Clearly Maine and Stephen's assumption about religious faith was that it was something you were born into but only remain in as an adult by an act of will or 'choice'. That is to say, if the Brahmos ceased to believe in the idols of Hinduism, and the caste-based hierarchies which prohibited inter-caste marriages, they were no longer 'Hindu'. The context to their assumption was the process of secularisation and loss of faith among intellectuals in England at this time (cf. Chadwick 1975). However, in India, this notion that 'members' of religious communities could 'opt out' of their groups was anathema to the vast majority. The defenders of orthodox religion included western-educated Indians like the Brahmos, but they sought to defend the rights of their communities to expel renegades rather than allow them to abandon their faith through legal provisions enacted by the colonial state.

In the outpourings of anger and disgust that met the publishing of the original Bill between 1868 and 1872, petitioners questioned the wisdom of the categories, the licence it allowed dissenters, and the inability of 'native communities' to respond with any potency. An earlier legal enactment had already severely affected the ability of religious communities to restrict the rights of renegades. This was the 1850 *Lex Loci* Act (XXI of 1850), or, the 'law of the place'.[24] One of the provisions in *Lex Loci* was that 'the Courts of the East India Company would no longer uphold any forfeiture of rights or property' or the 'right of inheritance' which was being denied by reason of a 'Native renouncing or having been excluded from the communion of any religion, or being deprived of caste'.[25] Thus, despite religious identity being the basis of a person's legal rights, *Lex Loci* ensured that these rights were made partible; the right to religion being different and separable from, say, the right to property. Further, a Hindu convert to Christianity could avail of the joint family property by virtue of having been born a Hindu, and could choose by virtue of his Christian identity to pass on his property through a will to his heirs (as opposed to his joint family). Religion did not absolutely determine one's rights to inheritance, and despite social sanctions, the verdict was that the courts would *not* uphold the rights of religious communities to deny or punish their wayward wards. This was an indicator of the extent to which the law was willing to re-categorise what combination of the elements of religion-by-birth, 'customary practice' and 'conscience' were to determine the civil rights of the 'natives'. It was thus hardly surprising that the primary justification provided by Maine was that the law of civil marriage he was proposing was 'only a small extension' of the principle of the *Lex Loci* Act. This 'charter of religious freedom' was to serve to relieve natives of 'the greatest of all civil disabilities, the disability to contract a lawful marriage'.[26]

The legal historian J.D.M. Derrett has criticised the way in which the British manipulated the category of who was and who wasn't a Hindu:

> The net was indeed elastic therefore the mesh was not fine enough to allow all Hinduised tribes to escape, for it was advantageous that they should be governed by ascertainable rules; but it was fine enough to catch every non-Muslim, -Christian, -Parsi, and -Jew native inhabitant, unless he could prove positively that he was governed by certain and precise customs unambiguously binding upon him in derogation from the personal law. [...] [I]n vain did the Jains plead that Hindu rules were inapplicable to them as they had texts of their own. All were lumped together (1978(b): 77–78).

While the legal definition of 'Hindu' as a general residual category was different from the question of the voluntary 'opt-out' category of the Act, the response to the proposed colonial legislation was to defend the boundaries of 'Hinduism', not so much from the innovations of the Brahmos as from the British interceding on their behalf. This interference presented the British as dictating the terms in which 'dissent' within Hinduism was to be defined and articulated. Many petitioners therefore argued that the Brahmo innovation of non-idolatrous marriages was perfectly acceptable to 'Hinduism'. For instance, P. Srinivasa, the Principle of Sadr Amin of Vizagapatam, argued that there were 'two general forms of marriage ritual prescribed in the Hindu codes'. The first, sanctioned by the Vedas and meant for the 'three regenerate tribes', was invariable. The second, prescribed in the later Puranas, varied a great deal. '[I]ts forms are as numerous as the various sub-divisions of the sects of the people who compose the fourth class, commencing from the forms given in the *Puranas*, and ending with the simplest ceremony of joining hands in token of marriage…'[27] Other members of the Brahmo Samaj who sought to distance themselves from the Keshubites were similarly keen to emphasise that the marriage ritual was indeed in full accordance with the *shastras*, and they reiterated their subsumation within 'Hinduism'.[28] Hindus objected to the Bill, not because it created 'sects', but rather because the Brahmos were claiming that 'Hinduism' could not tolerate such diversity and, therefore, to validate their practices they had to seek recourse from the British.

Even if the Brahmos' position within or without 'Hinduism' could be resolved to the advantage of the orthodox, the second problem the Brahmo Bill raised concerned the same lumping together, but with altogether different social consequences. As one petitioner, Dawur Rustomji Khurshedji Modi of Surat remarked: '[T]he Bill by using the words "Marriage between Natives of India" evidently contemplates to do away with the distinction of caste or creed'. Another writer argued that the 'fusion of castes and creeds' would do away with the divisions of society which have hitherto enabled alien races to rule India' and this, it was argued, was inconsistent with other British enactments which sought to perpetuate 'English dominion'.[29] Not only was the Bill presented as objectionable to the sentiments of 'natives', it is alleged by loyal subjects that it also threatened the best interests of colonial rule.

The writer of the article is emphasising the positive value of India as an organically integrated *and* differentiated society. The vision of a strengthened unified Indian 'race' capable of over-throwing the colonial state (the 'fusion of castes and creeds' being inconsistent with the perpetuation of English dominion) is only alluded to negatively. The article continues with the argument that 'cosmopolitan marriages' succeeded in Europe because of the 'absence of [the] spirit of isolation of various nationalities of that continent, and the absence also of those deep contrasts between them which divide the million races of this country.' It concludes pessimistically:

In Europe, intermarriages […] can only infuse into the new generation the same quantity of blood, the same intensity of force, and the same amount of vigour and spirit, or nearly the same. In India, on the contrary, the chief dread of them is the *loss of individuality*, the humiliation and decay that are consequent on an unequal match, an inferior union. And it is precisely this feeling which the present Bill can lead to in its ultimate practical consequences.[30]

These views encapsulate the wider import of this Bill. The petitioner seems to be arguing that the proposed reform will both 'strengthen' and 'weaken' Indian society. He tries to scare the British with the talk of nationalism, while also putting forward a fairly standard view of Indian society: it works by hierarchy/complementarity and the interdependence of communities. This sort of society is qualitatively different from European nations and the attempt to turn India into a modern European nation would cause political trouble for the British and also produce something that wasn't really 'Indian' any more.[31] Interestingly, marriages of choice are seen to affect the essence, and cause 'the loss of individuality' of the *community*, so that the distinctiveness of a group of people is seen as diluted.[32] As we shall see, in Delhi in the 1990s, love-marriages were believed to be caused by *too much* individuality—of individuals—who are assumed to no longer care for the values of their 'community'.

Another indication that there were those who sought to use this legislation and the debates it raised to redefine their collectivities comes from Uttaram Khubchand, a Pleader in the Sindh Courts. He says that among the educated Natives of Bombay Presidency there are 'four classes' firstly, 'those who are opposed to any innovation whatsoever'; secondly, 'those who simply want to purify the marriage ritual'; thirdly, 'those who wish to bring about an amalgamation of all the Hindu castes, so as ultimately to form one Hindu nationality'; finally, there are 'those who desire an introduction of foreign blood as the only means of improving the race, for which purpose they do not consider a mere acquaintance with western literature and science sufficient'.[33] The marriage Bill was thus interpreted as many things all at once. For some, it was a clarion call to defend the faith from the incursions of reformers (no innovation wanted), but for others, the debate provided an opportunity to recreate a more authentic and subsequently more modern form of the marriage ritual (those wishing to 'purify' it).

The supporters of inter-caste marriages argued that they would provide the possibility of a unified caste-less Hinduism of one people (a pan-Hindu 'nationality'). Finally, those supporting inter-community marriages argued that these would introduce 'foreign blood' and this was the 'only means' of improving the whole of the 'Indian race'.

Shifting the Goalposts

Henry Maine, famed author of *Ancient Law* (1861), 'Father of British Anthropology' (Macfarlane 1991: 141), and of the theory that societies moved from Status to Contract, was the driving force in the Governor General's Council which received the Keshubite petition in 1868. The fact that the Brahmos were seeking to repudiate their 'status' (in this case, caste community) and intermarry through 'reformed rites' in the presence of a Brahmo authorised not by religious authority, but by the state, was, in a sense, in keeping with Maine's theory of 'progress': from caste 'status' to civil marriage 'contract'. The fact that the Brahmos had emphasised their claim to be reverting to original Vedic Hinduism was overlooked. For Maine, what was much more relevant was the Keshubite rejection of the customary law of their status group (Hindus). Thus, their innovation regarding non-idolatrous and inter-caste marriage was interpreted, from Maine's perspective quite reasonably, as a plea for civil marriage.[34] The Brahmos' plea of conscience implied that there was no customary law that applied to them. They had left the old status (custom)-based system (which was multiple) and so the state had to provide a contract-based (and universal) alternative for them.

Maine had to acknowledge that the view expressed by Advocate General Cowie that the marriages of the Keshubites would be held to be invalid was not a legal judgement, but purely a legal point of view. He consequently had to work hard to convince the Council that there was an express need to legislate. He did this by arguing that under the earlier statutes, Sikhs were considered to be 'Hindus'. However, since Sikh marriages were clearly not celebrated in accordance with Hindu 'rites of orthodox regularity' (the principle that Cowie had upheld), this meant that they too were 'invalid'. Maine's suggestion was refuted by a large number of administrators. Amongst those who took issue was Thornton, then Secretary to the Government, Punjab. He pointed out that the Punjab Civil Code (which had been judicially declared to have the force of law in the province) already provided for 'the recognition of marriages performed in good faith, even though not performed according to the orthodox ritual of the religion to which parties nominally belong'.[35] However, Maine persisted and made the argument that across India, religions had a tendency to 'throw off' sub-sects which adopted new practices or doctrines. Thus, Maine argued, there was much more 'formation of new creeds and practices than prima facie appears', and the only instrument to control this was timely legislation.

Thus, intervention to validate the Brahmos' entirely modern invention of a 'primitive Hinduism' is justified on the grounds that Native religion in its traditional 'usage' was flexible and permissive. It was colonial legislation and the administration of justice through regular courts that had changed its true nature and made it 'immobile'. In order to restore to 'Native religions' their original flexibility that allowed the free formation of new creeds, the state had a duty to legislate them back into existence. But interestingly, Maine rejected the Keshubite scheme of legislating directly for them. As we recall, he argued that his reason was administrative: it was to prevent the state from having to entertain petitions from every new sect that was formed, and that new sects in the process of formation were difficult to define legally. With this justification, he invented a category of individuals who were not-community—an obvious step towards contract-based marriage law. This logic failed to recognise the often repeated protest that not a single section of the Indian population actually wanted a civil marriage law—that is, a law that dispensed with the sanction of religion in forming marriage contracts.[36]

There are some striking parallels between this debate over religion and marriage and the discourses on the prohibition of *sati* in the early nineteenth century that Lata Mani (1989) examines. For instance, she identifies the debate as one in which tradition and modernity were simultaneously constituted, because ideologically, *sati* was not primarily about women, but about what constituted an 'authentic tradition': a discourse about tradition which was entirely modern. Similarly, Maine's justifications for legislation are primarily about restoring to Indian religions that which colonial law had 'fixed' and thus perverted.[37] This perversion, for Maine, resulted in injustices that denied Brahmos the rights of marriage. Since it was 'equitable and according to good conscience', that all 'men should have a right to marry', it was justifiable for the state to intervene.

The interest in the Brahmos was furthermore not coincidental. It is worth noting in some detail Stephen's exhortation to the Council on the need to support the final Bill.

> Brahmoism is at once the most European of Native religions, and the most living of all Native versions of European religion...Brahmos, in common with Englishmen, believe that marriage should be a union for life, in all common cases, of one man with one woman; and that the most numerous body of the Brahmos go a step further, and are of the opinion that marriage should be regarded in the light of a contract between a mature man and a mature woman of a suitable age, and not as a contract by which parents unite together children in their infancy. [...][T]he Progressive Brahmos are opposed to infant marriage and to polygamy far more decisively than the Conservative party [the Adi-Brahma-Samaja]. The former, in particular, adopt the European view, that marriage is a contract between the persons married; the latter retain the Native view, that the father can give away his daughter as he thinks right when she is too young to understand the matter.[38]

In this formulation, a crude trajectory of social evolutionism is set up. Europeans were mongamous and married according to choice. Polygamous natives married according to 'birth'. However, as we shall see in the final part of this chapter, this was not merely a 'colonial construction' but also an argument that many of the 'native' petitioners were insisting upon.

Despite Maine's argument about the original flexibility of Native religion, the self-appointed spokesmen of the latter were not willing to tolerate any challenge from dissenters, and put up a determined resistance to interference in their rights to excommunicate, expel or similarly disable their constituents. The fact that this legislation was being supported by the colonial state in favour of a group of urban, educated 'reformist' Hindus was viewed as a particularly irksome challenge to religious autonomy. But while the final Act of 1872 demanded a declaration of the repudiation of all the major 'native' religions along the lines of 'I am not a Hindu'...', this was in fact a concession to the strength and force of 'native' opinion. For the latter, far more objectionable was the original version of this declaration, found in Maine's draft of the Native Marriage Bill. The declaration went:

> I, A.B., am a Native of British India. I do not profess the Christian religion, and I object to be married in accordance with the rites of the Hindu, Muhammadan, Buddhist, Parsi or Jewish religion.[39]

The objection to it was founded on the widespread dissatisfaction that a civil law of marriage was about to recognise the principle that 'natives' had a right to dissent to their marriage ceremonies without first explicitly renouncing their religion. The implication was that the state could bear witness to this dissent (in the form of a written declaration) and that 'native communities' had no right to deal with such matters themselves. Any two 'natives' (other than Christians) willing to make this declaration could marry each other through a civil marriage in the presence of a Registrar. Such a marriage was to be held valid, despite 'personal laws', which indicated the contrary.

It soon became clear that this law was primarily designed to permit and legitimate inter-caste and inter-community marriages. The right to object to the 'rites' of a marriage ritual was held to enable any individual to contract a legal marriage: one could object to the rites and marry whomever one pleased *without* having to go beyond the social pale, through the gauntlet of excommunication. For the leaders of 'native' religious communities, dissenters could no longer be punished because of *Lex Loci*, but *Lex Loci* was primarily about outcastes and converts. Maine's Native Marriage Bill allowed dissenters to remain 'Hindus, Muhammedans', etc. and thus brought dissent into the body of 'communities'. The principle was that you remain a follower of a religion, and yet select according to an independent 'conscience' (in all likelihood groomed by English education), which rites you were willing to conform to and which not. This was seen as the thin edge of the wedge. Religion/law/custom and 'rites' could be expeditiously separated out and reassembled to cater to the abstract principles of colonial jurisdiction under the guise of social reform.

In the case of the law for civil marriage, there was little political 'exigency' as most counsels of 'prudence' argued the other way. Though, this is not entirely true. For instance, Stephen's description of 'Brahmoism as the most European of religions' cited earlier was a way of identifying those Indians most amenable to the colonial style of governance, and way of life. Neither was the state able to co-opt significant sections of the population to its support, but on the contrary it managed to antagonise large sections of 'native' communities which had initially been asked to pronounce upon the measure. Certainly, the most convincing argument about why Maine in the first instance and Stephen after him bothered at all with this law was that both of them believed in the need to transform India through legislation. As Viswanathan (1998) has pointed out, Law Member Stephen developed in India 'juristic notions of individual rights for a culture in which the customary laws were organised around the beliefs of communities'. Apart from Act III of 1872, he also enacted three significant legal provisions: the Evidence Act, the Contract Act and the revised Code of Criminal Procedure. Further, she says that:

> ... in the exercise of good, sensible English laws, Stephen imagined the possibilities of a 'moral conquest' more palpable than physical conquest—a possibility that he described in terms of 'a new religion'. Even more than Macaulay, Stephen fervently believed in the eventual displacement of Hindu and Muslim customary laws by English law (or what he called the 'gospel of the English')... (ibid.: 109).

During the eight years of Maine's stint as Law Member (1862–1869), an astonishing estimated 211 Acts were passed. Stephen, who took over from him (1869–1872), was similarly prolific. After ensuring the safe passage of Act III of 1872, Stephen retired and the new Law Member, Hobhouse, was strongly advised to slacken the pace of legislation because it was feared that it was fast outstripping public opinion in India (Jain 1972: 542). This fear was not unfounded. There was public outrage at the provisions of the Act. What is salient about this outrage, however, is that the decision of the Council to obtain Native opinion prompted Indians to take a much more active and assertive role in voicing their outrage. The colonial state was forced to make considerable amendments to all the Bills that were proposed and that was in no small measure due to the forceful petitions they received.

Public Morality and Not-Community

The Council published all the versions of the proposed Act in order to ascertain how the 'natives' would receive it. Representatives of the state were told to obtain the opinions of 'native gentlemen' whose thinking might have some weight in their communities. This served as the instigation for thousands of people to pronounce judgement upon the Bills. The respondents were only marginally concerned with the Keshubites, and their status as outcastes, innovators of ritual, or reformers of Hinduism. Far greater attention is paid in these petitions to the problem of 'public morality'. The greatest fear that is repeatedly expressed is that the Act would introduce and encourage marriages based on 'lust', and that this would lead to profligacy and immorality. The colonial state, consisting as it did of Europeans who were accustomed to marrying out of choice, were told by these respondents that 'native society' could never countenance such a state of affairs which threatened to do away with 'all distinctions of caste or creed'.

The proposed new marriages were discussed as if they affected not just the immediate families, castes, lineages, villages or urban neighbourhoods of those embarking upon them, but rather the entirety of the population. Such debates presented the morality of the 'native community' [40] as consisting of a homogenised and conservative sexuality of the urban educated and privileged upper castes, which was then juxtaposed against the moral world of Europeans. Curiously, however, the imminent state of moral corruption seen as a consequence of the passing of a law for civil marriage, appears from the petitions already to exist, prior to the enactment of the law. Clearly then, this was not a case of the law bringing into existence marriages of choice, but rather the law legitimating unions that had already existed but which were nonetheless being kept firmly outside the social pale.

An examination of the petitions shows that the concerns revolved around three sets of themes. The first was the decline in public 'morality'. The second was a preoccupation with the corruption of the young; more specifically, ignorant women being tricked and forced into marriages by men of 'bad character' and young men of 'status families' falling in love with 'harlots' and 'dancing girls'. Thirdly, the petitioners were worried that the law would legalise the offspring of such unions and create contestations between 'legal heirs' and the illegitimate issue of such inappropriate unions. The petitioners in large part constituted a western-educated segment of Indian society quite similar to the Brahmo reformers. These defenders of the faith were mostly influential magistrates, Pleaders and subordinate officials. A critical reading of the petitions representing the righteous moral world of 'native society' thus allows us a window through which to view what was increasingly being constituted as a not-community of immoral marital choice and sexual desire.

The 'Allahabad Brahmo Samaj', one of the first groups to respond to Maine's Bill, set themselves apart from the Keshubites and argued that in discarding the religious obligations in marriage, the law would 'loosen the bonds of morality and disorganise the framework of society'. They said that even an orthodox Hindu who kept many mistresses would never acknowledge 'any woman' to be his wife unless he was wedded to her according to the orthodox marriage rites. However, it was painfully evident to them that

> … love is blind, and when a man becomes passionately attached to a woman he totally forgets himself and is apt to sacrifice his wealth and honour for the gratification of his carnal desires. There are innumerable instances of orthodox Hindus having kept Mahomedan and European mistresses and lavished enormous sums of money upon them. There are cases of Rajahs and Maharajas who have taken Mahomedan or European wives having turned Muslims or Christians when pressed by their mistresses to marry them after the fashion of their respective creeds.[41]

Since the proposed law did not even necessitate conversion to any new faith, it made it much easier for such men of 'impure desire' to submit to its requirements 'when pressed by the object of their love', labouring as they most surely did under an 'infatuated desire'. Love, and passionate attatchment in the above formulation, are equated with 'carnal desire'. Further, the possibility of gain from marriage to women possessing wealth or owning property could easily induce such 'regular orthodox men' to take 'immoral women' for their wives. Such a law, the petitioners argue, would countenance 'indiscriminate prostitution' in 'every rank' of society.

The core of the Allahabad Brahmo argument is that 'women of the town' and 'corrupt women' would choose to live with their paramours as husband and wife. They concede that many people do lead such a life. However, the proposed law would allow such people to ignore community sanctions and have what they describe as a 'mock marriage' with a certificate to prove it. The 'Allahabad Institute' plays on these fears to warn that 'society will be torn asunder when a Mahomedan woman will be introduced into a Hindoo family'.[42] If such marriages were permitted, Muslim women would defile the inner sanctuaries of caste-Hindu homes. Instead of being ejected from all social communion into not-community, such women would demand the right to live as members of the Hindu household.

The petitioners almost without exception play on the notion of Brahmanical purity and hierarchy, and the abomination which constitutes any challenge to this authority. The assault on caste Hinduism is defended with the strongest rhetoric. One group argues: 'If a woman of the Brahman caste co-habits with a man other than a Brahman, the parties, together with the issues of such illicit intercourse will all go to hell'.[43] Babu Kali Prassana Banarji argues that the issue of inter-caste unions would be looked upon by Hindus 'with hatred, and treated as bastards and [would] never be allowed to remain within the pale of the Hindu community'.[44] S. Srinivasa Rao, Principal of Sadr Amin, is more careful to alert the British to their own concerns. He explains:

> When a dozen Brahmans marry Pariah women, or Pariahs marry Brahman women, the Native society would be as bad as an European society would be when a dozen young noblemen marry the daughters and sisters of hangmen and cobblers.[45]

Further eulogising the rigidity of caste in India, Banarji says: 'India, as she now stands is proud of her unmixed blood which would scarcely be found in any other part of the world; the chastity of her women is almost proverbial, but it is with deep regret that our Hindu brethren look upon the contemplated law'.[46]

The myth of 'pure' and 'unmixed blood', notably linked to the 'chastity' of 'India's women' (rather than the moral uprightness of India's men) is used as a justification to prevent legitimation of inter-caste and inter-community marriages.[47] The petitioners all implicitly or explicitly use the particular case of Brahmanical and high-caste codes of purity, but extrapolate their effects to all communities; in the above case, to all of India. Indian women as reproducers of moral communities come to be worshipped as upholders of the 'pure tradition', and because of this privilege they are also in need of constant surveillance and protection by the men of their communities; and men of the nation.[48]

This image of a 'pure' and unsullied nation of Indians was however constantly contradicted by evidence provided within the petitions themselves. For instance, a number of petitioners seemed to imply that such marriages or sexual relationships, although socially illegitimate, continued unabated. One petitioner sought to prove that the law legitimating such unions was unnecessary by revealing the extent of inter-caste unions that were not held to be invalid. Writing about marriages solemnised 'at the caprice of the parties themselves', he claims to be able to identify 'hundreds of marriages throughout the length and breadth of the country that will, according to the Hindu standard, be considered null without hesitation. But they are not the less legal'.[49]

Inevitably, the vast majority of opponents to the measure appeared to be fighting a war on two fronts with both flanks liable to attack. On the one hand, the colonial state was upholding the principles of religious freedom and choice which were anathema to those who upheld the principle of marriage by birth, so crucially linked to Hindu philosophical and religious ideas about *dharma* and caste. On the other hand, there was the admission that members of even the most orthodox Brahman community were availing of this choice through polygamy, concubinage and 'prostitutes'. What was important for the petitioners was that no legal avenue should be created to enable these relationships to be made legitimate. As we shall see, it was a difficult position to sustain.

One petition argued that the law would fail to protect 'women' and would interfere with the '*purda* system' in the land. The 'Residents of Bareilly' complained,

> Women of this country are generally uneducated and do not possess sufficient discrimination, and men of bad character would have no difficulty in inducing them to go before a Registrar and then and there have the marriage ceremony performed with the assistance of three or four witnesses, and the ceremony once gone through and the rubicon once passed, the husbands will be enabled to force their wives to cohabit with them, no matter whether or not they are consenting parties to the same.[50]

This, they stated without further elaboration, would 'interfere with the *purda* system', presumably referring to the breakdown of seclusion when women start living with men of their choice. Others like the Allahabad Brahmo Samaj made the argument that a 'girl' never 'gives herself' nor 'takes' for herself a husband, but is always given as a gift by the father or guardian to the husband. Female choice in marriages is thus constructed as more deviant than male choice. The 'Allahabdis' pointed out that there were women who wished for the children of their paramours to inherit their property. This Act would no doubt prompt such women to seek 'legal divorces' from their husbands and in marrying their lovers, legitimate children who would otherwise have been held to be illegitimate. Evidently there were those who did give themselves and take husbands for themselves.

The concern with female agency was initially framed in the language of protecting uneducated women from men who were clearly of bad character. However, there was a split in the rhetoric with women described as both 'innocent' and 'immoral'. The petitioners stepped up their assault on the sort of women who would avail of the law, and increasingly characterised them as 'prostitutes'. The Allahabad Brahmo Samaj submitted that under this law women might bring their paramours into the same house containing her other relatives, and that this would 'licence' immoral women to live openly with their paramours. Their own draft of a Bill presented to the Council sought to pressure the Council into including in the final Act the following clause: '...[T]he woman is not a prostitute, nor the man her paramour, and the cases do not come under the category of abduction, seduction, elopement, enticement, or the like, as are punishable under the Indian Penal Code'. A similar concern prompted the *Som Prakash* newspaper, on 17th April 1871, to run a story that argued that the bride and the groom to a civil marriage should, prior to the solemnisation, obtain a 'certificate' from one of the priests of their creed stating that they had led a 'virtuous life'.[51]

Thus the characterisation of women was that they were both 'pure' but nonetheless prone to immorality. They were in need of male surveillance because they could themselves become profligate and immoral. One petitioner, Rattan Chand, felt that the Bill would be viewed as

...giving colour to female freedom, and depriving the high-born classes of the control which they are, under the *Dharma Shastra*, entitled to exercise over their females. A female, for instance, of 18 years of age has nothing more to do to shake off the yoke of her male relatives, than to declare herself as professing none of the five religions enumerated in the Bill. On mere declaration of this fact she is left under this Act, entirely her own mistress, and can choose a husband for herself, not only from her own caste, but from any one whatsoever.[52]

From this he argues that the end result of the Bill would be a step towards 'demolishing the whole fabric of [the] caste system, and to make Native females free like English ladies'. By way of suggestion, he felt that the Act should call for a confrontation between a woman and her parents before she was permitted to solemnise a civil marriage. This would have the commendable effect of inducing in the woman 'a little shame' at having gone away 'from under their paternal roofs'. The idea of 'a little shame', so simply put yet so ominously pregnant with possibilities of threats and violence to the girl, reassures Rattan Chand that if this confrontation were to be written into the law, it would act as a sufficient check to such marriages.

At times the picture that emerges from the petitions is that the greater threat to women came not from the men they sought to marry, but rather from their own families who would oppose such marriages. Lachmi Narain, an Honorary Magistrate, did not believe that people could wait a lifetime before they discovered that their daughters would shame them by having civil marriages. He argued that this freedom could never be countenanced, and that the result would merely lead to an 'increase in infanticide'.

When ... the uneducated respectable people of all classes and creeds, see that their daughters have legal liberty to go to the Registrar and declare to marry a man of any caste or religion in an open *kachari* [court], without the consent of their parents or guardians, they will unquestionably prefer infanticide. [...] Parents would rather kill her in her cradle than allow her when of age to disgrace the family.[53]

The 'Residents of Moradabad' also felt that such marriages would lead to female infanticide, and would additionally inhibit the salutary effects of female education that Indian reformers were seeking to introduce. They point out that 'people, fearing the result, will rather keep their daughters ignorant, than give them an opportunity of corresponding with a stranger and then fulfil their wishes before the Registrar of Marriage'.[54] If there was a need for families and communities to protect women from these dangers, the law also raised the question of a still more serious threat: the danger to young men. The image that was projected was of affluent or high-status men using the law to satisfy their lust. This image of innocent young men of 'family position' falling prey to the allures and delights of the flesh is one to which some of the members of the Council proved to be sympathetic. A petition from the Mahomedan Community of the Town and Suburbs of Calcutta expresses these fears and underlines their validity by pointing to a speech made by one of the members of the Council, Inglis, in which he is lauded for having defended their concerns. Quoting Inglis, they argue that this Act would afford 'clandestine marriages' which were the cause of 'serious evils'. Inglis is quoted as saying:

I think there is ground to fear that advantage might be taken ... by designing parties to entrap young lads of family position, infatuated with some dancing girl, and utterly reckless of consequences, into a marriage which can only end in disgrace and ruin. The extraordinary influence frequently obtained by women of this class over young men is well known to all who have seen much of Native life. Men under such influence would not, I believe, hesitate a moment while their frenzy lasted to make the declaration required by the Act to obtain their ends.[55]

Interestingly, they discuss his argument to explain why this Act would lead to unhappiness. Marriages under its provisions would be of a very different nature to the 'half marriage now occasionally contracted' by people in such circumstances. Their subsequent lives were not affected by these marriages. However, a marriage under the new Act would be binding and could not be dissolved except under the provisions of the Indian Divorce Act. Further, the man can contract no other marriage during the woman's lifetime, and the children to the marriage would inherit under the Indian Succession Act. If one views this argument from the perspective of the communities, it is clear that they are concerned that young men should not be trapped by a marriage conducted in haste. From the perspective of these young men however, the question is whether such 'half-marriages' were marriages of convenience, or whether they were love-marriages which were necessarily 'half' because they could not obtain social legitimation. If they were love-marriages, then the fact that young men could be made to remarry and fulfil social obligations was an important right of the family or 'community'. To avail of the act would provide a safeguard from this interference and would protect such marriages from being dissolved through community pressures.

As if to reiterate the fact that the Act would allow men to choose one marriage (of love) over another (of caste obligation), the 'Inhabitants of Allygurh' argue: 'It is possible that some men of respectable family might fall in love with a woman of different caste, and, solely in order to secure the object of their love, might make the declaration referred to. [...] The man would be unable, during the life of the woman, to marry into his caste or family, which would result in the total destruction of his lineal respectability and genuineness'.[56] The constant emphasis on the 'inability' of the man to contract a second marriage belies a more significant possibility, which is that the men may refuse to have arranged marriages and by availing of the Act wherein bigamy is punishable, would preclude pressures to such 'second' marriages. This would clearly be to the peril of community. Lineal respectability is ensured through legitimate heirs. Since there was no way of legitimating and securing such love-marriages prior to the Act, 'communities' had the prerogative of insisting upon marriages that they arranged.[57]

Hiership under the Indian Succession Act would thus enable men to disinherit their joint families. The joint family could no longer disinherit converts or outcastes, and now such marriages could further disrupt inheritance in the Hindu joint family. As another petition put it, if an 'orthodox Hindu man keeps a public prostitute as his mistress and wish [sic] his children by her to inherit his property to the prejudice of other lawful and legal heirs, he would easily take advantage of this Act'.[58] Clearly, it was not simply about a choice of whom one wished to marry, but also about whom one wished to legitimate as one's own: the joint family or the lover.

One petitioner, S. Vyjia Ragavalu Chetti Garu, pointed out a case in which a married Hindu man 'took an unmarried woman into his protection'. Upon the death of his 'childless wife' the 'concubine' became 'mistress of his household'. "When the old gentleman saw his end approaching, he took the greatest possible trouble to examine the law books in order to see how he could make his 'concubine's' son the lawful heir to his property; and if only a law of the description now proposed had existed, he would have married the woman on his deathbed so that the boy might benefit of his property through his mother.... It is no doubt true that the old gentleman might have married a young girl of his own caste and have begotten or regularly adopted a son, and so cut off his divided family from all hope of inheritance. But this would have been much less mortifying to the family than the stigma of his marriage with a dancing girl with its attendant loss of caste and position."[59]

Love that sought legitimation through marriage was seen to threaten the disruption of loyalties and kinship bonds through a challenge to caste boundaries and lineage. More tellingly, Garu's formulation describes the woman in a progressively derogatory manner. When she is brought to the house, she is a 'woman' under his protection. When she takes over the running of the household as his mistress she is described as his 'concubine'. However, in describing the hypothetical inter-caste *marriage* between the old gentleman and this concubine, she becomes a 'dancing girl'.

The 'Residents of Bareilly' leave out the rhetoric, and instead of condemning those who led immoral lives they tried to reason with the Council. They make a candid admission: 'We do not object to a man of one sect cohabiting privately with a woman of another, but what we do object to is that such cohabitation be not authorised by a legal enactment, for in that case the issue of such marriages would be illegal'.[60] So long as the community could control the proper transfer of inheritance, these liaisons, though disapproved, could always be ignored. By providing a form of marriage for such relationships the Council was inevitably going to disrupt the delicate balance between sexual immorality and social legitimacy, but the *illegality* of issue of such unions according to customary law would create an untenable conflict.

As the Council's meetings in 1872 began to indicate that the Act was going to be passed despite the voluble objections, some petitioners like Kali Prasanna Banarji felt it more prudent to suggest devices through which the application of the Act could be limited. In February 1872 he submitted a petition requesting that steps be taken to ensure that eloping couples did not have the chance to marry undetected. His argument centred on the Bill's suggested minimum residence period of five days before and after a couple could file notice in any district in the Registrar's Court. This period, he said, was so short that it would afford 'a marvellous facility to stolen and illicit marriages'.

> For example, A eloped with B, a Hindu widow, to a distant place, lives there for 5 days, and sends up a notice to the Registrar, and making the necessary declaration, marries her. The persons whose interests would be prejudiced by such a stolen marriage would have very little chance of detecting the plan before the marriage was consummated, and would seldom undergo expenses, vexations and troubles of long journeys and suits, to reclaim one who has already lost his or her caste by the consummation of such a marriage; for there are very few persons so vindictive by nature who would brave all these difficulties and deft public exposure only to punish one for whom they might still cherish some affection and who, after all, could not be restored to them and to the community at large.[61]

In order to give persons interested in the marriage sufficient time to publish and file counter-notices, and to provide a 'tolerably effective bar' to such marriages, he suggests that the period for notification be one month, and that the notice be published in English and vernacular *Gazettes* and papers for one month prior to the celebration of the marriage. Others like Garu suggested a period of twelve months so that the couple could only marry in a place where both parties are known by inhabitants and relatives, thus discouraging 'run-away' marriages. Banarji's more moderate suggestion was partially accommodated in the final Act. The residence period was extended to two weeks prior to notification, and two weeks after notice had been submitted. However, the Council ensured that notices were not published at large. The strategy of the petitioners to discourage such marriages through public notices that would alert the families but also cause a 'little shame' at such infamy was rejected by the Council and restricted to notice being given in a publicly accessible Registrar's book.

A Secular Law of Civil Marriage: 1872 to the Present

Act III of 1872 was perhaps most remarkable because, as one petitioner pointed out, even the Brahmos had not appealed to the state for a civil law of marriage. Despite this it was passed, though in a severely amended form. Various concessions such as extension of the notice period and increased age of majority were written into the law. The demand it made on people wishing to have inter-caste or inter-community marriages was that they had to place themselves in a position of not-community through a categorical renunciation of belonging and professing any of the 'major' religions of India. This renunciation was primarily a declaration of social 'not-belonging' because it was a concession to the objections of the major communities that they could not countenance the state witnessing dissent that was in contravention to their customs. Hence the declaration in the first Bill, regarding objections to the rites of marriage of a religion, was changed to a declaration of not belonging to a religious group in the final Act. This change of words only makes sense in the context of a consensus that the 'traditional' religions were not 'faiths' subscribed to by individuals but rather the constituent social 'communities' of Indian society. If two people were willing to exile themselves from the communities of their birth, the law would be willing to witness that choice and conduct a civil marriage. It could be argued then that the only difference to the situation prior to the passing of the Act was that those who contravened caste and community injunctions were excommunicated by their communities. After the Act was passed, that same condition of not-community was attained, but this time through a declaration asserting self-exile. For many people in India, the situation was difficult to comprehend: how could anyone be of 'no religion'?[62] The conditions of Act III of 1872 and the orthodox backlash as evidenced in the petitions promised severely to limit its use by those who wished to have love-marriages.

Yet, its passing has been so widely ignored that even in a com-prehensive work of Indian legal history from the seventeenth to the twentieth century, the first law to introduce civil marriage in India does not even warrant a single mention (Jain 1972). Despite the growing academic interest in reform movements and the law in the nineteenth century,[63] there are only two works (Mahmood 1978; Basu 2001) that address the history and import of this very significant and indeed symbolic legislation. Act III of 1872 was a forerunner and the basis for the Special Marriages Act, 1954, the civil marriage law for independent India. It underwent an amendment in 1923 which made it possible for Hindus, Buddhists, Sikhs or

Jains to inter-marry without renouncing their religions.[64] This was clearly a move towards permitting 'pan-Hindu' alliances without demanding that 'Hindus' inter-marrying should have to renounce 'Hinduism'. However, Christians, Jews, Muslims and Parsis were still subject to the earlier Act, as was any Hindu who sought to marry these latter adherents. After 1872, legal challenges to the law were made, specifically in the area of inheritance and succession. As Hari Singh Gour, a legislator who spearheaded the amendment of the law in 1923 argued, 'What is this; for one purpose [marriage] you say, I am not a Hindu, and for another purpose [succession] you claim to be a Hindu'. The law made self-excommunication a prerequisite, yet for the purposes of inheritance, persons could continue to avail of the benefits of their own personal laws. In 1923, the amendment permitting inter-'Hindu' marriages was materially driven and intended to replace co-parcenary rights and other rights concerning the Hindu undivided family with a position in which the person so marrying would become a divided co-parcener. The new clause stated: 'The marriage solemnised under this Act of any member of an undivided family who professes the Hindu, Buddhist, Sikh or Jain religion shall be deemed to effect his severance from such family'.[65]

Two years after India's independence, the first Prime Minister Jawaharlal Nehru's with Ambedkar as Law Minister, introduced a Bill into parliament which eventually amended Act III of 1872 into the Special Marriage Act of 1954, despite opposition in the Lower House of Parliament.[66] In the new 'special' law, the controversial declaration, caricatured by critics of the law in the 1950s debate as stating 'I am not a Hindu', was dropped. The civil right to marry whomever one pleased was no longer conditional on a repudiation of religion, and the Special Marriage Act thus constituted a properly civil *and* secular law of marriage. The Special Marriage Act is also extremely significant in Indian Statute Law because it is seen as an attempt to lay down a uniform territorial law for all of India.[67] If India does acquire a Uniform Civil Code, as promised by the Indian Constitution,[68] the Special Marriage Act, 1954, would form the basis of this future marriage law.

The Special Marriage Act legalised inter-community marriage in the wider sense of the term as it included all the religious communities residing in India. Further, there was also a provision for marriages already solemnised to be registered under it if so desired

(Mahmood 1978: 9). Consequent to such a marriage or registration, those parties would be limiting the application of their personal law to their family affairs as well as to the succession of their properties, without renouncing their religion or sub-religious faiths (Mahmood 1978: 14). The law in theory was perfectly indifferent to the religions of the parties availing of its provisions.

At the same time as the Lok Sabha debated the Special Marriage Act, another law was also being discussed. The Hindu Marriage Bill sought to introduce the legal validity of divorce and inter-caste sacramental marriages between the quasi-'Hindu' categories described earlier. Prior to 1955, if such a 'Hindu' wished to have a religious ceremonial inter-caste marriage, he or she would have had to do so under the Arya Marriage Validation Act, 1937. This Act had been passed to support the Arya Samaj's positive stance towards inter-caste marriage.[69] Like the Brahmos, the Aryas also sought to reform Hinduism, and the ritual of inter-caste Arya Samaj marriages was one of its innovations. The Arya Marriage Validation Act was passed on precisely the same grounds on which Act III of 1872 had been opposed. Aryas wishing to have inter-caste marriages with other Aryas were not willing to make the declaration of not-community or 'no-religion' that Act III of 1872 demanded, because in their view they were Hindus. Hence between 1937 and 1955 any Hindu wishing to have an inter-caste marriage without repudiating Hinduism could only do so by becoming an Arya Samaji.

To prevent such a situation from arising and to assist 'Hindus' who wished to have a religious marriage rather than a civil marriage, the Hindu Marriage Bill was introduced and passed in parliament in 1955.[70] This Act had three direct effects. Firstly, it provided legally for *religious* marriages between Hindus, Buddhists, Sikhs and Jains of any caste. Secondly, it introduced a provision for divorce that applied equally to men and women, and thirdly, it enshrined the principle of monogamy for all Hindus irrespective of the forms of marriages. The debates over the Hindu Marriage Act were much more fraught and bitterly contested than those of the previous year over the Special Marriage Act. This was because the latter was viewed as catering to an urban westernised elite without seeking to impose their liberal values on a conservative populace, whereas the Hindu Marriage Act concerned a large proportion of the population. Many Members of Parliament (MPs) argued that on top of inter-caste marriages destroying the fabric of social life, divorce would now definitively destroy the Hindu family.[71] Further, the debate once again raised the issue of a civil code for all Indians. It was felt that the Hindu Marriage Act was communal in that it created uneven rights and privileges amongst the different communities and their personal laws. For instance, N.C. Chatterjee argued

> ...this Bill is contrary to the Fundamental Rights laid down by the Constitution of India, because it discriminates by law against a community or a particular religion. What right have you to enact such a law? What right have you to say that monogamy must be made compulsory for all Hindus, for all Hindu men and for all Hindu women? If you honestly feel that this is a blessing and polygamy is a curse, then why not rescue our Muslim sisters from that curse and from that plight? What right have you to enact that this shall be compulsory only for one community and not for others?[72]

Another MP, Khardekar, launched a scathing attack on Chatterjee's 'communalism'. He made a parody of Hindu right-wing politics of the post-independence period, and argued that it was the politics of the Hindu Mahasabha and Jan Sangh (the predecessor of the Bharatiya Janta Party) that made them oppose the Bill on Hindu marriages rather than any true understanding of the spirit of Hinduism.[73] The charge of communalism is one that remains with us sixty years after Independence. Indeed, one of the election platforms of the right-wing BJP before they became the ruling party at the national level in 1998 was the introduction of the Uniform Civil Code. The opposition to their rhetoric came from the left and from various minority groups who saw the BJP's attempt to legislate a Uniform Civil Code as suspect, and a veiled attempt to impose 'retrogressive elements' of Hindu law on the rest of the Indian population.[74] The tensions between the state and the communities-as-political-actors at the national level in India today are part of the same historical process in which various ethno-religious communities have, on the one hand, struggled to retain their powers over their members, and, on the other hand, had to contend with judicial enactments that increasingly expanded the power of the civil state over their sacramental customs and beliefs. The process that Das (1995) has described as the state 'colonising the life-worlds of communities' and 'communities colonising the life-worlds of individuals' was as much in evidence in 1872 as it is in the post-independence period.

Indeed, as Bétéille has so ably shown, it was due to the insistence of Ambedkar that the 'individual' was made the repositore of rights in post-independence India. He rebuffed attempts by other parliamentarians to make the village the basic unit because he believed that this was the stronghold of caste and faction which would inhibit individual accomplishment (1991a: 228). These democratic principles are safeguarded in the Special Marriage Act, and it is an instance of the state displacing and levelling the authority of ethno-religious communities in favour of individuals: in effect, the state successfully colonising the life-world of communities.

The salience of 1872 to a work on love-marriages is that while the Keshubites wanted to create a Brahmist community, their dissent created a theoretical and, subsequently, legal space for not-community. Although both the Keshubites and the Council steadfastly avoided a discussion of 'love', the petitions saw all the three Bills as permitting an altogether new form of marriage in India, for them, marriages based on 'lust'. Those entering such marriages are represented as morally corrupt, a threat to 'native' religious and social values, and the colonial state's legislation is viewed as 'making Indians into Europeans'. The fact that such illegitimate unions had always existed, oftentimes sanctioned through customs such as bigamy and concubinage, was completely ignored. Instead, desire and sexuality in 'native society' were sought to be erased from the records, and in their place was inserted the characterisation of a corrupting amoral social world created by colonial legislation.

The 1872 Act got caught up in all manner of paradoxes, not least the paradox of a colonial state interfering with the rights of communities to arrange marriages for their members. The cautionary progress from Maine's original Bill to Stephen's Act shows that there was an enormous amount of accommodation that was made prior to the final enactment. Paradoxically, Nehru's government, the first of a free and democratic India, was in a much stronger political position and did not need to concede to the demands of orthodoxy while enacting the Special Marriage Act. This is why the Special Marriage Act is primarily a secular law of civil marriage. However, this does not mean that society was in the least bit transformed by the passing of the Special Marriage Act. Rather, in the case of the 1954 Act, the accommodations take place after legislation in the actual way in which the law is both administered and transformed to suit 'Indian' exigencies. This is why, as we shall see in the next chapter, a District Court (where both civil and Hindu marriages are registered) in Delhi in the late 1990s dramatises many of the same anxieties about the role of the state in legislating 'personal laws', the rites of marriage and the nature of choice, love and individual conscience that we see in 1872.

To conclude, Maine was at least partly right (and anticipated much of today's academic writings) when he said that without compensating legislation, legal process would rigidify caste and religious divisions and empower communities at the *expense* of individuals. The many objectors to the Bill were also largely correct. A hierarchical and differentiated caste society could only thrive in the modern world with the active support of state-endowing communities such as castes and religions with definite rights and entitlements at the expense of individuals. 'Public morality' as they saw it (concerns that centred around the control over women and property) would indeed be undermined by a genuinely open civil marriage law. Both colonial and post-colonial governments have been inconsistent, but the story of this Act has been repeated many times over in different domains and the result is that communities defined on the basis of caste and religion are now *more* powerful and coherent political identities and agencies than a hundred years ago. This fact is illustrated in the next chapter because a law which now empowers individuals (or couples) directly is undermined in practice by exactly those forces and for exactly the same reasons as the Bill was opposed in 1872.

Notes

1. The Brahmo Samaj was founded in 1828 (originally as the Brahmo Sabha) by Ram Mohan Roy, popularly known as the 'Father of Modern India', a social reformer who began campaigning in 1815 for the eradication of *sati* in India. The Keshubites, as we shall see later in this chapter, formed one faction of the Brahmo Samaj, and were referred to at the time as the 'Progressive Brahmos' as opposed to the 'Orthodox Brahmos'. Kopf (1979), among others, has written extensively on the far-reaching influence of the Brahmo Samaj on Indian society and the reform movements of the nineteenth century.

2. Because of inconsistencies in the transliteration of Indian words in the primary sources, I have standardised the spellings and removed the accents as per contemporary Indian-English. (for e.g. 'Keshubites' for 'Kesobites', 'Brahmo Samaj' for 'Brahma Samaj', 'shastras' for 'shaster'). In quotations the spelling remains the same except for the absence of the accents: so, 'Bráhma-Samája' becomes 'Brahma-Samaja', 'Hindú' is 'Hindu', etc.

3. The National Archives of India, Legislative Department, May 1872, 'Act III of 1872', 'From Babu Kali Prasanna Banarji, to Hon'ble J.F.D. Inglis'. Henceforth, all references from this file of the Legislative Department will be abbreviated and denoted as NAI, 'Act III of 1872', with the relevant document number/title and date.

4. The Indian Majority Act, IX of 1875 was passed eight years later and set majority at 18 years of age for men and women (Derrett 1978(a): 295).

5. NAI, 'Act III of 1872', No. 148, 11 September 1868.

6. NAI, 'Act III of 1872', No. 151, 18 November 1868.

7. NAI, 'Act III of 1872', No. 173, 4 September 1868.

8. NAI, 'Act III of 1872', No. 150, 10 September 1868.

9. NAI, 'Act III of 1872', No. 173, 4 September 1868.

10. NAI, 'Act III of 1872', No. 156, 27 November 1868.

11. Other conditions included the consent of the father or guardian if the girl was below 18 years of age and the prohibited degrees were to be 'degrees of consanguinity or affinity prohibited by the custom which would have regulated marriages between them had the Act not been passed'. Further, bigamous marriages under this Act were to be punished under the Indian Penal Code. NAI, 'Act III of 1872', No. 233, 'A Bill to Legalise Marriages between Members of the Brahma Samaja'.

12. NAI, 'Act III of 1872', No. 237, 11 July, 1871. A small detail like Stephen's embarrassed admission that he had not even read the Adi-Brahmo Samaj petition is a sobering reminder of just how arbitrary the colonial law making process could be. If he claimed not to have even known that there was indeed a split in the Brahmo Samaj, then he couldn't have paid much attention to the purported reasons for Maine's extension of the provision for civil marriages to all 'natives'. By extension, he could not have known that one of the main justifications for the introduction of the first Bill (Native Marriage Bill) for civil marriage was the perceived instability of the Brahmo Samaj.

13. Interestingly, the third Bill proposed that consent be obtained if the boy were under 21 and the girl under 18. The raising of the age (from 18 to 21) at which a girl could independently contract a marriage of her choice was another compromise to the orthodox opponents of the measure. It must be noted that this is a period when the most

common (and legal) age of marriage for Hindu girls was 10. Indeed, shortly after the passing of the law, Keshub Chandra Sen's daughter was married before she reached the age of 14—a cause of yet another bitter division within the Brahmo Samaj. NAI, 'Act III of 1872', No. 332, Vide Appendix Y, 'An Act to Provide a Form of Marriage in Certain Cases'.

14. *The Special Marriage Act, 1954* (1997), Universal Law Publishing Co. Pvt. Ltd., Delhi.

15. Kopf mistakenly assumes that Act III was called the 'Brahmo Marriage Bill', and that it legislated 'at the stroke of a pen' the Brahmos 'out of Hinduism' (1979: 105). In fact it was exactly the opposite—the final Act does not even contain a passing reference to the Brahmos. Clearly, Kopf was thinking of Stephen's Brahma Marriage Bill which never saw the light of day.

16. The Office of the 'Registrar of Marriages under Act III of 1872' was initiated by the Act, and the local government was authorised to appoint one or more Registrars whose domain was the domain of the territory subject to its administration and was to be deemed his 'district'. NAI, 'Act III of 1872', No. 332, 22 March 1872.

17. NAI, 'Act III of 1872', A Bill to Legalise Marriages between Certain Natives of India not Professing the Christian Religion, 18 November 1868.

18. NAI, 'Act III of 1872'; No. 148, 11 September 1868.

19. Ibid., (my emphasis).

20. Quoting from Thomas Strange's Hindu Law, they argue that these 'elements' are the formal gift of the bride, the acceptance of her hand in marriage and finally, the ceremony of *saptpadi* (literally, seven steps). NAI, 'Act III of 1872', No. 158, 26 November 1868.

21. The fact that Maine had to legislate for the whole of India, just because he could not define the Keshubites, was mocked in some 'native' newspapers. One editor was alleged to have asked how Maine imagined he could define a Hindu, 'there being no judicial or legislative definition of that comprehensive term'. NAI, 'Act III of 1872', No. 225, 'Summary of Opinions on the Native Marriage Bill', *Vide* Appendix O. 25 July 1870.

22. NAI, 'Act III of 1872', No. 173, 4 September 1868.

23. NAI, 'Act III of 1872', Abstract of the Proceedings of the Council of the Governor General of India, 16 January, 1872.

24. This was not meant to affect the principle that the courts in India used, which was that 'the greatest part of the civil rights of Natives in India is determined by the religion which they profess'. NAI, 'Act III of 1872', No. 156, 27 November 1868.

25. Ibid. Unsurprisingly, this concession in the Act was inserted after the Governor General's Council received a memorandum from Christian

missionaries in Calcutta. They sought to encourage conversion by relieving converts of the not insignificant consideration that, if they were converts from Hinduism they would never be granted their share in the joint family property. Though this provision had already been provided for in Bengal (S. 9 of Regulation VII of 1832), *Lex Loci* was to extend the principle to the rest of India, except the Presidency Towns (Jain 1972: 521).

26. NAI, 'Act III of 1872'; No. 156, 27 November 1868.
27. NAI, 'Act III of 1872', No. 203, 29 May 1869.
28. The 'Allahabad Brahmo Samaj', as if to drive the point home said: 'The Brahmos are not Christians, nor are they Mahomedans, nor Jews, but they are Hindus. Your petitioners' religion is a form of Hindu religion and their rites are therefore no other than Hindu rites'. NAI, 'Act III of 1872', No. 170, 24 January 1869.
29. NAI, 'Act III of 1872', No. 225, Native Opinion, 8 November 1868.
30. Ibid. (my emphasis).
31. It is also interesting that he appears to be saying, in Durkhiemian terms, that India has 'organic' solidarity and European nations 'mechanical'.
32. See Susan Bayly (1999) for a detailed discussion of the assimilation of European racial theories by Indians in the nineteenth century.
33. NAI, 'Act III of 1872', 'From Uttaram Khubchand, Pleader, Sindh Courts, to Secretary to Government, Bombay', 5 October 1870.
34. One wonders whether this was a situation that the Brahmos could have envisaged, particularly in the light of Christopher Bayly's observation that Maine was 'read by and indirectly influenced Indians' (1991: 393).
35. NAI, 'Act III of 1872', No. 216, 10 November 1869.
36. NAI, 'Act II of 1872', No. 154, 23 November 1868.
37. It is striking that Maine himself seems to anticipate the argument of postcolonial Indian historians.
38. NAI, 'Act III of 1872', Abstract of the Proceedings of the Council of the Governor General of India, 16 January 1872.
39. NAI, 'Act III of 1872', No. 154, 18 November 1868.
40. When quoting petitions, I use the term 'community' to refer to these elected or self-appointed groups of spokesmen.
41. NAI, 'Act III of 1872', No. 170, 24 January 1869, Allahabad Brahmo Samaj, Signed by Nilcomul Mitter and others.
42. NAI, 'Act III of 1872', No. 168, 2 December 1868.
43. NAI, 'Act III of 1872', No. 195, 16 August 1869. 'Proceedings of the Meeting of the Principal Residents of the Town of Bareilly'.
44. NAI, 'Act III of 1872', [No number or date given], p. 245. 'Petition from Babu Kali Prasanna Banarji'.
45. NAI, 'Act III of 1872', No. 203, 29 July 1869.

46. NAI, 'Act III of 1872', [No number or date given], p. 245. 'Petition from Babu Kali Prasanna Banarji'.
47. O'Hanlon, in her examination of debates about widow remarriage also points to this 'feminisation of tradition' and draws attention to male petitioners who chastise Hindu widows as prostitutes while failing to draw attention to the men who actually consorted with these women (1991: 83).
48. I found no evidence of any direct contribution from women.
49. NAI, 'Act III of 1872', [No number or date given], p. 248. 'Petition of Rattan Chand'.
50. NAI, 'Act III of 1872', No. 195, 16 August 1869, 'Proceedings of a Meeting of the Principle Residents of Bareilly'.
51. NAI, 'Act III of 1872', No. 241, 22 April 1871. 'Extract from Report of Native Papers for the Week Ending 22 April 1871'.
52. NAI, 'Act III of 1872' [No number or date given], p. 249. 'Petition of Rattan Chand'.
53. NAI, 'Act III of 1872' [No number or date given], p. 243. 'Petition of Lachmi Narain'.
54. NAI, 'Act III of 1872' [No number or date given], p. 250. 'Petition of the Inhabitants of Moradabad, signed by Salag Ram'.
55. NAI, 'Act III of 1872', No. 325, 6 March 1872, Signed by Abdool Baree, Chairman of 'Meeting of Mahomedans of the Towns and Suburbs of Calcutta'.
56. NAI, 'Act III of 1872', No. 330, 12 March 1872, Signed Raja Jaikishun Doss, Secretary of British India Association, North West Province.
57. Here I am using the term 'community' to refer to parents or extended families, or small groups of brothers, or local descent groups, or caste *panchayats*, or village groups, depending on very variable circumstances.
58. NAI, 'Act III of 1872', No. 170, 24 January 1869.
59. This particular petition clearly had a great impact on the Council because it is his suggestion of raising the age of marriage without parental consent to 21 years of age which found its way into the final Act. NAI, 'Act III of 1872', [No number given], 12 February 1872, Signed S. Vyjia Ragavalu Chetti Garu.
60. NAI, 'Act III of 1872', No. 195, 16 August 1869.
61. NAI, 'Act III of 1872' [No number given], 1 February 1872, p. 245.
62. NAI, 'Act III of 1872' [No date given], No. 193 'Proceedings of Meerut Debating Society'.
63. For example, Chatterjee (1989); Chandra (1998); Chowdhry (1996); Forbes (1979); Sen (1980–'81); Singha (1993); Mani (1987); O'Hanlon (1991) and Poonacha (1996).
64. Government of India, 1974, *Law Commission of India, Fifty-Ninth Report on The Hindu Marriage Act, 1955 & The Special Marriage Act, 1954.* This

was again amended in 1974. Hindus, Buddhists, Sikhs or Jains could intermarry without having to suffer any economic penalty so that they could continue to benefit from Hindu law for the purposes of succession, and so that their agnates would no longer be excluded from rights in joint-family property inherited by someone availing of the Act. To clarify the situation, if a person married under the Special Marriage Act, in the event of intestate succession, the Succession Act would apply (not the personal inheritance law). The changes brought about in 1974 ensured that if both parties to a marriage were 'Hindu', then Hindu law would continue to apply both with regards to undivided property and divided property.

65. In simple terms, this clause ensured that there was a statutory (a compulsory legal) severance of a person marrying under the Act from the joint family. This was meant unambiguously as a further deterrent against persons resorting to such marriages. It must be noted that a person retained all inheritance rights (anything willed to him or her) as if they had never married under the Act.

66. There is some confusion over the name of the law. Mahmood implies that 'Act III of 1872' was already known as the 'Special Marriage Act' by the time it came to be amended in 1923. However, in my own archival work of 1872, I did not encounter this name other than the general description that the Act catered for marriages in 'special' instances. Even the final Act is entitled 'Act III of 1872'.

67. Speech in the Lok Sabha by the then Law Minister Mr. C.C. Biswas when introducing the Bill to a parliamentary vote. Lok Sabha Debates, 1954, 19th May, 1954, p. 7797. Article 44 of the Indian Constitution expressly enjoins the Indian state to 'strive towards and provide' its citizens with 'a Uniform Civil Code' which would provide equality before the law and equal protection of the law to all its citizens.

68. In recent years, the introduction of a Uniform Civil Code has taken on more sinister tones with Hindu nationalists having promised that when they have a clear majority in parliament, they will enact a new law for all Indians, thus displacing all personal laws. This has been a particularly contentious proposal, with feminists and civil rights activists arguing that any revision of the law by Hindu nationalists will be biased against women and minorities. See for instance Pathak and Sunder Rajan (1989), Agnes (1996), and Tharu and Niranjana (1996).

69. The Arya Samaj was started in 1875 by Swami Dayanand Saraswati, a Shaivite ascetic from Gujarat. The teachings of the Samaj are directed towards a re-interpreted and modernised Hinduism. Dayanand believed in the infallibility of the Vedas and subjected Hindu customs and beliefs to the test of Vedic authenticity. His followers rejected polytheism, idolatry, caste, child marriage, Brahmanical claims of superiority, pilgrimages, horoscopes, the ban against widow

remarriage and even restrictions on foreign travel (Jones 1989: 30–32).

70. Reba Som (1994) has argued that Nehru capitulated on many of the 'progressive' elements of the Hindu Marriage Bill and allowed the orthodox opponents in parliament to limit its provisions. It was over this Bill that Ambedkar resigned from Nehru's cabinet in September of 1951 because he felt that far too many concessions were being made to orthodox religion. It is noteworthy that the Special Marriage Act was also being debated in the house, and often the two acts were opposed together because they were seen as a threat to 'Hindu' India.

71. For instance, a recurring issue in the parliamentary debates on the Hindu Marriage Bill was whether or not women should be permitted the unilateral right to demand a divorce. In the words of 'experts' such as Sir Gooroodas Bannerjee, quoted amongst others by N.C. Chatterjee of the Hindu Mahasabha and MP from Bengal: '[Marriage] is regarded as one of the ten sanskars, or sacraments, necessary for regeneration of men of the twice-born classes, [castes] and the only sacrament for women and Sudras [low caste, "untouchables"]'. To introduce divorce then, was to deny women the chance of rebirth in their karmic cycle. From Lok Sabha Debates, 1955, 'Hindu Marriage Bill'; 29th April, 1955, p. 6845.

72. Ibid.: 6838–39.

73. Ibid.: 6878–79.

74. The BJP government in the state of Uttar Pradesh has revised the social science textbooks to say that laws which supposedly 'favour women' like the Widow Remarriage Act, 1956, the Hindu Women's Property Act, 1937, the Special Marriage Act, 1954, and the Hindu Marriage and Divorce Act, 1955 'are causing tension and strife within families'. In *The Times of India*, 'Women's Worth: Parivar's Brand of Liberation', by Lalita Panicker, 5-7-1997, p. 10, New Delhi.

ॐ

2

Legitimating Love: Tis Hazari and the Judicial Process

> Give me a man that
> buys a seat of judicature
> I dare not trust him
> not to sell me justice
>
> Translation of an Urdu *shairi*[1]

Olivia Harris has pointed out that 'anthropology characteristically chooses as its field of study those who are at the frontiers of legality, and those for whom the relationship with the law is at best ambivalent' (1996: 3). In this chapter I examine the law entirely from the perspective of the purveyors of various services within the court, and from the viewpoint of those who must avail of these services in order to marry: namely, the love-marriage couples. The touts and lawyers whose services I detail provide some indication of how complicated and fraught the process of marriage really is. Unsurprisingly, 'law as process' looks very different from 'law as statute'.

Following from the way in which the Marriage Room actually functions, I examine the state of 'not-community' that comes to be stamped upon the movements of love-marriage couples who enter the court. It is usually at this juncture, and for the first time, that their desire comes into conflict with an impersonal public which is strongly disapproving. While I am able to show in the first part of this chapter that in theory this public considers love-marriages in the court to be a good thing, the actual experiences of couples indicate that we should be wary of such generous assessments. Further, the process of having a 'court-marriage' (a civil marriage or the registration of a Hindu marriage) is subject to a number of contestations, some of which concern themselves with the illegitimacy of love as a motive for marriage; but most of which are more recently concerned with the inflection of 'sexuality' with 'secularity' (Ritu Menon's terms 1999: 31). By this I refer to the unsavoury politicisation of a couple's domestic sexual life which uses their sexuality to make a political point about 'secularity', or 'secularism', as it is understood in the Delhi of today.[2]

Delhi is famed for the beauty of its ancient parks and gardens which are regularly frequented by lovers.[3] In recent years, however, there is a growing trend to identify heterosexual pairs as romantically linked 'couples' and 'westernised lovers' and to police public morality. During my fieldwork in December of 1997, the Mayor of Delhi, Mrs. Shakuntala Arya, a stalwart of the Rashtra Sevika Sangh—the women's wing of the Hindu supremacist Rashtriya Swayamsevak Sangh (or 'RSS[4])—issued a dictate over the reigning in of 'public displays of affection' in the city.[5] She remarked that 'holding hands, kissing and hugging in public were obscene' and should be 'banned'. Threatening to impose the Obscenities Act on couples found in each other's embrace, she argued that such behaviour was an 'imitation of western morals' and did not suit 'our *bharatiya sanskriti*' (Indian culture).[6]

In February of 1999 and again in 2000, the youth wing of the BJP went on a rampage in nearby Kanpur, in Uttar Pradesh, blackening the faces of couples and shaming them for 'celebrating Valentine's Day' because this was a symbol of the 'west' which was corrupting Indian youth.[7] Police allegedly joined in by arresting couples on Valentine's Day.

This was followed the subsequent year with similar protests in Delhi and other north-Indian cities, taking the form of ransacking restaurants which were preparing special romantic Valentine's Day events as well storming greeting card shops and burning their cards in the streets. Soon, the Shiv Sena in Bombay took up cudgels against Valentine's Day celebrations. Now it has become an annual event, punctuating the calendrical cycle of protests across metropolitan India, widely anticipated and hungrily covered by the national and international print and televisual media, and with the occasional desultory police *bandobust* (arrangements) on the streets in case of trouble. Interestingly, Valentine's Day protests are not restricted to Hindu protests alone with reports in the last couple of years of a Muslim group that have also jumped on the bandwagon.[8]

The old fashioned card (often sent anonymously) has in the last five years been superseded by the extraordinarily affordable and widespread use of mobile phones and text messaging, with card producers complaining of a massive fall in profits. Indeed, the complicity of mobile phones in allowing intimate and immediate personal access to loved ones without the embarrassing potential of dissenting family members picking up landlines and thus being alerted to fledgling romances, have become so ubiquitous that in April 2007, some Sindhi leaders called for a ban on the use of mobiles by all Sindhi youth. The precipitating circumstances were two love-marriages of Sindhi girls to Muslims in Bhopal, Madhya Pradesh.[9] The spokespersons for the Sindhi community in Bhopal identified two other facilitators of romance that were to be banned: parental gifts of so-called 'two-wheelers' (i.e. scooters) which provided independence and mobility to their college-going daughters and the wearing of *dupattas* and scarves (particularly wrapped around the head and face when riding a scooter), which allowed girls who roamed with impunity around the city to cover their faces and thus remain incognito.[10]

The 1st of January, 'New Year's', and to a lesser extent Valentine's Day, are occasions when young urban couples go out for meals, walks, movies and post pages and pages of saccharine, stylised and fairly florid confessional messages in special New Year or Valentine's Day listings in the English language newspapers.[11] Radio stations have programmes of all-day *ishq* (love) talk with endless Hindi movie romantic hits, and listeners phoning in to dedicate songs, more often than not to their spouses rather than their lovers.

The question raised by the Valentine's Day annual protests are to what extent these celebrations represent a new form of expressing romantic love for Indians in the big metropolitan cities. I am in no doubt that the true significance of Valentine's Day, in its current avatar, is more a result of its visibility through the advertising hype in the media along with the incommensurate news attention afforded to small groups of protesters who seem to struggle to find streets full of couples whose faces they can blacken or who they can attempt to de-couple (hence the resort to restaurants and card shops as these tend to be easier targets to locate). While I do not deny that many young couples go out on Valentine's Day to talk and drink a coffee together in the air-conditioned comfort of expensive coffee shops in the cities, one gets the sense that the themed events target the exceptionally wealthy urban elite who are eager to consume the iconic styles of New York in New Delhi. This isn't to my mind about 'westernisation', but rather about the consumption of western styles and languages of cultural significance on one's own terms (indeed, on one's own turf). The outcome is that Valentine's Day celebrations in cities like Bombay are more *maha-kitch* (for e.g. Hindi 'Bollywood' songs to accompany the red roses), than a groundswell of young lovers staking their claim to western-style, public forms of intimacy. In my own work with love-marriage couples in Delhi, not one of my informants ever mentioned celebrating Valentine's Day (indeed, I am fairly certain that the vast majority wouldn't have known what I was talking about) though some in the University mentioned receiving romantic cards on New Year's Day. What they did speak about was how important it was for them to try and see their loved one (or speak over the phone) on the day of religious festivals that were saturated with social significance such as Diwali, Holi or Eid rather than risk detection by going out to restaurants or to events in the evenings only to find oneself an easy target for censorious aunties or wolf-whistling groups of young men.

The political trend against courtship are notably directed at expressions of romantic love (which is often equated with carnality), and which is increasingly viewed as somehow 'un-Indian' and a result of 'foreign influence'. While this doesn't change the way lovers court, the vitiated public consensus *vis a vis* romantic love and love-marriages, and the increasing politicisation of inter-community relations, does have a bearing upon the ways in which couples are treated in public spaces, and more specifically, in the court. For the most part, however, neither the defence of 'Indian Culture' nor communalism alone can begin to express the ways in which the court is a place of enormous contradictions. What is striking about the Marriage Room in the court, and what I seek to examine in this chapter, is the observation that what the law allows is not the same as that to which society is willing to confer its assent. At the same time, I explore the notion of the law as refuge to show that despite its contradictions, it serves to temporarily protect many couples from separation.

In Delhi, 'public conceptions' of love are predominantly negative. 'Love' is described in Hindi in two ways: *adhyatimik pyar*, or spiritual love, and *sharirik pyar*, or bodily love. In Urdu, the word *mohobbat* is roughly equivalent to the Hindi *pyar*, but there is another category of love which is *ishq*. *Ishq* combines a sense of both spiritual and bodily love, as it is used in Sufi devotional worship and refers to a desiring subject seeking union with God. Its emphasis on desire and passion thus gives it a different ontology to the Hindi *adhyatimik pyar*, which is unambiguously 'spiritual'. In Delhi, women are described as being eminently capable of spiritual love, whereas men are constantly suspected of being susceptible to its less noble counterpart: bodily love. Further, *adhyatimik pyar* is viewed as a thing of the past, with young people today being obsessed with *sharirik pyar, chumma-chatti* ('kissing and licking') and 'holding hands' *hath pakadna*. The interesting thing about the distinctions drawn between spiritual love and bodily love is that they map onto other dichotomies such as the morally righteous past and the degenerate and corrupt present. Love-marriage couples themselves use these categories to differentiate between 'Indian love' and 'Western love', where the former is spoken of as 'spiritual', a 'meeting of minds' and *'heartfelt'*, while the latter is described as *'just physical attraction', 'meeting of bodies'* and disingenuous. By describing romantic love with the metaphors of religious devotion, love-marriage couples represent their love as 'pure' and unconcerned with the worldly matters of caste, status and religious difference. The widespread popularity of the discourse on love being a symbol of the corrupt 'west' is symbolically inverted with the representation by love-marriage couples, that *their* love, unlike that in the 'west', is spiritual and other-worldly.

'Steel-proof' Marriages

The court in Delhi provides legally for marriages solemnised under what is known as the Special Marriage Act, 1954 (43 of 1954), and the Hindu Marriage Act, 1955. As already discussed, the Special Marriage Act was based on the legislation during colonial rule and its amended version provides a form of marriage which can be availed of by any Indian irrespective of the faith which either party to the marriage may profess. The other form of marriage in the court is the registration of marriages solemnised under the Hindu Marriage Act, 1955. The appeal of marriages solemnised or registered under both these Acts is that they provide the couple with legal proof of their marriage in the form of a certificate. Thus the law provides forms of marriage for those who do not wish to have their marriages solemnised through religious ceremonies (i.e. those wishing to have a civil marriage) and those who wish their marriages to be solemnised 'before God' (i.e. through a Hindu marriage in a temple) and which is subsequently registered in the court. The desire to celebrate marital union through a religious ceremony 'in the presence of God' is linked to the notion that true 'love' is 'pure' and spiritual.

Of the two forms of legalisation available, it is commonly assumed that caste strictures make it very difficult for inter-caste couples to marry through religious ceremonies as the priests would refuse to solemnise such unions; this is why most couples avail of the Special Marriage Act. For instance, Tahir Mahmood says that 'in these instances [of family objections] the parties turn to the civil marriage law under which such a marriage can be easily solemnised' (1978: 54). However, my own assessment was that it is civil marriage which is much more difficult to solemnise in Delhi, and that Hindu Marriage is by far the easier. This is one of the reasons why many couples who come to the court asking for a 'court-marriage' are sent off to a temple where the marriage is ritualised. These temples usually come recommended by the touts and lawyers, as having *pujaris* (priests) who are not averse to solemnising love-marriages. Further, the court functionaries and the Sub-Divisional Magistrates (SDMs) actively and persistently encourage people to have Arya Samaj marriages which are then registered in the court under the Hindu Marriage Act of 1955. The Arya Samaj, while being well known for its anti-Brahman stance and the simple sobriety of its marriage rites which can sanctify inter-caste unions, is equally famed for its ritual of *shuddhi* conversion ceremony whereby a non-Hindu can become a Hindu. This legacy notwithstanding, the Arya Samaj is widely viewed as a purely religious organisation, and its more political past does not affect the perception that they are a reformist group of modern Hindus who accept inter-caste marriages. In addition, a number of people interpreted the Arya Samaj's willingness to convert Muslims, or indeed any non-Hindu, as a sign of its 'openness'. The Arya Samaj recognises all religions and all can marry under its rites. In this way, a modern continuation of the old *shuddhi* 're-conversion' ceremony, which is integral to the larger 'Hinduisation' goal of the Arya Samaj, is not only made palatable, but almost a virtue to the modern Indian public.

Such conceptions of what constitutes 'public good' and what constitutes 'effective action' are critical to an understanding of love-marriage in Delhi. In my public interviews a number of people felt that love-marriages taking place in *mandirs* (temples) like the Arya Samaj could be easily dissolved due to family and caste objections. Temples were still within the reach of the community, which would do its best to break up marriages. Couples should rather go to the court where the signatures of both parties is taken. As one man explained, the court made such marriages 'steel-proof', meaning, as strong as steel. 'If the girl's family is rich, they can always break up an Arya Samaj *shadi* [wedding]. But if it is done in the court, nobody can touch them. The court will say, this marriage was done in law, "*kanoon*". You cannot break it up. It becomes *steel-proof*.

The law, or *kanoon*, is imagined as an objective impartial authority that is powerful enough to contest 'communities' trying to break up marriages, though in many instances this is far from the truth. This is one of the reasons why couples continue to come to the court rather than go to their nearest Arya Samaj temple. Further, there is little awareness about what a court marriage may involve. Most couples I spoke to in the court had no idea of what laws were available to them, nor what law their marriage had just been registered under. From their perspective it was much more a case of couples being asked by lawyers and touts what caste or community they came from, and what proof of age and residence they had. Depending on this, the lawyers would decide whether or not they could have a marriage, and what form it would take.

Popular discourse also validated love-marriages through the examples of famous figures. In answer to one of my questions about when 'court-marriages' first began, I was surprised to find a number of people identifying Indira Gandhi's marriage to a 'Muslim', 'Firoze', or in other versions 'Firoze Khan' (the name of a noted action-hero in Bombay films) as the first instance of love-marriage in India. Indira Nehru married Firoze Gandhi (not 'Khan'), a Parsi, on 26th March, 1942.[12] One man argued that Indira Gandhi married a Muslim from a slum in a court-marriage. Another respondent, B. Kumar, a Valmiki sweeper said that the 'problem' started when Indira and 'Firoze Khan' fell in love and 'crossed the boundary' (in Hindi: *sima par kar di*; had sexual relations). When they told Indira's father Nehru ('the first Brahmin Prime Minister of India') he was shocked.

He said to her: 'How could you do such a terrible thing? What will people say?' But Nehru was such a man; he thought Hindus and Muslims were equal. He said 'In the interests of the unity of India,[13] I will accept this love-marriage'.[14]

This story came up in a number of contexts. In one instance it was vigorously defended by an advocate of the court who said he had just read a feature on this Hindu–Muslim court-marriage in connection with celebrations of India's fifty years of Independence in 1997. The most interesting context of the story was the narration of an event in which a Hindu woman married to a Muslim was campaigning outside Delhi for the parliamentary elections. During clashes with BJP candidates, this member of the Communist Party of India was publicly slandered in the BJP's pre-election campaign as having had a 'court-marriage' to a Muslim. Apparently she turned this to her advantage by retorting in her speeches that even Indira Gandhi had married a Muslim and look how far she got in life.[15]

Clearly then, to say that someone has had a 'court-marriage' is to throw into doubt its social legitimacy. It invokes all the secrecy and intrigue that does in fact surround the Marriage Room like an aura of doom. As one couple told me, they could never forget the fact that in the early 1990s (when they got married) the Marriage Room in the court was also the Divorce Room. They sat awaiting the call from the Registrar for their marriage, while other couples waited for their marriages to be annulled. The inauspiciousness and inappropriateness of this was lost on the court. It was almost as if these 'special marriages' in the very nature of their contentious existence needed to be reminded of the provisions for divorce.

Nishar, a Muslim auto-rickshaw driver was convinced that inter-community love-marriages were a social evil. He argued that the Mughals spread war through such marriages. He recounted how Babar, the first Mughal, took Hindu wives and built side-by-side a *mandir* (temple) for them and a mosque for himself. Nishar argued that society could never accept this because both faiths had been dishonoured by Babar's marriages. By refusing to convert his Hindu wives, Babar had 'insulted' Islam, and by taking Hindu wives in the first place, Nishar argued that Babar had dishonoured Hinduism. The widely disseminated school text-book view of 'real' Mughal history is that the Mughal strategy of recruiting aristocrat (Rajput) wives was a 'secular' achievement and a virtue. Nishar's construction shows how this sort of history is being widely disseminated by *Hindutva* ideologues, and even in popular consciousness inter-community marriages are increasingly coming under attack by being 'Ayodhyaised'.[16]

Ramji, the peon who works in the court Marriage Room, is not so convinced that the law should meddle with custom. He said he has seen better days in the court; days in which it was considered shameful to even enter its premises.

In those days, if you stole something you would get five shoe-beatings.[17] If you left a woman, you would be put straight onto the back of a donkey and paraded around. Today the boys and girls come running here. They fall in love, they do a *love-marriage*, and neither does the father know nor the mother. There is so much injustice in this world. In this society, a *Harijan* girl and a *Rajput* boy[18] can get married. Is there no difference between poverty and wealth? The way you speak, the way you walk, the food you eat... all that is different. Today even a sweeper writes his name as *'Sharma'*.[19] They say they can do it because *Hindustan* is a free country. Is that any reason? How can you challenge the natural order of things? Milk will always remain milk; water will remain water.

To counter such views, others in my public interviews argued that Hindustan is indeed a free country, and that is why people should be allowed to have love-marriages, whether in the court or in temples. On the one hand, court marriages are viewed as a *'steel-proof'* guarantee that a couple will not be separated by their dissenting families. Individual freedom to marry who one pleased was viewed as an important part of being a modern Indian. Equally, such marriages were viewed with suspicion and fear and were seen to carry with them an enormous baggage of a fraught history. Love-marriages in Delhi continue to personify the ambivalences of community and caste relations through their unions.

Tis Hazari

The ambivalence of popular perceptions of love-marriages is concretely manifested in the court buildings of Tis Hazari. Tis Hazari is Asia's largest district court complex.[20] It is located in Civil Lines, a few roads away from the walled city of Old Delhi. The complex is enormous and consists of three main buildings connected by endless corridors. Outside, whether in the blistering 45 degrees celsius heat of Delhi's summer, or in the freezing chill of winter, one finds advocates and touts sitting under make-shift tin roofs with a few permanent brick chambers for the more well-to-do. They are supplied with cups of 'mobile-*chai*' (tea brought to their tables), snacks and *pakodas*, cold drinks and meals by attendant 'mobile' vendors and restaurants. The back wall of the building is covered with a 20-foot-high pile of rusted and mangled old metal furniture from the court rooms, with monkeys gambolling over the building and periodically eating the records inside.[21] Outside, adjoining the car park, is the Delhi Traffic Police's graveyard of confiscated or crashed vehicles. With more fatal accidents on Delhi's roads than those of all India's other cities combined, Tis Hazari looks more like a wrecker's yard than a court. The front is however more suitably juridical: it is the famous Tis Hazari lock-up. Police trucks from around the city stream in in the mornings, ploughing through crowds of nervous relatives, and handcuffed defendants are escorted by the police to the magistrate's courts.

6. Photograph of the sign outside '137-C', Marriage. Room, Tis Hazari Courts, Delhi; April 1997.

The Marriage Room in Tis Hazari is known as such, and is referred to by its room number: '137C'. The Marriage Room is the official place where civil marriages are solemnised by a Sub-Divisional Magistrate, and where Hindu Marriages are registered.[22] Outside is a large sign that says in formidable print: 'Beware of Touts', with the friendly advice that the marriage procedure costs a mere fifteen rupees, so 'why be a victim and pay more?' Ironically, even the warning cannot prepare you for the onslaught of harassment from the Marriage Room touts. Any couple entering the court is immediately approached and asked if they are there to get married, and services are offered to help navigate the complicated and difficult process. One tout in particular refused to accept that I didn't want to get married myself but that I was actually quite interested in learning about the Marriage Room and love-marriages in Tis Hazari. This for him proved to be quite a conundrum. Over the months that followed, he took me through the gamut of possibilities as to *why* a woman would hang around the court and what it *really* meant. There were few women who worked in or visited the court. One young advocate told me that she never stayed on the court premises after 3.30 p.m. because this was when the lawyers started drinking in their chambers. Besides, she never walked down the corridors alone, but was always accompanied everywhere by a male *munshi* (a lawyer's clerk). There were also contemporary 'courtesans' who plied their trade within the premises, showing me their telephone books with judges, lawyers and traders alike counted among their clients. I soon learnt that Tis Hazari was a place of dirty dealing of all sorts. While I was working there, two of the Sub-Divisional Magistrates who solemnised marriages (and outside whose offices I spent many of my days) were arrested on charges of running a scam involving the issue of passports and forged documents. They were bailed (but not exonerated) and were back to work within a week. During the time I was working at Tis Hazari, there were two gun-fights in the court premises, bringing the violence of urban India into the no longer sacrosanct premises of the judicature.[23]

Delhi also has an escalating problem of crimes against women. I heard from an advocate about a case that had apparently hit the news sometime in January or February of 1997. A judge in the Kakardooma court across the river Jamuna in Delhi was taking *in camera* evidence of a woman who had been raped. 'He kept asking her, "Then what happened, then what happened". Then he himself *selected* that *ledies* [lady]. He raped her.'[24]

As I was working on love-marriages, I soon began to hear stories and rumours about court practice in Tis Hazari. Initially, I took them to be well-meaning warnings about my own status in the court. I was advised not to drink tea with the touts, because people in Delhi were known to 'drug women and rape them'. One female advocate who worked with a Civil Liberties group in Delhi forewarned me about male advocates making passes at women in the court.[25] Another lawyer told me a story about a case that took place sometime in 1993–94:

A young couple who had eloped came to the court to get married. Here they met an advocate who agreed to help them. He sent the boy off with his assistant to have the affidavits made. The girl was left with him. The advocate said to the girl, you are under-age. I'll have to do a check-up on you. He took her into his chambers and shut the door. He lifted her clothes and said: So you are eloping with him? If you sleep with him or if you sleep with me, what difference will it make to you? Then she was raped. The boy returned to find her crying. Both of them committed suicide. This story was reported in the press.[26]

Stories such as these were recounted to illustrate the vulnerability of the couples who came into the court declaring love as their motivation for marriage. Sometimes their desperation was so evident that even if there were no incidents as extreme as this, the lawyers and touts were able to scare them into doing their bidding. The court attracts couples who bypass the rigid controls of their ethno-religious communities and seek assistance from the legislative apparatus of the state in their attempt to legitimate their love. By virtue of being not-community, they are uniquely vulnerable to the violence and excesses of both, their communities and the state.

The process of court-marriage

The association of love-marriages with 'court-marriages' makes them seem all the more socially deviant. Courts in India are liminal places. Mostly, people feel that the courts are traps into which they fall, and until they have no money left to bribe a judge or pay the lawyer, the court will continue to wreck their lives. As Cohn argues with reference to Indian courts in the colonial period: 'There is apparently no quicker way of driving an opponent into bankruptcy than to embroil him in a law suit. Most people would go to any length to avoid going to court' (1987: 568–569). And like the litigants, the love-marriage couples too are perceived to come to Tis Hazari with reluctance and heavy hearts. Mr. Sharma, a tout, explained the situation to me:

> They come here to the court out of *majboori* [compulsion]. The girl doesn't want to, but yet she becomes his lover. Most of the boys are *goondas* [thugs]. They scare the girl. She runs away with him. Then reality hits her. Her people reject her. *Young blood* doesn't think until the eleventh hour. The meaning of love is sacrifice. Yet love-marriages are selfish and self-gratifying. The girl can no longer return to her maternal

home. The reality is, she can't even say anything. Society won't *leak* the information about her marriage. They try to cover it up by burying it. The shame is too much.

Mr. Sharma is the very embodiment of the danger warned against by the sign outside Room 137C, asking 'why be a victim and pay more?' Sharma works outside the court rooms where both civil marriages are solemnised and Hindu marriages are registered. As a tout, he has no legal training and has learnt the law entirely through its practice.[27] He told me that there are three sorts of love-marriages: *'Special marriage'*, *'Hindu marriage'* and *'No-marriage'*. The first, civil marriage (under the Special Marriage Act, 1954) is a 'thirty-day business'. By this he refers to the requirement for a thirty-day period of notice to the Registrar of the intention of the couple to marry. The second, *'Hindu marriage'*, is a 'two-day business'. On the first day, the couple is taken to an Arya Samaj temple where they are immediately married. On the second day that marriage is registered in the court. The third form of marriage provides no business for Mr. Sharma. It is a marriage before the gods with personal vows or symbolic gestures such as placing garlands around each other's necks, or the man filling *sindhur* (red powder used to indicate the marital status of a Hindu woman) in the parted hair of a woman in a temple. Such marriages according to Sharma have no legal standing, and as such, provide no security against separation.

The thirty-day business of civil marriage requires the couples to give notice of their intention to marry. This notice is pasted by the clerk of the Marriage Room on a corridor outside; a wall of infamy, where names and photographs can reveal caste identity and religion, and critically, addresses where the couple can be found.[28] These notices are also sent to the addresses provided by the couple, ostensibly to check whether either of them has been previously married (and not divorced) and whether either of them is under-age (under 18 for the girl, under 21 for the boy). Inadvertently, the judicial process of sending notice exposes the secrecy of couples marrying against the wishes (and often, without the knowledge) of their families and communities. So 'complicated' is the business of civil marriages that the work of the touts and lawyers is to claim to try and safeguard the well-being of the couple (for not inconsiderable sums of money). This is done by slipping money to the clerks either not to put the notification on the board, or by peeling it off so that it is not readable. Further, the notice must be intercepted so as not to reach the family, but according to Mr. Sharma, this cannot be guaranteed as the post-office is not 'reliable' (it cannot be relied on to subvert the notice-sending process) and often the notice will reach the families despite bribes meant to ensure that it doesn't.

The Sub-Divisional Magistrate has the legal discretion to demand further proof of residence under the Special Marriage Act, and the local Station House (Police) Officer is often asked to send someone around to establish whether or not the girl or the boy live where they claim to have lived for the previous thirty days.[29] This adds another twist to the tale, as *havaldars* (constables) will often need to be bribed into not visiting the home and stating that the couple do indeed live wherever they claim to. However, it sometimes happens that when dissenting parents get wind of all this, either through the child's absence from the house or through the *havaldar's* visit or through the notice of intended marriage, they immediately rush to the police station to file a kidnapping case, saying that their son or their daughter is missing and they suspect that they have been kidnapped, a phenomenon I examine in greater detail in Chapter 3. Often the family will do this in utmost secrecy and strings will be pulled to ensure, in Mr. Sharma's words, that 'society doesn't *leak* the information'. The hope is that the police will use their power to recover the boy or the girl and the whole matter will be hushed up. Such gossip, if leaked, will certainly jeopardise the social status of the family with knock-on effects on all marriageable youth in their kin group. A love-affair and an aborted love-marriage can sabotage a family's chances of arranging a match for other offspring. All this information is reeled off to people who are about to enter the Marriage Rooms to make enquiries, and it is not uncommon to find them so daunted by the intricacies of the legal system that they hire the tout or the lawyer to help them navigate through it.

The tout and the lawyers make their (invariably large) profits out of the system by convincing their clients that the ins-and-outs of the marriage process won't be revealed to them through the official enquiry desks. This is easily done because, to a certain extent, people expect all legal procedures to be hugely bureaucratic; but in addition to this, the process in Tis Hazari is now finely tuned to ensure limited access to information. So, for instance, a form for a civil marriage is only issued against the production of an official ration card.[30] Obviously, this form does contain some of the requisite information about the legal requirements of the Special Marriage Act, but ration cards are prized possessions and most young couples will not be able to smuggle them out of their homes.[31] So if someone is belligerent and they don't want to avail of the services of the touts and lawyers, the latter just sit back and watch with amusement as they charge around endless corridors looking for the right rooms (many of which aren't numbered), trying to attract the attention of indifferent clerks, and trying to procure any information about the legal process. Mr. Sharma says that there are few 'high-class' people who come to Tis Hazari asking to have 'thirty-day marriages'.[32] He always tries to dissuade them from it because it ruins business if he has to go through the elaborate process with them, and furthermore, it is to his disadvantage if there is such a long waiting period in which the 'girl can change her mind', the families can find out and stop the marriage, or the couple themselves can find another lawyer or another tout who may undercut his price.

For all these reasons, the most convenient and *best* way to have a love-marriage is 'Hindu marriage'. This involves a ritual ceremony ('*riti-rivaz ki shadi*') in an Arya Samaj[33] temple, the ingredients of which are photos that are evidence of the marriage, taken by the photographer attached to each of these temples, and affidavits saying (*a*) that the couple is marrying under Hindu *riti-rivaz* (customs and traditions), (*b*) that they are both Hindu (and if either or both are not, that they have 'converted' to Hinduism through the *shuddhi* ceremony and have taken Hindu names), (*c*) that they are above the ages of 18 for women and 21 for men,[34] and (*d*) that have left home of their own free will and have taken nothing from their homes except the clothes they are wearing. This affidavit is then attested by a Sub-Divisional Magistrate. Finally, the Arya Samaj has a system of maintaining registers of all marriages performed, and they provide certificates of marriage with serial numbers that correspond to their registers, thus making it difficult to deny that the marriage has taken place. This certificate along with the affidavits and the photographs are then submitted to the court, and within a day the marriage is registered and a certificate provided to that effect.[35] This two-day 'business' constitutes the second form for love-marriages.

The third (*'No-marriage'*) is the most foolhardy way. It is to run away from home, get married in a temple that doesn't provide a certificate or photographs; indeed, sometimes, not have a marriage at all but merely display marital status through co-habitation, *sindhur* in the parted hair of the woman (in the case of a Hindu), and glass bangles on her wrists. For Mr. Sharma, well versed in the tactics of dissenting families and communities, this is a very bad option indeed, because invariably when the family catches up with the couple they will succeed in breaking them up through arm-twisting and blackmail. For the families of eloping couples, it is usually a better option to be able to deny categorically that any marriage has taken place, and various alibis are easily found to explain away their child's absence from the home during the period when they eloped. Mr. Sharma told me one story about how he had helped marry a young couple. They had been found out by the girl's family, who were powerful people and who opposed the marriage. The girl's father and brother brought her to court where she gave a sworn statement before the Magistrate that she had been drugged by the boy and Mr. Sharma before the Arya Samaj wedding and, as such, she had not married of her own free will. Mr. Sharma was apparently arrested along with the boy and thrown into jail. This change in the girl's statement is constantly talked about in Tis Hazari; *'larkiyan bayan badal dete hain'*; the girls change their testimony. This for the lawyers and touts means big trouble. This is one of their justifications for exhaustive, and occasionally voyeuristic, enquiries into the affairs of the boy and the girl, to *test* whether they will stand up to the pressures that lie ahead.

The role of the lawyers and touts

The touts and advocates who work outside the Marriage Room are perhaps uniquely positioned in a relationship of ambivalence towards the wider legal profession. This is because, at the district court level (in cases other than runaway couples seeking civil marriage), business is transacted not through impersonal relations with lawyers, but rather through members of one's kin group, or members of one's own religious or social community who are lawyers and advocates in the court. Most people arrive at a lawyer's desk through personal recommendations: Sikhs seek out Sikh lawyers, Muslims head for Urdu signs outside the lawyers' chambers, and caste surnames help people to identify where in the labyrinth of the court they may find the advocate whom they have come to see. Love-marriage couples, on the other hand, very rarely come to the court with any idea of what they need to do, how they should proceed, and whom they should approach for help. Further, they are wary of precisely the sorts of kinship ties that most other people seek out, and this is one reason why they are more likely to hire a tout or lawyer who does not belong to their own community or caste. They run too much of a risk if the lawyer happens to know their families and lets on that their children were in the court trying to get married.

The lawyers (who often work in teams of two and three) and touts (who usually work alone) are well aware that couples come to them with different circumstances and they clearly enjoy categorising their cases according to the dangers involved, the money earned and the tragedy of the lovers. Touts like Mr. Sharma who worked independently, while lacking the professional garb of a lawyer, were nonetheless respected for their wealth of experience in the court and the networks of relationships that they have built up with clerks and other court functionaries. Sometimes, if a 'case' got too hot for them to handle, they would pass it on to the lawyers, who would at least have the legal standing should trouble arise and they be asked to give evidence. Touts provided a comprehensive service, meeting the couple outside the Marriage Room and accompanying them through the labyrinthine corridors of the court, from one room to another where different aspects of the bureaucratic procedure were initiated, processed, and through the good offices of the tout, completed. The difference between touts and lawyers was that the lawyers would only occasionally accompany the couple in their run-around. Both touts and lawyers supervised the making of affidavits, the illegal 'production' of various sorts of *'proofs'*, and coached couples about their 'rights' and the manner in which they should respond if they ran into trouble during the solemnisation or registration process with the Sub-Divisional Magistrate or the police. It is striking that neither the touts nor the lawyers were allowed to set foot into the actual Marriage Room. Their services were thus entirely 'unofficial'.

Some couples in the most desperate of cases would have had to leave home without any preparation, either because of the unexpected discovery of their '*affair*',[36] or because if they remained, there was the risk of being forced into an impending arranged marriage.[37] Such couples required specialised services and it was the touts and lawyers who provided them with it. For a start, they needed to be able to trust the lawyers '*as-a-friend*' and divulge all the details about their families' 'objections'. Anticipating trouble is what these lawyers did best, and since they often had more than their fair share of it, they sought to minimise their risk by putting the couple through a lengthy, though '*friendly*', interrogation. Sometimes, the services provided would include boarding at the lawyer's home, or being provided a suitable alibi address so that they could not be tracked down. As the lawyers enjoyed telling me: each case was dealt with on its own merits. One couple who had eloped from Jammu to Delhi were made to send an attested copy of the marriage certificate to each of the parent's homes *and* to their local police stations. The lawyers wrote out the statements for the boy and the girl, to which they then affixed their signatures. This measure was taken because both sets of parents had filed kidnapping charges on their offspring's lover: the girl's family insisting that the boy had kidnapped her, and the boy's parents accusing the girl of having kidnapped him. It was now up to the couple and their lawyers to prove to the police that the certificate of marriage was not false, the photos not posed, the witnesses ready to corroborate the couple's story,[38] and it was up to the families to prove that their child had been forced, was insane, was underage, or somehow not of sound mind and balanced judgement.

On a number of occasions the lawyers and touts worked on credit if the couple were too poor, or could not provide the money in advance. Their insurance would be the addresses of the parents and since very few couples would be foolhardy enough to allow their parents the chance to 'buy-off' their own tout or lawyers, they would almost invariably be able to collect their dues with ease.[39] Perhaps most interesting of all was that they would be willing to accompany couples to their homes in a bid to convince their families. They argued that since most of the couples were lower-middle or working-class, the presence of a lawyer or a *munshi* from the court would inevitably confer a sense of legitimacy to the marriage in the eyes of the parents, and deter them from more desperate measures such as filing police cases or getting the community to help them break up the marriage. The services were so intimate that Mr. Sharma showed me a sheet of paper in the file he always carried with him, on which he had painstakingly written out in poetic Hindi a ten-point letter of advice to the couples he married.[40] Amongst others was the advice that in an argument, the man and the woman should try and lose rather than win; that neither of them should chastise the other for mistakes of the past; that they should never sleep until fights had been resolved, and that they should try to express at least one loving sentiment to each other every day. In this way, touts such as Mr. Sharma sought to sell themselves as surrogate 'family' and 'community' to the couples they encountered.

Despite the comprehensive service that they provide, the lawyers who worked on marriages in Tis Hazari were considered the lowest of the low in the prestige hierarchy of lawyers' status in the court. They even disparagingly called themselves '*thor-maror wallahs*' (breakers and fixers) of the legal system who were willing to manipulate it to get a couple married. The reason they cited for their low status is that the Marriage Room at Tis Hazari was probably the only place in the court where, technically, lawyers were not required. A Sub-Divisional Magistrate at Tis Hazari told me that he didn't wish to talk about the lawyers' involvement in the marriages at his court because there was no need for lawyers in marriages, and they were never allowed to enter the SDM's office with the clients. The lawyers marshalled the Advocates Act in their defence, quoting Section 27 which they claim says 'lawyers can be engaged anywhere'.

The reasons that other lawyers cited for their disrepute was that Marriage Room lawyers completely lacked any professional ethics. For instance, the allegation was that these lawyers, while avowedly supporting love-marriage couples, were not averse to providing their services to families seeking to catch renegades or helping families to legally annul marriages already solemnised. One case to which I was witness involved a young couple who were so sure of the threat to their marriage that they fled to Nepal in the hope that the Indian police could not follow them. The parents approached some lawyers in Tis Hazari who hired 'a college friend' of one of the lawyers, a senior Delhi police officer, who took time out from the police force to hunt the couple down in Nepal and restore them to their families in Delhi.

If the lawyers and touts did indeed provide an elaborate service for couples and their families alike, it was not for want of remuneration. The lawyers and touts made three assessments of the clients they encountered. The first was: how vulnerable is the couple, and consequently, how desperate are they to have a court-marriage. A correlate of this assessment was the 'reading' of their client's caste and class status, which also gave the lawyers and touts an idea of how powerful the couple's families were and what the basis of the opposition to the marriage might be. The second was how intelligent they were, and how much of the legal procedure they might know. Finally, there was the important consideration of money: how much would the couple be willing to pay for services rendered?

The number of actual certificates and paraphernalia necessary for a civil marriage or a Hindu marriage registration varied according to the amount of money a couple could afford, and their degree of street-credibility or naiveté. Hence, the very poor could be told that a court-marriage was an affidavit, and they would be made to pay fifty rupees and would sign and leave the court with a piece of paper that was 'proof' of nothing other than the advocate's or tout's trickery. Sometimes women found, when abandoned by their husbands, that their court-marriages were 'false'. A prostitute in Tis Hazari told me that she had been told to leave her husband by a man who loved her very much and wanted to marry her. She did, and they came to Tis Hazari where she signed a piece of paper and thought she had had a *'court-shadi'* (court-marriage).[41] Only after he left her did she discover that a *'real court-shadi'* was a registered marriage, whereas her 'marriage' consisted of merely signing an affidavit that she could not even read.[42]

The middle class on the other hand were made to pay for their proof. So, for instance, one lawyer replied to my question about fees by saying that it depended on how the couple came to the court. Small talk would involve saying, where did you come from, and how did you travel here...

If the boy has his own scooter or bike, I know that he is wealthy enough to pay x amount. If they came by car and he carries a mobile phone, then I know I have found a good client. If they came in a Blueline then, well, he can only pay a few thousand rupees. I will ask them to trust me and tell me everything, because only if I know the full story can I help them. They will try not to tell me the details, but I will say, why don't you have your ration card? Or, why are you afraid your parents will find out? Who are you running from? I will try and find out what objections the family has to the marriage.

Then, armed with this information, he would be in a position to extract more money. The lawyers and touts played on the theme of vulnerability, saying that they themselves were taking such a big risk getting involved in such a messy case, and so on, until the picture painted for the couple would be as grim as the scenario they had presumably escaped from. What option did they have but to believe the lawyers and touts that their 'proof of age' for instance, was not suitable for the court, and that they need go to the hospital by the court for an X-ray and a 'certificate'?[43] The X-ray 'certificate' would say that from the bone structure of the girl, it was the opinion of the doctor that she was above 18 years of age. All this cost would then be added on to their final bill. The lawyers' and touts' total charge for a marriage could thus vary quite considerably depending on the client's status and gullibility. There turned out to be an amazing range in the 'cost' of the legal procedure (which, as the sign warned, was in theory a mere fifteen rupees), the bare minimum being 1,000 rupees, while the more affluent would be charged in the region of 20,000 rupees. One advocate boasted that he had extracted a full 30,000 rupees from one man, and jokingly related how, when he subsequently discovered the full extent of this individual's gullibility before the law, he felt that he could have got at least twice that.

The manner of assessing the age of a couple in a country where many people do not have birth certificates or similar 'proofs' allows considerable manoeuvrability of the rules concerning the minimum age of marriage. If a couple is under-age, the lawyers can always manage to find a doctor to say that the girl is above 18, especially if she *looked* the age. These deceits can be tricky because if the parents oppose the marriage and produce other proofs of the girl being under-age, then the marriage could *theoretically* be declared by the court to be void. Even though under-age marriage is a crime punishable by law, the punishment under the Hindu Marriage Act is simple imprisonment which may extend to fifteen days, or a fine which may extend to 1,000 rupees or both. The courts are reluctant to prosecute couples under the Hindu Marriage Act because under-age marriage is viewed as too widespread a phenomenon to punish only those who come to the court for their marriages. The accepted legal position is that non-age is *not* a ground under the Hindu Marriage Act which renders a marriage void or voidable. Under the Special Marriage Act, however, non-age marriages are categorically declared to be 'null and void'. This is a powerful reason for the touts and lawyers to convince couples to use the Hindu Marriage Act as opposed to the Special Marriage Act because the age requirement is viewed as being far more flexible under the former law.

Another example of the ingenuity of the informal economy of Tis Hazari was the response to the 'zonalisation' introduced by the government in an attempt to break the nexus of corruption in the district court. Initially nine Marriage Officers in nine different rooms in Tis Hazari (to take over from the one SDM in 137C) were appointed to deal with couples whose residence fell within their 'zones'. In August 1997, these offices moved to their respective 'zones'.[44] There was no sign-posting of this outside 137C and scores of people would come there every day assuming it was still the Marriage Room for all of Delhi. They were invariably told about the zonalisation and sent to the information desk on the ground floor to learn which zonal office they should go to. Typically, the information office was manned for only a few hours in a day, and so was almost never attended. Those who returned to 137C to say there was no one at the desk to provide information, were told the staff were too busy to attend to enquiries. Outside, the touts and lawyers waited for the couples to capitulate and hire them for their services.

The zones in the notification were described as follows: (1) West District, (2) D.C. and West, (3) Nand Nagri, (4) North Delhi, (5) Central, (6) North District, (7) East, (8) South, and (9) North–West. It was bewildering for everyone because the zones did not relate to established, generically understood, geographical locales and literally no one in the court other than the touts and lawyers, could tell a person into which district fell his or her residence. Again, a notice was pasted with these details outside 137C, but within a couple of days it had been peeled off the wall and the only people who had the zonalisation details and the knowledge of where exactly the zonal offices were, were the touts and lawyers who guarded the information jealously. 137C became the Marriage Room archive of registers where I subsequently spent many weeks assessing the archive, and was able to observe the ways in which information was rationed out to the public. People would be told, 'your office is somewhere near the Britannia Bread Factory on the Ring Road'. Or, 'it is in Saket'—a huge area rather than an address. Members of the public continued to go to 137C and it acted as an excellent touting ground to get clients who, with better information, might otherwise have gone directly to their local area office and bypassed the 'system'.[45] However, a number of the lawyers decided that the boom in marriages over the previous few years was now being complemented by a boom of divorces.[46] Since the divorce courts remained centralised at Tis Hazari, and because their networks of contacts remained there, they reasoned that this was their new calling, and became divorce lawyers.

Processes of social legitimation

As we have seen, love-marriages tend to be equated with 'court-shadi', which are typified in the image of an eloping couple (*bhag-ke shadi karna*: to run away and marry) who get married without any of their family present. This is then associated with a perception of the corrupt and chaotic district court, where the perceived illegitimacy of the union is ironically confirmed through the manipulations of the process of registering its legitimacy. However, the due process of these marriages is only half expressed in their legalisation through the court, and, hidden from the general public's purview, is the far more important and significant domestic struggle in which couples seek to gain the acceptance of their parents and families.

The certificate that is provided in a *court-shadi* is necessary proof of marriage and is used as a lever to bargain with the parents and family to agree to the marriage. Secrecy is of the utmost importance because if the families are strongly opposed to the marriage they will almost certainly create trouble for the couple, who may then have to go on the run. It is very rare that people come to the court with their consenting families to be married. It is important to note then, that while from the standpoint of the law a civil marriage does legally legitimate the union of a man and a woman, the couples rarely see it as an end in itself. It marks the beginning of a long battle in which they most often return to their respective homes and pretend that nothing has happened; awaiting an opportune moment when they can start breaking the news to their family and garnering the required support to socially legitimate the marriage.

For some couples who are aware that one or both families will never concede to their choice, the court-marriage or registration marks the beginning of their elopement and their struggle to keep one step ahead of their families in case they try to track them down. These marriages would often be the sort considered the most socially unacceptable: that between Hindu and Muslim, high and low caste, or rich and poor. In such instances, the opposition from the family that considers itself socially ascendant can be so severe that the entire community may be mobilised, and police cases lodged to aid the retrieval of the child. If the couple has not succeeded in getting a legally valid wedding certificate it is very likely that the family will attempt to ensure that they never see each other again. Mostly, however, the couples do obtain the certificate, and this, along with numerous statements, are submitted to the police or the court which gives them leave to go their own way.

In a tiny minority of cases, the family is so powerful that despite a legal certificate of marriage or registration, the marriage is made void under the legal clauses regarding, under-age marriage consent, unsoundness of mind, 'unfit for marriage or the procreation of children', or 'recurrent attacks of insanity or epilepsy'.[47] The dynamics of elopement are treated in the next chapter; but I want to emphasise that the process of getting one's family to accept the marriage is as fraught and delicate as the most sensitive political negotiations imaginable. Anything can go wrong, and the sense of tragedy, betrayal and abandonment on both sides can be so severe as to inspire some of the acts of destruction that do occasionally take place.[48]

The picture presented here is one of bewildering complexity. However, while the touts and lawyers are capable of mediating the process of court-marriage and negotiating all the bureaucracy, they are less concerned with the more subjective goals of the couple. Sometimes this indifference can create insurmountable problems for the couple; for instance, in the event that it is an inter-community marriage. When Mr. Sharma described the three forms of marriage for me, I posed the question: what if the couple are a Hindu and a Muslim? Well, that was no problem, he replied. They would go to the Arya Samaj *mandir*, the Muslim would be converted through a *shuddhi* ceremony, and his or her name would be changed in an affidavit of conversion, saying that the conversion was of their own free will. They would then be married under the Arya Samaj rites and their marriage would be registered the next day under the Hindu Marriage Act in the court. But what if the Muslim did not wish to convert to Hinduism? Well, he reasoned, I would tell them that it is only for the marriage, and to get the certificate. It is not a '*real*' conversion.

There were a number of couples who seemed to have no problem with religious conversion through an Arya Samaj *shadi*. For many inter-religious marriages, giving the 'marriage' a religion was much more important than hanging on to one or the other. Invariably, the girl converted to the religion of the boy, and this was a widely accepted principle. More prosaically, as one man put it, 'the one who holds the stick owns the buffalo'.[49]

The problem with the expediency about advice such as that concerning conversion was that, even if the couple was comfortable with the 'quick' and 'easiest' court-marriage available to them (the Arya Samaj *shadi*, and the consequent registration under the Hindu Marriage Act), it was difficult to see how such a marriage would perform the two-fold function required of most '*court shadis*' by the couples themselves. This, simply put, would be: (*a*) safe-guarding the couple from being separated, and providing legal 'proof' that they are married, to police and the court where kidnapping cases have been anticipated; and, (*b*) using this certificate over a period of time to 'convince' their families that the situation was now irreversible, and to convince them to 'accept' it or compromise and host the '*love-cum-arranged*' marriage. While the conversion of the Muslim would fulfil the first requirement, it is difficult to see how it could leave open the possibility for the second. The Muslim side, it would seem, would have substantial cause to be less than forgiving to the couple.[50]

For Mr. Sharma, the Arya Samaj marriage between a Hindu and a Muslim seemed to be about business considerations. But what could explain the attitudes of court functionaries towards the Special Marriage Act? For instance, a young clerk in his early 30s who worked in the Marriage Room at Tis Hazari said to me:

> We try to help them. We tell them that they should get their parents to understand. That they should not do this. Those who we say this to, they fight with us and leave! What is a civil marriage? After all, it is only a *sarkari shadi* ['government marriage']. It is a marriage on a piece of paper. A real marriage is when there are rituals, when everyone is there, when everyone participates.

So for him there was a scale of preference, with an arranged marriage on the top, the Arya Samaj *shadi* next, and the Special Marriage Act *shadi* last. The couples come to the court to get married. There they must fight with officials and functionaries who seek to convince them to go back to their respective homes. It would seem to be an impossible situation.

For many couples, the fact that they were getting married without the presence of any of their family members was traumatic enough. My own role as a researcher working in the courts and the temples was fraught with ethical dilemmas: some couples were clearly too terrified or too traumatised and suspicious to talk to someone whom they had never seen before and who they feared might reveal the fact of their marriages to their families. A few were keen to talk, and they usually asked whether I could tell them if 'love-marriages' were 'successful'. A number of times, I was asked to confirm statistics: 'Is it true that 95% love-marriages are failures?' 'Is the success-rate 1%?' Coming from people who were starting their lives together in such difficult circumstances, such concerns drove home the fact that there was very little to console them or give them confidence in their marriage, either at home or in their social worlds.

Love-marriage couples' demeanours indicated their grief. There were often tears over the fact that such an important occasion in a person's life should take place outside of the remit of the family. Often the couple would be dressed in ordinary clothes, sometimes without any jewellery or flowers, and they would explain that they didn't want their parents to suspect that there was anything amiss. Some would arrive with a change of clothes and then revert to everyday wear after the marriage. Most people had 'fill-ins' who played the role of the girl's father gifting her in marriage, and accepted the obeisance of the couple after the ceremony. The photographers who worked inside the Arya Samaj temples provided an expensive next-day service of marriage photos. Most couples were urged to hire them if they hadn't come prepared with a camera, as such photos would be useful as further *'proof'* of the marriage. The couples would be made to pose for photos and would be urged not to cry and to smile because it shouldn't look as if the marriage was taking place without their consent. The touts and lawyers would console the couple: 'The families will just shout and scream for a few months. After that they always accept the marriage. A compromise will be found.' In cases involving inter-religious marriages, or marriages between high and low castes, their advice was usually more cautious: 'Your people will shout and scream for a few years. Then you'll have your first child. Everything will be forgotten'.

Note on court data

The Tis Hazari marriage archive now occupies the old Marriage Room, '137 C'. It is maintained so as to be able to establish whether or not a marriage has taken place. Every now and again, the clerks will receive a note in the archive and will try and dig out the records requested.

Tahir Mahmood, in his definitive paper on the history of civil marriage law in India, provides aggregate data of civil marriages solemnised or registered in 27 districts in the state of Uttar Pradesh, from the years 1954 to 1973 (1978: 51–52). Such data are extremely important when trying to assess the effectiveness of any law, and since none was available for Delhi, I took up the task to collate this information, and also to try and see what sorts of historical data one could glean from the records.

My work in the archive took approximately two and a half months. There were two clerks in the Marriage Room archive, whose assistance and kindness were invaluable. Soon after I ploughed through the many cupboards I discovered the source of their indifference to their records. Pages, sometimes entire registers were damaged, defaced or removed.[51] Registers were moved around so much that it took days for the clerks to locate any one book. This was the reason behind their phlegmatic treatment of anyone 'harassing' them for marriage records. Sometimes, for each year there were overlapping registers for the same period implying that two registers were being maintained. Equally, there were years in which records were left loose—for instance, in 1995, twenty-one unbound records of the Special Marriage Act (or SMA), or 1994, seventy-two loose records. Sometimes, there were serious errors and overlaps in the serialising of the records. For example, in the year 1986, the records for the Hindu Marriage Act (HMA) Registration jump from serial number 1583 to 4583—an overlap and an error which if undetected would claim 4,629 marriages instead of 1629 for that year. Similarly, registers sometimes ran seamlessly from December into January of the next year (for example, the file for HMA 1971 starts with the serial number 220), and were often desperately incomplete (see Table 2.1). However, it is important to recognise that during the time when I was doing my fieldwork, the Marriage Room was undergoing great changes through zonalisation, and this in turn was the work of conscientious magistrates who sought to purge the court of the advocate-tout canker. It was clear even then that the resources available to the judges in Tis Hazari were poor and that zonalisation might help turn things around for the better.

Table 2.1 Records of Marriage Registration at Tis Hazari (Delhi)

Year	Civil Marriage (Act III 1872; Special Marriage Act, 1954)	Hindu Marriage (Hindu Marriage Act, 1955)
1933	2	
1934	2	
1935	3	
1936	4	
1937	8	
1938	5	
1939	5	
1940	10	
1941	13	
1942	18	
1943	14	
1944	12	
1945	14	
1946	15	
1947	27	
1948	42	
1949	43	
1950	43	
1951	38	
1952	61	
1953	56	
1954	87	
1955	73 □	
1956	38	
1957	76	12
1958	98	13
1959	47	19
1960	92	42
1961	88	43
1962	111	51
1963	no records	49
1964	no records	78
1965	136	132
1966	117	166
1967	124	233
1968	149	381
1969	184	707
1970	229 □	219 □

(Table 2.1 Continued)

(*Table 2.1 Continued*)

Year	Civil Marriage (Act III 1872; Special Marriage Act, 1954)	Hindu Marriage (Hindu Marriage Act, 1955)
1971	235	516 □
1972	212	697
1973	317	788 □
1974	347	1,153 □
1975	367	1,210 □
1976	526	1,218 □
1977	509	1,256
1978	482	1,366
1979	409	1,329 □
1980	456	1,247 □
1981	453	no records
1982	355	1,819
1983	360	1,814 □
1984	318	1,862
1985	no records	1,773
1986	no records	1,629 □
1987	418	1,631
1988	398	1,884
1989	444	1,863
1990	474	2,024
1991	499 □	2,611
1992	457	2,805
1993	181 □	3,234 □
1994	378	2,799
1995	367	3,053
1996	285	3,407
1997	169†	1,065‡

□ *incomplete records extant for that year*
† *records end on 20/05/97 due to 'zonalisation'*
‡ *records end on 21/4/97 due to 'zonalisation'*

When the records are so haphazardly maintained it isn't merely their accuracy, but also their entire *raison d'étre* that must be called into question. The Marriage Room archive was under-resourced, under-staffed and almost deliberately poorly maintained by the clerks. This is explicable only if we recognise that the Marriage Room in Delhi is subject to all manner of political constraints, where dissenting families can demand that some marriages be denied, and others be recognised as valid. Since Delhi is the nation's capital, high-profile political and business figures may find their children eloping to the court, or may themselves marry in it.[52] The records

Figure 2.1: Graph Showing Relative Increase Over Time in Marriages Registered
under the Special Marriage Act ("SMA") and the Hindu Marriage Act ("HMA")[53]

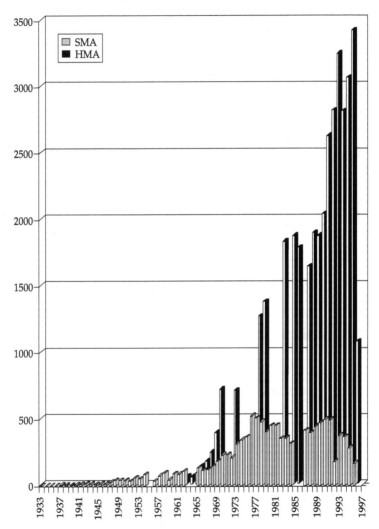

in the Marriage Room in Delhi's Tis Hazari can be relied upon
to provide sufficient time and space within which the validity of
a marriage can become subject to negotiation, such that delicate
political matters may be held in abeyance, so that matters can be
satisfactorily resolved.

Nonetheless, one fact that does emerge from the records is that the number of marriages registered under the Hindu Marriage Act is increasing dramatically, whereas there is a rather more steady increase in the annual number of civil marriages. This situation was made even more evident when I was permitted to look at the registers of marriages maintained by a single Arya Samaj temple in Jangpura, Delhi. The annual records for this single small temple registered around 3,000 marriages solemnised each year in the 1990s. This is dramatic (albeit tentative) evidence for the hypothesis that inter-caste Hindu marriage is greatly on the rise. Of course, these would also include the majority of 'arranged-marriages' for the followers of the Arya Samaj. However, when one considers the vast number of Arya Samaj temples in Delhi (an incredible total of 350 temples in the Delhi Metropolitan Area) and the large numbers of marriages being ritualised therein, and when these are compared to the much smaller number of marriages registered each year in the court under the Hindu Marriage Act (never more than about 3,400 for all of Delhi), it is possible to hypothesise that most of the love-marriage couples having Arya Samaj marriages do not choose further to legitimise these through a court registration. This could imply that even the Hindu Marriage Records listed in Table 2.1 aren't accurately reflecting the extent of love-marriages in Delhi. Furthermore, as I have already pointed out, neither the court records nor the Arya Samaj records include love-marriages conducted under Muslim personal law and registered as *nikkahs* across the city. Taken together, all these factors would go some way towards explaining the evident popularity of love-marriages and the inability of the records to even begin to accurately represent this.

Another fascinating and unusual form of marriage that one encountered at Tis Hazari were 'mass-marriages' organised by the state. The Government of Delhi's Social Welfare Department arranges marriages for women who express such a wish and who are wards of the state by virtue of living in *Nari Niketans* (Women's Refuges) and the 'After Care Home'. In such marriages, the Department advertises in the newspapers for 'bachelors of all religions', and vets all the respondents thoroughly as if the Department were the parents of the girl. Amongst the many considerations for suitability were matters such as family stability, income and job prospects (the Department encourages government employees to apply), and rigorous health checks which included an

HIV test and a sperm count.[54] The marriages are then 'arranged' in the court and the couples married under the state's own law – the Special Marriage Act. After this, religious ceremonies are held, and generous benefactors in Delhi help the Department ensure that each girl is *'properly settled'* with all the necessary household items and clothes she may require. Additionally, each groom can bring fifteen family members and guests to whom the Department bestows the honour and respect given to bride-takers through a substantial feast to celebrate the marriages.

As is evident, the records of the Marriage Room do not necessarily signify that the marriages registered therein are 'love-marriages'. A number of circumstances require that marriages which are parentally arranged be registered in the court – for instance, in the event of foreign travel or as proof of marriage for the purposes of obtaining a passport.

Samina

From the lowest echelons of the court employees upwards, there was the widespread sense that civil marriages were false marriages, and that they represented nothing more than government interference in a matter best left to the gods of religion and ritual. The clerk in the Marriage Room expressed the view that civil marriage was a 'paper marriage', or in his words, 'only a *sarkari shadi*' or 'government marriage'. Further, a number of people associated Hindu–Muslim 'love-marriages' with 'court-marriages', as we have seen from the constant references to Indira Gandhi's 'court-marriage' to a Muslim. However, in practice, there are relatively few Muslim couples who come to the court as most inter-caste Muslim marriages would be performed by a *kazi*. In the case of a Muslim marrying a non-Muslim, the more standard practice is to have a *kazi* perform the wedding, and if needs be, convert the non-Muslim spouse to Islam.

When Muslims did come into the court for civil marriages (either because they wished to register their marriage under the Special Marriage Act or they wished to solemnise their marriage under the same), they were almost always urged to go to the Arya Samaj temple and have a Hindu marriage, or to go to their *kazi*. It was clear that in addition to a couple's liminal status as not-community, the fact that one or the other of a couple was Muslim meant that they were more than likely to have difficulties in solemnising or registering their marriages. Despite the fact that the Special Marriage Act provided for the registration of any marriages solemnised under religious or other rites, the lawyers and court functionaries maintained that there was no provision for Muslims in the court. As I have already shown, the process of court-marriage is extremely open-ended and allows all manner of cynical manipulation. If anyone wishes to obstruct a couple, they can do so with considerable ease. A Muslim girl, Samina, who had dramatically escaped from her home in Udaipur, attempted to have her marriage to an American non-Asian boy registered in Delhi under the Special Marriage Act. The couple had to go to one of the new zonalised courts in Delhi. Samina's story illustrates the helplessness of not-community when the fact of having to abandon community is compounded by an uncooperative and obstructive officer of the law:

> We went to the court and asked the clerk for registration [under the Special Marriage Act]. He gave us a form—it said Hindu Marriage Act on it. He said, get an affidavit, photo of marriage and certificate from temple and come back. I said to him we have already had a *nikkah* and want to register it under the Special Marriage Act. He said, take the *nikkah* to Patiala House Courts to get affidavits from a Notary Public, hire a lawyer and pay him 1,000 rupees and come back tomorrow, your work will be done. We were doubtful that a Muslim *nikkah* could be registered under the form he had given us (Hindu Marriage Act) so we waited to see the SDM. He seemed very annoyed with us. I said to him, this is a Hindu Marriage Act form; I want to register our marriage under the Special Marriage Act. He said, 'Go and have a *nikkah*!' I said, its already been done, but I want a legal paper to say we have registered under Special Marriage Act. He pointed to the form we had been given by the clerk and said: With this you can get it registered in two days, okay? Get an affidavit, convert saying you are a Hindu, and I'll give you the certificate in two days. I said, look, I don't mind waiting for the month it takes for Special Marriage Act. He said, okay, file it and wait!

For the Special Marriage Act registration, Samina was required to get a note from the Station House Officer (SHO Police) to say that they were living where they claimed to be. The police agreed to do the investigation, but asked for a note from the SDM requesting the police for address verification. This, the SDM refused to do.

Somehow, Samina managed to get the police to certify that they had been living there, and with all the formalities complete, they returned to file their notice under the Special Marriage Act. Over the next few weeks, they made five futile trips to the court only to find the SDM absent or refusing to see them. Finally, their lawyer convinced the clerk to help, and they phoned in advance, checking whether he was in before they made another trek to the office. She says, by this point everyone in the court knew about her case, and she could hear discussions among the clerks about the fact that she was a Muslim marrying a Christian.

> When the SDM agreed to see us, he said: 'He's a Christian, you are a Muslim. Where are your parents?' I replied that they lived in Udaipur. He said, 'Okay, get them along with you and I'll get you married.' I replied that my parents would come for the wedding (which would be a month later), but for the time being, I asked him to accept our notice.[55] He said: 'No, I won't accept your notice!' I asked what legal reason he had for refusing to accept our notice. He said, 'you are from Udaipur, you don't belong to Delhi.' I said that the SHO report and our rent receipts proved that we had been in Delhi for over a month and could submit notice. So he turned to Peter [Samina's husband] and said: 'You're not an Indian, you are an American!' So we showed him Peter's Delhi immigration entry stamp in his passport proving he had been in Delhi for the past three months. When he still kept saying that he would not accept the notice, Peter said: 'Tell me what is the reason? We've done everything according to the law!' The SDM replied: 'I am the law'.[56] I got so angry, saying what reason do you have, what is your reason, and he just told us to leave or he would call the police. I told him I would feel safer if the police were there when I was in his office. He took the declaration form and wrote 'Failed to prove residence' on it. We tried to see the Deputy Commissioner, but the SDM sent his clerk with three men to stop us. They stood outside the Deputy Commissioner's door and barred us from entering. We just left. What could we do?'[57]

There are many possible interpretations of this experience. For one, the SDM might have been angling for a bribe, but that doesn't seem plausible because some mention would have been made to Samina and her husband through the intermediaries of their lawyer or the clerks. Another possible explanation is that the SDM considered himself a pious man and was against love-marriages; by refusing to cooperate, he was indirectly expressing his disapproval of the marriage. However, this thesis too we must reject because it is obvious from his willingness (indeed, his eagerness) to register the marriage under the Hindu Marriage Act (should both of them convert to Hinduism) in no less than two days, that it was not the marriage *per se* that he was against, but rather it was something to do with both of them and their request for the Special Marriage Act registration. The argument that the SDM found civil marriage too abhorrent to be in a position to solemnise it has some currency, but for the most part it is unlikely that he would expect to get away with not solemnising any civil marriages when that is an important part of an SDM's job description. There is the possibility that the SDM objected to the fact that Samina and Peter were an inter-racial couple, but this theory too falls by the wayside when we consider the insistence that a Hindu Marriage Act registration would not be a problem.

The final argument, then, is that the man was what is called in India a 'communalist': someone who hates members of other ethno-religious communities and who has a militant and aggressive posture when dealing with them. It is a label that is easily applied, but it has some explicatory potential too. The SDM obviously was uneasy about the fact that Samina, as a Muslim woman, was not willing to convert willy-nilly to Hinduism for the sake of expediency. For those Hindus who are in sympathy with the so-called 'Hindu Right', Samina's refusal to convert is seen in itself as being evidence of her own 'Muslim fundamentalism'. We can certainly identify the SDM as being right-leaning simply because, as an upholder of a secular law, he was stepping out of line by suggesting to Samina and her husband that they convert to Hinduism. Equally, it is possible that he was agitated that Samina's husband, an American, had been through a conversion ceremony and become a Muslim (as they had had a *nikkah*). This too might have seemed to him to illustrate Samina's 'fundamentalism' and he was perhaps merely suggesting Hindu conversion as a tit-for-tat response.

The Sub-Divisional Magistrate's emphasis on Samina's parents accompanying her to the court is explained by Tanika Sarkar in the context of the gendered ideology of Hindu supremacist groups:

> Parental permission is ...vital in marriage arrangements, where self-choice is discouraged. This accent on parental discipline shapes an obedient filial and feminine identity, maintains the caste and class boundaries of the families, and rules out transgressive miscegenation, without overtly referring to caste ideology as such. Thus social hierarchy is

maintained without making the ideological apparatus explicit, for parental counselling is portrayed as an emotional imperative (1999: 99).

Samina was fortunate in that she had the bold and quick-witted sense to lie that her parents would accompany her for the actual solemnisation, but that the SDM should accept their application in the interim. In marriages of choice where such parental consent is known to be impossible and where the SDM remains intransigent, love-marriage couples would be forced to take the only way out—convert and marry in an Arya Samaj marriage.

Returning to my earlier point about the two-fold function of *court-shadis*, Samina and Peter had had a *nikkah* because they had been forced to elope and were too scared to sit out the thirty-day period for the Special Marriage Act notification without any legitimisation of their union. It made sense to them that Peter should convert because it was Samina's family that was opposed to the marriage, not his. That is, the fact that Peter converted to her religion might be read by her family as a true sign of commitment to their daughter and their own values. This may have made them more amenable to accepting her back within the fold once tempers had cooled. At that point, it would be utterly devastating to her parents if they discovered that not only had she married a Christian, but that both of them had become Hindu and married in the Arya Samaj. However, there was the fear that her family would manage to pressure the *kazi* into denying that the marriage took place. It was clearly important to Samina to have a legal document to consolidate the authority of the *nikkah* ceremony. However, despite repeated attempts to get the Sub-Divisional Magistrate to capitulate, they were ultimately unsuccessful. Here, unlike most love-marriage cases, the condition of liminality is exacerbated by, on the one hand, Samina's family which was in hot pursuit of the couple, and on the other, by the refusal of the law to provide them its sanctuary and their failed attempt to make the marriage '*steel-proof*'.

Rashmi

Another couple I worked with had submitted their notice for marriage under the Special Marriage Act in November of 1992 at Tis Hazari. The boy, Mustafa, went home to his village in Uttar Pradesh to convince his family to accept his decision to marry a

Brahmin Hindu girl from Delhi, Rashmi, whom he had met four years previously. The day after the submission of the notice the girl's father who was posted in the north-east of India received a phone call. The caller said, 'Do you know, Mr. Jha, your daughter has filed her name for a registry marriage with a Muslim?' Luckily her father approved of the marriage and was dismissive of the caller's obvious attempts to incite trouble. In the meanwhile an old man visited Rashmi's family home in Delhi. Her brother asked him what he wanted. The old man reported that he was from Nari Seva Sadan, which he claimed was an organisation to 'protect Hindu women'. He had come to 'save' Rashmi from her impending marriage to a Muslim. Finally, there was a phone call for Rashmi from a lady who claimed that she was Mustafa's first wife's friend, that he was already the father of two children, and that she was calling to try and save Rashmi from being 'trapped' by him. Rashmi explained:

> Once we filed our names in Tis Hazari, people figured out that it was a Hindu–Muslim marriage. The RSS-*wallahs* and the VHP-*wallah* have this cell in Tis Hazari. I don't know what 'cell' means. Maybe it means they regulate these marriages, scanning and all, for inter-religion and all. They try to prevent such marriages. At the time of the wedding, Mustafa had some friends in Delhi, some of them were linked to the Congress. They had their own *goons* [heavies]. After all the phone calls and the trouble we told these guys to be ready in case we had problems on the day of the wedding in the court. It was just after Babri Masjid.[58]

Rashmi's experience of the court indicates clearly the infiltration of the procedure surrounding the Special Marriage Act by political groups in sympathy with the Hindu nationalist cause who exploit the fact that civil registration of a marriage necessarily throws the couple's relationship into the public domain. In this case, Rashmi and individual members of her family were directly approached in an attempt to intimidate them and prevent the marriage. An interesting array of methods was used to weaken the family's resolve to support Rashmi's choice: her father was asked whether he had no shame as a Brahmin Hindu in allowing his daughter to marry a Muslim; her brother was warned that his sister was in need of protection and that the marriage should be stopped at all cost; and she herself was given false accounts of the man she had known for four years. All these various attempts at coercion reflect the fundamentals of communalist Hindu social theory, namely, that a daughter must never be allowed to shame herself by transgressing community boundaries, that a sister must needs be protected within that community, and lastly, that a Muslim male is polygamous, and necessarily an adulterer from a Hindu nationalist's perspective.[59]

It was common to hear from other love-marriage couples I interviewed about Hindu–Muslim marriages bringing forth dissuasive activity clearly sponsored by organisations of the Hindu-right, which certainly seems to validate Rashmi's claim that the RSS or VHP, or both, had representatives operating within the court in order to provide information about mixed marriages. Under these circumstances, a Hindu–Muslim couple are faced not only with the likely approbation of their families, but are also exposed to the politicisation of their private lives, more often than not leading to an intensification of their sense of social exclusion.

Durga

In Nangloi, on the outskirts of the city, I met Durga. She was organising the women of the *gully* (lane) in her *busti* to go to the local electricity board billing centre and protest against rising electricity bills. Someone who knew her sister mentioned to me that Durga had had a love-marriage. This is how Durga represented her 'story' to me:

My path had been drawn in another direction. For three years I knew I was to marry a man from Karol Bagh. After that I said to my mother I wouldn't. My relatives began to tell her that no matter how much dowry you give those people, they will never be satisfied by it. They will ask for more and more, and then if you can't give it, they may burn her in the kitchen. That is what these people do! The boy had a *chai* stall. They were as rich as kings compared to us. I began to think like my relatives and told my mother: marry me to a lame man, blind man or a poor man. I will be happier there. Some women in the *gully* used to hear me saying this. One neighbour mentioned it to a man. That man came up to me one day and said, so, you are poor? Do you want a job? I said yes! He used to do *duty* with my brother in a *factory*. So he told me to go on a certain day to a certain place, where a girl called Pushpa would give me the forms and a contract to assemble electric switches at home. He said, don't tell your mother because she will stop you from going. After you sign the forms she too can work with you and you will make some money. I went there on the assigned day. There was no Pushpa there, but this man was there with another man. He pointed me out to the other man. I said, you were going to make me meet Pushpa here? What's happened? He said, she couldn't make it, we'll have to set another date.

The next time I went, he took me to such a place where there was a lot of typing going on. It was a court. I didn't know at that time that it was a court. I am not so educated, I can't read or write, I am an ignorant woman, what did I know of what was going on? I never venture out of the house alone! So there was a lawyer sitting there, and she said to me: Will you sign these papers? I said, yes, why not! They made me sign some papers. Afterwards I learnt that that was a lawyer, and that that was a court. It was Tis Hazari. After I was made to sign, the lawyer said to me: 'You are now married to this boy.' I said when did I marry this boy? They said, 'The papers you just signed, these are all *shadi* papers, and that's how you are married.' Then his friends said to me, 'If you don't do the right thing, your brother will kill him.' If you don't accept him, he will die. His life was put in my hands. I was angry, so I just went home. I had a terrible headache for a month. My head just hurt and hurt. I was so upset. I couldn't even tell my mother that I had gone to get work making electric switches and this is what they did to me. One day, when I was sitting outside in the *gully* reading a book. He came up to me. He started saying, I want to meet you, I need to talk to you. I said, no! I don't want to talk to you. I ran into the house. Then some days later, I began to think that I'll have to get married somewhere, so why not meet him and find out who he is, what he does, why he wants to marry me. So I went to meet him. He introduced himself to me by saying I am a poor man, I want to marry a woman just like you. So I said to him, I am of the lowest of low castes; I eat pig! Would you accept this? Would you eat *roti*'s made from these hands? Would your mother keep me in her house? Can we live together happily for the rest of our lives? He said yes to everything. I said, I don't go out of the house. Will you do the daily shopping and bring food and clothes for me? He said yes. You see, he was from a village in Uttar Pradesh. He wanted to marry a girl from Delhi. Then later, when I presented him to my family, everyone accepted him. That was a month after the Tis Hazari *shadi*. Now we are very happy. I am a *Rajasthani regar*. That is a *secool caste* [scheduled caste], and we tell everybody we are *Rajasthani*. He has been incorporated in my caste. He is really from the *sonar* [goldsmith] caste. But nobody around here knows this. I feel very shy to say to people that I have had a love-marriage. You never know how they might take it.[60]

In my interview with Durga, my responses were those of genuine shock. This story validated everything I had heard in Tis Hazari, about women being tricked into 'false *shadis*' and the law failing miserably to act as a safeguard. The whole issue of consent in a marriage was made into a nonsense by Durga's narrative. Luckily for her it all ended well and she and her husband are deeply happy. However, it seemed to capture the spirit of all the critics of love-marriages. As Mr. Sharma had once said to me, 'the girl is tricked into marrying the boy'. What better story did I have to validate the fact that women are sometimes mere pawns in the charade of a love affair? Durga's husband could just as easily have blackmailed her into living with him and then discarded her. Indeed, a number of people in my public interviews argued that love-marriages are the beginnings of prostitution. When the man has used the woman for his lust, he leaves her. There is a phrase that is used to describe such cases in Hindi: *na ghar ki, na ghat ki*, she is no longer of the home, and no longer of the *ghat* (river bank where women collect to bathe). A woman with such a fate can no longer return to her home; neither can she expect to be accepted by society at large. She is shunned, and to earn her own bread, she turns to prostitution.

Later, however, when I re-examined her narrative I began to see something very different going on in it. Durga said to me on numerous occasions that she didn't know how to read and write. She said that she was a poor and ignorant woman who never went out of the house. Yet she signed her name on the papers, rather than putting her thumb impression which is what most illiterate people in India do. This in itself is not surprising because many people do learn how to sign their names without being able to read and write. However, it was her inability to read the forms that she signed in Tis Hazari which bolstered her claim to ignorance regarding the court *shadi*. She was tricked into thinking they were forms for her contract to assemble switches. She could not read them, so she just signed them. However, when describing the time when he comes to meet her, a few weeks after this incident, she says I was sitting in the *gully* reading a book. Furthermore, whenever I met her, she was writing things down and it struck me that this claim to ignorance about what was going on at the Tis Hazari incident could have been a gendered response to the stigma of being a woman who had had a love-marriage. It was important to Durga not to appear as if she had had a part to play in having a court *shadi* because to do that would leave her open to allegations of being *tej*, a fast woman. Seen in this light, we can reinterpret her narrative to see how it expresses the contradictions between having fallen in love with a man and having to deny her agency so as to appear like a traditional 'good' woman.

Durga talks of her husband as a stranger. He was a friend of her neighbour, who told him there was this girl who wanted to marry a poor man and that she was breaking off the arranged match her mother had fixed. But she also mentions that he worked in a factory with her brother. How was she to know this? Did the neighbour act as a go-between, telling the two of them about each other, or did he come to her house to visit her brother and meet her there? Her mother had arranged a marriage with a comparatively rich man. In the light of this, her family, in all probability, would have had difficulty accepting her choice of husband, who lacked the status of the Karol Bagh boy. Were the shenanigans at Tis Hazari a ploy on her part to plead innocence and yet to present her family with a court certificate which proved that she was married to him already? Her plea of ignorance and victimisation in the narrative might have made them more tolerant of the marriage, because at least she didn't knowingly bestow the gift of her sexuality to a man of her own choosing and thus, no shame at least was brought upon the family.

After the Tis Hazari marriage, his friends say that her brother will kill him if she doesn't accept the marriage. Here too, she presents a picture in which her hand was forced, so to speak. She says elsewhere that she felt sorry for him. He too was somebody's son, somebody's brother. He didn't deserve to die. And after all, she did have to get married somewhere! This justifies her own intervention in going to see him. Here she tests the limits of an inter-caste marriage by asking the sorts of questions that would evince a straightforward response. I am a low caste girl, she says. I eat pork! But why did she take the responsibility of talking to him herself? Why not send her brother or mother to ask him about himself and to decide whether he was suitable arranged-marriage material. If it was a matter of such indifference to her who she married, then there was nothing to lose from getting her family to intervene. Obviously Durga cared for him and her denial of her love makes her rebellion all the more significant for us. It would never do to have a court *shadi*, but to be tricked into one achieved the two-fold goal of a love-marriage: a legally valid certificate to ensure that she was not pressurised into marrying elsewhere, and she had a month at home to be able to convince her family to accept him as her husband, thus giving a marriage which had some legal validity the social sanction and blessings of an *'love-cum-arranged'* marriage.[61] This explains another inconsistency in her story: Durga says that everyone accepted the marriage in her family, but when I asked her what gifts were given to her and her sister she replied that her sister had been given gold *tops* (earrings), furniture, clothes and other things. When I asked again what she had received, she was upset and said 'Nothing. You see, I married in a different way to my sister, so my family gave me nothing'. While the image she presents is one of family acceptance, the truth of being punished for her love-marriage, despite her attempts to protect herself, is much more tragic, and indeed, much more widespread.

Legal and Social Ambivalence

Tis Hazari is a place of enormous contradictions. It seems to bring together two extremes of the love-marriage phenomenon: on the one hand, it captures the isolation and social estrangement of couples who come to the court in order to seek refuge in the law and validate their marriages. It thus serves to mark the beginning of a potentially life-long social excommunication. On the other hand, the value of secular law *as a refuge* remains an indispensable factor in maintaining a democracy in India. While couples who seek to marry under the Special Marriage Act are often victims of communal prejudices which are quite capable of permeating the annals of the law, they can also be seen as asserting their right to personal choice. No longer constrained by community, they are nonetheless more markedly determined as *not-community*.

The simple difference between Act III of 1872 and the functioning of Tis Hazari in the 1990s (via the legislation of 1954) is that, what began as a debate about the rights of communities to detach renegade members is now about the individual's right to repulse the incursions of politicised communities into the civil machinery of the state. From the very inception of debates on laws that legitimated inter-community marriage in the 1860s, the 'native' community was outraged, and this outrage has not yet abated. This is the key contradiction made manifest in the Marriage Room at Tis Hazari: that what the law allows is not the same as that to which society assents.

Durga personifies this contradiction. She realises that she cannot openly marry the man of her choice and constructs a complicated scenario whereby she presents herself as a victim being tricked into a court marriage and thereby disavows any sense of personal responsibility. She is aware of the standing of legal proof to a marriage—providing as it were, a shield against separation. She has consciously manipulated the social discourse which dictates that love-marriages must take place surrounded by deceit and exploitation in order to assert her own right to choose her marriage partner. Further, it is worth noticing that her lies are at her husband's expense. She constructs a veil of virtue for herself by presenting him as a scoundrel. In so doing, she creates a middle ground, a moral grey area in which her lack of 'true consent' is set up as the fate of a woman in the evil city of Delhi. Her complicated fabricated story nevertheless makes room for a compromise. Her family did not give her a dowry or give her a 'proper' wedding, but neither did they reject her or try and destroy her marriage. No longer of the home, and no longer of the *ghat*, she has nevertheless succeeded in creating a life for herself with the man she loves.

Notes

1. Recounted by an advocate in Tis Hazari. *Shairi* is an Urdu poetic art form.
2. 'Secularism', as Nandy has pointed out, means different things to different social classes in India. For what he calls 'non-modern Indians' the word implies accommodation of religion in public life, and more or less equal respect for all religions. India's 'westernised intellectuals' on the other hand, use the term to imply the abolition of religion entirely from the public sphere (1990: 74). There is a third meaning that we must make note of, as it is widely used, and is one that has evolved in the more recent past, particularly since the BJP came to power in parliament in 1998. In this configuration of 'secularism', it comes to be used rhetorically to imply the illegitimacy of the views concerning religion of the class whom Nandy calls 'westernised intellectuals'. In this interpretation, 'tolerance' of all religions is interpreted as 'appeasement and favouritism' of Muslims and Christians; the retreat of religion from politics comes to imply the irreligiousness and illegitimacy of the 'modern' and by implication of all intellectuals critical of Hindu religious nationalism. Take for instance

Ashok Singhal's (the leader of the Vishwa Hindu Parishad suggestion that the award of the Nobel Prize to Amartya Sen (a 'Hindu') was 'a Christian conspiracy to propagate their religion and wipe out Hinduism' from India. Underlying this rhetoric is the assumption that those who do not publicly declare their *Hindutva* (or 'Hindu-ness') are 'secularists' and thus open to attack since they pose a threat to the Hindu nation. (Singhal's quotation from *Economic and Political Weekly*, vol. XXXIV, no. 28, July 10–16, 1999, Letters to the Editor, 'Religion and Politics of Hate', p. 1858.)

3. See Dalmia for an exploration of Krishna Sobti's novel *Dilo-danis* ('Heart and Mind', 1993) which uses the urban setting of Delhi and its spaces and seasons to evoke the romantic emotions of the protagonists (2006: 183–207)

4. The Rashtriya Swayamsevak Sangh literally means 'Association of National Volunteers' and is a paramilitary organisation founded in 1925 (S. Bayly 1999: 297). The women's wing was established in 1936 when Lakshmibai Kelkar persuaded the RSS leader Hegdewar to support its establishment. Like its male counterpart, it subscribes to a Hindu supremacist credo that is fiercely anti-Muslim. Its gender ideology consists of a 'call to motherhood', and members are trained in martial arts and worship the icon of an armed goddess—a figure taken from nationalist iconography. For more on the RSS, its women's wing and its political and gender ideology, see Sarkar and Butalia (1996), and Sarkar (1999).

5. In *The Pioneer*, 'Lovers Skip a Beat Over Heartless Diktat', 20-12-1997, pp. 1 & 3, New Delhi.

6. While the English translation 'Indian Culture' sounds amorphous enough, the term '*bharatiya sanskriti*' is a lot more problematic. It is used to connote a Brahmanical tradition that has been reworked and reinterpreted by the Hindu Right to provide a political and moral template that conflates nationhood and religious identity and culture. Thus *bharatiya sanskriti* implies that Hindu Brahmanical history and culture is the correct and only version of true 'Indian' identity. All other versions, including Islam and Muslim culture, are branded as foreign, and by implication 'anti-national' and a threat to 'Indian culture and life'. (See Anitha et al. 1996, for transcripts of interviews with women ideologues of the Hindu Right.)

7. *http://www.southasiatimes.com/article/May2000/culturec.htm*

8. For instance, a Muslim women's separatist group in Srinagar, Kashmir have stormed shops fully veiled, burnt Valentine's cards and posters and raided hotels believed to be used by unmarried couples, alleging the corruption of Muslim youth through such un-Islamic practices. See International Herald Tribune, 25th July, 2007, *http://www.iht.com/articles/ ap/2007/07/25/asia/AS-GEN-Kashmir-Sexual-Assault.php*

9. One of the cases concerned that of Priyanka Wadhwani who married Mohommed Umer, a Muslim. Umer converted to Hinduism in an Arya Samaj ceremony and took the Hindu name 'Umesh' prior to their wedding. Predictably, his conversion was mocked by Sindhi leaders, and condemned by Muslim groups alike, the latter, for not having converted Priyanka and had a *nikkah*. Interestingly the Bombay High Court where the couple sought protection, passed an order restraining the Bhopal police from arresting Umer on charges of kidnapping (having ascertained that Priyanka was a major and was marrying him of her own free will) and additionally ordered that the Bombay police protect the couple. See *http://timesofindia.indiatimes.com/articleshow/1895094.cms*. In response to the inter-community marriages, the local BJP has set up a Hindu Kanya Suraksha Samiti (crudely, 'Hindu Organisation to Safeguard Girls') and have called for changes in the law that allows such marriages.

10. See *http://www.expressindia.com/news/fullstory.php?newsid=84748*

11. For example, a standard entry into these message columns contemplates the love-giving potential of humble vegetables: "My heart is like a cabbage, divided into two; my leaves I give to others, my heart I give to you".

12. Clearly the fact that Parsis have Persian names led people to believe that 'Firoze' could only be a Muslim. The marriage was initially opposed by the secularist Nehru on the grounds that Firoze had a very different 'background' and Mahatma Gandhi, who shared a surname with Firoze, was said to have intervened. They were married through semi-orthodox Vedic rites, supposedly valid for 'mixed marriages'. Orthodox Hindus at the time were outraged that Nehru's daughter (a Brahmin) should have been allowed to marry a 'fire-worshipper' (T. Ali 1985: 123–27).

13. In Hindi, *Desh ki ekta ke liye*.

14. As I was interested in how people perceived gender relations between love-marriage couples, I posed the question of how Indira's surname (which was originally Nehru) came to be Gandhi? B. Kumar explained: 'See, Firoze Khan, he was a Muhammedan. So Mahatma Gandhi adopted him. That is how he got the name Gandhi, and that is how he became a Hindu. You see, Bapu [M.K. Gandhi] had no children, so he made Firoze Khan his son. Then Firoze and Indira had an arranged marriage'. Thus, as we shall see later in this chapter, even the 'first' political 'love-marriage' is popularly perceived as needing re-socialisation through an arranged-marriage.

15. Discussion with Asha Lata of the All India Democratic Women's Association, Delhi Branch.

16. Ayodhya is the mythological site for the birthplace of Ram, the Hindu god whose worship has come to characterise the recent form

of assertive Hindu religious nationalism (van der Veer 1994). It is also the place where Hindu nationalists destroyed a mosque and vowed to build a 'Ramjanmabhoomi temple', or temple to commemorate the birthplace of Ram. For many academics, Ayodhya (as a 'critical event') marks a definitive turning point in modern Indian life, and serves as a marker of the communalisation of politics in India today. See for instance Jeffery and Basu (1999), Tharu and Niranjana (1996).

17. Being hit on the upper body by a shoe is considered a truly deadly insult because caste hierarchy and Hindu physiognomy combine to make the feet the most impure, and the head and upper body the most pure in a Hindu's body. Shoe-beatings invert this hierarchy and in so doing, pollute both the body and the reputation of the person.

18. Harijan is the Gandhian neologism for 'untouchables' (now known as Dalits). Rajput is an upper -caste Hindu group.

19. Sharma is a Brahman surname.

20. In the *Times of India*, 'Tis Hazari Lawyers Protest, Litigants Suffer Again'. 11-7-1997, p. 5, New Delhi.

21. It is something of a standard response of the clerks in the record's archive at Tis Hazari, that anything that couldn't be located in the mountain of dusty records and files 'has been eaten by the monkeys'.

22. From the oldest records in the Marriage Room going back to the 1930s, it is clear that this place once registered marriages of Parsis and Christians. However, these registers had fallen into disuse, and nobody seemed aware of the possibility of such marriages being registered in the Marriage Room.

23. In the *Times of India*, 'Man Shot Dead in Tis Hazari Complex', 10-7-1997, p. 5, New Delhi. In the light of this incident, the former Delhi Bar Association Secretary Rajeev Khosla ruefully admitted, 'the recent shoot-out cannot even be termed as a security lapse since no security exists there'. Further, one advocate reported that 'an undertrial threw chappals [slippers] at a judge recently' (in the *Times of India*, *Delhi Times*,'Security at Tis Hazari Non-Existent say Bar Association Members', 11-7-1997, p. 1, New Delhi). Five months later, and despite the hue and cry that the first killing caused, there was another in which two persons were gunned down and a third seriously injured. One of the accused was arrested and produced in Tis Hazari and was described as a 'registered bad character' by the police as he was involved in 'over 30 murder, attempt to murder and other criminal cases' (in the *Times of India*, 'Three Accused in Tis Hazari Shoot-out Arrested', 4-11-1997, p. 5, New Delhi).

24. This story I have been able to verify as being true.

25. Indeed, one (short-sighted) advocate, for instance, said to me, 'You look like a film star. Why don't I get you some work in the movies?' Another tout argued with me, 'Why do you get angry when I speak

lovingly to you?' It was an impossible situation, and no matter what I did to try and induce some degree of professionalism in my working relationships, there was no respite until I actually finished this phase of my fieldwork and ceased going to the court.

26. It is interesting that the enormously successful 1988 Hindi film *Qayamat se Qayamat Tak* (loosely translated as 'From Calamity to Calamity') uses precisely this theme of a couple on the run from their dissenting families. The girl is raped, and unable to seek retribution because of their already shameful circumstances, the hero and heroine take their own lives.

27. Like many of the other touts in the court, Mr. Sharma was literate but uneducated and was respected by trained 'marriage' lawyers as being greatly experienced in the 'marriage business' and able to recall complex cases of law from memory. This alleged 'status' was tempered by the essential illegitimacy of touts in the court, whose slightest misdemeanour made them prone to being ejected by the clerks upon the orders of high-handed Sub-Divisional Magistrates or District Commissioners, all of whom periodically sought to purge Tis Hazari of its canker. The lawyers, on the other hand, were utterly secure of their livelihood as their trade union was perhaps one of the strongest in Delhi.

28. According to the Special Marriage Act, 1954, the notices are legally required to be displayed in a 'notice registration book' available to members of the public at certain times in the day for inspection. The display of these notices on the wall, ostensibly to save the clerks from dealing with public inquiries, a task which they admittedly despise, serves to advertise marriages in a much more public way. Interestingly, the notices were pealed off so frequently (by couples and the touts) that at one point a board with a metal mesh (secured with a padlock) was erected on the wall so that notices could not be defaced.

29. When a couple seek to marry in secret, they often give a friend's address as their own to avoid the risk of notices reaching their parents. The legal requirement as to residence is that a person should reside for thirty days prior to submission of notice in that area in which the marriage seeks registration. The decision to involve a Station House (Police) Officer usually arises if the Sub-Divisional Magistrate believes the couple are eloping.

30. The rationing system started under the British in India during the Second World War. Ration cards are part of the Public Distribution System of independent India. Prior to the introduction of National Identity Cards, ration cards were one of the few means of asserting proof of residence (the other proofs being passports or driving licences). Since the ration cards allowed people to buy provisions (such as kerosene, rice, oil and wheat), at government subsidised rates from

local 'ration shops' they are important both as a means of subsistence and as widely used 'proof' of identity and residence.

31. The requirement to submit ration cards to obtain official documents was probably introduced so as to ensure that touts and lawyers don't get hold of the forms; but in a predictable twist of irony, it is they who buy the forms from the clerks and it is the couples who often can't get them legitimately and are forced to buy them from the touts. I suppose this system is beneficial to all: the clerks don't need to accept bribes from the public (after all, a complaint could jeopardise their job) and they know that the touts can be trusted not to make official complaints about them. They can seem efficient in following their orders to the book and provide only those who have ration cards with forms. In the meanwhile, everyone else gets them when they employ a tout or a lawyer to marry them. The ration-card system ensures that couples eloping to Delhi in the hope of marrying at Tis Hazari cannot even obtain a form to get married. If they were to produce their ration card, they would be advised to return to their own areas in order to get married, or fulfil the thirty-day requirement after registering at a local police station.

32. *'High-class'* because marriages under the Special Marriage Act are marriages that do not require a ritual ceremony. Thus, when a couple enters the court and asks for a 'civil marriage', the assumption is quickly made that they are educated and know about the Special Marriage Act. It could be argued that their comfort with the lack of a religious ceremony is viewed as so different from the mainstream that this, in itself, qualifies them as *'high-class'*.

33. The Arya Samaj claims to be doing a service to the community. One of its members, R.N. Sehgal, said in a Doordarshan T.V. programme (Dir. Harish Chawla, 28-5-1997), *'We assist the Court Marriages. We get affidavits from the couple and marry them through the Hindu Marriage Act'*. Among their 'salient activities' the Arya advertise in a flyer *'All kinds of marriages, National, International and Intercaste are performed as per Vedic Rites and Marriage Certificates issued which are acceptable out of India also'*.

34. Note that the age qualifications for Hindu marriage are the same as that of the Special Marriages Act.

35. Arya Samaj temples across India provide this service, though it is worthy of note that in Bombay, the registration of an Arya Samaj marriage at a Registry Office isn't considered necessary, as the Arya Samaj certificate is seen as proof enough of the marriage. This goes to prove the thesis that the procedure in Delhi has developed because such temple marriages (despite all their precautions) are easily annulled, and it is only a combination of the two *'proofs'*, the Arya

Samaj certificate and the court registration, that ensure the marriage isn't easily made void.

36. The destructive use of the English term *'affair'* is used to imply a whole spectrum of meanings, from illicit childish unconsummated flirtation to actual sexual relations.

37. Occasionally, I saw couples arrive in the court literally with bag and baggage in hand, having just stepped off the bus at the Inter-State Bus Terminus which was around the corner from Tis Hazari.

38. The Special Marriage solemnisation and the Arya Samaj temple marriage both required the presence of two witnesses. If the couple were on their own, then any passer-by, other couples, the 'temple photographer' (who took photos for the couples of their marriage ceremony) and, occasionally, even the touts and lawyers would be asked by the couple to sign as witnesses.

39. Some evenings, after the day's work in the court, Mr. Sharma would set out by bus to visit some of the couples who he had married years earlier and who still owed him his 'dues'. I was able to accompany him on a number of these trips and this served as an important network through which I was able to meet a heterogeneous mix of couples who had already married and were now adjusting to married life.

40. It was lovingly entitled: 'The rules of a happy married life' (*'sukhi vaivahik jeevan ke niyam'*).

41. The term *'court-shadi'* was used as frequently as *'court-marriage'* by Hindi and English speakers alike.

42. The wiliness of the touts and lawyers can only be contrasted with the ways in which people themselves seek to manipulate the system of court-marriages. Sometimes, illegal (and invalid) second marriages that seek to legitimate a relationship despite probable social opposition to it, are falsely registered as civil marriages. The interesting thing is that when someone does wish to have a second marriage while concealing the first from the court, they do not necessarily conceal this information from the lawyers. One day an advocate who also worked in Tis Hazari came to the 'marriage lawyers' with a woman, saying he wished to marry her but, unfortunately, he did have the small problem of a wife who should be shielded from this information. Of course, such a marriage would legally be declared null if the previous wife decided to take up cudgels with the husband.

43. The lawyers would often dismiss the 'proof of age' that the couple had by lying that it was not acceptable in the court. If, for instance, one of them had a Madhya Pradesh driving licence, they would say it won't work in Delhi. If the couple had a school-leaving certificate with proof of age on it, the lawyers would scare them that using the certificate would reveal which town they came from. Unless the couple were able to assert that their proof was proof enough, the lawyers would

have their way. The 'hospital X-ray' refers to a bone ossification test, and the 'certificate' is the statement of the doctor on the estimated age of the client.

44. The Gazette notice informed the citizens: *'The Government of the National Capital Territory of Delhi has set up 9 offices of Deputy Commissioners and 27 Sub-Divisional Magistrates with a view to bring the administration at the door step of the people. These offices which have been functioning since 1st January 1997 are ultimately to be one-window offices for all Government Departments at the District and Sub-Division Level for day to day administration, in response to the repeated public enquiries, the names, "offices", telephone numbers and board functions are given below: [...] Functions: Issuance of various certificates: SDM's offices will issue SC/ST/ OBC [Scheduled Caste/Scheduled Tribe/Other Backward Caste] physically handicapped, Lal Dora, Insolvency, Birth, Marriage Registration, Income certificate etc'.*

45. Even after finding the office there was no guarantee that a person would be able to get his or her work done. When I visited one of the offices listed as a Marriage Office, the clerk and the secretary were adamant that it wasn't any such thing. However, another Gazette notice had stated that not only was it a Marriage Room, but that it had been functioning as such for the past six months. Finally someone confirmed that I had indeed come to the right place, but the Sub-Divisional Magistrate was out. When would he be back? 'Don't know...'. The marriage lawyers argue that the disadvantage of zonalisation was absenteeism among the Sub-Divisional Magistrates. When the nine offices functioned within Tis Hazari, the Sub-Divisional Magistrates were more accountable to the District Commissioner, whereas now, they could run the courts like their personal fiefs. Considering the vested interests of the lawyers in the previous centralised set-up, it is difficult to assess this criticism except to say that it does seem to be borne out in the experiences of many of the couples I worked with.

46. In the past few years, Delhi has been described as the Divorce Capital of India.

47. *Delhi High Court Rules: The Special Marriage Act, 1954, and the Hindu Marriage Act, 1955.* 1996. Pioneer Publications: Delhi.

48. The most common is 'double suicide' of the boy and the girl that I have touched upon in the introduction when speaking of custodial deaths. This phenomenon was eulogised by the 1981 Hindi film *Ek Duuje Ke Liye* (loosely translated as 'Made For Each Other'). In this, the opposition to the couple's marriage causes them to jump off a cliff. The Hindi lyrics of the hit song from the movie: 'I was made, you were made, we were made for each other', found their way into the suicide notes of many couples. (I am grateful to Tarun Bharati for this information.) Occasionally, however, the circumstances in which

couples died in Delhi made it difficult to accept the thesis of suicide, and prompted the question of whether it was actually murder. For instance: 'Man kills girlfriend, himself in 'suicide pact' (in the *Times of India*, by Lalit Kumar, 15-4-1997; p. 3, New Delhi), in which the police were refused permission to investigate the allegation of possible murder because the deaths happened on an Air Force Base, where the boy's brother-in-law was a Flight Sergeant who owned the gun with which the boy is alleged to have killed the girl and himself after the two families refused to entertain talk of their marriage. Indeed, these are plenty of instances such as the 2007 death of Rizwanul Rehman where the police themselves have been investigated for their alleged complicity with the families and their role in the death. See the PUDR report 'Courting Disaster' on all *www.pudr.org* for details of a few cases of police harasment and complicity.

49. In Hindi, '*Jiski lathi, uski bhains*'.
50. This of course works both ways. So for instance, a Muslim boy marrying a Hindu girl would need her to convert before the *nikkah* (Muslim marriage contract) is read and the same goes for a Muslim girl and a Hindu boy. In both scenarios, the Hindu family would find the marriage even more difficult to accept because of the conversion. This is why, in theory at least the Special Marriage Act provides a more agreeable form of inter-community marriage.
51. Some of the thick cardboard covers of the registers, and the pages inside were so savagely torn that I was soon convinced of the clerks' earlier euphemistic complaint that the 'monkeys had eaten the records'. Also, during my research, I found the draft of a letter, dated in 1972, inside a register that gives some indication of the earlier state of affairs: '*We are in urgent need of 4 steel almirahs* [cupboards]. *These almirahs are required to keep the record of Marriage Room. At present this record is lying on the floor of the Marriage Room so please arrange to supply at the earliest'*.
52. Amongst the records that I encountered were a great many of prominent Indian public figures, including the marriage of the one-time President of India K.R. Narayana, and of the politically ambitious daughter Priyanka, of the late Rajiv and Sonia Gandhi. A great many members of the political left are also registered under the Special Marriage Act, such as the marriage of Safdar Hashmi.
53. Missing or incomplete records have not been entered.
54. Interview with Mr. Kale, Social Welfare Department, New Delhi, on 6-5-1997 and 19-5-1997. The girls in the After Care Home have been abandoned or abused by their families. As a result, the Department is very careful about vetting all the prospective grooms. The first question that they are asked if they have been short listed for an interview is why they wish to marry a girl who has no family and

belongs to an *After Care Home*. A common reply is that the boys have left their hometowns and by the time they are ready to settle down they are considered 'over-age' back home. The emphasis on the unsullied procreative powers of the men was explained to me as an important consideration only because the social liminality of girls in refuges might attract unwanted proposals from families unable to arrange marriages for boys who were already known to have 'problems'. Divorcees and widowers are also avoided (in north India, the frequency of dowry abuse, bride-burning and neglect of new brides conspires against divorcees and widowers as suitable boys for re-marriage) unless there is sufficient evidence that they can provide a stable family for the girls. Most of the girls in the refuges have been given some vocational training and are usually working. Once every month, they are invited back to the refuge which functions after marriage as their *maike* or natal home.

55. Samina thought that in a month she would be able to find two people in Delhi to act as her parents.

56. This extraordinary declaration from the SDM is a braggardly display of the ground reality articulated and accepted by officials and citizens alike: that the boundary between state and society is utterly porous and that in the same way in which the law appears to somehow 'adhere' to the person of the magistrate (so that he can declare 'I am the law'), so also we witness his social identity merging into his role as adjudicator. What is interesting is that while Samina may be indignant about this, there is no avenue for recourse and on some level she must accept this as being the final outcome of all their troubles. This phenomenon, where government officials inhabit the garb of both public official and private citizen at one and the same time, has been widely commented upon amongst those producing ethnographies of the state in India; see, for instance, Fuller and Benei (2001), A. Gupta (1995), Brass (1997) amongst others.

57. The reason they went for the registration was primarily because the *nikkah* was in Urdu, and they would need an English translation to accompany it for the American Embassy. Since they were moving to America, it would make life a lot easier to be registered under a Special Marriage Act which provided an English-language certificate. It is also possible that they were advised that the Special Marriage Act gave better protection to women (in the event of divorce) and enshrined monogamy. Registering their marriage under the Special Marriage Act would override the Muslim Personal Law which presently applied. Samina and her husband never did succeed in getting their marriage registered under the Special Marriage Act, though she has subsequently succeeded in emigrating to America.

58. Babri Masjid is the mosque that was demolished by mob action following a militant campaign by the BJP, RSS and VHP. The demolition of the mosque took place in Ayodhya, Uttar Pradesh, on 6th December 1992, and was followed by waves of riots across urban India.

59. There is a vast and rich literature that deals with the body, gender and the nation, that supports the argument that religious nationalist discourse in India sets up the hated Muslim 'Other' in order to better define itself. For example, R.Menon (1999), Sarkar (1999), Alter (1996) and Mazumdar (1995).

60. Translated from Hindi into English.

61. The complex of the '*love-cum-arranged*' marriage is explored in detail elsewhere in the book.

3

Kidnapping, Elopement, and Self-Abduction

kitni-kitni larkiya	How many girls
bhagti hain man hi man	Have eloped in their thoughts
apne ratjage, apni dairy main	In their sleepless nights, in their diaries
sachmuch ki bhagi larkiyon se	There are many, many more
unki abadi bahut badi hain	Than the ones who actually run away
kya tumhare liye koi larki bhagi?	But has any girl run away for you?
kya tumhari rato main	Is there not a single red-gravelled path
ek bhi lal moram vali sadak nahin?	In all your nights? [1]

Away from the court, and inside the home, love-marriage couples seek to obtain the consent and legitimacy of their two families. This chapter is the 'other-half' of the court- marriage, as it explores some of the more intimate strategies that love-marriage couples use in order to complete the marriage (through a negotiation with community). However, in a large proportion of cases, opposition to the choice of an offspring leaves the latter little option but to leave home and chart their new life without their families. This chapter examines elopements, abductions and kinship relations evidenced in love-marriage cases, and through this explores the ways in which gender conditions the agency of love-marriage individuals.

'Love-cum-Arranged' Marriage

Most couples in Delhi have a court or religious marriage in utter secrecy and return to their respective homes as if nothing had happened. Here they continue to stave off proposals of arranged marriages often under the pretext of wanting to further their studies, do various career-oriented courses, or get a job and be 'properly settled' in life before having to marry. These considerations would be acceptable to the parents as they usually enhance the status of the offspring when trying to arrange a marriage. During this very difficult period, the spouse may be gently introduced to the family as a *'friend'*, or colleague, and every attempt is made to present this person in the best possible light. Sometimes allies may be found in sympathetic siblings, relatives and family friends who would be taken into confidence, and whose task would be to *'convince'* the parents and community, usually over a period of some years, to *'agree'* on the suitability of the person's choice of partner. Great care would be taken by the couple not to seem to have already made a choice, or to be 'in love', so that the family was never given cause to suspect why their attempts at arranging marriages were being so repetitively foiled.[2] As time wore on, the preference of the child would be revealed and the parents would be placed in a position of either forcing the child into an arranged-marriage, or making the child's *'choice'* their own.

In a large proportion of cases, the parents eventually decide that they have no other option but to accept the person that the child has *'selected'*. In this scenario there are two possibilities. The first is to try and 'arrange' a marriage or a reception with the parents of their child's spouse. This is often an unsavoury prospect, because unless the child has married someone who happens to be of the same status (religion, caste and social class), the conjoining of the two families is bound to lead to conflict over the nature of the marriage ceremony or reception and over the sensitive business of advertising to one's relatives the fact that this is an arranged marriage with a difference. Far better is the second scenario in which the parents of the boy hold their own ceremony or reception, and the parents of the girl do likewise. This can often be the occasion for elaborate deceit, with parents renaming their in-laws with appropriate caste/religious names, and disguising the true identity of their child's spouse with appropriate forms of dress and coaching on behaviour. When the couple are presented to the parents' social world, an image of coherence and order is presented. This for many people is the only acceptable form of love-marriage, because here the couple's choice is definitively legitimated by the parents through the process of compromise. Such marriages are the ideal for many a young couple and are suitably known as the only acceptable form of love-marriage: *'love-cum-arranged'* marriage.[3]

This 'second marriage', while being predicated on the choice and agency of the couple-in-love, is nonetheless domesticated and brought within the purview of parental authority and control and the reciprocal obligations of the child. Importantly, such love-cum-arranged marriages avoid the devastating sanctions of the couple being excommunicated, but in the act of supporting the child, leave the parents open to community sanctions. If word gets out that their child's spouse was in fact not of the same caste, community or class, and that the marriage was therefore, in all probability, a love-marriage, the parents and family could themselves be excommunicated.

While the negotiations for a love-cum-arranged marriage take place in the sanctuary of the immediate family, an elopement, on the other hand, is a public declaration of a love affair and the intention to live together as man and wife. It is often the first time that couples make their relationship public by virtue of their disappearance from their homes. It is usually impossible to contain news of an elopement, though the families might try and provide alibis while simultaneously hunting the couple down. The moment such cases enter public discourse, they are viewed as abominations. The actions of the couple are read as evidence of callous, unthinking and irresponsible individuals expressing their freedom and selfish lust with scant regard for their families' wishes and feelings. The reason for this is that an elopement is viewed as a definitively public act that forecloses the possibility of a *love-cum-arranged* marriage. Most people in Delhi make a distinction between a love-marriage and a *love-cum-arranged* marriage. In the latter, the social order that had been disrupted by 'love' is seen to be restored through the arranged marriage. An elopement on the other hand upsets the social order with its implicit declaration that 'love' couldn't wait for an 'arrangement'.

This damning condemnation is not merely limited to the couple, but has the effect of weakening the family's honour and reputation too. The sense of shame and dishonour quickly spreads and entire families and kinship groups are vulnerable to being held responsible for individual acts of 'rebellion'. Chowdhry (1997), for instance, discusses this with reference to violence inflicted upon love-marriage couples and their families in Haryana. This explains why, for many parents of eloping couples, the only option is to disown or disinherit the child. In responses instinctually echoing a thousand Hindi film refrains, the father of an eloping child shouts to his wife: 'Don't mention that name in front of me. I have no child. My child has died!'

The Dead Girl Who Came Alive

True life, however, bears down hot on the heels of even the most melodramatic Hindi movie. In a newspaper report by Anju Sharma, we are told:

In a bizarre case, a dead girl has literally come alive. The 'dead girl' who had been cremated by her parents a few days ago, appeared in the Patiala House District Courts yesterday along with her husband. She claimed that she had married against her parents' wishes and wanted the court to intervene in the matter.[4]

The 'dead girl', 19-year-old Munesh Solanki, had eloped with a boy in the neighbourhood on the 7 March 1998, and had married him 'against the wishes of her parents'. Her father registered a missing person complaint in the Najafgarh police station and a massive search was launched to find her. In the meanwhile, the Janakpuri police found the body of a girl who had been brutally murdered. It seems that when Munesh's parents heard about this unidentified body in the Subzi Mandi mortuary in Delhi, they went and claimed the body as that of Munesh. They checked several identification marks and told the police that they were absolutely certain that it was their Munesh. The body was cremated the next day. On the 25 March, Munesh sought intervention from a magistrate pleading that her parents had cremated someone else. Munesh's case clinically exemplifies the desire (even if metaphorical) to make dead someone who is clearly known to be alive. It is noteworthy that Munesh emphasises the fact that she was marrying against her parents' wishes (rather than without her parents' knowledge), and that she had had to elope to be able to be with her husband Rupendra.[5]

In most elopement cases, despite making their relationship visible, the couple paradoxically are themselves invisible: they are on the run and hiding from literally everybody. They leave behind in their homes families that can only recount with surprise and shock the standard narrative to press reporters of how they discovered that their child had just 'gone'. However, as in Munesh's case, there are some indicators that the parents are rarely so ignorant about why their child has left home or where she might be. More often than not, the child will have eloped due to some precipitating event within the family, most commonly an engagement for an arranged marriage or an argument over their own choice of spouse. What becomes interesting for us is the pattern of lies that emerges from a study of love-marriages. It is almost as if the family is socially bound to declare their ignorance about the child's whereabouts and must do so in very public forums such as police stations and press reports.

The parents must file a police case to try and recover the child, and it is through these 'First Information Reports' (FIR) filed at the police stations across the city that press reporters are able to pick up and publicise cases in the news. The predominant representation is that of the family and their story of how their child went missing. Here, the couples themselves are not represented, and the entirely one-sided nature of the reporting ensures that at their most public exposure, love-marriage couples are not represented as having eloped for love, but rather as victims of crimes such as kidnappings. In Munesh's story, this 'representation' extends to her family's decision to kill her symbolically and cremate the body. Munesh and her husband, although not physically harmed, seek protection from the court because they recognise in these actions a grim warning and an explicit threat to their continued social and legal existence.[6]

My own attempts to meet love-marriage couples were riven with the problems of eloping couples seeking to remain invisible to their families and the police, and therefore perhaps constituting some of the most anthropologist-shy people one could try and work with in Delhi. The result was that I had to lie in wait for them to appear in the courts and temples, much as might the families, the police and the media. Occasionally, they would tell me a little about themselves and their lives, but mostly I had to depend on them contacting me in their own time, rather than being able to follow their progress in such tense and critical times. This was the most difficult time to work with couples and I too was spellbound by their ability to appear and disappear from my life. Indeed, I soon came to realise that this was a weapon of the weak. They had chosen 'self-exile' in order to extract themselves from their people and to prevent themselves from either being excommunicated (pushed out), or locked within through marriages arranged against their will.

What follows is an ethnography of an elopement: that of Zahra and Nadim. They were both still 'underground' and so it was impossible to talk to them. Their story was obtained through a few press reports (through which I was first alerted to the police case that was being investigated), and interviews over three months with the police officers, and various members of the family and friends of the couple.

Running Away or Being Taken Away: The Semantics of an Elopement

The print media reports elopement cases very frequently, and while the substance of each story may indicate the contradictory evidence involved, the story itself tends to categorise the event as a whole, and name it one or the other: elopement, kidnapping or abduction. Only very rarely are missing person complaints filed. The popular perception is that unless you give the police a crime to solve, or have sufficient influence to get them to launch a manhunt, they will write the case down and forget all about it. One avenue for pursuant families is to file a case of theft by accusing the couple of having decamped with goods, money and jewellery from the family home. However, the most popular form of retrieval is to file a kidnapping or abduction case. The Indian Penal Code defines kidnapping as:

> Whosoever takes or entices any minor under 16 years of age if a male, or under 18 years of age if a female, or any person of unsound mind out of the keeping of the lawful guardian of such minor or person of unsound mind, without the consent of such guardian, is said to kidnap such minor or person from lawful guardian.

Abduction is defined as 'Whoever by force compels, or by any deceitful means induces any person to go from any place is said to abduct that person.' The main difference in law between a kidnapping charge and that of abduction is that the victim in the case of the former is considered a minor and is taken away from their legal guardian, and in the latter, the victim is an adult. In practice, however, the two terms are used interchangeably in Delhi. If the parents can manage to file a kidnapping case even when the child is an adult (usually by lying about the age), they have the added advantage of retrieval being accompanied by the police handing the child over to them, as they are legally his or her guardians. In abduction cases, the police are obliged upon re-trieval to ask the man or woman whether they went of their own free will; there is no obligation for the police to return the person to the parents against his or her will.

The categorisation of cases as one or the other, or as elopements, quite obviously comes from either the family of the missing person or the police when a report has been filed.[7] That means that from the moment love-marriage stories enter the media in stories of elopements they carry the heavy baggage of contested events described from the vantage and perspectives of interested parties. The media uses and mimics the categorical terminology of the parents or the police, and reiterates its symbolic context in order to create moral opinions about the event. A missing person complaint implies that the person has just gone, and it does not implicate anyone else in the case. Some families do file missing person complaints when their children elope, but invariably these are the people who genuinely do not know that the child has eloped, or don't know with whom. One of the reasons why people prefer to file kidnapping cases is that if one does know about the affair, then retrieval is very important. This is best achieved by naming the eloping partner as the 'accused' so that the police may find the couple more easily.

While it is generally considered to be a much greater tragedy if one's daughter elopes, it is also the case that parents of eloping sons may seek to track them down. Daughters who elope are seen to spurn the protection of their fathers and brothers and declare their sexuality through love-marriages. They bring shame and dishonour, not just to themselves, but also to all their female kin, whose arranged-marriages may be jeopardised by the stigma of belonging to families where the girls are given so much slack that they are able to elope with men of their choosing. However, eloping sons also bring shame and dishonour to the patrilineage. During my research, I encountered as many cases of love-marriages being broken up by the boy's family and the boy being married elsewhere, as the other way round. This is because unless retrieval is within a few days, the public stigma of an eloping girl having potentially lost her virginity could make it difficult for parents to arrange her marriage elsewhere. Men, on the other hand, can more easily recover from the stigma of a 'love affair'.

Both families of the couple frequently file kidnapping and abduction cases. This can be for two reasons. The first more obvious reason is that both sides object to their child's choice. The other reason is that even if, for example, the man's kin have no objections, they still run the risk of being implicated in the elopement by the case filed by the girl's family. They then risk being accused of acting as accomplices who conspired with the boy, and this leaves them open to arrest and interrogation by the police. To prevent this scenario, both sides file pre-emptive kidnapping or abduction cases. The linking of one's child's name with that of the 'accused' in a police report is nonetheless seen to be scandalous—even if it positions one's offspring in the relationship of an unwilling victim of the accused—and especially if it is repeated in the press. The families however, see themselves as having little option in the matter. As I will show in this chapter, a kidnapping/abduction complaint at least momentarily contests their child's agency in having eloped. In addition, the charge carries the added benefit of the possibility of putting the 'accused' behind bars, if and when the two are caught.

Very often, a family that files an abduction case knows a lot more about the circumstances of the case than they are willing to admit. A family that may have been surprised to find their case in the next day's newspapers, may now find that they must court publicity either to reiterate their view about the event being an abduction, or to counteract other views that this was really an elopement. This creates a paradox: on the one hand, the case attracts attention from various quarters including political animals who are invariably brought in (or step in of their own accord) to politicise the proceedings and speed up recovery of the child. On the other hand, the family's withholding of vital information from the police (for example, the fact that their child was having an affair with the 'accused') seems to imply that the retrieval of the child occupies an important though subordinate position to a more pressing concern. This is the need for families to transform and make honourable the dishonour they have been subjected to through the scandal and shame brought with the inevitable gossip that their child has eloped. Put differently, to call an elopement an 'abduction' (or 'kidnapping') is to contest its meaning and throw it into confusion, momentarily gaining a reprieve in which to turn the situation around. So long as the child remains missing, the honour of the family and community remains violated, but only in the sense of being victims of some ill-defined crime that took their child away from them. Retribution can ensure the restoration of honour, hence the allure of delaying the judgement and keeping the question of what 'really' happened under interminable negotiation. Everyone knows that some elopements do get reversed if the couple get caught, and with sufficient pressure exerted, either the boy or the girl may be made to confess that they were actually kidnapped or abducted. In this way, the family still retains the potential to restore their honour and redefine the event.

The press in Delhi provided an amazing array of stories that illustrate this paradox. As in the story of the 'dead girl' coming alive, the stories all take for granted a high level of intrigue, violence and 'love' both inside and outside the family, as an almost normal state of affairs. This is striking because it contradicts the well-versed characterisation of Indian life as rigidly defined by community authority and the lack of individual choice. The affairs that lead to love-marriages are portrayed as remarkably 'natural' and perhaps even inevitable, however hard the families try to prevent them. Take for example two news reports about a 'kidnapping' that went drastically wrong and inadvertently caused the death of an accomplice. The first is a report from the *Times of India*.[8] It tells us that a girl called Reena was reportedly abducted from her home in Ghaziabad, on the outskirts of Delhi, by six armed men, led by her cousin Kishanpal (aged 21). The men scaled the boundary wall to enter the courtyard and held a gun to Reena's mother's head. Reena rushed to save her, but was 'bodily lifted by one man while the others severely thrashed Rati [the mother] with pistol butts. Even as Reena was being carried away, her mother chased the abductors through the streets.' When she shouted *'chor, chor'* ['thief, thief!'] one of the men fired a shot in her direction and, missing her as the bullet grazed her cheek, inadvertently shot one of their accomplices in the head.

Reena's cousin's involvement in the case is revealed by the investigating police officials who claim that Reena and her cousin 'were having an affair'. Reena's relatives however, strongly deny this and argue that what seemed to others to be an affair was merely Kishanpal 'teasing' Reena. Her grandfather says: 'I had thrashed Kishanpal's father Raja Ram, a few days ago, because Kishan had teased Reena.' Another newspaper portrays a similar scene, but points out that Reena and Kishanpal were not merely teasing one another, or having an affair, but had earlier eloped, and Reena had been caught and brought home by the speedy intervention of other relatives. Additionally, it reveals that Reena's father Kaniyalal had been trying to get his daughter married: 'Kaniyalal had reportedly fixed up Rena's [sic] engagement with someone which allegedly led Kishanpal to kidnap the girl before her parents could marry her'.[9] It is clear from this that the parents' motives were to stop Reena and Kishanpal from getting married to each other. Kishanpal abducts Reena to ensure that she gets married to no one but him. The plot, all in all, is hardly perplexing and it is not wholly unreasonable to assert with some certainty that Reena was herself aware of her lover's plans to rescue her. The excessive force may be due to enormous opposition from Reena's family and the expectation of resistance. However, Reena's family's insistence before the police that Reena isn't in fact romantically linked with Kishanpal is clearly a lie. At worst, they could have asserted that she no longer liked him, even though at one stage the two had eloped. Their denial of any affair leaves us questioning the truth of the matter. However, before I move to the central problematic of these cases, let me briefly recount one final story that appeared in the Delhi newspapers. The news item details the misadventures of a 15-year-old girl.

The report of a young schoolgirl being abducted by Maruti [a popular upper-middle class car] borne youth drove the Malviya Nagar police into a frenzy this morning. The entire exercise, however, proved to be much ado about nothing with the girl returning home in the afternoon and claiming to have merely gone to a temple.[10]

The alarm was raised by two of her school-friends who were walking with her to school. We can confirm two facts from the rest of the story: that she did go somewhere with some boys, and that it was assumed for some reason to have been an 'abduction'. When she returns, she claims to have merely gone to the Kalkaji temple and to have spent the 'entire day there'. The tone of the article is designed to imply that the girl is having an affair (as if a young girl would go to a temple and spend the whole day there). The event is considered to be newsworthy because her parents thought she had been abducted when in fact she was found to have been on an assignation with a boy. The reporter is clearly amused by the attempts to redefine the event. Her 'boldness' in keeping to her story and not buckling under the pressure over her so-called abduction is represented in the article as a sign of her complicity.

When the girl returns home she is confronted by her family, friends, community and, of course, the police: all in a 'frenzy'.

She had perhaps tried to give her friends the slip but was caught getting into the car, or perhaps her friends told her family that she had gone with some boys in a car. The parents, fearing that their daughter had eloped, or perhaps fearing the shame of people discovering that their daughter had gone missing with some boy, decide to file a case for 'abduction' in the hope of swiftly retrieving her and safeguarding her honour. For her part, she must stand by her alibi. The possibilities expressed in the article do not include an admission to what was going on (a love affair?). It is alluded to, but not named or discussed. For her part, the girl bolsters her innocence with the idea of a devotional experience spent in a famous temple.[11]

What is interesting in both these stories is the unmistakable implication of the girl having been coerced by one or more men.[12] One girl is 'bodily lifted and carried away' by her armed boyfriend, and another is 'abducted' by Maruti-borne youth. Yet, from the evidence in the articles, we can safely conclude that both the girls went with men they knew. In Reena's case, it was the person she had unsuccessfully tried to elope with; in the second case, the girl explicitly denies having been abducted, therefore, protecting the boys, leaving the writer of the article to make the innuendo about her moral character. The only matter we are left to consider is not Reena's complicity in leaving with her rescuers, but rather the whole kidnapping that Kishanpal sets up and her own struggle that caused the men to bodily lift her and carry her away. In the second case we can ask a similar hypothetical question; was the abduction a staged event? Was the sense of coercion an integral element in the ritual of an 'abduction'?

I do not wish to deny the possibility that Reena, despite her initial affair with Kishanpal, and elopement, may have been pressurised, blackmailed or quite simply convinced by her family to opt for an arranged marriage. Equally, she may have decided of her own accord that she did not wish to consort with Kishanpal any longer. Hence, the armed kidnapping may well have been a genuine abduction. Equally, I am not saying that the Malviya Nagar girl was definitely not forced into the car. These things happened with such frequency in Delhi that one would be naïve to imagine that they were not possible. However, while these remain possibilities, and while there are no further clues as to what 'really' happened in these two incidents, I hope to use them as ciphers for other cases where I did have a chance to make more intimate assessments.

Zahra's Self-Abduction[13]

The previous day, Riaz had had an exam. He had come home late and immediately fell asleep in the living room that he shared with his older sister Zahra, and two younger sisters. The next morning, he was awoken by his father. On the floor by his bed was his sister's *dupatta* (scarf) and slipper. Outside the room, by the steps to the road was her second slipper. His father said to him: '*Beta*, what is this *colour* on the floor?' pointing to the liquid spilled everywhere. Riaz looked at it and at his sister Zahra's *dupatta* and slippers and replied: 'Papa, it is not *colour*. It is blood.' Riaz said they looked everywhere for Zahra. He realised what had happened. 'Papa is a *property dealer*. He has a lot of enemies. There are many *cases* over our disputes, *cases* over land. Papa buys land and *cuts colonies* on it. Someone had even put a *rape case* on papa. The enmity went back a long way. So papa thought that some *against party* has done this to us. We thought she had been killed or carried away by thugs. Papa called the police.'

The police learnt that Zahra had woken as usual at 5.30 that morning and read *namaz* with her mother at 6 AM. At 6.30, when her mother went to lie down, she began her daily chores. When her father woke to pick up the newspaper from the front door, he saw the blood and woke Riaz. This is when they called the police. The police started making their interrogations. Sub-Inspector Alok Prasad said:

Everyone said what the family said. That the girl was very innocent and decent. The type who never leaves the house, and who reads *namaz* daily. A *religious type* of girl. We asked if she was with someone, whether she was having an affair with anyone—but they gave us no proof that it was at all possible that she could have left on her own. The dog squad was unable to pick up any scent. We were puzzled. She went missing at a time in the morning when the street is full of people. Yet nobody had seen anything. There had been a violent struggle, someone had been hit, and that is why there was all the blood on the floor and in her *dupatta*. In the small room where the incident took place, and where all the blood was, there were 3 people sleeping, and none of them say they heard a thing. This is the reason why our *mind diverted* a little. We thought that the chances were that this wasn't an abduction.

The next day's newspaper headline announced: 'Cops suspect no foul play, relatives allege abduction'.

For Riaz and his family, the police's attitude made them very angry. He said:

> They started saying, *nahin ji* [no sir], the girl must have gone on her own will. That means they began to slacken. So what if I was sleeping there. The blood was also there! We had said from the word go that we suspected papa's rival. When someone says 'we suspect him' they should catch him and investigate it. They should find the girl. *Open* [solve] the *case*. After that you can take evidence from the girl and she can tell you what the *reality* is. The case slowed down, because from there [from the rival], *note-vote* [money] started moving hands. Instead of being questioned and locked up, the police are visiting him in his house and saying 'Rizvi *sahib* this, Rizvi *sahib* that!'

For many people, the police's inaction in a case so gruesome as this was deplorable. Zahra, like many Muslim girls in her locality, was from a 'respectable' family and as one shopkeeper told me, 'She was *shy*! Those people aren't even too *modern*. They keep *purdah*. She hasn't studied very much—maybe up to the *higher secondary* at the most.' There was considerable amount of public sympathy for the family.

Despite the clear motive of the prime suspect, and the fact of all the blood, the police doggedly pursued the theory of Zahra having left her house on her own.

> The possibility of an *affair* was utterly obvious right from the start because it was a girl in her early 20s. Then we had our first breakthrough. Someone said 'it was possible' that she was having an *affair* with a tailor called Nadim. We interrogated 60–70 people in all. Mostly people felt it wasn't an abduction. 30% said it could be Rizvi [the rival property dealer], 20% said it could be someone else, but the remaining 60% [sic] were saying that in their view the girl had gone on her own. We learnt that Nadim was actually a good friend of Zahra's brother Riaz. They played *cricket* together, and Nadim used to come and go from Riaz' house frequently. We also learnt that more recently they had had a fight, and that Zahra's people had beaten Nadim up.

The first indications of something being amiss came from Nadim's original testimony. When he had been interviewed on the first day after the abduction he had denied even knowing Riaz. In the meanwhile, Zahra's family was horrified that she still had not been found. They organised a demonstration of some 2,000 people in the centre of Delhi, in front of the Commissioner of Police's office, and a three-hour demonstration later that night, in front of the local police station investigating the case. They shouted slogans: 'Delhi police hai hai' ['shame, shame'] and demanded that some action be taken so that the girl be recovered. The pressure on the case kept mounting. The Commissioner was called by Sushma Swaraj, a BJP minister who demanded that the case be solved and action taken against the rival. Rizvi and his associates were called into the police station. According to the Sub-Inspector, he told the police in a very straightforward manner that he did do dirty deals of all sorts, and that he was Zahra's father's enemy. However, under no circumstances would he ever have planned to do something to someone's children. The police believed his story and let him go.

At Zahra's house the situation deteriorated with every day that passed. Riaz described their condition to me:

My father cried, 'my daughter, my daughter!' For 9 days he cried and cried. People said—'Asad *sahib*, eat something. How can you function if you don't eat?' He would just cry. My mother was running around. She was crying. Over there she was having goats sacrificed everyday in Nizamuddin.[14] Over here someone said, go to this *Baba* [god-man]. His fee was 5,000 rupees and his brother-in-law takes it. The *Baba* said she is in Aligarh, in this street, at this house number. *Mumma* [mummy] came home. She went to other *Babas*. They were all saying things like four men have taken her. No *Baba* said anything about Nadim. Anyway, we hired a *taxi*, put a cousin and one of my friends in it, and sent them to Aligarh to look for Zahra. For two days they searched for her. The *gully* existed, the address was correct, but there was a lock on the door. Nobody had lived there for ten years. Our neighbours knew Zahra. They helped us a lot. They sent over 15 kilos of *Rajma* [a type of bean]. Each bean … if you count it, you can just imagine how many there would be. These were counted and each bean was prayed over with a *dua* [prayer].[15] Everybody sat and read the *dua*. At night there was no food because we were all sitting there reading, praying, crying. On the day the whole story emerged, I saw no tears. Nobody cried that day. To the point that when someone asks about it, it just hurts.

The entire family remained in a state of extreme anxiety and torment. 'Crying and praying', they kept vigil with other members of the neighbourhood and community who came forward to share their grief and keep alive their hopes that Zahra would be recovered. In the meanwhile, the police took Nadim in for interrogation. He stuck to his story of not even knowing Riaz. When he was confronted with evidence that they played cricket together, he said he did know him, but wasn't a friend. He had never been to Riaz's house for instance. Again, this conflicted with the information the police had.

At this point, the mystery deepened. The police received a phone call from Zahra's father Asad to say that they should stop the interrogation and release Nadim immediately. He assured the police that Nadim wasn't 'that sort of boy' and that he was well known to Asad. Furthermore, they were told that interrogating him 'wouldn't solve the case'. Alok Prasad says they continued the investigation, but merely as a formality, and allowed Nadim to leave. Their persistence with Nadim, and their unwillingness to arrest and charge Rizvi seemed evidence to Asad that the police were trying to protect Rizvi. With 'pressure' and influence, the case was transferred out of their hands and into the charge of the District Crime Cell.

The effect of offending the pride of the local police was stupendous. They were now absolutely determined to find the proof that indicted Nadim. He was kept under observation, and found to have spent each day away from home, returning only at night. At 4 AM the next day the police picked him up along with his two brothers.

We asked them *politely* what was going on. They of course, refused to say. Then we showed them our force. Our informant was very reliable, so we knew we had the right clues. He finally started talking and told us where Zahra was. We raided the place but she wasn't there. We posted teams at all his relatives' homes. We finally found her at his cousin's friend's house across the river. That is how the story was opened. We took the two of them to our main police station and called her father. We told him, 'Asad *sahib*, Zahra and Nadim are both here.'

At the other end of the phone there was shocked disbelief. Riaz says: 'Papa heard Nadim's name. I had just walked into the room. He said to me—"*bhai*, the way it is now, the case has been opened".

I said: "Where is Zahra?" He said, "Do you want to go and meet her? She is with Nadim that friend of yours. The two of them have been caught." I said, …then I will not come. If you wish to go please go." Then he asked my mother, my little sisters; everyone said no. Papa wanted to take everybody's view—what does the family think.'

Armed with the family's support, Asad went to the police station and spoke to Zahra. Riaz says:

> He asked her: '*Beta* [daughter], is this under pressure? Have you been through some *drama*, and been tricked into this? *Beta*, tell me, is this with your consent?' She said in an arrogant voice, 'yes, papa. I have tried many times to say something to you but I never succeeded.' Papa heard this statement and just stood up. He said, '*Beta*, it is like this. From today I have no relationship to you, and from this day onwards, you are dead to me.' Saying this he just came home.

Alok Prasad was witness to the meeting between father and daughter in the police station. He said that when he told Zahra her father was there to meet her, she started crying and said she didn't want to see him, she was too scared. She was forced to see him and when he asked her what she wanted to do with her future, she said she wished to remain with Nadim. Her father said: 'What has happened has happened. You have turned our honour to dirt. Now you can do what you want to do.' Zahra was so terrified that she could not even bring herself to say to her father that she and Nadim had been married for the past three years. It was left to the police to break this news to him.[16]

A roof-top romance

Sub-Inspector Alok Prasad learnt the rest of the story from Zahra after her father had left the police station. It seems that she and Nadim had been having an affair.

> Even though she had to keep *purdah*, and even though Nadim's house was 600 metres away across an open ground, she had a roof and he had a balcony… She would come up to her roof and he would emerge on his balcony, and they would signal each other. Then they would go to their phones and speak. Nadim's family was so upset by their phone bill that they had their phone-line cancelled. Still he would see her signals and go and call from the local phone booth.

At some point, Riaz found out about the affair and beat Nadim up. Anticipating trouble from Zahra's family, they had a *nikkah* ceremony in Nizamuddin. Nadim was careful to keep the *nikkahnama* [*nikkah* certificate] and their court affidavit with his aunt who lived on the other side of the city. In the event that they were found out, at least the proof of their marriage could not so easily be destroyed by Zahra's family. The romantic in Alok Prasad comes out: 'They [Zahra's people] were good and proper *crorepattis* [millionaires]. Like in the films, it was a *rich-girl-and-servant type affair*'. The headlines the following day were suitably amended: 'Kidnapped Delhi girl found to have eloped'.[17]

Even after their marriage, they continued to live in their own homes. Then disaster struck. Zahra got pregnant. It is not known whether she wanted to have the child, or whether it was already too late to abort it. In any event, she decided to leave home. She confided in her teacher, a young woman not much older than herself, who came to the house to give her tuition since Zahra was in *purdah* and was not allowed to go to college. The two of them conspired to buy the blood from a private clinic and make her elopement look like an abduction. Apparently Nadim was not involved in the plan. Alok Prasad explains her motives:

> She thought, that if I run away, people will immediately start to suspect. So to *mind divert* them, they did this. Because there was this enmity with the *property dealer*, they thought that they could *mind divert* people so that they think she has been taken by thugs, and is dead. She wanted her family to *chapter close* her. Her family will have the impression that some bad elements have done this. There will be no shame, and their *line of action* will be in another direction. They *adjusted* the blood from someone in a *nursing home*. The teacher gave her the blood when she visited that evening. The next morning, Zahra poured the blood on the floor, soaked her *dupatta*, threw her slippers and went out on the street. She sat in a *cycle-rickshaw*, then caught an *auto-rickshaw* and arrived at Nadim's relatives' house in Seelumpur.

When Nadim's relatives read about the case in the newspapers and realised that a police case had been lodged, they panicked and tried very hard to convince Zahra to return. She adamantly refused. On the third day, they phoned Nadim and told him she was with them. He too apparently tried to convince her to return but she refused. The morning when he was finally arrested was the day they had planned to leave the city for his village.

During the period of my initial fieldwork, I never spoke to 'Zahra' or 'Nadim'. They were still in hiding, even though the case had been withdrawn. Sub-Inspector Prasad indicated that Nadim's family had only recently come in to ask the police to get Zahra's family to stop threatening them. Clearly, the insults will continue and the dishonour will take some years to recover from. This notwithstanding, Riaz had a very amiable discussion about Nadim with me:

> See really, I have no complaint against Nadim. He did what he did, but he was a friend—he is distant from me. But the sadness concerns our sister, whom we trusted so completely! The truth is, I had never seen her misbehave either on the *telephone* or in a look. She never even used to pick up the *telephone*! How could we have suspected what was up? She never used to open the house door, saying, whoever is expecting visitors may open it. This sort of behaviour would instil confidence in any man. And she tricked us. That is why I have no love for her.

Riaz admitted that when the case was solved, his father's brother tried to prevail on Asad to accept Zahra's choice and marry the two off in a lavish ceremony. Asad was both affluent, and a powerful member of their *biradari* (endogamous caste group or lineage). People would have to accept his decision, and in all probability, would not seek to excommunicate him. However, although the broken Asad was seemingly amenable, his son Riaz openly confronted his uncle's sagacity and politely told him to leave these matters to the nuclear family. No marriage was held and Zahra to this day remains unforgiven.

An anatomy of an elopement:
The blood of one's own

Zahra's elopement was ripe with the symbolism that allowed her family to believe that Rizvi had abducted her, and caused the police to suspect that she had eloped. The blood was meant to indicate her wounding in a struggle, and the gruesome violence to which she had to succumb in order for her kidnappers to take her away. For the police, it was the presence of so much blood and the absence of any witnesses to the struggle that alerted them to the possibility of a set-up. The blood was a part of her that she leaves behind in her home, forcing the reflection that she has come to great harm, and that she may never again be seen alive by her loved ones. Her kin must grieve that part of her which made her kin; her blood or *khoon*. The blood invokes the fear that her kidnapping is probably only a prelude to the extremes of violence reserved for women whom men seek to dishonour. It is this notion that Zahra is clearly invoking by her self-abduction.

Zahra, we learn from Riaz, was well aware of the predicaments their father had been subjected to when Rizvi had a 'false rape-case' filed against Asad. Riaz told me that the rivalry between his father and Rizvi was so intense that it was the sort that they could even kill for. The Police Commissioner, 'ministers', 'everyone' knew about these two businessmen who 'keep filing false cases against each other'. According to Riaz, the 'rape-case' had been trumped up by Rizvi who paid a woman to say that Asad had raped her. However, the charges were dropped when the woman failed to show when the case came to trial. Proudly Riaz says that his father put the news about his success in the newspapers by 'buying the *media*'. Ruining a rival's reputation by alleging rape is only a small step away from abducting and actually raping his daughter. The symbolic repertoire that underlines Zahra's thinking clearly existed, and she manipulated it to her advantage. The rival Rizvi had already been seen to stoop low; this event would be used to prove his guilt.[18]

Her family, for their part, fell for the ruse, hook line and sinker. According to Riaz, some friend of their father consoled him when Zahra was still missing with the reassuring thought that, '…at least it was a girl they took, not your son', playing on the commonplace assumption that daughters come and go, but sons must never be taken away.[19] To this, Riaz claims his father replied:

> If my *rival* took my son, I would not be this upset. This is a matter concerning my daughter! Is there no difference between a boy and a girl? A girl is forever stained by the suspicion that the thugs may have done something to her.[20] If my son had been kidnapped and his hand cut off, that would still have been better than this. My son can even sleep outdoors at night. It is no problem. But a girl at some level makes one burdened.

Zahra burdens her father because she is a girl. Her father must recover her, but he and everyone else around already recognise and articulate the view that her honour is already stained by the mere suspicion of what the thugs may have done to her. Zahra is around 20 years old and single, so her honour, if indeed violated, may never be restored in time to get her an arranged marriage. But ironically, we know that her 'honour' has been 'violated' by her own consent, because we know that she is pregnant by a man she gave herself to, in marriage and in sex. Her staged abduction thus serves as symbol of the dishonour that she herself feels she has brought upon the family, and that she herself seeks to disguise. Rather than make them and herself suffer the inevitable public shaming, and possibly also to avoid detection and capture, Zahra excises herself from the family. The blood serves as evidence to disguise this operation, and makes it appear as if the excision was caused by a rival determined to dishonour her father.

It is the protection of her sexuality that burdens her father, as much as the obligation to marry her off. Yet it seems as if Zahra wants her father to believe that her honour and her life are in grave danger. If she hadn't left the blood, we can imagine that the suspicion would have fallen immediately on an elopement, or a 'non-violent' abduction. The latter could involve imagined scenarios like kidnappings for ransom alone, which would have been 'read' as less dangerous to her honour than the scenario she created. In her set-up, she leaves enough room for the possibility that she has already been killed in the encounter with the thugs. Her slippers testify to her reluctance to leave. A girl from a 'respectable family' would never leave home without sandals or slippers on her feet. Walking barefooted on thoroughfares is considered a sign of poverty. Her *dupatta*, the piece of cloth that a woman drapes over her bust and trails over both shoulders, or wraps over her head and shoulders, is a powerful symbol of a girl's modesty. The *dupatta* is worn by women with the *salwar-kameez* and whilst many young girls may not wear it at home, most would certainly never be seen without it outside the home, or by non-kin within the house. If a man were to snatch or pull a woman's *dupatta*, it is symbolic of disrobing her, because it allows the shape of her body to be exposed to the male gaze. Zahra leaves her *dupatta*, purposefully soaked in the blood, to indicate perhaps that she has been stabbed in the chest or brutally assaulted. Nadim's mother, who claims to have been unaware of the extent to which her son was involved with Zahra, told me about her first response to the news in the neighbourhood of Zahra's abduction: 'We heard that she left without three full pieces of clothing! She left her *dupatta* behind. From that, the evidence was created that yes; someone has taken her away! When we heard this, even my eyes filled with tears.' Seen from another perspective, the pregnant Zahra leaves her honour behind in the vestige of her *dupatta*. The blood in it is marked as representing her struggle to defend her honour, and the fact that she left home without it drives home the fact that the dye, so to speak, has been set.

When Zahra has been caught and brought to the police station, this theme concerning the possessions she took when leaving home is further dramatised and elaborated. At this stage, the truth has been revealed and everyone knows that Zahra and Nadim have been married for three-and-a-half years. According to Nadim's mother, who is keen to establish that she is not greedy for Zahra's family's wealth, Zahra took off the single gold ring she had worn for years and her tiny gold earrings, and tried to return them to her father, Asad. Asad was deeply affected by this. He allegedly said: '*Beti*, whatever you have done you have done. But if you try and give these things back to me you will wound me. Please don't take them off'. In this simple exchange we can unpack so much of the tragedy of elopements. Zahra feels that she must sever all ties with her family, not because she wants to, but because it is her only way of proving that she loves her family and is sorry for the pain she has caused. To take anything with you other than the clothes you are wearing is considered an unparalleled act of calumny. The obsession with taking or not-taking things with you when you elope comes from the context of a girl 'leaving' home at marriage and being bid farewell with her gifts and dowry.[21] The dowry is often viewed as a symbol of the love that a family carries for their girl. The girl who is given a good dowry measures her family's love for her through it. It is taken at the time of *bidai*—the ceremony when the girl is taken by her husband, and is bid farewell from her maternal home. It is also, typically, a traumatic moment for all concerned.

By focusing attention on the little jewellery that she wears, Zahra draws attention to the fact that she left home without a dowry. In seeking to return the jewellery to her father, she emphasises the fact that he bids her farewell in a police station without the jewellery that she is rightfully expected to wear as a bride. In returning the jewellery she reverses the relationship between a father and a daughter at marriage. Not only does she leave without dowry, but she also returns the few items of jewellery that were given to her as a young girl. Her act is symbolic of a declaration that she is not worthy of dowry and that she expects none from those whose love she knows she has betrayed. Her father, seeing this, gets distraught. For many people in Delhi, the lack of jewellery on a woman's body appears as though her men-folk have left her 'empty' or 'naked'. He reads the symbolism of both the dowry that was never to be, and the reverse-dowry. She shows her un-bejewelled 'empty' body to her father, and this sight is too much for him to bear. Underlying all this is the symbolism of a poor husband and a rich father. Zahra asserts that her husband takes her for who she is, without a *cowry* in dowry. As for Asad, he is pained to realise that his daughter will never wear the jewellery he could have gifted her, and that in all probability, her husband (a tailor) would not be able to cover her in gold the way he might have. As Nadim's mother said to me: 'She [Zahra] did what she had to do; what was written in her destiny. But even as a person starts to do these things, they start to regret it. And she is going to regret it for a long, long time.'

Making and breaking kin:
Who was Zahra's *walid* (father)?

In the police station, another mystery concerning this case began to emerge. This was the fact that in Zahra's *nikkahnama* and affidavit, she had put down her grandfather's name as her father. This completely baffled Alok Prasad, and when narrating this anomaly, he started straying perilously close to mainstream Hindu views on Muslim kinship. He said to me: 'People had told Zahra that Asad was her brother not her father and that her father was someone else. In these people, [Muslims] if say the mother or the father are not the same, then they can marry. So for instance, if you have the same father and two mothers, or the same mother and two fathers, even these people can marry.' Despite this completely baffling explanation as to why Zahra wrote her grandfather's name as her father, I was able to learn from Nadim's mother that it was because Zahra was indeed Asad's sister. They had been orphaned when Zahra was still a little baby, and subsequently, Asad, who was 20 years her elder, with his wife, shouldered the responsibility to bring her up as their own daughter.

When I spoke to Riaz about the anomaly in the wedding certificate, he was reticent about suggesting explanations for why she had done this. I was working on the assumption that she didn't wish to put a name that was recognisable to people at the mosque or the court, considering that Riaz kept telling me what a famous and well-known builder his father was. Later, according to Alok Prasad, Zahra panicked that this 'error' could be argued to make their marriage invalid, and so she told them that six months previous to her elopement, she had another *nikkah* in which Asad's name was put down as that of her father. Clearly, Zahra was left with no illusions about her family's objections to her relationship with Nadim, and she was determined to leave no stone unturned in ensuring their position in law before the elopement. Nadim's mother, however, says that Zahra only said she had had a second *nikkah* out of embarrassment in having to reveal to the police before her father that she regarded her biological father as her 'real father'. The second *nikkah* never took place. For Asad, the shame of hearing about his daughter's marriage certificate was enormous. Obviously, Zahra's explanation was accepted, and the police officers like Alok Prasad left to speculate what murky relationships Muslims like Asad had to girls they claimed as their daughters.

Having given her the full status of his daughter, she still denied him his right as a father—to be written into her marriage. The rejection (however unwitting) is telling, and emphasises an aspect of elopement that we may otherwise have overlooked. Eloping couples excise themselves from their families, rather than waiting to be thrown out. They choose their spouse over their families, and go into self-exile. They make and break kin at will. The danger that this is seen to pose cannot be underestimated. In Zahra's case, the breaking of her tie with Asad was foregrounded by the tragic demise of their parents and her subsequent fostering as his 'daughter'. In Alok Prasad's eyes the tragedy of Zahra's story was that an elopement broke in a matter of a few days the trust and love of family built up over a lifetime. This sense of tragedy still plagues Zahra; according to her mother-in-law: 'She really regretted not having put his name on the certificate. In the police station he said to her, "*Beti*, you have even forgotten your father's name?" The one, who has cared for her from her childhood, she doesn't even think of him in her heart as her father. The pain must be so immense for him.'

Interestingly, everyone who narrated Asad's dialogues with Zahra to me, emphasised his use of the word *'beta'* / *'beti'* (an endearing way of saying child/daughter) whenever he addressed her. It was as if Zahra's accuracy in identifying her biological father was a denial of her social father; and it is as if his assertions of disowning her (*'beta*, it is like this. From today I have no relationship to you, and from this day onwards, you are dead to me') are made despite his enormous love for his daughter, who he cannot but help address as *'beta'* even as he seeks to sever forever the bond between them.

Lies as particular versions of the truth

As I learnt more and more about Zahra and Nadim's story, with each surprising twist and turn, I began to wonder whether it was at all conceivable that Zahra's family were more directly involved in her elopement than they made out to be. Many of the clues as to who knew about Zahra's affair with Nadim and who didn't came from discussions about the nature of relationships within the family, and the way in which young people regard their family as opposed to their friends. These innocuous leads would allow me to directly ask about 'talk' that led me to believe that Zahra's family did in fact know full well about Nadim's affair. After all, there are two aspects of Zahra's story as told by the police that leave enough room for doubt that her family was indeed aware of, if not colluding with, her elopement. Firstly, they instantly named a suspect and staunchly denied Nadim's possible involvement. Secondly, Asad tried to get the police not to investigate Nadim—seemingly attempting to cover up the elopement with their own version of Zahra's abduction.

If they did know about Zahra and Nadim, then was it possible that their opposition to the relationship caused Zahra to elope that night or early that morning? Was it possible that it was Zahra's family and not Zahra who sought to disguise the elopement as an abduction? So intriguing was the story that, despite assurances from Riaz, Sub-Inspector Alok Prasad and Nadim's mother, I kept wondering whether, in fact, it wasn't Zahra who got the blood, but her family. Of course, Zahra's confession that she got the blood from the teacher need not be evidence of anything other than her own willingness to go along with her family's attempt to save their honour.[22] The truth unfortunately, will never be known.

However, what I can prove is that the family was keen to hide the fact that they knew about the affair between Zahra and Nadim. Whenever I interviewed Riaz, the overwhelming sense that he sought to convey to me was of a family in which there were no secrets, and in which the parents were utterly supportive of their children. He said that his father Asad deeply regretted that he had been influenced by conservative family members to keep Zahra in *purdah*, and for this reason he would often say to her that he had to make it up to her one day. Zahra's tenacity and will to study privately (when she went into *purdah*) rather than be married off pleased Asad so much that it was one of the reasons why her five younger sisters were all sent to school and never kept in *purdah*. The image Riaz invokes is one of a traditional family that trusts its daughters enough not to have to keep them in *purdah*. Riaz uses the idea of Zahra in *purdah* to emphasise the rigid control under which she was brought up. He says that she never went anywhere alone and was always chaperoned by his mother or by him. His parents were not guilty of giving his sister too much slack.

On the other hand, he also wants to make the case that she kept them in the dark about her affair with Nadim. He says that when Zahra was in the police station, she was asked who knew about the affair at home. According to Riaz, she replied that nobody did. He reports his version of events at the police station; with Zahra saying: "'My mother used to say to me: *beta*, you will be married soon. If you don't feel like continuing your studies, or if there is anything you want to say, then say it *frankly*. That *mummy*, I want to get married, or *mummy*, I have found a boy I want to marry. Our mother was a friend to us. I even thought to tell my mother, but I could never do it out of fear". So the policeman said to her: "where will you find a mother like yours—who asks things to you in such an *open* manner? You have done something very wrong. Asad *sahib*, whatever you said in your statement was totally correct—you never falsely tried to implicate someone else. The only mistake was the girl's and it was their [Zahra's, Nadim's and the teacher's] *planning*"'.

While it certainly could have been the secret of the three of them, Riaz let slip that he did know of the affair. I asked him why he had broken off his friendship with Nadim when he heard of their affair, and he struggled to maintain his composure. 'Yes, one second. It was.... See the thing is.... In the locality, boys were saying that Nadim has befriended me because of my sister. I went to him and said that I have heard you are besotted with my sister. I asked him because I thought that since I was helping him people were perhaps jealous of him.[23] So he cried and said, "how can you think this of me? I can't even think such thoughts." This happened last year. I said to him, I am not your enemy, but nor do I remain your friend. You remain at your home, I at mine.' I then asked him whether he spoke to Zahra about it. Riaz said: 'I told her look, there are many other girls, but the boys don't link him to any of them. Why do they link him to you? She started crying in front of me and said: "*Bhaiya* [brother] how can you think this of me?"' Once he had admitted that he knew of the affair, other revelations began to emerge. For instance, he says that when Zahra went missing, the first thing he did was to send a friend, Naren, to see if Nadim had skipped town with her. Clearly, Nadim was the first suspect who came to mind, and yet he said nothing of this to the police; instead he bolstered his father's assertions that this was certainly an abduction masterminded by Rizvi. Yet, to the police and to me throughout my earlier interviews, Riaz had sought to maintain his ignorance of the affair.

Riaz's perspective was that Zahra had not said anything in the house about her affair with Nadim. This is entirely possible. Girls are often described as being too scared to say anything, or name their lovers, because usually action will be taken to subvert the affair. However, as it turned out, this was untrue. On the day of one of my interviews with Riaz I was with Kamiyar whose wife had been 'abducted' from him by her family. He put it to Riaz that girls don't disclose these things because if they do, their parents' will prevent them from getting married. Riaz replied that he did not disapprove of love-marriages, and even though Islam enjoined its women to keep *purdah* and thus resist any interaction with men who are not immediate kin, he also said that Islam doesn't stop you from marrying the person you like. This was not the sort of family in which there would have been threats to kill Zahra, beat her or force her. Nobody would have blamed her for destroying the *khandaan* (literally, dynasty). They would have simply advised her against the match, and if she insisted, they would have arranged her marriage to Nadim and wished her all the happiness. Zahra's 'mistake' according to her brother, was that she never even put her wishes before her family; she gave them no chance to accept her choice. Instead, she went ahead and eloped and 'did all that *drama*' which ruined the family name.

However, it turns out that everybody other than Zahra's father, Asad, definitely knew about the affair. Nadim's mother and brother catalogue in detail the squabbles they heard of between Zahra and her mother, who was utterly opposed to the marriage. Riaz's flattering description of what Zahra allegedly said in the police station regarding her mother's open-minded attitude towards love-marriages was not borne out by my own interview with her. I asked her whether, with hindsight, if Zahra or Nadim had approached her and said that they wished to marry, would she have allowed it to happen? She firmly replied in the negative. 'No. No. How can it ever be?' she said. 'He isn't even of the same *biradari* as us.' Riaz underplayed the importance of caste differences. For him, more important than caste was a man's education, of which Nadim had none. It was on these grounds that he felt that Nadim was not worthy of Zahra. For Nadim's family of Sheikhs, Zahra's caste of Saifies were fellow Muslims first and foremost. Nadim's mother argued: 'They are *Mussalman* and we are *Mussalman*. There was no caste problem. But she has lived in luxury. She will have to *adjust* here.' Even after what the family had been through, Zahra's mother was not willing to pay lip service to the position of perhaps having accepted Nadim as her son-in-law. If Nadim's family is to be believed, Zahra was put in *purdah* only after the affair had become known to members of her family.

Nadim's family explained that Riaz's friendship with Nadim was very close, and that he was regarded as a son in Nadim's family. This was because Riaz himself was having an affair with a girl, and it is at Nadim's terrace that they would rendezvous. Riaz would spend hours of any given day at Nadim's home. When Nadim apparently asked Riaz to take his proposal to marry Zahra to her father, Riaz flatly refused and broke off all contact with Nadim. As Nadim's brother says: 'It is the way of the world to spread muck about others and keep oneself looking clean'. Riaz and his mother did their utmost to supervise Zahra and keep her away from Nadim. Even Zahra's younger sisters knew of the affair, and had seen Zahra spend time with Nadim on his terrace. A month before Zahra eloped there was yet another conflagration. One of Zahra's younger sisters said to Nadim's sister: 'I know who she comes to visit and why she comes to your house'. Apparently Nadim's sister replied, 'I don't know who she comes to visit. If you do, then catch them.'

Clearly, more and more people were learning of the affair, which by now had become an open secret. The most indicting piece of evidence comes from Alok Prasad who in other parts of the interviews insists that Zahra's father was ignorant of the affair, but here unwittingly exposes Asad. He says to me at one point: 'See, what was revealed at the end of the case was that the parents knew everything about Zahra's affair, and they even had *proof* of the girl's relationship. They did not want her to leave because they had initiated talks for her engagement with two or three families and were trying to get her married.' This confirms the suspicion that not only would her family have known about the affair, but they were seeking to arrange a marriage for her before things came to a head. Clearly, they must have suspected an elopement when she went missing.

The remarkable nature of her story made me wonder whether it was indeed similar to the story of Munesh Solanki in that the family discovers that their daughter has eloped and makes (to use Riaz's phrase) 'some other *drama*' from it. That is to say, was it conceivable that Zahra did elope that morning and that her family did the '*drama*' to make it appear that she had been kidnapped? If they knew that Zahra had eloped, they were trying to keep that out of the public focus, and instead indict someone who was anyway an enemy. In doing this they could either retrieve her themselves (with the police and the media set on a false trail) or they could mourn her and blame Rizvi and the police when she couldn't be found, thus symbolically killing off the renegade. Most indicting of all was their determination to control the police investigation. They held demonstrations and vigils to demand Rizvi's arrest, and they used 'political influence' from an MP to pressurise the local police through the Delhi Commissioner of Police himself. Curiously, they intervened when Nadim was taken in for questioning, leaving room for the suspicion that they didn't want Nadim to confess that Zahra had eloped and thus give the game away. Finally, it was their doing that the case was transferred to a police team of their choosing, a move that does nothing to indicate that they are anything but guilty of at least some of the '*drama*'.

Despite all disclaimers, we can safely conclude that Zahra's family was only too aware of her affair. We can only speculate as to whether she did tell them about her marriage or her pregnancy. More interesting is the way in which they sought to mani-pulate stereotypes about the good daughter they had ('a *religious-type* of girl', kept in *purdah*). Equally, we can see how she herself manipulates the stereotype of an abducted woman through her symbolism of the *dupatta* soaked in blood. If it was indeed Zahra who put the blood, then we have here a portrait of a self-abduction, designed to prevent the dishonour heaped upon the girl and boy, as well as both their families.

The Question of Agency

Elopement and abduction can be seen to sit at two extremes of a scale demonstrating 'agency'. One elopes of one's own free will, and one is abducted in clear violation of one's will. Despite these simple and adequate definitions, we are faced with the problem that in Delhi, cases of kidnapping often look at first like elopements, and cases of elopements can look like abductions or kidnappings. Of course, on the face of it, this does not help the police, nor does it help us to better understand elopements. What I am going to suggest, however, is that it is no accident that this confusion exists and thrives.

The police compare versions of events from different people, looking for inconsistencies to get at a socially acceptable version of the 'truth'. While these serve to represent a consensual version of 'what happened', the actual process of evaluating the different confessionals from various actors is plainly much more complex. The police were alerted to Nadim's involvement with Zahra be-cause he lied about his friendship with Riaz. However, they do not come up with a satisfactory 'truth' about whether or not Nadim was an active participant in the elopement. The police obtained from Zahra a version of the truth (she, after all, 'knew' what really had happened), and accepted her testimony as such because they had already exposed her lie (regarding her relationship and secret marriage to Nadim) and found a 'motive' for her leaving home. She was assumed to have no further motive to lie, because she had no honour to protect by lying any further, and nobody hypothesised as to whether she was covering up her family's guilt, as opposed to having indeed put the blood there herself. She had to present herself before a magistrate and assert that she had left home 'on her own'.

Here too, she was in all likelihood protecting Nadim who would be an easy target to vent the wrath of her family. By saying she left alone, Nadim was not implicated in her 'elopement'. Ironically, then, we have not just a self-abduction, but a lone elopement too. For the media, there was no room for anything but a narrow version of the truth. The news was that a girl who pretended to have been abducted had really eloped; and that at the end of the day, she was caught out.

Seen in a different light, however, Zahra's confessional in the police station and before the magistrate in court, are declarations of agency that stand in a diametrically opposite relationship to what she seems to express through the abduction that she herself staged. In the court she has to articulate and assert that she acted out of her own agency. The staged event in her home, however, was a deliberately inarticulate representation of her acting out of coercion. For the police, the court and the media, agency is about who was responsible for the event. Zahra accepts responsibility and that is where the police leave it. For us, however, it must mean something more than what is clearly only half the story. That is the only way in which we may begin to apprehend the paradox that Zahra did elope, but that Zahra never wanted to have to confess that she did.

Once Zahra had been recovered, the case was declared by Alok Prasad to have been *opened* (i.e. closed). But this was not strictly true. The case would have been *opened* if we knew exactly from where the blood came. Whoever put the blood on the floor that morning was responsible for transforming the elopement into an abduction. As I have shown, there was sufficient cause to believe that it was Zahra, but equally, there was a mounting pile of evidence which implied that it could have been her family. In the event that it was the latter, Zahra's corroboration of their story would have served to re-establish some shared ground with her natal family. In the light of the involvement of Asad's rival, however, it would have seemed logical that the police would have wanted to unearth who had staged the abduction. However, Alok Prasad's meticulous arrangement of the narrative concerning his investigations left this aspect of the case purposefully ambiguous.

When I pressed him about the blood he laughed and described the scene in the police station. Zahra and the teacher were questioned together and were asked by the police: 'Who got the blood?'

Both of them denied having obtained it, and when the police threatened them to tell the truth, both blamed the other. The police made no investigations at the nursing home directly opposite Zahra's house, and a few hundred metres away from the police station. Clearly then, the police felt it was not important to discover who had actually put the blood where it was that morning. Further, the sensitive manner in which Alok Prasad handled the case (he never let word get out to the press that Zahra was pregnant, or that she had been married for over three years) indicated that he was sympathetic to the emotional and social quagmire that Zahra's elopement had created.

The fact that we do not have a clear idea of who staged the abduction is as revealing as if we did. The unearthing in a police station and then a magistrate's court of some truths such as Zahra's love affair, her secret marriage and her pregnancy, were far too shameful for her or her family to have to deal with. In such a fraught and destructive situation it served all concerned to agree on versions of the truth is which responsibility for the chaos was shifted elsewhere. In doing so, everybody had a chance to deny the agency they had in events that had gone so desperately wrong. This need to shift the blame is something that Alok Prasad clearly recognised and accepted. It allowed a space for reconciliation, at least as a hoped-for possibility, in the future. It is because he steadfastly refused to investigate who had actually obtained the blood that Rizvi, Asad's arch rival, was able to call off their feud and empathise with his 'friend' over the tragedy of an eloping daughter. If Zahra had put the blood there herself, her family would know that it was their honour along with her own that she sought to protect in her web of deceit. But if it was her family who staged the abduction, then Zahra's acceptance of the blame might serve as a basis for her family to forgive her.

Notes

1. These lines are taken from Alok Dhanva's Hindi poem, '*Bhagi hui larkiyan*' ('The Girls who Eloped'), published in his collected poems '*Duniya roz banti hai*' (1998: 41–46). The translation is my own, though lines 7 and 8 are from the translation done by B.K. Paul and Roma Paul, in K. Satchidanandan (1993: 83–87). I am grateful to Tarun Bharati

for bringing Alok Dhanwa's poetry and the Paul's translation to my attention, and to Aishwarj Kumar for finding me the original poem in Hindi.

2. Singh and Uberoi point out that women's magazines in India warn female readers that if romance and courtship hasn't culminated in marriage by the age of 20, a girl should opt for an arranged marriage before she misses the boat (1994: 101).

3. My description of *love-cum-arranged* marriages derives from my informants' discussions and use of this term during my fieldwork. However, Uberoi describes the same phenomenon as 'arranged love marriage'. She specifies two different forms: where a person's choice is subsequently endorsed by the parents and where a couple proceed to 'fall in love' with each other after an arranged marriage (Uberoi and Singh 2006: 36).

4. In *The Hindustan Times*, '"Dead" girl appears in court, with a husband: Says she eloped; family "claimed" wrong body, cremated it' by Anju Sharma, 27-3-1998, p. 1, New Delhi.

5. Incredible though this story is, it was by no means the only one of its kind I encountered during my fieldwork. For instance, a similar case surfaced in Jaipur in which a married woman (Rajkumari) whom the police had registered dead (and even recovered and identified her skeleton) and whose husband and five accomplices were arrested on charges of murder, appeared before a duty magistrate and confessed she had eloped with her lover Rajkumar to Bihar and that she hadn't been killed and was very much alive. See *The Hindustan Times*, '"Murdered" woman appears in court', 31-5-1997, p. 7, New Delhi. In both these stories, the more terrifying question that isn't asked in either of the two articles is: who were the dead women whose bodies were found and why were they unclaimed? The ability of the police to find dead bodies or skeletal remains of hurriedly buried women hints at the terrifying reality of commonplace and sometimes lethal violence against women whose mobility between parental and natal homes makes it easy to conceal their absences and even their deaths.

6. This is reminiscent of Strathern's reminder (drawing from Gell) that 'person's do not exist independently of concepts of them' (2005: 84); so that 'a woman is a mother to a child not through her physical presence or acts but as a term in a relation'. In this instance, by seeking to make the daughter dead, her parents attempt to erase her existence as part of the terms of the relation. They leave her physically unmolested but attack instead the concept of their having a living daughter. If her part of the relation could somehow be erased, her love-marriage would not be their problem. Of course, the difficulty is that real or symbolic death does not erase a relation; what it generally does is to make the representation of that concept of the relation one-sided; which in this instance

would free up the parents to reinvent and represent their daughter in a better light.

7. This can raise problems for diligent police officers who may suspect elopement but who are pressed to file a kidnapping/abduction charge. In the case of one of my informants, the local Station House Officer filed a missing person complaint after she ran away from home. The precipitating event was her mother's discovery of a note on which she had written the English words 'I love you' to her tuition-master. After her disappearance, her father insisted on going up the police hierarchy until a sympathetic senior officer leaned on yet another local Station House Officer to accept a 'kidnapping' case, because the girl was under-age. This was triumphantly discussed in a Hindi newspaper article at the time. *Dainik Jagran*, 1992, '*Teen mah purav agva ki gayi chhatre ka surag nahin*' ('No trace of the schoolgirl abducted three months ago'), 18-7-1992, New Delhi.

8. The *Times of India*, 'Armed men abduct 19-year-old girl, kill accomplice by mistake', 13-4-1998, p. 4, New Delhi.

9. The *Hindustan Times*, '18-year-old girl kidnapped at gunpoint in Ghaziabad', 13–4–1998, p. 5, New Delhi.

10. In the *Hindustan Times*, 'Abducted Girl Returns', 23-1-1998, p. 5, New Delhi.

11. Interestingly, for many young couples, *dargahs* (mausoleums) and temples like the one in Kalkaji were the perfect place to meet and spend time together. In the face of social scorn, lovers seek the blessings of saints and gods.

12. Indeed, the gendering of elopement is so forceful it would seem, across India, that we even find instances where women seeking to elope with other women must do so by mimicking the dominant form. Thus, 'A 19-year-old girl masquerading as a man kidnapped a teenage girl from her home at Bokakhat in central Assam. On the basis of an FIR filed by the girl's father, the police arrested the abductor on Wednesday. The kidnapper, identified as Kiran Tanti of Hatpani Tea Estate, had kidnapped Biju Kalandi of Naharani Tea Garden of June 21 and wanted to marry her, the police said.' In *The Asian Age*, 'India Notes: Girl kidnaps Another Girl', 26-6-1998, p. 3, Mumbai.

13. Though this case received widespread press coverage, I am withholding details of this, as well as details of the identity of all the people involved. In my interviews with members of the public in the area, and through off-the-record interviews with the police, I learnt of some aspects of the case that were common knowledge, but had been withheld from the press for fear of causing more scandal. It is to use this very valuable information that I have chosen to maintain the confidentiality of the case. As one police officer valiantly said to me: 'It is the girl's reputation that I have to protect'.

14. Nizamuddin is the area in Delhi named after the fourteenth century sufi saint Nizammudin Auliya.
15. A *dua* is a prayer to God for help. It was a measure of the family's desperation that they offered up an individual prayer for every single bean in the sack—as if it were a string of prayer beads.
16. The police presented the couple before a magistrate, with their marriage certificates and proof that Zahra wasn't a minor. She gave her statement that she had been married to Nadim for some years and that she had left home of her own accord. The magistrate discharged them with the ruling that 'no case has been made out' and the original abduction case filed by Zahra's family was cancelled.
17. The headline states the area of the city where she comes from. I have replaced it with 'Delhi'.
18. The use of women's bodies and their honour to steal a victory over one's enemies is as prevalent in India as it is in celluloid Bollywood films where the villain rapes a woman to establish the extent of his villainy. Take for instance a newspaper article in April 1998, which describe two separate cases reported in a single day, in Delhi. One woman was raped by her husband's brother after an argument. The latter was unemployed and because of this, 'there were constant quarrels in the family'. Another woman was raped by her husband's friend, who 'had an argument over some trivial issue' and subsequently, 'caught his friend's wife and raped her'. In *The Hindustan Times*, 'Two Women Raped to Avenge Insult', 16-4-1998, p. 3, New Delhi.
19. This, of course, is quite a literal representation of the idea that a daughter will be incorporated into her husband's kin, and to some extent, will be 'lost' to her father at marriage. A son will live with his parents and swell the ranks of his lineage through the birth of his own sons.
20. In Hindi, the phrase used was *'Larki pe dhag lag jathi hain'*, *'Dhag'* literally means 'stain'.
21. There is another legal context in which this has resonance. Families of eloping children invariably file theft charges along with those of abduction and kidnapping, alledging that the abductor took jewellery or money too, thus adding a further criminal element to their actions.
22. Indeed, one reason why I maintained this thesis was that literally within 10 metres of Zahra's house is a medical clinic/nursing home where blood would have been available to them even at 8.30 in the morning when they discovered Zahra had eloped. Further, I was frustrated to discover that despite the seemingly exhaustive investigation, the police had failed to get any evidence whatsoever about where the blood did in fact come from. Of course, everybody could have realised that if Asad and his family had put the blood there when they discovered that Zahra had eloped, they would be charged with misleading the police. Furthermore, the transfer of the case, at a

point when things were really hotting up, indicates that Asad did not want the case to '*open*'. If it was not meant to be resolved, perhaps it happened only because the local police took offence at the transfer, pursued the case and managed to rough up Nadim enough for him to reveal Zahra's whereabouts. We can see how its public unravelling with the police having found the eloping couple could have come as a surprise to Asad. Zahra, who has irreversibly damaged her reputation by having eloped, is made responsible for the blood, as if it was she who sought to disguise her elopement, not her family. Of course, this is merely a theory, and when I put it to people such as Alok Prasad, they went to great pains to insist that this was not the case. Additionally, Riaz went to great lengths to convince me that the police would have nailed his father if they thought he was guilty of 'having created such a big *drama*'. I am cynical of this argument. The transfer of the case, their wealth and willingness to bribe (Riaz says his father 'bought the media' to publicise his innocence in the rape-case), and their alleged political connections could have ensured that their version was the one that was released to the public.

23. Riaz had loaned Nadim an electric generator to ensure an uninterrupted supply of electricity. Without this, Nadim was losing business because the continuous power failures in Delhi meant that he could not use his sewing machine and stitch the clothes of his customers in time for the Muslim festival of Id.

4

Failed Love

Lake of sorrow
Ocean of tears
Valley of death
End of life

(A warning painted with hearts on the back of a Delhi auto-rickshaw, 1997)

An Anthropological Analysis of
Agency in Love-Marriage

All love-marriage biographies involve degrees of 'success' and 'failure', arising from a mediation of the principles that bind community and define not-community. This chapter explores the extent to which 'success' and 'failure' for love-marriage couples is determined by the compromises they make as regards their personal or individual desires when these come into conflict with social norms and the determinants of 'community'. This process of compromise, as detailed in the previous chapter, is described as a negotiation between community and not-community, and it is this negotiation which I will utilise to posit an analysis of agency for love-marriage couples. Agency is often mistakenly interpreted as implying a combination of freedom and efficacy, without the all-important counterpart of accountability. An anthropological analysis of love-marriage biographies points towards the conceptualisation of agency as a double-edged sword: in Delhi, persons are viewed as both agents of self, and agents of groups. This allows us to see how actions aren't just unmediated acts of 'individuality', but are simultaneously actions of persons-as-accountable to groups to which they are assumed to belong.

I must point out that the definitive and judgemental 'end-edness' of the terms 'success' and 'failure' are misleading, and are being used as social categories, not social facts. In the two love biographies presented here (Subhash and Indu; Kamiyar and Priya), the love was said to have 'failed'; but of course it may just have failed temporarily, with life throwing up changed circumstances and new and different opportunities for reunion and 'success'. I saw this 'end-edness' and its continuous invocation in discussions of love-marriages as integral to the need to establish closure—as if a more nuanced assessment (for instance, 'some marriages succeed in some ways and fail in others') was quite unacceptable to my informants. This is explicable with reference to the very definite criteria by which marriages are open to social adjudication in India. The criteria are concerned with the domestication of female sexuality through primary marriage, the role of the marriage in forging appropriate affinal and kinship relations, and the appropriate expansion of the social group through the birth of children, in particular, males. Since love-marriages invariably are assumed by their very nature to 'fail' on the first two of these three counts, they are virtually doomed to the stereotype that all such marriages are 'failures'.[1]

Such is their own insecurity over this matter that, when hearing that I was a 'researcher', numerous couples in the court or the temple would approach me, often on their wedding day to enquire whether love-marriages *could* be '*successful*'? Clearly, they themselves were unable to disregard the social consensus that unhappiness, separation or divorce was on the cards. In this chapter, I use the terms 'success' and 'failure' to indicate those love-affairs that are able to consummate themselves in marital togetherness, and those that fail in achieving such a consummation. I am omitting the inverted commas, and use the terms as a shorthand for the discussion that follows.

The agency of couples is evidently present in both cases of failure and success, but it is noticeable that these are made more explicit (by my informants) when love fails and when there is little to gain from keeping matters disguised or undisclosed. Central to this chapter is an attempt to examine the issue of agency through the perspective of failed love. Strathern argues that one way of examining agency would be to ask 'what constitues *effective action?*' (1987: 23, emphasis mine). Although these exceptional cases of failure (*in-effective action*) serve to shed light upon less dramatic ones, it is wrong to assume that these latter instances represent a counter-foil of 'normalcy' against the exceptional failed love instances. Most love-marriages involve some degree of emotional or social trauma, leaving a sense that 'normalcy' is a privileged state that they only rarely achieve. Failures highlight instances that aren't evident in other marriages and also allow us to see how inadequate mediations between the community and not-community cause failure. In the final analysis of these two biographies, we are able to separate out some of the elements consisting in agency which outweighed the others, making a negotiated settlement—the ultimate goal of most love-marriages—virtually an impossibility.

The previous chapter on elopements tried to deal with the paradox of women creating victimhood in order to conceal agency—the complex resolving itself as a tempering of agency. Thus, actions that seem on the surface as illustrating 'agency' must be much more scrupulously investigated because this is neither a clear-cut demonstration of individual will nor a rejection of corporate values, but rather comprises a careful and deliberate calculus of action. The singular intentionality that the word 'agency' assumes is deeply antithetical to the ways in which most people actually conduct their lives. In elopement cases, women may choose to adopt strategies of oppressedness to stave-off social disapproval that would otherwise condemn the un-negotiated act. Strathern points to this complexity when she argues that the impact or efficacy of actions is registered by 'what people compute to be the intentions behind it' (1987: 23). Thus, the intentionality *and* effect of the action ('agency') is to be found in the anticipation (and predetermination) of the reaction.[2]

In seeking to determine the extents of community and the negotiations of this by individuals, this chapter once again re-examines the mutual exploration of the boundaries between community and not-community through the issue of agency. An anthropological examination of agency in love-marriages should primarily be about the ways in which the complex of love-marriages are a contested site in which agency (in the sense theorised by Alfred Gell, where agency implies 'doing')[3] is invoked and revoked *within* its social context. This balancing (invoking, revoking, stressing, and disguising) is what I describe as the calculus of love. Consequently, I am not concerned with the 'principles' of love, romance and courtship in their abstraction, but rather examine the ways in which agents (informants) use notions of 'love' as having a bearing on their actions. I am concerned with the social relations and contested actions that come about due to 'love'; in other words, I examine how love-marriage couples go about negotiating and balancing their 'love' against other equally important factors—for instance, their sense of familial obligation to their parents and their own sense of honour. Equally, I examine the ways in which individuals and couples are the loci of *both*, the cause and effect of action (Strathern 1987: 24).

Failed love-marriages, such as I am about to describe, highlight the actual dialectic of mediation in love-marriages. The negotiations of love-marriage couples are driven by the needs and exigencies of their social relationships; therefore, it is only correct that they should be examined in that light. Rather than providing solutions to the 'problems' of agency, Strathern points out that academic work provides a suitable range of issues that encapsulate a particular problematic with regards to 'agency':

Are persons the authors of their own acts? Or do they derive their efficacy from others? ... [W]hat is seen as the origin of particular events, outcomes, sets of behaviour? The concept of agency is a shorthand for these questions. It refers to the manner in which people allocate causality or responsibility to one another, and thus sources of influences and directions of power. To ask about agency is also to ask about *how people make known to themselves that ability to act* (ibid.: 23, emphasis mine).

As Strathern describes it, we need to explore the ways in which love-marriage couples make known to themselves their ability to act, but equally, we need also examine the ways in which others make known to them the limits of their actions and the fact that they will be brought to account. Thus, agency as 'effective action' is tempered with 'accountable action', and this makes explicit the ways in which love-marriage couples are constrained; both in the manner in which they build their relationships, and the ways in which they construct their actions.

Strathern's attempts to explore agency lead her to examine 'personhood', and it is striking that she comes to the discussion of Melanesian personhood in the *Gender of the Gift* (1988: 348–49) from McKim Marriot's transactional analysis of Indian social relations. Marriot's conclusions about the 'divisiblity' of South Asian personhood provides one strand of my own attempt to conceptualise agency in love-marriage. In his model, persons in South Asia are not thought of as 'individuals' (indivisible bounded units) but 'dividuals'—absorbing and giving out to other persons heterogeneous material influences 'that may then reproduce in others something of the nature of the persons in whom they have originated' (1976: 111). In the case of love-marriages, circumstances demand that persons maintain a capacity for being *both*, biomorally affected 'dividuals' and 'individuals' acting as such. The dialectic for love-marriage couples is that they must juggle these two categories such that in some contexts they explicitly need to act as indivisible bounded units (often to safeguard selfhood), while in others their selfhood is transactional and dependant on their ability to transform themselves both internally (for instance, in transforming their romantic love into a sense of obligation) and socially. I retain the use of the term 'individual' because I do not wish to imply that love-marriage couples as 'dividuals' transcend the historical facts of legal personhood in urban Delhi, or that they are somehow subsumed within a Dumontian collectivity, but ask the reader to bear in mind that when I speak of individuals I mean both the capacity for boundedness, and the capacity for expansiveness.

The significance of Marriot's construction for the argument in this book lies less in its material and biomoral sphere and more as a principle of transactions in 'selfhood'. The dilemmas of love-marriage agency are well encapsulated by the maxim of actions causing mutual realignments between self and social relations. Selfhood in India, as Das has rightly pointed out, is constituted through two processes: an individual's attempts to 'break through the limits of community and live on its margins', as well as through the community's attempt to 'colonise the life-world of the individual' (Das 1995: 15–17). In other words, both individual and community are consubstantiated in the selfhood of persons. This has an obvious and pertinent relevance to love-marriage *couples* (the same principle that applies to individuals applies to couples, i.e. what they are is a result of both self and social relationships), such that the 'couple' as an entity come to possess *agency and personhood* because, in this conception, they are linked. The usefulness of this particular construction will be made obvious in my analysis of the ethnography where I sometimes talk about the agency of the individual lover, and at others of the agency of the loving couple.

In order to think about agency in love-marriages, I posit a five-fold conceptual model of ethics or values which I hope would encompass and 'embed' agency in the specific context of love-marriage in Delhi. It is the negotiation of these five factors in the selfhood and social relationships that is the primary goal of the love-marriage individual/couple. These are:

1. Honour as a code of individual and social conduct
2. Sexuality (as a source of shame and strength)
3. Legal 'Rights' (Individual and Community 'Rights')
4. Consent (as a means of representing agency)
5. Love ('Loving' as Agency)

The deployment of these concepts, in complex and overlapping ways, provides the context for an examination of the agency of the men and women whose love failed. They do not form a hegemony of categories, but constitute the subjects of debate through which I examine agency in love-marriage. 'Love' is thus viewed as a source of agency in a transformative process, not in the sense of transforming emotions or 'cultural forms', but in the anthropological here-and-now of transforming social relationships.

As we shall see, there aren't specific gendered parallels between these five factors: which is to say, for example, that the men do not uphold honour while the women safeguard their sexuality, but rather, that all the four people discussed in the love-biographies that will follow seem to be following radically different strategies from each other.[4] In itself, this is a fact of enormous significance because it indicates the apparent lack of a joint strategy (and its concomitant disadvantages), and the diverging conceptions of love, honour and power (both social and legal) that prefigure such different strategies. Love-marriage, it would seem, fails because externalities prise apart the notional conjoining and appropriate balancing of legal agency, love, honour, sexuality and consent, making it impossible for the couple to find a mediated compromise of each.

Agency Generalised: Honour, Sexuality, 'Rights', Consent and Love

It is necessary, however, to add a small caveat here; to alert the reader to the complexity of the problem at hand in this study of urban values and agency. An anthropologist familiar with the diversity of social groups, castes and ethno-religious communities in north India would no doubt pour scorn upon an attempt towards a homogenising discourse of pan-community honour (*izzat*), or female sexuality (*shakti*). Both terms when used in Delhi have specific cultural, linguistic and political meanings. For instance, *izzat* is an Urdu word meaning 'honour', and it has strong Muslim connotations.[5] *Shakti* is a Hindi word invoking the 'power to create and destroy', associated with Hindu female goddesses like *Kali* and *Durga*. *Shakti* is often described as existing in all things and beings, but as a feminine principle, it is especially active in women. In Hindu nationalist formulations from the turn of the 19th century onwards, *shakti* has been invoked for political ends such as the revitalisation of the nation characterised as 'Mother India'.[6] However, as we shall see, both *izzat* and *shakti* are widely used in their more generalised sense by many people in Delhi; *izzat* to imply 'caste honour', women's modesty, and the correct recognition of hierarchy, and *shakti* to indicate the potentially potent aspects of a woman's strength.

There is enormous diversity in a modern city like Delhi, but this fact should not detract from the formidable consensus against love-marriages, and in favour of groups and individual agents maintaining and upholding what people describe as all that is '*social*' (hierarchical social structure and values). During my fieldwork, the notion of *izzat*/honour in conjunction with *sharam* (shame) cropped up repeatedly as something of a definitive north Indian principle that both guided and justified the actions of those who opposed love-marriages. *Izzat* was used across the board, and occasionally with no regard to narrowly defined 'caste' (a matter of 'religion' and 'ritual'), but rather to 'secular' considerations of class status and standing, both increasingly important preoccupations in the urban milieu of Delhi.[7]

For a number of anthropologists, *izzat* is of critical importance because it overlaps with 'credit' and therefore has an explanatory value in economic terms, but equally because it is spoken of in such immediate and emotive terms. It seems to serve as an overarching reference point that is used to explain the morality behind the sense of obligation that underpins the functioning of the social order. *Izzat* represents one's lineal respectability and is a register of the social judgements of one's actions. It serves as a resource of power, status, rank, authority and, most valued of all it serves as an indicator of authenticity. To be without *izzat* is to be a person of no social value. The most common punishment for dishonour (*beyizzati*) is, consequently, ostracism—the denial of respect through the termination of social intercourse.

Izzat is recognition from others. Due to its association with ritually and socially appropriate behaviour, *izzat* is adjudged by others, and bestowed by others. It is maintained through the proper transferral of a girl's sexuality from father to arranged-marriage husband. It also invokes practices of veiling, separation and avoidance, and associated forms of proper behaviours that are gendered. For men, *izzat* lies in the maintenance and defence of the honour of the patrilineage against all external threats, be they in the realms of politics, kinship or religion. For women, it lies in the 'shyness' and shame of female sexuality, such that a woman's sexuality is both undermined and controlled. Minturn speaks of the ways in which *izzat* is held to lie with the father's lineage, who are 'charged with the obligation of raising virtuous daughters' (1993: 202). Thus even a married woman who dishonours her husband's home through an extra-marital liaison is not usually punished by her husband's kin, but rather is sent back to her natal home for appropriate disciplining and shaming.[8]

The sexuality of an unmarried girl is of particular importance to her father because a proper arranged marriage involves his lineage's gift of a virgin to the bride-takers. Virtually every ethnographer of the *purdah-belt* draws attention to the fact that a love-marriage, an affair or a dalliance can bring forth crushing penalties upon the girl, or upon both the girl and the boy (Mandelbaum 1993; Freed 1971; Lindholm 1982). In many instances, they report that it is expressly desirous that the girl be killed by her father and brothers so as to establish 'closure' over the dishonour that has already been caused (Minturn 1993: 212–16; Das 1997: 214; Chowdhry 1997). Parry, in fact, points out that historically, amongst some Rajput clans, female infanticide was a solution to the dangers posed to the patrilineage by female sexuality.[9]

Most of the ethnographers of north Indian society would, it seems to me, concur that marriage is an event that evokes anxiety and is fraught with risks. It is a rite of passage for the individual and is a liminal time for the kinship group as lineages and individual families re-negotiate their *izzat* and subsequently, their standing, and where propitiating rituals are instantiated. In marriages, *izzat* is flaunted, disguised or lost altogether. As a social celebration, marriage has exacting criteria for the ways in which one's family name is definitively enhanced or permanently destroyed. What is interesting about marriage and its relationship with *izzat* is that marriage is an arena in which achieved rank (personal or family reputation, prestige in job, educational qualifications, career prospects of a prospective spouse) can be and is converted into status (the 'permanent and immutable attribute of groups'), albeit through the 'surreptitious' mechanisms of hypergamous marriage alliances (Parry 1979: 271). In other words, marriage has the potential to transform achieved capital into kinship capital, and thus retains an unparalleled importance in both individual and group aspirations. The downside of this process is that an inappropriate love-marriage 'wastes' achieved rank and even lowers group status in the all-important arena of *izzat*. This explains why parents of children who have had love-marriages bemoan their fate and all that they were able to achieve for the child because it was never reciprocated by being converted into positive and enhancing *izzat* and kinship capital, and instead was used to disgrace and dishonour the family and the social group.[10]

Das (1997) provides an interesting assessment of honour amongst Punjabis by arguing that honour for them is about overcoming natural urges—indeed, using 'masks'. It is thus honourable for a mother to ignore the crying of her own baby and to be seen to cuddle only the children of her sisters'-in-law. This establishes the pre-eminence of the moral and social value ascribed to communal living in one household (an action that brings honour), whilst denigrating the 'natural' (and divisive) bonds that evidently exist between a mother and the children she feeds at her breast (an action that is to be avoided as dishonourable). Acts that arise from the biological stratum are not to be denied, but are merely to be ascribed a 'back seat' (preferably out of sight of others) and underplayed, to establish a concurrence with the predominant social form. Thus 'love' and desire, which are seen to be 'natural', are not denied (for instance, however immoral, it is acknowledged that some men visit prostitutes because it is in their 'nature'), but are meant to be kept away from public view.

This explains why some parents may even turn a blind eye to their own child having a romance, but are incensed and outraged when confronted with the actuality of a love-marriage. I met a number of couples where the boy's parents had coerced him into an arranged marriage despite their knowledge of his love for someone else, and had explicitly assured the son that he could carry on with his girlfriend, so long as he fulfilled his social obligations towards his parents, wife and affines.[11] The argument is that if 'love' must exist, it should be veiled (remain in *purdah*), and should not be flaunted through a legitimating 'marriage'. It is quite striking then, that the debate about concubinage in the 1870s is essentially the same in the 1990s, though it must be added that it is quite possible that fewer women in present-day Delhi are willing to accept the status of 'concubines', lovers or illegitimate second 'wives'.

Also of interest are the ways in which the issue of 'consent' of the marrying couple is manipulated and occasionally entirely co-opted by the family concerned to force their offspring into arranged marriages. Equally interesting is the predetermined emphasis of many love-marriage couples on obtaining their *parents'* consent prior to their marriage. When juxtaposed with the manipulation of individual consent in the context of the court or temple during the process of a love-marriage (Chapters 2 and 3), we have seen that the issue of consent isn't as simple as the legal notion makes it out to be. 'Consent' is often invoked as a means of breaking up the marriage through legal loopholes. Cases of marriage are made voidable due to the allegation that either the girl or the boy was under-age, insane (and not capable of giving 'informed consent') or was forcefully or fraudulently led into the marriage. In police cases involving kidnapping/elopement, the issue of consent is manipulated to 'prove' a lack of agency. However, the counterpart to this phenomenon is the desire of couples to marry *only* with the consent of their parents, thus indicating that the issue of consent (and its representation of agency as an ability to declare the efficacy of a person) is linked to the efficacy of others. The efficacy of a couple derives as much from others as it does from themselves, a feature that will crop up repeatedly in this chapter. Furthermore, the contest between individuals and groups over which unit constitutes the appropriate repositories of 'rights' (the post-independence legal system dismissing the group or 'community' as an appropriate unit of agency, and giving legal precedence to the individual) is examined in this chapter.

One aspect of *izzat* that hasn't been sufficiently explored is that it is crucially a corporate value. One's personal *izzat* (or indeed, the *izzat* of a nuclear, or 'joint-family' household in the city) can be enhanced alone, but it can also be damaged or ruined by the actions of others such as the extended family or, more often, the entire clan or lineage (or even the reputation of the whole 'village' from which the family descends)—be these units scattered over the city or located in the rural hinterlands. When honour is lost, there is a sort of domino effect upon the *izzat* of all the kin. A striking example of this was during my fieldwork when the love-marriage of a Muslim woman to her lover (a previously married Muslim man belonging to a lower caste in the same village) outside Delhi became politicised and received extensive media coverage.[12] Following this, it was declared that none of the affines who normally arranged marriages with her people would accept women from that village again. Not only this, it was reported in the press that as a punishment for her brazen acts of defiant sexuality, all her female kin, who were already married, were sent back to their natal homes by their husbands as punishment for the collective dishonour that they brought by virtue of their kinship to her. Events such as these serve to constitute groups and emphasise the nature of marriage as a site of critical importance in securing or safeguarding honour.

However, it is important to note that it isn't just women who are meant to guard against dishonouring the lineage. Geeta, a woman I worked with, had eloped with her lover Ajay, and lived with him for four years (we will see more of them in the concluding chapter). However, Ajay was forced by his family to agree to an arranged marriage, principally through threats that if he didn't he would jeopardise the honour of the family and ruin his sisters' chances for marriage. His girlfriend's mother told me that another factor was the large dowry his marriage would net from the village girl whom he was being betrothed to, because this would then be 'recycled' to provide the dowry for his younger sisters' marriages. However, the fact that Ajay was publicly known to have a lover, with whom he had had a child, jeopardised his sisters' chances anyway, and up until I left Delhi the parents had been unable to arrange their marriages. Thus, the corporate aspect of honour can serve as a significant deterrent for many love-marriage couples who are reluctant to heap dishonour upon 'innocent' family or lineage members.

Finally, we come to the parameters of 'love' itself in our attempt to understand agency. As I already pointed out in Chapter 2, the meanings ascribed to romantic love (*pyar, ishq, mohobbat* are dependent upon the context in which they are used, with couples describing their romantic love as almost spiritual and 'pure' of physical contamination, and families viewing it as an anti-social sentiment that subverts the smooth functioning of the social order. However, there also exist valorisations of 'love' that present it as enabling, empowering and even as a social phenomenon of political significance.[13] Again, these are problematic generalisations because I often encountered couples who were engaging in 'love-marriages' (marriages of choice) but who would themselves berate 'love' (interpreting it in the corporeal, sexual sense) as selfish, and would qualify their marriage with more positive resonance's such as 'same caste marriages', or as temporary measures before their 'arranged' marriage (in other words, a love-cum-arranged marriage).[14] Other than this, there is the issue of what love means in Delhi, and broadly, this can be characterised as love as failure (*gham*, or 'the joy of eternal longing', the longing of the lover for the beloved, which almost by definition is never a means to an end but an end in itself), and love as success (the ecstasy of lovers uniting, love as a means to an *affair* or more commonly, marriage).[15]

Gham is characterised by Majnu ('the one possessed') in the popular and ancient folk tale of 'Laila & Majnu' (Nizami 1997), a man who is contemptuous of temporal success and who would rather be regarded as a complete 'failure' in life than as someone who surrendered his longing for his beloved, Laila (Mukhia 1999: 868–74). Indeed, while my informants never once used the Urdu word '*gham*', they elaborated this form of near-mystical devotion to the beloved very frequently, as did members of the public who occasionally denigrated and personified lovers as their most famous male icon, 'Majnu'. Thus a 'Majnu' dreams obsessively about his beloved but is unaffected by the likelihood of failure or the social scorn and disgrace to which he is subjected.[16] Instead, he derives a particular satisfaction from the act of yearning itself, and is unable to bring his love to fruition. The denigration of Majnu is not universal, and occasionally this form of love was valorised because it flourished through self-sacrifice and self-destruction, rather than culminating in success and subsequent social disruption. It does not represent a challenge to the status quo against love-marriages, because such love was doomed to failure. On the other hand, love as 'success' is not about the pleasures of 'longing', but the joys of actual togetherness and union.

In some ways, love as failure and success can be seen as love that is conceived as spiritual (felt in the spirit) rather than love as corporeal (felt in the flesh [Mukhia 1999]). These distinctions are important for our notions of negotiated agency because the conceptualisation of love as spiritual or corporeal has differing effects upon its ability to establish social legitimacy. Moreover, it is striking that spiritual love emphasises a moral (rather than a bodily) union and it thus represents itself as a synthesis of the notion of the individual lover (a capacity for expansion *as well as* a capacity for boundedness). In the notion of spiritual love, as represented by love-marriage couples, the physical boundaries of the body are represented as self-contained and intact (an 'individual'), but there is an exchange of *moral* substance ('pure' love) between the beloved and the lover. Thus, the 'bio' and 'moral' aspects of Marriot's 'dividual' can be strategically separated in order to represent something of a socially acceptable form of conjoining. Sexuality and desire (love as 'success' in consummation), on the other hand, implies 'dividuality'—the reconstitution of self and society through the contact of body parts, exchange of fluids and substances, and the emotional and social intertwining implicit in a love affair.

Agency and Legal 'Consent': Subhash and Indu[17]

Love-marriage couples are constantly stereotyped as having no regard for 'community' and corporate values such as those of 'honour'. In this section I examine a love-biography of a couple who were forced to separate because Subhash could not bring himself to dishonour his girlfriend's father. Their love and plans for marriage were destroyed when Indu was engaged (and subsequently married) to a boy of the 'same caste' by her parents in an arranged marriage. Subhash could not bring himself to break up his girlfriend's engagement to another man and/or elope and marry against her father's wishes. He sacrifices his love in order to maintain the honour of both their families. Despite the fact that Subhash and Indu were Brahmins, Subhash was at pains to point out that they were not of the *'same caste'*, nor were they of the same regional background. Subhash belonged to the Shukla *gotra*, while

Indu was a Kashmiri Pundit. Furthermore, Subhash came from a much poorer family than Indu, and this was a sticking point for her family. A jealous protector of his girlfriend's honour, Subhash now had to entertain the thought of her as another man's wife, and this drove him to attempt suicide three times in so many months, following the marriage. Ironically, Indu's sexuality which was so troublesome to her parents during her love affair is eventually transformed into a resource and a 'right' in her unconsummated arranged marriage.

Subhash, a poor boy living on the outskirts of Delhi, first met Indu in college. She was walking down a corridor when her photograph accidentally fell out of her book. Subhash jumped at the opportunity to be chivalrous. Photos, in the romantic courtship of the young, are precious things in Delhi; and being given a photo, particularly by a girl, is a clear symbol of reciprocating love. Girls, for their part, must be vigilant that their photos never fall into the hands of boys who may blackmail them. Equally, a boyfriend who is trusted with a photo must be a boy of good repute, for, should things go wrong, there is always the danger that he may use the photo to terrorise the girl and seek to dishonour her to her parents. Subhash says: 'I thought, girls should at the very least be careful with their photos! I returned it to her. She was very impressed. She said: "Other boys may have misused it".'

Subhash says that '*by-friend*' (as a friend) they used to talk in class, but that he hadn't found the courage yet to '*propose*' to her. When he did, he gave her a note. It said: 'I may or may not be right in this. It's not that you aren't worth loving'.[18] This sort of oblique 'proposal' follows a conventional pattern of male courtship in Delhi where professions of love are preferably ambiguous. The reason for this is that a declaration of love from a man is often assumed to automatically initiate a relationship because 'decent' women (the sort one proposes to) are seen as the recipients of desire rather than as desiring subjects themselves. However, men need to safeguard themselves from increasingly assertive women rejecting their love. If a woman declines, the man may feel it incumbent upon himself to ignore this and safeguard his sense of pride in ensuring that she does not give her love to anyone else. The Hindi phrase occasionally used to describe this sort of attachment in Delhi is '*marenge lekin chhodenge nahin*', which means, I would rather kill her than let her go.[19] Subhash, however, waited patiently for Indu's response. On the 3rd of April 1995, she gave him a small note on which she wrote that she liked him a lot. What did it say? 'That she *accepted*'. What did she accept? 'She accepted my proposal. She started loving me. She said, *"I-love-you"*.'

The playfulness of their affair continued unabated for two years, with Subhash visiting Indu's home when her parents were out, and Indu's siblings learning of her romance. At this point, both of them initiated dialogues with their respective parents in an attempt to alert them to their intention to marry and get them to agree. Subhash's father seemed amenable but Indu's parents remained angry and intransigent. Subhash explained this with reference to her 'living standard' which he described as being considerably higher than his own. Indu felt confident that she would eventually convince her father, and that he would concede to the marriage 'for the sake of the happiness' of their future children. Furthermore, she always maintained that no matter what, they would not marry without her parents' consent. It is clear in the case of Indu and Subhash that parental consent absolves them of all wrong-doing—so much so that the couple agree that they will not marry until this consent has been obtained.

This, however, wasn't meant to be. In July of 1997, Indu told Subhash about a *rishta* (marriage proposal) that had arrived in her home. She wanted Subhash to be aware of it. He explained the course of events to me:

> Following the exams, in July, it was her birthday. She told me that by January 1998 we would have to get married. I was happy, because I thought if we leave it too late, we won't be able to do it. Then she said, 'Before January my father will come to your home with the *rishta*'. See, the talk of her birthday which I liked so much was this: that before January, she would make her father agreeable and he would come to our house. She was still somehow determined that we would marry with their blessings. [...] After the exams, I spoke to my father in 1997. My *daddy* understood that I loved her a lot. [...] My sister told my father. My *daddy* asked me only one thing: what is her *caste*? I said to him, '*daddy*, what her *caste* is, I don't know. All I know is that she isn't of our *caste*.' In fact, she never ever asked me my *caste*. Till today, I know her *caste* only through my friends. We never spoke of it because it wasn't important.
>
> My father said: 'Now see, you have grown up so much that even if I forbid you it is possible you will still go ahead—and if I say yes, then

how do I say yes?'[20] So he said: 'We will marry you to her, but the only thing is that her people should be willing. Because, when we bring a girl of another home into our home, then at the very least her immediate family should be willing, if not all her people. Because when a girl goes from one home, then it is a question of the honour of that home.' So *daddy* was *agree*, and we both were very happy. We thought that if things were being settled so well, then the rest will also follow.

On the 21st of November we met. It was a Friday. I met her at her home. Her parents were not there. [...] On that day she said that she had told them [her parents] that if they didn't arrange our wedding by January, then she would marry me, and then they shouldn't say that they hadn't been warned.[21]

The 22nd was a Saturday, and the 23rd was a Sunday. We never used to phone each other on Sundays because on Sundays my *daddy* and brothers would be home and over there her *daddy* and brothers would be home, so we couldn't speak. Only Sundays. On every other day we spoke to each other all day. Then on Monday the 24th morning I got a call that she was engaged. As soon as she said this I put down the phone. After this on the 31st [of January, 1998] she was married...

Clearly, with hindsight, Subhash and Indu should have known better than to trust her parents to agree to her love-marriage to a lowly electrician. Such was the young couple's confidence in having their way that even when they met to discuss the *rishta* that had arrived in Indu's home, they didn't take any preventative steps, such as safeguarding their relationship in law through a secret court or temple marriage. Subhash felt that their marriage could only be initiated through an appropriate exchange of honour between the two families; not through the legal overwriting of family honour through a disgraceful court-marriage. Indu's cajoling of both Subhash and her parents illustrates her dilemma. She makes Subhash 'happy' (on her birthday) with her reassurances that she will make her father come to his house with a marriage proposal in the properly deferential manner that a bride-giver must adopt towards the bride-taker. This subordination, of a rich man to Subhash's poorer father, is pleasing to Subhash because it indicates the fullness with which the love-marriage will be domesticated as a 'proper' arranged-marriage, and the completeness with which he is able to fulfil his own father's conditions that the marriage must only take place with the girl's parents' approval. Subhash's father draws an interesting boundary between the necessary 'minimum conditions' for an honourable union between his son and Indu (his own calculus of honour), such that even if her entire kinship group isn't agreeable, then at least her own parents must be willing to ratify the marriage. This clearly illustrates the ways in which the nuclear family in the city may find it necessary (or inevitable) to dissociate from its larger social moorings in order to voice support or acquiesce to the love-marriage of a child. Implicit in this scenario is the symbolic inversion of status for Subhash's poorer parents, and the powerful ability of the union to enhance the status and *izzat* of Subhash's family.

For Indu's father, it is one matter to subordinate himself in the ritually appropriate ways of bride-givers to bride-takers when the affines in question are those of his own choosing. It is another matter altogether to have to enact this subordination to those whom he deems unfit for such an honour. Indu's real dilemma, therefore, lies in protecting Subhash's honour from her own father's dismissal of it. In the early years of a love-affair this is a particularly common phenomenon, where the purported 'equality' of a couple-in-love is protected from the starkly hierarchical and status designs of their families. However, despite Subhash's stated indifference to Indu's caste (to the extent that he claims it was never directly discussed between the two of them), it would be incorrect to assume that this indifference to 'difference' and hierarchy shows that couples like Subhash and Indu are so imbued by the *noblesse* of their love that they are somehow devoid of status or *izzat* value judgements.[22] For instance, Subhash, being a Brahmin himself, was particularly sensitive to his own lineage honour and would have been repulsed by any hint of himself or his father being dishonoured by Indu's people. The stereotype that such couples are devoid of all honour is therefore only one part of a complicated illusion. The mere fact of choosing one's own partner does not mean that couples are indifferent to honour as they still want their marriage to be an 'honourable' one. The fact that love-marriage couples must proceed in unorthodox ways when trying to arrange their marriages certainly makes the issue of honour a more delicate one, a fact that Subhash's father clearly recognises. It means, among other things, that negotiations between two sets of parents have to be indirect (through the couple) even if they do tacitly agree to the marriage. The couple also feels obliged to pretend to be indifferent to caste status. In this configuration, caste status is seen as a worldly matter whereas the justification for their love is that it is spiritual.

Indu was clearly more than just a 'traditional Indian girl' who confronted her parents with her desire to marry Subhash. Even though they were both from Brahmin families, they never considered themselves *'same caste'* because castes from different regions are not ordinarily compatible, and certainly have no regularised marriage exchange. The differences between their families in class terms was perhaps more of a hurdle for the couple. Indu accepted the vast economic difference between her own wealthy status as the daughter of a businessman and Subhash's meagre position as an electrician and the son of a lowly government servant. For her, honour came after love, and she was willing to challenge her parents through a court-marriage. Subhash, for his own part, ran his electric goods and repair shop in the front portion of the family quarters. If he challenged his parents by going ahead with his marriage to Indu, he might have lost his only source of income. Interestingly, he discounted this possibility, arguing that his father never tried to teach his sons through harsh words or threats. Instead, he always supported them, and even when they did terrible things, he consoled them with words that were meant to give them courage and strength. Clearly, Subhash's love for his parents was as meaningful and abiding as his love for Indu.

Honour and sexuality: Appropriating agency

The suddenness with which Indu's parents arranged her engagement and threw their life into turmoil is familiar from the narratives of many of the couples I worked with. However, it is clear that the warning signs were there all along, and that they were perhaps wilfully misread. For instance, Subhash and Indu dismissed the *rishta*, presumably on the basis that girls in urban India are commonly allowed the power of veto in arranged marriages. Capturing the initiative, Indu's parents managed to destroy Subhash and Indu's dreams. Subhash says he was absolutely 'shocked' by the news of Indu's engagement. Indu kept calling him that day and pleading with Subhash to find them a way out of the mess. Subhash himself felt that he had no *solution* because the engagement had already happened. He described his conversations with Indu:

> She said: 'Subhash. There were thirty people who came to do the engagement. Thirty people. If there had been two-three, or four or five

then I wouldn't have let the engagement happen. But there were thirty people.' See, the thing was *Shakti*... She had fought off all the threats and they knew that she would not concede, and that she never would. Then when those people arrived, her father said, '*Beta* [my child], these people...' *Emotionally* they *blackmailed* her. That now, you can choose to dishonour your father or keep his honour.[23] So then all she did was cry. What answer can you give to your father? Whatever clothes they gave her to wear her mother and sisters had to put on her. [...] That's how she got engaged. She kept saying to me: 'Find me a *solution*. There must be a way Subhash, so that we can be saved from this. I can't marry him.'

At that time, I don't know what had come over me. I kept saying, 'No, there is no *solution*. Your *engagement* has already happened. From one house the matter has spread to another.[24] Now what can I do? Perhaps even my family won't accept this marriage, if I break things there and bring you here to my home.' My mind was in such a terrible state that I didn't even want there to be a *solution*. On the 25th and 26th we spoke. On the 27th my people sent me away to attend a marriage at my sister-in-laws. When I went there I went crying. I was too upset. After 2 days I returned. I kept thinking, if there isn't a *solution*, then what am I doing alive?

Subhash's honour and selfhood are dependent on him maintaining his own father's honour, Indu's family's honour and that of a third party betrothed to his beloved. To go ahead and marry Indu would be to dishonour everybody and in so doing, to ruin his own sense of self. The sheer weight of impossible scenarios and socially suicidal '*solutions*' makes the contemplation of self-annihilation a constant and recurrent theme for many love-marriage couples.[25] Both Indu and Subhash find themselves separated—not so much by external force, but by the emotional bonds and appropriate behaviours demanded by the rules that they themselves in great part subscribe to. Indu could have denounced her father and dishonoured him before the 'thirty people' who came for the engagement by refusing to go ahead with it. Such disgrace at the hands of a daughter could certainly have had the potential to prevent the arranged marriage. Equally, Subhash had two months between the engagement and the wedding to find a viable *solution*. His treatment of Indu's engagement as a final and definitive act that transferred her honour from one home to another, considering their circumstances, is an extreme and unusually rigid reading of the situation. Engagements do break off, but usually with some amount of scandal in their wake. This wasn't a scenario that Subhash was willing to entertain. Tellingly, Subhash admits that after he heard of the engagement, he didn't even want there to be a solution. Evidently, he sees dishonour as an impossible solution, be this through a love-marriage in a court, or in a love-marriage subsequent to a broken engagement with a 'third' family. In this way, their desires are thwarted, but this happens in part through their own agency.

Subhash claims that Indu had the requisite strength (*shakti*) to resist her parents, but faced with disgracing a father amidst an entire community of elders, she chose to sacrifice her own person to the honour of her parents. In the anthropological literature, the interaction of *shakti* with honour perhaps serves to explain Indu's choice. Honour and *shakti* (in this construction, female sexuality) are not mutually exclusive. Minturn argues that for Rajput women 'the psychic strength surrounding sexual energy is a hallmark of upper-class women... [...] High status women should possess high standards for honor, so that their behaviour will not disgrace them and their family. The combination of much *Shakti* and much honor is the ideal for Rajput women' (1993: 201-2). Indu's *shakti* (as psychic strength) initially opposed her father's honour, but faced with a *fait accompli*, *shakti* transformed its ends to serve honour. Thus Indu went ahead with the engagement, drawing upon her strength to bear her role as obedient daughter. Even so, it is important not to elide the pressures exerted upon her when her father chooses to '*emotionally blackmail*' her with the option of disgracing him forever, or doing his bidding.

Subhash points out that Indu possessed much *shakti*, even though it was domesticated through her father's honour. In this scenario, Indu's arranged marriage provides an opportunity to examine the legal conundrum that arises over the issue of agency and consent in arranged marriages. Firstly, as I have already pointed out in the contexts of court and temple love-marriages, the idea of 'free consent' is deeply problematic and virtually impossible to discern. Many couples only just accede to the expediency of a marriage, and most dislike the expressions of 'free consent' that it legally demands because this implies a challenge to the withheld consent of their families. Indu says to Subhash that whatever she does, she does for the happiness of her parents. This sense of sacrifice isn't necessarily borne out of coercion. Furthermore, she permits her agency to be appropriated by her parents, such that her strength and honour in resisting their pressures is now theirs to domesticate.

In light of this, to what extent is Indu legally bound to a marriage that she accedes to under pressure, rather than bestowing her 'free consent?' Legal experts in India believe as regards the Law of Agency[26] under the Hindu Marriage Act, that if a son authorises his father to choose a bride for him and negotiate his marriage, then he may not have the marriage annulled on the grounds that this choice was unsuitable to him or that he was misled by his father (Uberoi 1996a: 332). The ambivalence of the law lies in the term 'authorised', because it is widely assumed that parents have the social legitimacy (and by implication, 'authorisation') to arrange their children's marriages. Derrett (as quoted in Uberoi) pins down this transformed notion of consent in the context of the social forms of arranged and child marriages in India:

> ... [T]he consent of the bride and groom is really their consent—if at all it can be considered such—to allow marriage negotiations to go ahead on their behalf, and not to express consent to a contractual arrangement with a particular person (Uberoi 1996a: 331).

Furthermore, Uberoi points out that it has been argued legally that consent is implied in a person's participation in the marriage ceremony, in the words recited in the ceremony, and that even when it may be proved that a person partook in the marriage ceremony but did not consent to it, the courts would not allow a decree to nullify such a wedding, because the state and its legal system are 'understandably wary of lightly invalidating marriages' (1996a: 332). In such a situation, the marriage may not be what Indu wishes, but it is what she intends as she goes through the engagement and marriage. It may be something she does reluctantly, but it certainly isn't unintentional. In other words, her desires and her actions are divergent, and since the law only accounts for actions and ascribes a fixed-ness to the meanings of certain actions, she is now legally married to the man of her parent's choosing, and the legal consequence is that she is seen to have expressed her agency through this marriage.[27] It would appear as if the young couple were doomed never to be together again.

'The *real-meaning* of marriage':
Making moral relationships

Subhash was initially unable to do anything but mourn. However, when he returned to Delhi from the family wedding, he returned with a *solution*. This was that he, or some male members of his family, would approach Indu's father with his proposal to marry her. 'I thought that I would threaten and coerce them saying I will bring disgrace to them [by revealing details of their *affair*.] Your own daughter won't deny it, so how can you?' However, by the time he came up with this, Indu had been sent away to Jammu by her parents, and when she got back to Delhi she seemed distant and resolute. Subhash tried to convince her but she replied that he should stop bothering her because she was doing all this for the happiness of her people. He urged her that they still had time, that the 'wedding cards still hadn't been printed'. She replied that her father had already booked a *banquet*, and had given one *lakh* (100,000) rupees to the groom's family, as a sort of pre-dowry. Subhash said to me: 'She made it seem that she was under pressure, but also that she didn't wish to resist it. I kept saying, "I have brought a solution", but she didn't want to know what I had brought.' They spoke to each other over the phone after this, but two weeks before the wedding, Subhash told her that he would never speak to her again or show her his face. He kept his word and on the day I spoke to him he said it had been precisely 102 days since he had last spoken to her.

Subhash's only potential *solution* to their problems had consisted of him threatening Indu's parents with the possibility of dishonour by proving that their daughter was having an *affair* with him. In seeking to make Indu his wife, he was not trying to prove himself worthy of her, but rather sought to prove that she was unworthy of any other man, having already given herself to Subhash. In trying to win the woman he loved, he threatened to dishonour her. This again was a common enough blackmail strategy adopted by love-marriage couples, where the man would threaten his girlfriends' parents with public disclosures of the *affair* with their daughter. This wasn't a very attractive 'solution' for Indu, who probably had hoped that Subhash would suggest a court-marriage, or at least an elopement. But Subhash was in the final instance unable to justify to himself such a socially reprehensible act as a court-marriage or a love-marriage that wasn't suitably domesticated by both families. Instead he provides a guarantee of Indu's future marital security by returning all signs of their love (letters, gifts, etc.) so that in a moment of weakness he would not be tempted to ruin her and her parents, and probably destroy her marital home.

While anthropologists and Indian historians have pointed to the difference between the marriage ritual (historically, prior to the puberty of the girl) and consummation rites (after puberty, when the girl joins her husband) in north Indian society,[28] the conflation of the two and their implications for the moral meanings of marriage have only begun to receive any attention. Uberoi (1996), for instance, has provided an arresting 'judicial ethnosexology' gleaned from the recorded observations of judges in the Indian legal system, adjudicating upon Hindu arranged-marriages.[29] She argues that while the marriage ritual can be theoretically approached in two ways—marriage as sacrament and marriage as contract—it is the *consummation* of the marriage (rather than the religious ritual) that is increasingly seen to be of critical importance in initiating a new 'moral relationship' between the husband and the wife. This initial sexual encounter (ideally, between complete strangers who meet alone for the first time on their '*suhag rath*' or night of consummation), establishes for the husband of the virgin bride the rights to her sexuality and the control over her body. The bride, for her part, is assumed to reciprocate undying devotion in return for her 'sexualisation'. Her sacrifice permits her to make demands upon her husband, such that he protects and provides for her. Uberoi's analysis of marital breakdown as seen through these judgements may have a special bearing upon the wider relevance of our reading of the meanings of marriage in India today.

It is instructive to compare the arranged marriage scenario, where emphasis is placed upon consummation and, as Uberoi points out—towards creating a new 'moral relationship' between husband and wife—to this ethnography of love-marriage, where the contested arena is the social form of the marital ritual itself. As we have noted earlier in the book, the *validation* of the relationship in the latter case lies in domesticating a relationship seen to be based on love, desire and sexuality into a ritually blessed and socially sanctioned love-cum-arranged marriage. The greater emphasis then is not on sexualisation or consummation (which is usually presumed to have taken place in any case), but rather on the social significance of establishing moral relations between kinship groups. Thus, there is a striking inversion of metonymic significances attached to each type of marriage. In love-marriage cases, the energies of the couple are seen to be directed towards disguising their premarital love and sexuality, with a concomitant emphasis on the social display of the marriage ritual itself which is used to validate the illegitimate love union. In arranged marriages, it is the fruition of an assumed dormant sexuality that validates the marriage ritual and fixes upon the sexual conjoining of the couple on their 'first' night.[30]

This is not, however, a straightforward and uncontested reading. In instances where the love 'fails' there is an entire range of meanings that gets ascribed to the process of getting married. Firstly, Subhash regarded Indu's arranged-'engagement', and not the consummation of her marriage, as definitively creating a moral relationship between the two sets of kin, such that his reflections to substantiate his point centre around the imagined publicity that the boy's mother would give her son's engagement, and the kinship term ('*bahu*' or daughter-in-law) that she would lovingly (and prematurely) use for Indu. The '*engagement*', during which *rings* (bought by the respective parents) are exchanged in the presence of the kinship group, serves then to publicly ratify the terms of marriage and the acceptance of both sides to the union. This public display implies for Subhash the gift of his beloved to another man; and he sees her as another man's wife from this point on. Indu, on the other hand, expects him to stand by the moral relationship created by their mutual commitment of love, and her reported words reveal her dismay that Subhash so easily interprets the engagement as a final (albeit tragic) *solution* to their affair.

In a bitter twist of fate however, Indu's parents have emerged the biggest losers in their daughter's marriage. In their enthusiasm to ensure the public face of marriage, they overlooked the rare possibility of the marriage itself failing to consummate. When I asked Subhash's best friend Gopal how Indu was faring and whether he had spoken to her recently, he surprised Subhash by saying he had met her the previous day in a temple, and that she had told him of her deep unhappiness. Gopal was nervous about speaking of Indu in Subhash's presence (due to his fragile state of mind), but the fact that I was present somehow justified his astonishing revelation:

She isn't happy. Even her husband is of this *type* of *nature* that he says this marriage wasn't with his consent. He wasn't *interested* in marriage. He says he wanted to live his life *free*.... The people of his house said that it was their duty to marry him—then after that he could do what he wanted—live whatever life he wanted. Indu asked her in-laws: 'If he wasn't interested in this marriage, then why did you ruin my life?' So they said: 'See, we thought it is our duty to marry him. We thought that after he gets married he will reform, he will understand what its *real-meaning* is...' But there was no change. In fact, people say that what happens on the first night, even that hasn't happened. I think that what she is saying may even be true. Because, she says that even lying together on the bed, we aren't together. Even if we are together in a bedroom, we aren't together. She says that her situation has become so bad that her people are now talking about divorce. They are saying, that hardly any time has passed since the marriage, and that they should take a divorce straight away.[31] If she is not getting peace in that home, and if she is not getting what we sent her there for—then what did we do her marriage for.... When the boy himself does not *accept* you, then what are you doing there? Are you there only to wash the dishes? Her in-laws are laying down the rules for her. They say, 'Okay, if our son isn't doing it, even then you should live with us, and for us.' Indu says: 'Why should I live *without-husband* here? No woman would live under these conditions.'

Clearly, Indu's in-laws believed that their son's intransigence towards marriage could be reversed when the marriage was consummated. The *'real-meaning'* of marriage that they refer to is sexual intercourse with his virginal wife. Here, Uberoi's message regarding the moral meanings of consummation are striking, because not only is the boy assumed to be transformed (they use the Hindi term *sudhar jana*, which means 'to reform') through the sexualisation of his wife (and himself), but equally, the lack of consummation is seen to have a disturbing effect on Indu's peace of mind, and she is viewed as unfulfilled and 'not having got what she was sent there for'. Indu is portrayed as a woman who has been 'wronged', and whose existence *without-husband* is a euphemism for a sexually unconsummated marriage.

An arranged marriage of such unseemly haste did not permit for the usual enquiries into the 'background' of the boy. Not that such enquiries would necessarily reveal the requisite details, but at least people would feel satisfied that some attempt had been made to ensure the reputation of a boy to whom one married one's daughter.

I often heard it said that in swift marriages, the spouses are joined in marriage almost immediately, and possibly with the sort of people about whom more detailed enquiries would have revealed their unsuitability. In those instances when the marriage does go wrong for reasons that might have been foreseeable, the parents are held to be particularly culpable for having sacrificed their offspring's happiness of a lifetime for the expediency and haste of a few weeks. In this instance too, Indu's parents would no doubt have been held responsible for having made such a ruinous alliance.

From Gopal's report of his conversation with Indu, her strategy to deal with this anomalous situation was remarkable. Having been forced into conjugality with a man she did not know or love, Indu now claimed a right to *his* sexuality that she was being denied. The illegitimacy of sexuality in a love affair was now juxtaposed with the *shakti* of a married woman, wronged by being denied her husband's attentions. Indu's parents supported her because an unconsummated marriage is considered 'unnatural' as procreation can never be achieved. Indeed, the 'weakness' of the husband empowers the wife, just as the deceit of the bride-takers' challenges and charges the bride-givers to seek retribution. Clearly, while an unmarried woman's sexuality is of grave concern to her father's honour—such that he may sacrifice her wishes to ensure that she is passed on to a suitable affine—the awakening of a woman's sexuality in marriage is a right that even her father would be willing to demand her husband fulfil. When a husband fails to consummate his marriage and domesticate his wife's sexuality, he renounces his rights to her productive capabilities too. The trade-off is clear—if he is unwilling to impregnate her, she is unwilling to act the coy bride and slave over his parents' every whim and fancy. The allusions to Indu's husband's sexuality (he does not *like* her, she doesn't awaken any *interest* in him, the marriage wasn't with his consent) are left unanswered. Gopal observed that Indu once asked her husband if he was perhaps not 'interested in girls' at all, and instead of defending his '*izzat*', he merely replied: 'Please don't discuss this *topic* with me'. Clearly then, *izzat* is not just about female modesty, but has a structural pairing that is only rarely challenged, and consequently, rarely made visible: male virility.

Subhash too found this revelation traumatic, and was eager not to discuss the *topic* of Indu's unsatisfied sexuality. He said that he was so possessive about Indu that when they were having their *affair* he had forbidden her to go out even with her own brother. 'I didn't like it if she spoke to any men. Once she went for a *picture* [movie] with her brother. I felt really bad. I told her never to go again with any *gents*. Not that my thinking was wrong. I just forbade it.' For his part, this talk of Indu's unconsummated marriage was like rubbing salt into his wounds.

'She has become the *izzat* of another home'

Subhash is upset at being subjected to a discussion about Indu's conjugal situation, but nonetheless he doesn't seize the opportunity that this news presents him with. If Indu is seeking separation from her husband, and if her parents are supporting her because the marriage has remained unconsummated, then perhaps Subhash and Indu could be reunited in her secondary marriage. For Subhash, a secondary marriage with the woman he loves is hardly going to redeem his loss, or allow him to maintain his family honour. Rather, he takes the situation philosophically, seeing in her sacrifice his own, and seeing the loss of her *izzat* to him, in her conjoining with another man, be this ritually or physically. For Subhash, the meaning is in the metaphor, not in the act itself, and just as he took Indu's engagement to imply a 'marriage', he now saw the non-consummation of Indu's marriage as a matter of her own individual *kismat*, rather than a source of potentially renewed hope for their love. Whether or not the marriage was consummated was not the issue at stake—what clearly mattered was that her primary marriage had taken place elsewhere. When I asked him why he didn't have a court-marriage when Indu begged him for a *solution*, he replied that it was because *his* father was willing to marry them so where was the justice in disgracing him by having a court-marriage. Clearly the true source of Subhash's inaction was the criteria laid down by his father. His father had warned him that his own honour lay in Subhash's ability to negotiate in such a way that Indu's father gave her to them in marriage. Subhash's agency during the period prior to Indu's marriage was closely linked to that of his kin group. His agency in loving Indu is made accountable to the honour of the group, such that his self as agent and self as agent of the group temporarily merge in the hope that Indu's father will gift her to his people.

Further, he was warned not to dishonour both families through an elopement (and inevitable subsequent fracas), such that Subhash would have his people's support so long as he ensured that Indu and he were married properly, with full rites in a 'love-cum-arranged' marriage. This is why Subhash shied away from the precaution of a quiet court-marriage that would only ever have been declared in precisely such circumstances as Indu's overnight engagement. Most people know that a court-marriage is one important weapon to ward off an arranged marriage and to coerce one's parents into organising a love-cum-arranged marriage. Subhash knew that his own father would never forgive him for bringing dishonour by breaking up Indu's engagement, and that now that those two families had been '*linked*' it was futile to imagine Indu's father conceding to his own 'inter-caste' marriage to her. As he said: 'She has become the *izzat* of another home'.

His only weapon against Indu's father was to reveal the details of Indu's affair with him, and shame her parents into submission. It is the control over her sexuality that he can contest, but in so doing, he will only heap dishonour on his own father. To demand a wife by arguing that she is of loose morals and subsequently should not be allowed to marry elsewhere, is hardly likely to enhance one's own family status as the recipients of that woman's sexuality. As we have seen, a woman's sexuality and psychic energy (her *shakti*) is ideally harnessed by the honour of her father and then her husband's patrilineage. The combination of much *shakti* and little honour would have done nothing to recommend Indu to Subhash's own people. In the end, her parents are faced with the potential disgrace of a daughter who is what is frequently described in Indian matrimonial columns in untranslated English as an '*Innocent Divorcee*'. This does not imply the lack of culpability in the breakdown of the marriage. Rather, it indicates that the woman has emerged from her marriage 'innocent'—as the man was either impotent, unwilling (and possibly in love with another woman) or homosexual. An '*innocent divorcee*' is considered of dubious moral standing simply because, having failed properly to harness her sexuality (*shakti*) with honour in a primary marriage, her sexuality can no longer be given as a 'true gift' (the 'gift of a virgin' or *kanya dan*) as she has already forfeited the right to a ritually sanctioned marriage. Furthermore, her claim to '*innocence*' is always open to suspicion. Who is to know what really transpired behind the closed doors of a marital bedroom?

Far from living in a different moral universe, as popular discussion tends to imply, love-marriage couples share all of the prevailing constructions of sexuality and the moral meaning of marriage. For Subhash, Indu's marriage saw the gift of her virginity bestowed by her father upon another man. Now, even when the possibility of a love-cum-arranged marriage presents itself (Indu's parents might be more willing to allow her to marry her boyfriend if she has had a divorce, because the divorce would make a second marriage difficult to arrange in any case), he sees himself as being asked to pick up that which another man has already '*touched*'. Worse still, he sees Indu's husband as having rejected her—making his own position more demeaning. While it isn't unusual for a Hindu high-caste man to have a secondary marriage with a 'virgin', the popular Brahmanical notion that a woman must only be given in marriage once and that her sexuality may only ever be received by one man, is still very prevalent in Delhi today. This is not to say that divorced or widowed women do not remarry, but simply that remarriage is still relatively difficult and stigmatised particularly among high-caste groups. For a high-caste woman, a primary marriage is indissoluble and inviolable. A Brahmin girl like Indu can expect to go through such a marriage only once in her lifetime.[32] But these generalisations mustn't be overstated because they are frequently contradicted in practice. If Gopal is to be believed, Indu is challenging her marriage from within because she does not shy away from the possibility of a divorce and a secondary marriage with Subhash. Equally, while Subhash vows never to marry and assiduously counts each day that passes since his last phone call to Indu, his best friend Gopal is confused by the inflexibility of his principles. He argues that if he were in Subhash's shoes he wouldn't think 'what was wrong and what was right because you are getting your love back!' He says that if he loved a girl then he would '*accept*' her even after a primary marriage.

Subhash's agency lies in stasis because he presents himself with two irreconcilable values: that of honour and that of his beloved's polluted sexuality. He is unable and unwilling to re-negotiate his own sense of honour. He gains in honour because he is seen to have sacrificed his base desires for a greater common good—the respectability and honour of all concerned. In so doing, however, he does not relinquish his claims of absolute and undying love for Indu, but instead seems to imply that he has opted for love as failure, in which the pining for the beloved—the love that is felt deeply and abidingly in the spirit rather than debasing itself in seeking consummation—is the only end he seeks. Indu, on the other hand, negotiates her sexuality by treating it as a means to an end: a marriage to Subhash. She opposes her parents by declaring her choice to them, and stands firm until they give her no choice other than to surrender to their will. However, after the marriage she does not accept her circumstances, but rather finds ways in which the marriage can be dissolved, such that she may be free to marry of her own choice the second time round. Her undomesticated sexuality is thus used as an important resource (it is a tool that she can use in her divorce) which may even allow her to achieve her own ends (a marriage to Subhash). In this she is foiled, not so much by her parents, but by Subhash's discomfort in her negotiations of her own sexuality, advertising the fact that she is a woman who lacks modesty. He sees her engagement as an act of betrayal, but from Indu's perspective the engagement was in the final instance an act of sacrifice designed to express her own sense of decency and obedience (the surrender of her sexuality) to her parents. This is a blow to Subhash's honour as the caretaker of her sexuality. Thus, the failure of their love lies as much in their tragic circumstances as it does with their own conceptions of acceptable and unacceptable negotiations of Indu's sexuality and Subhash's sense of honour.

Indu and Subhash's story illustrates some of the ways in which we may assess the breakdown of a love relationship. In the next love-biography, we look at the precipitating factors that are brought to bear upon issues of honour and legal rights which get balanced against love. Here, the negotiations are also about the sexuality of a Hindu girl (Priya), but additionally include the sexualisation of her Muslim husband (Kamiyar) through commonly held communal stereotypes about Muslim men and their aggressive sexuality towards Hindus. The discourses of *izzat* that are invoked are seen to be unequal and hypocritical, with both families having instances of love-marriages amongst Kamiyar and Priya's older siblings. This again leads us to explore the issue of balancing 'individual' and 'community' rights in heavily charged and politicised Hindu–Muslim love-marriages.

Claims to Modernity;
Claims to 'Rights': Kamiyar and Priya

Kamiyar was a modern-day hero. Far from shying away from the individualistic allegations that face love-marriage couples, he boldly asserted to me that marriage is indeed *'for the individual'*, *'not for society'*. While this may seem unsurprising, coming from the mouth of a 24-year-old man who challenged his wife's captors by climbing a 210-foot microwave tower, it was an enormous departure from what most of the couples were saying to me. The implied indifference to social pressures was perhaps a show of bravado, but nonetheless a significant attempt to express resistance to the exigencies of family honour and social form.

Indeed, it was a sense of precisely this insolence that brought forth the most vitriolic criticism from some members of the public in attendance at the foot of the tower. This is how a principal of a college in Uttar Pradesh (self-styled as 'MA in Sociology and World Diplomacy') present on the ground below the tower vented his ire against Kamiyar's demand that his wife be brought back to him...

He says that the girl's parents kidnapped her. Parents kidnap their own child?! Parents don't have rights? They have fed and clothed and made adult their children. They have got some rights. At least take their views. You compel your parents that I want this thing. Those who have raised you for 20–22 years, they have no rights but a man who comes into your life after 22 years—and suddenly you decide to walk off with him? There is freedom, but parents also got some rights. They have their own izzat. They also live within society. They also want that we have only one daughter and we will celebrate her marriage with pomp, with our choice of boy, background and family.

Individual rights, after all, are only one aspect of the *rights in persons* widely regarded as held by one's parent's, family and social group. The impact that Kamiyar's declaration of his 'right to love' had on some people was quite extraordinary. One man said to me that Kamiyar had laid down a *'scale of affection'*, placing himself at *'maximum'*. No one could match this *'scale of love'*. He argued that from now on couples in Delhi would have this *'dialogue'*: 'The girl will ask the boy, do you love me? Do you love me as much as Kamiyar loves Priya? If you *agree* only then will I have *coffee* or *chaii* with you. You see, we have seen a *real Laila-Majnu.*' The heightened impact of Kamiyar's episode points to the sense that people in Delhi wanted (and needed) proofs of the existence of everlasting and constant '*real love*', unblemished and unfettered by social norms or history. The comparison with Laila and Majnu is made because it is a story of lovers opposed by virtue of their birth who withstand the scorn of society and remain true to their love. The love of Laila and Majnu knows no laws, and like Romeo and Juliet, ends with the union of the lovers in death. The story is so popular in India that Rajadyaksha and Willemen's encyclopaedia of Indian films lists no fewer than seventeen films with the title Layla-Majnu (1999). However, Kamiyar distanced himself from representations of himself as a caricature of a lover (a mad 'Majnu' who was content to love his beloved without seeking success) and instead sought to present his tower protest as a political act.[33] My interviews with members of the public indicated that in the spirit of street entertainment he was nonetheless widely perceived as a '*roadside-Romeo*' or filmy-hero, and that the private '*drama*' enacted in public held great promise for a career in Bollywood, but not for the return of a wife.[34]

The college principal insisted that this was not the way to go about having a love-marriage, and this view found many sympathisers. In climbing the tower, they felt that Kamiyar had shamed not just his own parents, but also Priya and her people. Further, by demanding that his wife be brought to him before he descended from the tower, Kamiyar was exposing himself to an interesting array of criticisms.

For a number of people, the defence of a daughter (or sister) during conflicts with her husband's family after marriage is an important 'right' to which she is entitled. The natal family is there to protect her interests against those of the husband's family. The tensions between affinal relations are so widely prevalent that people in Delhi say that even a 'third man' (a stranger) will come forward to safeguard the honour of the *ladkiwale* or the girl's side.[35] A husband must be suitably contrite when he goes to collect his wife from her father's home, and he must consider her brothers' or father's demands as to her treatment prior to the girl conceding to join him. The 'right' to collect your wife is not entirely conceived as an individual right, but rather a corporate one—a right of the patrilineage, counterpoised and balanced by the strength of her natal kin.

Interestingly, as if to underscore the widely prevalent notion that the natural people to protect a woman's interests are her natal kin, a number of people discounted the possibility that Kamiyar's wife might be any in danger at her parental home. This view, disseminated in equal measure by public reactions to the incident reported in the press, and off-the-record statements from high-ranking inspectors of the Delhi police, served as a justification of the state's inaction in establishing Priya's circumstances during Kamiyar's high-voltage protest. Others dismissed Kamiyar's claims to having married Priya by arguing that if he had indeed married her (and marriage being an inviolable institution), then his people would be gathered together to help him retrieve her. In the absence of his family (his mother and younger brother appeared at the tower only on the fifth day of his protest), it made more sense that he was a madman, or a besotted lover, and that his claims to a 'wife' were unsubstantiated. Besides, as strangers (or 'third men'), they were more inclined to believe that the girl's side had been wronged, and thus to extend their sympathy to them rather than to the man on the tower.

If there was sympathy for the girl's family, it was directed at the fact that not only were they expected to deal with a Muslim son-in-law, but also with the publicity that came with the tower protest. Priya's people were Thakurs, and as a result were widely acknowledged as placing a high premium on the *izzat* of their women-folk; a stereotype that was cited as being extensively reiterated in the characterisation of Thakurs in myth, folklore and especially Hindi films. Even though no one I spoke to at the base of the tower knew who the family of this girl were, the public consensus was that no matter what, her people would kill Priya rather than allow her to ruin the family's honour. This notion was fuelled by Kamiyar's written statements that Priya's brother-in-law, Hanuman Kumar, was a violent 'history-sheeter'[36] and had numerous murder and kidnapping cases filed against him in their home town of Kanpur and in the state of Uttar Pradesh. He also alleged that Hanuman had threatened his family with dire consequences and warned that if they tried to take Priya, he would retaliate by kidnapping either Kamiyar's younger brother or his toddler nephew. Taken as a whole then, the public debate about this case thus brings to the fore widely shared caste stereotypes about the defence of *izzat* and the conventional received wisdom about widespread criminality in northern India and, more specifically, in Uttar Pradesh.

The course of events was such that after their marriage in early November 1998, both Kamiyar and Priya returned to their respective homes. The night before they left, Kamiyar went to speak with Priya's mother (her father having died some years earlier), but she would not let him have his say and demanded that he leave immediately. Kamiyar had planned with Priya that if his attempt to convince her mother were to fail, then she should be prepared to spend her last night at her natal home. The next morning, they fled for Akbarpur and sought shelter at Kamiyar's *mama's* home (his mother's brother, i.e. his mother's natal village). The pattern of love-marriage couples seeking protection and support from the boy's maternal kin is clearly explicable through a brief analysis of the patterns of north Indian kinship. If Kamiyar's own parents were to allege that he was heaping dishonour upon them through his love-marriage, he would not be able to summon the support of his patrilineage, who would favour the adult decisions. However, the mother's brother, protector of his sister against the predilections of her husband and his lineage—and sharing as he does an intimate and familiar relationship with his sister's son—is an obvious and perhaps the only male ally to whom the young couple may turn. Innocent of the dishonour to another lineage, he may protect his sister's son against his father and act as an intermediary in subsequent negotiations.[37]

In Akbarpur, Kamiyar was received by his uncle and aunt, who tried to give the young couple some of the trappings of marital ritual. Priya was forbidden from entering the kitchen to help with the preparation of food—a compliment implying her exalted status as a new bride in her husband's home (no doubt, also symbolically implying that as a 'dangerous wife' she would need to integrate herself into her husband's lineage before she be allowed the delicate task of preparing food). The terrified couple managed to eat. By the evening, word had got out that they were in Akbarpur and during the night a mob of Priya's relatives, allegedly armed, entered the village to retrieve her. They stormed all the homes in the village, with Priya's sister leading the gang with the cry 'Where is my sister? Where is my sister?', until they found Priya and Kamiyar trying to escape. When they took her they warned Kamiyar not to file a police report and threatened him repeatedly. That was the last Kamiyar saw of Priya.

As far as Hanuman Kumar was concerned, Priya's *izzat* or honour had been saved as she had been tracked down before she could spend 'the first night' with Kamiyar. All Kamiyar's marriage papers and photographs, which had been locked up safely in a cupboard in his room in Kanpur, were taken by Priya's people after they returned from Akbarpur. Kamiyar alleged that they had pointed guns at his elderly mother and sister, and that his father was so terrified that he had escaped into the night, hiding on a neighbouring roof. Kamiyar's act of bravery on the tower was to make up for what he described as his *'mistake'*. *'I let them take her from me...'*, and for this he felt he could never forgive himself. In hindsight he wished he had fought them to the death, unarmed that night in Akbarpur. At least, he felt, they would never have been separated.

I managed to make contact with Priya's family. One of her brothers warned me: 'We are Thakurs. For us it is nothing to kill and be killed for our *izzat*.' He also spoke of the terrible shame Kamiyar had caused by climbing the tower. Apparently, they were trying their utmost to marry Priya off, but the nation-wide publicity had jeopardised these plans.

The corporate aspect of *izzat* has important consequences for *beyizzati* because it encourages the subordination of individual worth to the larger social good of the entire group. Equally, in arranging marriages for siblings of a child who has had a love-marriage, the new diminished status of the family's honour will play an important part in all negotiations, and in many cases such a match may be rejected outright as a statement of disaffiliation by those who come from truly *izzatdar* (honourable) lineages where such a thing would never be allowed to happen. I use the term 'allowed to happen' quite intentionally. *Izzat* is widely perceived to be underwritten by force. Its language is often that of violence, because *izzat* can only be redeemed through a violent expression of intolerance towards *beyizzati*. Prem Chowdhry is one of the few Indian academics to have drawn attention to the numerous instances in rural north India of direct violence (often culminating in death), perpetrated by male family members and inflicted upon couples, but more especially upon girls having inter-caste or intra-caste marriages.

She attributes this to the control of sexuality by 'patriarchal forces' who are concerned to ensure 'caste purity, caste status, power and hierarchy' (1997: 1019), and to the increased insecurity in property matters amongst rural communities due to the legal enablement of daughters to inherit property. It certainly is the case that such killings are more of a rural than an urban phenomenon, but it is striking that most of the reported cases of public beatings and executions are from regions surrounding the nation's capital; often only a few kilometres away. Many of the couples elope to Delhi before they are discovered and returned by extended kin networks to their villages to await their punishment.[38]

Oftentimes *beyizzati* need not even be intentional. The mere threat of dishonour to a daughter, sister or wife can provoke truly awesome acts of violence, such as those documented recently by Indian feminists and historians in the violence perpetrated against women by men of 'other' communities (dishonouring), but also by male members of their own kin (protecting against impending dishonour) during the Partitioning of the subcontinent in 1947 which I mentioned in the Introduction (Butalia 1998; Menon and Bhasin 1998). For now, I merely wish to reiterate the point that if *izzat* is attained at the critical juncture of an appropriate and well sought out status arranged marriage, it is also lost irrevocably through an inappropriate love-marriage, especially if it threatens to go public. Furthermore, if *izzat* is upheld by the group and supported by the threat of violence, it is no surprise then that in extreme instances individual love is sought to be stamped out through violence.

We must however beware of drawing general conclusions about love-marriages and these extreme instances of violence from the evidence of press articles because they are newsworthy to journalists (and interesting to the public), precisely because they involve extreme threats of violence that are then occasionally carried through. It is not just the case that instances of physical violence are given disproportionate exposure in the print and television media, but that such instances of extreme violence are the visible outcome of other less visible (to the ethnographer and the journalist) attempts to negotiate or resolve matters. In most instances, threats of extreme violence would be recognised as dangerous for both the executer and the executed because inevitably, the police would find it easy to attach blame to the family or kin group, and in cases of murder, it would send people to prison for many years. The likely scenario would be to bring all parties together in order to seek and find a better settlement. For instance, one common strategy would be for the couple to move away from their immediate kin and live in relative anonymity until the birth of their first child. Of all the love-marriage couples I worked with, only a small percentage received credible threats of physical violence, though most suffered great emotional violence and torment from having let down their parents or disappointed their elders.

In the violent cases found in the press, individual love or the loving-couple come to represent that which must be excised from the 'community' at all costs, and such violent displays of group solidarity play their part in reconstituting the relations within the group, re-establishing hierarchy between castes, and re-negotiating honour through vigilance in maintaining gender norms and 'traditional' values.[39] Such punishments represent the extremes to which communities and groups are willing to go in order to both terminate the agency of the individual lover, or the loving-couple, and to establish itself as the only moral claimant to exchanges of honour and sexuality. In other words, such actions represent the ultimate colonisation of the self-world of the individual by the group.

Dialogues of honour

While Kamiyar clearly hated Hanuman Kumar and regarded him as a powerful bully, when he did speak to Hanuman he was extremely conciliatory: 'I said to him, "make me your brother. Make me your younger brother! Forgive me!" I was just crying, just crying. "Take me into your home. Take me into your heart. Just give me back my Priya".' Clearly, there was nothing he was unwilling to do to get her back. The implication of begging Hanuman to make him his younger brother was clear. Kamiyar was willing to sacrifice everything, including the normal superior position of wife-taking affine in order to be accepted as a suitable spouse for his Hindu wife, Priya. Furthermore, he emphasises this point by constantly calling Hanuman's wife '*bhabhi*'. [40] If Hanuman was to make him his younger brother, he would also make him a Hindu. Hanuman of course replied that this was impossible. He pointed out that a Gupta Teli (a caste of oil-pressers, commonly 'businessmen' in

Uttar Pradesh) friend of his asked him for support when he was about to elope with his girlfriend, and in that instance too he had opposed the match because the girlfriend wasn't a Teli. Kamiyar replied with a claim to modernity: 'That is your opinion. Today the world is moving into the twenty-first *century* and you keep going on about Teli and Thakurwali [Thakurness]!'

Kamiyar's explanation about why Priya's people opposed the marriage of their daughter to a Muslim was that,

> [T]his whole thing about *izzat* is just an excuse. In the Faridabad case both of them [a couple] were Muslim, still they were opposed. If it weren't this, it would be an issue over *wealth*. If that's not an issue, then its over *caste*; if its not, then its over which *state* you are from. *Excuses* are plentiful. I have given them plenty of examples and asked them [Priya's people] 'Were all these people of bad character?' Indira Gandhi, Rajiv Gandhi, Akbar Ahmad Dumpy and Naina Balsawar... Imran Khan married a Jew![41] In Kanpur, there is a person of much higher reputation called Karana Singh. We know Karana *bhai* well. He married his daughter, [to the boy of her choice] and now she is coming and going [she hasn't been excommunicated, and visits her natal home as is the custom for all brides]—there is full *interchange* [between the two affinal families]. And these people are known to have much more *izzat* than Priya's family.

Although he doesn't specify whether or not the son-in-law of Karana Singh was a Muslim, Kamiyar's observation about *izzat* being a value amenable to negotiation (Karana *bhai* supported his daughter and retained his *izzat*) and even force isn't far off the mark. Equally, he found it offensive that the honour of his family was so easily denigrated just because they were Muslim, and was at great pains to point out that even though her family were Thakurs, his were Pathans (Khans) and were considerably more 'respectable' and of greater wealth and standing than hers. This is a reflection of Muslims being stereotyped today (first by Congress patronage which set itself up as 'protectors' of Muslims, and more recently, by Hindutva ideologues who depict them as a backward underclass), and the sense of indignation that many Muslims feel towards such stereotyping. Furthermore, in another outburst of extreme frustration, Kamiyar said to me: 'Hindus and Muslims they can do anything together. But not this. Not marriage. They can do anything behind *purdah* [in hiding], but if someone is *fair*, and someone brings it out *publicly*—then society will start prohibiting them. *That no, this is illegal.* So many people I know, they are Hindu-Muslim and they are *together. They are together!* But they can't say it.' These differing standards for social intercourse, marital exchanges and, indeed, religious worship were striking. It is a subject that has received attention from anthropologists such as Das (1997) and Chowdhry (1997) who point to the sharp demarcations between public and private morality in north Indian kinship relations, such that disclosures of private dalliances which spill over into the public realm 'impinge upon honour both private and collective, necessitating drastic action' (Chowdhry 1997: 1021).

Kamiyar pointed out that Priya's family worshipped regularly at the shrine of a Muslim saint, attending prayers on Thursdays, and always called upon the services of a Muslim *moulvi* (one who is acquainted with religious teaching and Muslim law) rather than a Hindu *pundit* (priest) whenever there was a crisis in the home. They partook in all the acts of good neighbourliness, for instance distributing *sherbet* to commemorate the memory of Hussain's martyrdom in Karbala on the occasion of Mohorram. It is important to note that this kind of 'syncretic' popular worship is a widespread phenomenon, but what is interesting is Kamiyar's invocation of it in the context of love-marriage. The usual assumption would be that Hindus and Muslims worship together but never consider this relevant to marriage. In a sense, Kamiyar is alluding to a historical past when marriages of Hindus with Muslim royalty (the marriage of Jodhabai, for instance) did allow for the syncretism of worship within the context of a mixed-marriage. However, none of this was necessarily influential in making Priya's family sympathetic to a love-marriage of their daughter to a Muslim. It was all the more surprising when I discovered that Hanuman Kumar, who was so determined to protect his wife's younger sister's honour, had in fact fought a very similar battle *against* Priya's male kin some years earlier. As it turns out, Hanuman himself had to struggle to be accepted as a suitable affine for Priya's elder sister.

He [Hanuman] kept opposing our marriage. I said '*Why*? You also loved *bhabhi!*' *That was a love-cum-arranged marriage. Means,* they applied a little *pressure* too! I have told you that they sent Muzzafar Ali to *bhabhi*'s house. [Muzzafar Ali is an alias for a famous politician who is also a nationally renowned gangster.[42]] See, actually *bhabhi* was studying in Lucknow. She and Hanuman came to know each other. An *affair* began. *Both of them were Rajput.* He sent a *rishta.* Now her father, a *DySP* [Deputy Superintendent of Police] was already dead. And the brothers were not in such a position as to set down too many *criteria* [marriage criteria] for their sister. Because he was a Thakur, they accepted. *But then they came to know that he was a history-sheeter and has been prosecuted for several murder cases—means—prosecution was there; like 307, 302* [penal code charges], after that they became *deadly against!* They said that there was no question of a marriage! How can we marry our daughter to a murderer? Our condition hasn't become that bad yet!

But then, *bhabhi's* love was *bhabhi's* love! She stopped eating and drinking—and insisted that if she was to marry, she would marry only him. [43] Hanuman was a *powerful* man, so he sent Muzzafar Ali—and he said to *bhabhi's* mother: 'As long as I am alive, no one can touch Hanuman'. She said: 'It's nothing personal! His *record* is bad'. So Muzzafar said—'See, if you don't accept things this way, we will bodily lift the girl and take her away'. They became compelled. Even though *bhabhi's* brother was a police inspector, what could a police inspector do to Muzzafar Ali?

Kamiyar's narrative of events makes clear his negotiating strategy. He turns the meaning of honour upon its head by exposing its inconsistencies and juxtaposing it with other important considerations such as those of social standing and respectability (versus Hanuman's criminality). By discussing Hanuman's virtually forced love-cum-arranged marriage, he balances his own unsuitability (in religious and ritual terms) with his evident suitability in terms recognised by Priya's own brother's and mother (he doesn't have a criminal record). Furthermore, he counters the allegation that his own love isn't important by pointing to *bhabhi's* dramatic and brazen attempts to blackmail her mother and brothers. Thus he presents Hanuman Kumar's love-marriage to *bhabhi* as both a source of potential hope and as ammunition to his armoury.

Defending Priya's honour:
'They are dirt. She is a lotus born in the dirt'[44]

Kamiyar, in his battle to safeguard his wife's honour, had to disconnect her *izzat* from that of her family. After all, if *izzat* is a corporate matter, then to insult your in-laws is to insult your own wife. He does this by arguing that she is utterly unique—a flower that blossomed despite all the muck around. Hanuman was discounting the dishonour of his own love-marriage by making the case that Kamiyar and Priya's (a Muslim–Hindu) marriage was truly dishonourable, rather than the discovery of their love for each other. Having your wife's brother-in-law, a criminal, accuse you of ruining his family's *izzat* was difficult for Kamiyar to accept. Hanuman Kumar was also projected as a crude muscle-man, while Kamiyar presented himself as polite and someone from a 'cultured background'; i.e. a person who was truly *izzatdar*. However, he was dealing with a person who was a known criminal, and this forced him to maintain a tough exterior and never show fear; an aspect of his strategy that was best symbolised by his act of climbing the tower and remaining there in death-defying conditions. In one instance, when Kamiyar was negotiating with Hanuman for the release of his wife, Hanuman swore at her. Kamiyar was so angry that he slammed the phone down and shouted '*F***-you sale!*' in the phone booth—a particularly interesting Hindi-English swear word that emphasises the ambivalences of the relationship between a man and his affines—in this case, his *sala* or 'wife's brother'.[45] Furthermore, the family had faced social ostracism from their own *biradari* since *bhabhi*'s marriage to Hanuman Kumar; not so much because it was a love-marriage, but because he was such a 'bad character'. Kamiyar reported that during the five years of his courtship with Priya, her brothers frequently tried to arrange her marriage but each time the criminal connection, once known, would put people off and the negotiations would collapse. Ironically, Kamiyar and Priya had Hanuman Kumar to thank for the time they were able to buy—and for the chance this gave Kamiyar to finish his degree and start earning so that he could support his wife-to-be, and prove his worth in the inevitably weighted negotiations that he was going to have to initiate with Priya's people.

Interestingly, in Kamiyar and Priya's case, Hanuman was unwilling to allow secular concerns (such as Kamiyar's career prospects) to impinge upon kinship honour, in the same way in which he discounted his own criminal record as being irrelevant to his marriage with *bhabhi*, simply because '*caste* was the same; everything was the same'.

As already pointed out earlier, the use of the English catch-all term '*caste*' (referring to the Hindi '*jat*' or '*jati*' meaning 'genus') rather unsubtly, but nonetheless effectively, elides the more specific kinship considerations that arise when arranging a marriage.

Marriages are not arranged willy-nilly within a *jati* or caste. Within *jatis*, lineages and *gotras* (clans, though occasionally this may refer to groupings of clans) are ranked hierarchically such that there are clear indicators of what constitutes a hypergamous, isogamous or hypogamous marriage, and subsequently, what one clan's ritual and status position is *vis a vis* another (Parry 1979). In pointing to the fact that their '*caste*' was the '*same*', Hanuman is able to present himself as a modern Hindu, who recognises the value of marriages of choice, so long as such marriages recognise the importance of '*caste*'.

Marriages also take into consideration the achieved status of the intended spouse, and of the 'background' of the family. I draw attention to Hanuman's statement, because in a number of instances during my research, I found people equating '*same-caste*' or 'marriage *by-caste*' with notions of appropriate arranged-marriage. Therefore, particularly in the case of love-marriages, it is of significance that the details of inter-caste relations, or intra-caste hierarchy, are glossed in urban contexts, such that the English terms '*same-caste*' or '*by-caste*' are meant to imply a 'proper' relationship, whereas in fact, if everything were (literally) to be the same, then one would assume that Hanuman was speaking of the most prohibited form of marriage; that within the same lineage or *gotra*! It is interesting that in an increasingly anonymous urban conurbation in which very few people would have the required information to assess a stranger's marriage credibility, love-marriage couples utilise this ignorance to their advantage. In his case, on a secular level too, it was clear that everything wasn't the same, and the wife of a late DySP, and his son, a Police Inspector, were deeply troubled by the possibility of such a close connection with someone who wasn't the same, but at least publicly, was from the other side (a criminal); whose '*record* was bad'. As Kamiyar argued:

> He's a man who is known to take money for *killing*. And he is saying that he is saving the *prestige* of Priya's family? One of Priya's brother's, even though he is married, he is living for the past 4–5 months with his girlfriend. She's a Christian. *Every man and woman in that family are doing on their own* [marrying or carrying-on with partners of their own choice], *but Priya is innocent; she can't rebel, she can't do anything, so they make her izzat into such a huge thing.* [...] This is the problem in our families. She is a girl, so force her into a marriage! She has been born so that she can marry according to our desire! In *Hindustan*, a girl has

no identity [*pehchan*] of her own. She is born, and she lives under her father's name. Then she is married to a man, and she lives under her husband's name. *She don't have her own recognition.* Priya can't say anything in her house. Her younger brothers drink and smoke, but she can't say anything! *See, a kid is smoking and drinking, it's not good for India. Is it good for India?*

It was because of this tainted family background that some people staunchly defended Kamiyar's more respectable attributes ('smart, intelligent, well-spoken, handsome and talented'). I heard a few people at the base of the tower joke that this Hindu girl's fate was looking up[46] if a boy as decent and well-liked as he was willing to marry her. It is salient that Kamiyar draws attention to Priya's 'innocence', and her inability to rebel. Her motivations are presented as the resignation of a girl born only to be married according to the whims of her parents. Her identity is subsumed by those of her male kin, and she is something of a second-class citizen in her own home. Her modesty and decency are the legitimate domain of all members of her family, while her brothers may 'drink and smoke' and indulge in such immoral activities as having affairs with Christian girls with no repercussions on the honour of the family.[47] At other times, Kamiyar would describe her as a 'typical Indian girl' or a 'traditional Indian girl'. Of course, we must note that Kamiyar sees no contradiction between this description and the fact that Priya married him in secret and eloped against the wishes of her family. Like Subhash, who went to great lengths to depict Indu as 'decent' and 'honourable', Kamiyar's characterisation of Priya must be seen as a valiant defence against the characterisations of women who have love affairs as being loose in their morals, or 'modern girls' with no regard for 'traditional' values.

Love-marriage honour: 'Are we ants or insects?'

Kamiyar's campaign to retrieve his wife had few supporters, but only in moments of extreme agitation did he reveal the extent to which he felt abandoned and betrayed by his own blood. He maintained to the press that Priya's people arrived at his parents' home armed to the teeth, and put a gun to his mother's head, demanding to know where the young couple had gone. They also broke open the locked cupboard where all Kamiyar's personal effects were kept, and took away his copies of their *nikkah*, affidavits for Priya's conversion to Islam, and photographs of the two of them. They then set off for Akbarpur to look for the couple, where they stormed the village and after a brief chase found Kamiyar and Priya.[48] Although I have no reason to question any of this, and indeed, while all of this was corroborated, I was interested to note that Kamiyar did not reveal to me one important aspect of that night's events. It was the fact that his elder brother Arif, who had also had a love-marriage to a Muslim girl, failed to protect him that night. Kamiyar felt that it was out of fear. Even though his own wife's parents had paid a gun-man to kill Arif when he had attempted to marry his love, Arif was unwilling to stand by Kamiyar and Priya's marriage:

> He also had a death-threat.[49] But that was his case; he was fighting for himself. Now it's my case; and now he has a kid and wife. So one day he has said to me, 'don't even expect a little help from me. I just cannot *support* you.' And you know, he has done something which has gone just against me! You know what he has done? When they came to take Priya, Arif told me that mummy and Fareeda [Kamiyar's 10-year-old sister] has been kidnapped. I estimated that 'no'—there was no such thing like that. The calculation done by me at that time was perfectly correct. He told me just to fear me. He came in person; they all came together to Akbarpur. It was like a mob you know. Word had gone around to everyone.

Kamiyar's brother had forewarned him not to expect any support. Kamiyar claims that he '*estimated*' that his brother was lying, and that the real reason that Priya was taken away was because her people were armed. Undoubtedly his family was forced—but as Kamiyar noted, even his own brother left him to fight his own battles alone. Perhaps he accepts that forced by the circumstances of protecting his own young family, Arif had to lie as he had been asked to, and convince Kamiyar that if he didn't hand Priya over, his own mother's and sister's lives would be in serious jeopardy. While this may well be true, Kamiyar was nonetheless protecting his own family (because in their honour lay his own honour?) by not publicly revealing the full extent of their complicity in being present in Akbarpur that night when they took away his wife. In so doing, perhaps he has been able to publicly mitigate his own perceived sense of alienation and abandonment. Equally, what this brief description also highlights is the extent to which the family had to turn in on itself in order to alienate Kamiyar, as that was the only way in which they could ensure their own honour and survival in such fraught circumstances.

Kamiyar was cynical about his family, and said that they were actively opposing him in their own way. They publicly denied all knowledge of the wedding between Priya and himself.[50] Finally, as if this weren't enough, his father told the press that his son 'was not mentally fit' and was therefore unable to legally contract a marriage. The press had a field day with this piece of news because it substantiated the argument that Kamiyar was mad, and that all his claims were false.

Kamiyar, for his part, was devastated, not just because it implied that he was mad, but because he was only too aware that one of the grounds for the annulment of a marriage is unsoundness of mind.[51] His father's testimony now added to other more systematic attempts to ensure the failure of his marriage. Over the next few months, he came to the decision that it was necessary to avoid speaking to his mother over the phone (as she pleaded with him to return and forget Priya), and that he had to avoid involving his family in his life or his troubles, as they were unwilling to support him. In more reflective moments he argued that from every side he was being told to consider the wishes, the honour and the lives of others and to sacrifice his self-interest for the sake of a greater common good:

My family's life is Life; But my wife, doesn't hers count as a Life?
Your *izzat* is *izzat*; But doesn't Priya have any *izzat* of her own?
Whatever you may be, are we ants or insects?
Do we not have any *decision*—do we not even have the right to live our lives?[52]

Denials and torture: Love-marriage strategy?

The greatest test to Kamiyar's resolve came not from his own family, or even from hers; it came from Priya herself. When Kamiyar descended from the tower, he had demanded that his wife be presented to a court, or that she be recovered from the unlawful custody of her family. Those from the National Human Rights Commission (NHRC) who asked him to descend and who promised him their full support were keen to establish that Priya was indeed his wife, that she was being kept against her will by her family, and that she was therefore in need of rescuing. Kamiyar, in his constantly anxious and weary state, was unprepared for a press-cutting that was handed to him. It was from a local edition of a national English language paper, but remarkably the same story was never carried by its Delhi edition. Somewhere along the line, it was felt that the article was either misleading or designed to incite those effervescent 'communal tensions' that are so regularly and conveniently invoked in the case of love-marriages. Kamiyar showed this article to me. He carried it around in his pocket and said it used to 'burn' him. He was keen that its contents should not be publicised as it could be used against his attempts to be re-united with Priya. The article headlined 'Priya Denies Marriage with Kamiyar' read as follows:

> The Kamiyar–Priya highly publicised love story took a new turn here when the so-called 'wife' of Kamiyar categorically denied that she got married with the former. Recently in Delhi, Kamiyar created a high-voltage drama remaining atop a microwave tower. According to Kamiyar, his wife Priya was illegally detained. Kamiyar also hails from the ... locality of the city. On Friday evening the circle officer of ..., Mr. Anil ..., along with the Additional city magistrate too, Mr. ..., visited the house of Priya for recording her statement. According to police sources, Priya categorically denied that she got married with Kamiyar. She also denied that she had any relations with Kamiyar. It is said that Priya also told the investigating officers and the magistrate that she was living with her parents of her own accord and the report was totally baseless that she had been kidnapped and illegally detained. While Priya recorded her statement with the team she was all alone. No member of her family was allowed to remain present there. It is said that she gave a one-page statement. Later Priya gave a somewhat similar version before the DIG.[53]

It was one thing for Priya to be held captive by her people, but surely when faced with the police and a magistrate, she could have asked to be allowed to join Kamiyar? However, Kamiyar pointed out that the two officials who took Priya's statement were Thakurs. The 'DIG' was known to Priya's family and was an immediate neighbour; it was unlikely that she would be able to say anything to an elder and highly respected neighbour known so intimately to them. Equally, her own brother's presence in the police force lent plausibility to Kamiyar's perspective that, had she found the courage to say that she wanted to join Kamiyar, she was presented with people whose allegiance to her family was unflagging and unamenable to negotiation.

Further, Kamiyar was implying in our conversations that the NHRC's solution of providing him a lawyer in the Supreme Court who would file a *Habeas Corpus* petition was not a path he wished to take. He gave two reasons. The first was that if he lost in the Supreme Court (and having already had his petition thrown out once by the Supreme Court on technical grounds, he was already cynical about the ability of the legal system to help him),[54] he would have no further recourse to appeal. This was a tremendous risk. Secondly, he was not entirely confident that his wife would be able to stand up in the Supreme Court and declare her love for him. He told me that if the judge allowed him a few minutes with her alone, he would be able to reassure her that things would be okay, and that she must not lie about the marriage, or about her family keeping her at home. But which judge would accept Kamiyar's argument that she was 'a typical Indian girl' from a small town, and would be scared out of her wits. As far as the legal system was concerned, Kamiyar himself could be trying to coerce her against her will—a far more likely scenario if she was indeed 'a typical Indian girl'. Kamiyar feared that Priya would have been 'mentally tortured' prior to the *Habeas Corpus* and would never dare to say that her own family was keeping her against her wishes, or that she had had a love-marriage with a Muslim boy.

It wasn't just Priya who was compromising Kamiyar's case to win back his wife. It was also the *moulvi* who solemnised their *nikkah*. Despite having photocopies of their *nikkahnama*, her affidavit of free and voluntary conversion from Hinduism to Islam, copies of Priya's school-leaving certificate, signed and attested copies from the office of the '*mufti*' (a jurist in the Muslim community) of Kanpur, and witness statements to all the above, the *moulvi* confessed that he was no longer willing to state that he had solemnised the *nikkah* in a court of law. He was willing to make this statement to the concerned authorities that the marriage had most definitely taken place, that he had in fact solemnised it, but that things had got to such a stage that he feared for his life and wouldn't make the same statement in public.[55] The *moulvi's* denial and Kamiyar's inability to produce the originals of the *nikkah*—because one set had been taken from his home by Hanuman Kumar and the other from his lawyer in Allahabad—conspired to make it appear as if the marriage hadn't taken place.

My own understanding of Priya's situation was that she had been deprived of all agency, and that being in the custody of her family, she was in no position to declare her desire to join Kamiyar. Kamiyar used to say that she had made him understand that what she was doing was the right thing, and that she was safeguarding his own family. She would say to him that if she escaped, Hanuman had promised to kidnap Kamiyar's younger sister and dishonour her like Priya had allegedly been dishonoured. Kamiyar's response was to question her concern with his people. 'Why is she so concerned with my *gharwale* [householders]? I am her householder! *To hell with both our gharwale* [members of their respective homes]. Do my people care about me?' However, I had to establish for myself that Priya did wish to rejoin Kamiyar. It took many months to organise for me to speak with her. When I did I was amazed by what I heard. There had been some indications that Kamiyar was being economical with the truth. Priya was being held to ransom by her brother-in-law, but she was trying to control the situation as best she could.

The 'half the body' metaphor

Priya's solution was to remain at home refusing to antagonise her people or give them any reason for complaint. These actions were designed to repulse allegations of her impropriety in having eloped with Kamiyar. She was determined to get them to accept her marriage to Kamiyar, and remaining with them was one way of winning their favour. I asked her why she made the statement she did to the police officers. Had she been tortured or coerced? No, she replied. I'll explain everything when I am with him. Do you want to join him? If you send a letter to the National Commission for Women they have agreed to send a team to get you out of your home and reunite you with Kamiyar. She replied with characteristic understatement: 'I want to be with him but I also want my people to agree to marry us.'

Priya was also upset with Kamiyar for mentioning her family's name in an interview he gave to a Hindi magazine which her family read. 'What was the need to bring up their names in the magazine? Will it help anything? They just get more annoyed.' I asked her repeatedly whether she had married Kamiyar, and she said that she had. She had also made the press statement, not so much because she was told to do so, but because it was part of her strategy to convince her people of her righteousness. She says that she was willing to wait until her family got ready to marry them. She didn't want rescuing. She wanted to be sent to Kamiyar like a bride, with all the *izzat* of her natal home behind her. When I mentioned this to Kamiyar, he shouted in frustration. 'She has told me she wants to convince her people. Will they ever be convinced?' Truly, I had to concede that having spoken to her brother and having followed Kamiyar's circumstances so carefully, I thought that she was being naive about her own family and their imagined willingness ever to accept this marriage. As Kamiyar said in one of the letters he threw down from the tower. '... *I tried my best to make reason our parents and family but failed. It was an effort which was a five year period. I think enough time to maybe reason God for anypurpose.*'

At some stage, however, it seems as if her family did agree to let her join Kamiyar.

> You know, that Hanuman had phoned [his parents] and said: come and take the girl. My people, when her people did something positive, then my people would create a problem. My people raised the problem. Why did it erupt so suddenly? Because my people didn't want it. And they used to say nasty things to Priya's brothers: 'Your sister is like this, your sister is like that. Why don't you make her understand?' If you say this to any brother can he tolerate it? And that too knowing that they are Thakurs! That's why I keep telling her, 'Why are you caring about our people!'[56]

My own sense is that this must have been after the first of the tower climbing incidents, where Kamiyar unashamedly exposed the level of her complicity in the love-affair and subsequent marriage, thus thoroughly shaming her people and making it difficult to conceive of an arranged-marriage to redeem their honour. Furthermore, it is conceivable that Phoolan Devi (India's celebrated 'Bandit Queen'-turned Minister of Parliament) intervened on Kamiyar's behalf with Hanuman, and convinced him to let Priya go.[57] Kamiyar's own people, smarting from the ignominy of Hanuman's bullying and bravado, could hardly resist the chance to thoroughly dishonour the latter by refusing to take their daughter-in-law into the house, alleging that she was of dubious morals and had been out to seduce their innocent son. This act of conciliation must have indicated to Priya that conciliation was still a hoped-for possibility, whereas for Hanuman, the dishonour that had been caused was probably irreparable.

Whatever the true circumstances surrounding this near-resolution, Priya felt that what Kamiyar had done was wrong. She felt that the only way was to win over her family and that she had to a large extent succeeded in this endeavour before 'suddenly, Kamiyar climbed the tower. After the second time, everything then went out of control.' After the second time, Hanuman's resolve against letting her go probably hardened. Kamiyar for his part felt that he knew the true situation—that her family were trying to fool her. He told me how the first time he spoke to her after Akbarpur she said, 'Kamiyar, forget everything, because people here have become ready to kill. It will initiate a blood bath between the two families.' Then he spoke to her and she agreed that they should move the court. The secular court offered them the only hope—it was the only *via media* between another elopement attempt (which would no doubt still heap upon them great dishonour and leave them in danger) and remaining a hostage of honour. If a court of law demanded that she be handed over to her husband, then at least she wouldn't bear the taint of having been responsible for any deaths in his family. Equally, it was unlikely that her family would go on a rampage if she had to go because of a court order. The most likely situation would have been that the court would have given the two families *the necessary reason* to reconcile themselves to the marriage of Priya and Kamiyar. It would have been the only reason that would not have involved a loss of honour that could have been prevented by the Thakurs. The power of the legal system would have merely been seen to prevail over the more 'traditional' ways of people. However, it is highly significant that the case never came to court. This does imply that there was sufficient will against such a judgement, or equally, that a judgement impinging upon the volatile issue of Hindu–Muslim relations would not have been politically expedient.[58]

In the *Habeas Corpus* appeal to the court, Kamiyar's lawyers state: 'The petitioner apprehends danger to her life limb [*sic*], and her honour and the petitioner may be exploited, harmed and even physically liquidated if she is not immediately released from the illegal detention of Respondent No. 7 [Hanuman Kumar]'. Kamiyar believes that as her husband it is his responsibility to safeguard her honour. His worst fear is that they will succeed in arranging a marriage for her, and she won't be able to get word to him, or he won't be able to prevent it physically. Considering the experiences of numerous love-marriages I encountered, where the families successfully arranged another marriage for their offspring despite a preceding court or temple love-marriage, this was not an unwarranted fear:

> She says to me 'I am coming,' 'I will come'—'the way I am enduring this, you must also endure....' She makes me understand. But my biggest fear is what if they do something in a week, ten days—then it will be terrible for her. Of course it will destroy my life anyway. But if they do this, I won't be able to bear it. That's why for everyone's safety she must get out.

It is striking that Priya and Kamiyar adopted such different strategies in their attempt to be together. It is quite likely that Priya went along with Kamiyar's plan to leave home because they both believed that they wouldn't be found out so quickly, and that their marriage would eventually be accepted. Equally it is conceivable that she believed that getting her people to agree to her marriage to Kamiyar was her only way out; even if this took years of perseverance. She chose to remain at home, but was this because she believed she would one day meet with success, or because she came to realise that their love was impossible? Her family vowed to arrange her marriage even if 'she goes and eats poison and dies!' When Hanuman took her away from Kamiyar in Akbarpur, he swore that they would kill Priya but never give her back to Kamiyar. Kamiyar in turn swore to defend her honour. In one of our discussions he said to me that her honour and their love meant everything to him.

> *Two people makes a body which is love. And if one of the body separates out then another* [the other] *person may get hurt up to that much that they can kill. This happens. Didn't it happen in America? A footballer whose wife married so he killed them.*[59] [...] My meaning is that I think these thoughts when I think I may be unsuccessful; that Priya,... I don't want to say it.... That she should go somewhere else.

Kamiyar also uses a widely recognised religious metaphor that is used particularly in the context of marriage in India. It is what Chakravarti has called a 'half-the-body' metaphor, and it comes from the ancient Hindu text by Brihaspati which says: 'Of him whose wife is not deceased half the body survives. How then can another take his property while half his person is alive?' (1998: 125). Chakravarti discusses this metaphor in the context of an eighteenth century debate on widowhood, widow remarriage, and widows' property rights where this text was used to make the argument that a widow, as 'half the body' of her husband, could not remarry and become 'half the body' of another man.

I believe the 'half-the-body' metaphor, while important for Hindu conceptions of marriage, serves as an equally important ontology for north Indian conceptions of 'love'. When Kamiyar makes the argument that 'two people make a body which is love', and when he validates the pain of separating out of this single body through reference to O. J. Simpson, he is drawing upon a reworked notion of marriage and he contextualises it within the modern world of romantic love, where the two halves don't make a marriage, but a body of 'love'. Equally, the sense of personhood and agency expressed in the reconstituted body of the loving couple is important, because it identifies the boundedness of the two-halves-as-one, and their separation from the rules and values of the rest of the world.

Also important in Kamiyar's discourse is the close link between notions of love and honour. It is a similar discourse to that of Priya's brothers and Hanuman Kumar who vowed to kill her but never to return her to Kamiyar, or who said they would marry her off even if she ate poison to save herself from that fate. Her honour is protected by the former; but of course, in their honour (marrying her off with full rites) lies the dishonour for the latter (one's legal wife is made to commit adultery). The source of dishonour for both the kin and Kamiyar is Priya's sexuality. To kill her would thus eliminate the source of dishonour for both sets of people. But for Kamiyar, '*Two people makes a body which is love*'. To kill Priya would be akin to a double suicide, a prospect which he cannot entertain. Priya's sacrifice of herself, and her love, for the honour of *her people* (she remains at home and is thus forced into an arranged marriage) is redeemed by the guardian of *her* honour (the other part of their 'body of love'—her husband Kamiyar). Ironically, of course, in so doing, he upholds the honour of the two families—his own (for whom Priya is a daughter-in-law, who would be committing adultery by remarrying), and her own (for whom she is a daughter with an already sullied reputation).

Love-Marriage Personhood

This chapter began with a discussion of what I saw as a theory of agency for love-marriages: the particular social contexts in which agency is invoked and revoked. Two love-biographies have been examined from the perspective of a five-fold parameter through which I have sought to discern the ways in which the complex agency of couples is best seen as a calculus of love: the weighing up of one act of agency against another, and the anticipation of the effects of one action upon the social relations affecting another. For instance, Indu is happy to make an issue of her unconsummated marriage because it provides renewed hope for togetherness with Subhash. Equally, Kamiyar advertises Hanuman Kumar's criminal connections in an attempt to gain the support of the secular state machinery which is supposed to safeguard his 'rights'. However, what we learn from both Subhash and Priya is that the notion of individual 'rights' devoid of parental support and family love are empty concepts for many Indians. It would seem that the ideal of the love-cum-arranged marriage is so strong that anything short of this is unacceptable, not just to the parents of such couples, but people like Subhash and Priya who seek to have these marriages themselves. However, this is only a partial reading, because it could easily be argued that while the ideal of a love-marriage is strong enough, people like Subhash and Priya succumb to the enormous pressures exerted upon them by their families to revoke their agency, such that the elaborate negotiations attempted by more determined people like Indu and Kamiyar truly enter the realm of the heroic.

Subhash's and Priya's agency can be summed up as a retreat into the social relations that withheld their agency, such that they are, once again, a part of their families. Indu and Kamiyar, on the other hand, declare their agency through a reinterpretation and careful mediation, of the very categories (sexuality, honour, 'rights', consent and love) that were used to appropriate their own personhood, and this allows them the possibility to challenge the social relations that served to constrain their agency.

These love-biographies are presented as social mediations between community and not-community. Yet there is a sense that I have not addressed the most glaring fact of these instances of failed love—the subjective pain and anguish that these couples have been through. How does their agency and struggle to have a love-marriage affect their personhood? Alfred Gell has argued that 'any one social individual is the sum of their relations (distributed over biographical space and time) ... with other persons'. He goes on to add:

> Our inner personhood seems to consist of replications of what we are externally, as suggested in the parable of Peer Gynt and his famous onion. So, bearing this in mind, it may not be so aberrant to suggest that what persons are externally (and collectively) is a kind of enlarged replication of what they are internally. Especially if ... we consider 'persons' not as bounded biological organisms, but use this label to apply to all the objects and/or events in the milieu from which agency or personhood can be abducted (1998: 222).

For Gell, personhood is the expansive potential of Marriot's 'dividual', affecting and being affected by all its transactions. In this sense, it is similar to Strathern's conception of agency in which the agent is the loci of both, cause and effect. I have argued that personhood in love-marriage is both bounded and expansive, and it is the dialectical negotiation of self-as-agent, and self-as-agent-of-the-group that both serves as a source of freedom and efficacy, and limits and constrains in making accountable the individual to the group.

Kamiyar states that marriage isn't for society but for the individual. However, if this were the case, then couples such as himself and Priya would need to quite literally ride off into the sunset, because all the relations upon which they have built their lives would be ruined. This is why, despite his valiant protestations, we need to recognise that love-marriage couples aren't trying to build 'a couple' who get married, but rather try to build a couple within a web of relations which are essential to their survival.

Similarly, with the five values (honour, sexuality, 'rights', consent and 'love') I have detailed, if a couple chose to pay attention to just one of them then they might find success in unambiguously (or relatively unambiguously) maximising them because a clear course of action could be obtained. What this study of failed love shows is that love-marriage couples consider marriage to require that these ethics be mutually reinforcing rather than mutually antagonistic. In trying to make them compossible, they cannot afford to take extreme views or fall back on a modernist discourse, but instead must seek to merge the agency of self with that of community. After years of separation, Kamiyar slowly began the painful process of re-building his life. Supported by his kin, he was encouraged to marry. After so many years of pain and feeling alone, he says that he felt so proud to see his parents smile and be happy on his account. It made him realise just how much his actions had affected them. His wife knows all about his past, and together they concentrate on building the foundations of a solid future for their child based on love and understanding.

Notes

1. Indeed, statistics are interestingly used, with many people in my public interviews converging on '99 per cent' to describe the 'failure-rate' of love-marriages. It must be noted that I was not asking for 'statistics', but many people felt the need to use them in their assessments. In the scale of things, the more 'unbiased' informants proffered '95 per cent' as a reasonable figure, and the most charitable suggested between '50 and 60 per cent' as a realistic proportion of 'failures'. Not a single informant in my public interviews suggested that love-marriages had a greater chance of success than arranged-marriages. However, this is not to say that such a view did not exist in Delhi, but that a sample selected for its arbitrariness (a stop-and-research method) yielded these particularly unequivocal accounts, indicating the preponderance of this viewpoint. Many Delhi University couples I worked with certainly had complete confidence in the 'success' of marriages of choice.

2. A good instance of how easy it is to misinterpret agency is when the reaction is not anticipated and comes as a surprise, or when an action is deliberately misleading. A couple coming to the court for a civil marriage, and who are discovered *in flagrante delicto* by their family(ies), may find it difficult to explain that their plan wasn't to elope (and in doing so advertise their agency) but rather, to safeguard their agency without having to declare it. Returning to one's parental home after a court-marriage indicates that action and intentionality may be usefully separated out by examining their complex in the sense described by Strathern.

3. Gell's dramatic proposition of examining 'art objects' as a 'system of action, intended to change the world rather than encode symbolic propositions about it' (1998: 6) is, I believe, instructive when dealing with 'issues' such as love-marriages that suffer from what could be described as 'symbolic overload'. By this I mean that love-marriages for the couples, their families and assorted members of the public, are imbued with contradictory and complex meanings that must be examined as evidenced in action (or agency; in other words, as social relations), rather than in some symbolic or semiotic abstraction. This is where my approach differs from those who examine the media, the construction of love and romance through pulp fiction and popular Hindi films. I find such approaches unconvincing because they don't tell us anything about how love is actually 'lived' by those that consume these works. Furthermore, it was evident to me that while people avidly consumed popular culture, their 'encoded messages' were never a matter of uncritical mimesis. This said, it is arguable that while films cannot be taken as an ethnographic description of attitudes to love or desire, they play a significant role in the ways in which love is *imagined*. For instance, despite my love-marriage informants' protests to the contrary, their language would often sound like it took something from Hindi films. Certainly expressions such as 'an Indian woman loves only once' or the oft-used quote '*chaar din ki chandni phir andheri raat*' ('Four days of moonlight, then the darkness of night') used to castigate love-marriages seem to derive something from public languages that are created to refer to love and bear the track of cinematic language (Veena Das, personal communication).

4. The lack of patterns in the agency of men and women can perhaps be attributed to the fact that this particular chapter deals with a particular sort of couple: those whose love hasn't been consummated in togetherness. While elsewhere there are gendered patterns quite obviously discernible (a girl who elopes might be seen to have been abducted), the lack of them here is important and partly explicable by the extremes of the circumstances involved. In other words, the fact that both couples were pushed to the limit perhaps inspires them into less conventional discourses such that they move beyond gendered and normative behaviour to a position of critical examination and occasional confrontation.

5. However, the maintenance of honour is a widespread phenomenon, and various groups use honour to pit themselves against each other in aggressive status and political matches. In rural contexts, a person or family may be dishonoured by *panchayat* decisions such as the levy of fines, or in more extreme instances, the blackening of a person's face, shoe-beatings and other deprecating punishments. The most extreme instances of honour violations are those in which women are molested

or raped, or vulnerable lower castes are made to suffer abominations by powerful landlords, such as the gang rapes of Dalit women or the forceful eating of human faeces by lower caste men. Honour is thus an important aspect of caste, but also of the *politics* of ethno-religious community. A Home Affairs Department Report on rape in Bihar notes that a stupendous 94.91 per cent of rape cases registered in the state between 1990–1996 were reported by Dalit women (In *The Hindustan Times*, 'Rise in Rape Cases in Bihar', by Mammen Mathew, 6-6-1997, p. 7, New Delhi.

6. The term enjoyed something of a revival when the feminist movement in the 1980s tried to use the term *shakti* to galvanise women through 'local metaphor', but found the term hijacked by women's groups on the far Right, who deployed them for their own divisive ends (Kumar, 1993: 145). *Stri Shakti* ('women's force'), *Grahak Shakti* ('consumer strength'), *Lok Shakti* ('people's power') are just some examples of the more visible contexts in which the term is widely used. Precisely because of its powerful meaning, it is particularly amenable to politicisation. Recently, the BJP used the 1998 Pokhran nuclear tests as evidence of Hindu India's '*Shakti*', destined to humiliate and humble the 'other' (in this configuration, Islam/Pakistan). 'INS *Shakti*', an Indian naval carrier, received particular mention when it was deployed to carry water for drought affected persons in Gujarat in 2000. Clearly then, the term is loaded, but capable of much metonymic adaptation.

7. Indeed, as Béteille has pointed out, in addition to caste, the things that count for status for urban Indians in 'modern occupations' are 'education, occupation, income, and the sub-cultures of the profession, the office and the association' (1997: 173). He argues that '[I]t is possible that a more permissive attitude towards caste in the selection of spouses is being accompanied by a greater attention to other restrictions such as those relating to education, occupation and income' (ibid.: 164).

8. Furthermore, Minturn makes the very important point that 'Most of the illegitimate children in the village are probably the children of their uncles or grandfathers, and these cases go undetected. It is only the case of the unmarried girl, the widow or the married woman who becomes pregnant in her parents village that cannot be covered up (1993: 202–203)'.

9. Speaking of the ritually superior clans in Kangra, he delineates the extent of the dilemma for fathers of daughters, who are bound to marry them upwards (hypergamy)—or among equals (within their *biradari* or clans of approximately equal status)—but, in so doing, are forced to accept the inferiority ascribed to the lineage of bride-givers with respect to the bride-takers: 'The mere existence of a nubile, but unmarried, daughter is shame enough in itself, for according to the sacred scriptures it is the binding—and supernaturally sanctioned—duty of a father to provide

a husband for his daughter before she reaches puberty. [...] If they leave their daughters unmarried, they incur both supernatural sanctions and shame in the eyes of the world, while they run the even graver risk of being totally dishonoured by the daughter's unchastity. Yet by giving their daughters in marriage they renounce all claims to absolute supremacy in the hierarchy. [...] Before the British took over the area, however, the Rajput aristocrats were at liberty to resolve this dilemma by resorting to female infanticide' (1979: 214).

10. I remember once hearing a Parsi woman on the radio (BBC Radio 4 in England) describing her son in the past tense as if he had met with some terrible tragedy. He was a tremendously accomplished pianist, she said. It was only later at the prompting of the host that it emerged that he was alive and well but married to a non-Parsi English woman whom the mother indicated was unsuitable and therefore unwelcome in the family home.

11. I examine two such instances in this part of the book. It is noteworthy that it was always boys whose sexuality was assumed to be capable of such dual roles. I never encountered a single case of a woman who was allowed, let alone encouraged, to continue with her love affair after a forced 'arranged marriage'.

12. See the *Times of India*, 'Caste Justice for Haryana Couple', by Shardah Uniyal, The Times of India Human Rights Cell, 16-5-1998, p. 11, New Delhi.

13. Gail Omvedt, in an article defending Arundhati Roy's description of the love between a Dalit man and a 'caste-Christian' in the Booker Prize winner, *The God of Small Things*, has argued that, 'Admitting the role of love and desire, the need for freedom in love, into a perspective on caste relations is an indispensable element in analysing it as a step to overcome it'. She criticises the women's liberation movement in India as being somewhat 'shy' about the issue of the right to love and argues that regular intermarriages will represent the ultimate collapsing of caste barriers: '[O]nly intermarriage to the point where a caste identity cannot even be fixed will destroy the system, and ...this will begin to be achieved only when boys and girls have the right to choose whom they will love and marry'. In *The Hindu*, 'Love Laws', 17-1-1998, p. 10, New Delhi.

14. Jeffery has pointed out that among the Pirzade of Delhi, 'shame' in love-marriages was so great that the boy's parents arranged the match as if they themselves had initiated the choice of spouse.

    '... [F]or public consumption, the ideal of the uninvolved bride and groom must be perpetuated' (1979: 105). This is very similar to what I have earlier described as what my informants called '*love-cum-arranged*' marriages. See also Uberoi (2006: 36).

15. I have found very little in terms of anthropological literature on 'love' in India (an exception being Dwyer's book on romance and love in Indian literature and Hindi film), and have been inspired by the theoretical categories of Harbans Mukhia's work on Urdu *ghazals* (the form of Urdu poetry which literally means 'to converse with the beloved').

He explores the artistic, aesthetic and socio-political representation of love in *ghazal* lyrics in north India, and provides some interesting illuminations on the conceptions of love in this literary form (1999).

16. Majnu is the typical extreme lover, but for Nizami, his creator, he is not the ideal nor the succesful one. This is because he goes too far in breaking with family and kin and destroys Laila's reputation by publicising his love for her (Meisami 1987).

17. The interview with Subhash's best friend Gopal took place in February 1998, and was followed by an interview with Subhash himself in April at his residence in a *busti* on the outskirts of Delhi. All quotations refer to an interview with Subhash Shukla (28-4-1998).

18. In Hindi: *'galti ho ya na ho. Aissi nahin jo mohobbat karne yogya na ho'*. By using the double negative, 'It's not that you aren't worth loving', Subhash protects his own ego by leaving open the possibility of a studied disinterest in her in the unfortunate event that his (potential) feelings aren't reciprocated.

19. In this regard, the increasing incidences of throwing acid on women's faces and bodies causing grievous disfigurements by men they know must be read as a crisis in the traditionally gendered norms of courtship in South Asia. Women rejecting unwanted advances from men are seen to be insulting to the latter and threatening male honour. In this configuration, the declaration of love itself is a gendered act which has the potential to force women into unhappy 'love' relationships. For details of circumstances of acid throwing cases by spurned suitors, see for instance *Hindustan Times*, 'Parents Demand Arrest of Accused: Acid Thrown on Girl's Face', 13-5-1997, New Delhi, p. 7; *Hindustan Times*, 'Awaiting Justice', HT Magazine, p. 1 and 4, 8-6-1997, New Delhi; *The Times of India* (Delhi Times), 'Burnt by Acid, Woman Struggles for Life', by Sreerupa Mitra Chaudhry, 4-9-1997, p. 1, New Delhi; for a case of kerosene burning see *The Hindu*, 'Jilted Lover Burns Woman to Death', 16-4-1998, p. 2, New Delhi.

20. The dilemma of the father is clear. Even if he wants to accept the marriage for the sake of his son's happiness, how can he do it without pitting his family's honour against hers? It is important to point out that in cases of couples seeking to arrange their love-marriage where one side or family agrees to the marriage, it is crudely and commonly assumed that the agreeable side has less honour (and reputation) to lose and the ambition to gain from such a match.

21. The insistence on parental consent is dropped and indicates that beyond a point, Indu feels that she must take a stance in the hope that the family may still capitulate; not out of happiness at the match, but out of pressure to avoid their own dishonour which will follow her love-marriage.

22. Parry has described how in Kangra, castes that have no regularised exchange reckon hierarchy through a 'transitive' process. That is, if an exchange defines A as superior to B, and B as superior to C, then A is superior to C although they do not share any exchange. The exchange of women, which defines and distinguishes a hierarchy of Rajput and Brahman clans, has no relevance in ranking castes because castes are endogamous and there are no systematic exchanges between them (Parry 1979: 93). In the context of Indu and Subhash, I have tried to ascertain their relative ranking of their castes, but have been unable to do so. Shuklas are considered a 'high-up' clan amongst Brahmans from Uttar Pradesh, and Kashmiri Pundits constitute a high-ranking endogamous clan of Kashmiri Brahmans. Most people I have asked have declared that in terms of hierarchy, Kashmiri Pundits and Shuklas are both 'equally high' (in caste).

23. The Hindi phrase Subhash used was: 'apne baap ki pagdi uchhal do ya rakh do'. Elsewhere, Subhash mentions that Indu's father ensured that she was not allowed to touch the phone to call for help or leave the house on the day of the engagement.

24. Subhash implies that any action the two of them took now also involved the honour of another home: that of the boy to whom Indu was betrothed.

25. As I have discussed earlier, many couples actually take the option of 'double suicides'. See for instance, The Times of India, 'Two Teenage Lovers Commit Suicide', 12-12-1997, p. 1, New Delhi.

26. As quoted in Uberoi, the law states, 'Qui facet per alum facet per se': ' or, 'He who acts through another acts himself'.

27. The legal issue of withheld consent to sexual intercourse within marriage in India is also of interest. Sexual intercourse without consent doesn't qualify as rape under criminal law. As Uberoi points out, 'consent to marriage is also, and simultaneously, consent to sexual intercourse so long as the marriage lasts' (1996: 324).

28. For instance, Dube (1996); Chandra (1998), and Sarkar (1993).

29. As she points out, it must be borne in mind that a sociological reading of judicial obiter dicta is prejudiced towards instances of marital disputes.

30. Parry, in his fascinating paper on marriage, sex marriage and consummation rituals are no longer separated by a period of years, in great part due to the legal prohibitions against under-age marriage, and the added convenience and limited expense of organising the two

in quick succession. In cities like Delhi, this usually takes place over a period of a few days, and in rural areas, over a few months. He explains this phenomenon as an ever-increasing anxiety over the virginity of the bride, and the parental difficulties of monitoring the sexuality of young people between the time of the marriage and its consummation. For Parry, the conflation of the marriage ritual with *bidai* (the ceremony of farewell for the bride at her natal home) ensures that the marriage is 'settled' from start to finish without opportunities for reneging, and bride-taking men expect to receive virgins. This may be one way in which we can think about the modern anxiety about the virginity of prospective brides, and about the added significance this gives the 'first night'. Equally, the work of historians like Chandra (1998) and Chakravarti (1998) shows that such ritual procedures were encouraged so as to prevent against the scenario where a girl's husband died after the marriage ritual but *prior* to consummation; thus making her a 'child widow' whose sexuality once 'gifted' was no longer available to be given again, and who would, in orthodox society, be expected to adopt the ritual and social injunctions applicable to widows in some (particularly high-caste) groups.

31. Like an arranged-marriage that takes place at the initiative of the parents, divorces are rarely initiated by the couple themselves. More frequently, the parents make the decision with their child and the divorce is so 'arranged'.

32. Dube says the valorisation of female virginity is one reason for the sharp distinction between the status of a primary and a secondary marriage where, in the first instance, the rituals and the acceptable limits of connubiality 'sacrifice and sacralise' the girl's sexuality, making her a full member of her caste and 'thus a complete person' (1996: 14). Thus, Dube's conception of the moral import of marriage lies in the gift giving and ritual actions, as opposed to Uberoi's observation that it is the consummation of the marriage that marks it with enduring moral significance for the 'meaning of marriage'. Parry (2001), adds to this with the argument that the added emphasis on the intimacy of the couple means that post-marital fidelity is possibly more of an issue than it was in the past.

33. In a letter to the President, he described his act as an '*aamaran anshan*' or non-violent fast unto death.

34. '*Roadside-Romeos*' are the Indian version of urban romantics who career through the streets of the city harassing strange women and singing ditties of romantic Hindi songs in the manner of what is known as 'eve-teasing'. The image of Kamiyar as a *roadside-Romeo* was soon displaced with the discovery of his mobile phone, because such a term generally refers to poor or working-class men and boys. Kamiyar could be seen using his phone from the ground below. This

delighted the crowd because it indicated that he was wealthy, and stories about his good looks and soft-spoken manner abounded. Since many popular Bollywood male heroes are Muslim, and since Delhi's print, television and radio media were assembled at the base of the tower, making quite a kerfuffle, it was generally assumed that this was some sort of stunt to gain the attention of Bollywood.

35. In Hindi: 'ladkiwale ko madat karne teesra aadmi bhi aage aa jayega'.

36. This term comes from colonial police jargon still widely used in north India to signal a 'bad character' known to the police.

37. It is striking that I never encountered cases of girls being protected by their maternal uncles in the case of love-marriages, and in one case where a girl did seek refuge with her uncle, he tricked the couple and handed her back to her father where the latter suffered a brutal and violent punishment. Even in Kamiyar's case, the mother's brother was only able to provide preliminary protection, and the fact that Priya was taken away, may even point to the possibility that while sharing love and intimacy with his sister's son, he is nonetheless impotent in effectively protecting him.

38. A small sample of some of the cases that I collected during my fieldwork are as follows. They include an execution of a couple with a steel mace and *chimtas* (a purificatory implement used to stoke a ritual fire), gang-rape of a young woman by four village men including the head-man, followed by cutting open her abdomen with a butcher's knife, and an 18-year-old boy bludgeoning his sister to death because she was to marry her neighbour in the court the next day. *The Times of India*, 'Relatives "sentence" two lovers to death', by Lalit Kumar, 12-4-1997, p. 3, New Delhi; *The Times of India*, 'Youth, Girl Killed for Falling in Love', 5-7-1997, p. 6, New Delhi; *The Times of India*, 'Sudaka: the Heart of Darkness', by Syeda Saiyidain Hameed, 18-8-1997, p. 13, New Delhi; *The Times of India*, 'Boy Stabs Sister to Death on Marriage Eve', 13-8-1997, p. 4, New Delhi; *The Hindustan Times*, 'Panchayat Members Flog Woman, Lover', by Amitabh Shukla, 24-3-1998, p. 5, New Delhi.

39. For instance, a common situation from my reading of press reports on such killings is that when one of the lovers is killed, the newly bereaved family demands that the *panchayat* sentence to death and kill the lover or spouse as they were equally responsible. Oftentimes, the police would get wind of these events days and weeks after both killings had taken place. There is a tendency to believe that the women are more likely to be killed, but my reading of this is that there are many more factors at play within the political–economy of the family, caste and the wider *biradari* or *panchayat*, and it is often these that play a determining role in how and why certain instances spill over into this sort of violence.

40. *Bhabhi* means brother's wife, i.e. Priya's elder sister. In referring to Hanuman's wife as *bhabhi*, Kamiyar is incorporating himself into Hanuman's kin, such that he stands in a symbolic relation of brother to Hanuman.
41. All these people had love-marriages. Akbar Ahmed Dumpy is a bureaucrat, and his wife was described by Kamiyar as a 'Miss India'.
42. In fact, shortly after this interview, Ali was imprisoned for numerous murder cases. The use of gangsters and hit-men in states like Bihar and Uttar Pradesh is so common that people in Delhi jokingly say that it is the only way in which politicians can work in the 'cow-belt'.
43. Here Kamiyar is explicitly mocking *bhabhi*'s double standards which saw her fast and in so doing blackmail her brothers, but which was incapable of understanding or supporting her little sister's love for Kamiyar.
44. In Hindi: '*Keechad hain. Keechad main kamal khilla hain*'.
45. Calling someone '*sala*' or wife's brother, indicates that you are sleeping with his sister (Kolenda 1990). In this context, adding '*f***-you*' is doubly insulting.
46. In Hindi: '*Uski kismat chamak gayi!*'
47. Of course, there may well be repercussions on the *izzat* of the family, but the important point to note is that nobody in Priya's family is about to safeguard against this loss of *izzat*.
48. An observant reader would notice that there is a discrepancy in the narrative here. This is that in written sources (such as Kamiyar's letters to the police) he says that Priya's family went to his home before coming to Akbarpur, whereas elsewhere he describes them going to the house after returning from Akbarpur to collect the marriage papers. I am not making too much of this simply because I have a feeling that they went to the house twice, and that as such, no discrepancy occurs.
49. Kamiyar had repeatedly been warned by a number of 'reliable sources', including well-wishers, that a contract was out on his life and that he would be killed if he dared return to Kanpur.
50. When Kamiyar was on the tower, the main issue for the press was whether or not he had married Priya, because only once this had been established could her whereabouts be investigated. It must be noted that the police and the public were particularly vigilant about ruining an 'innocent' girl's honour should Kamiyar have turned out to be an infatuated youth rather than a wronged husband.
51. For more on the legal aspects of insanity for marriage litigation in India, see Dhanda (1996), or *The Times of India*, 'The Insanity Formula for Getting Instant Divorce', by Darlington Jose Hector, 7-10-1997, p. 1, New Delhi.

52. In Hindi: '*Hamare gharwalo ki zindagi zindagi hain, Priya ki zindagi zindagi nahin?*
    Aap ki izzat izzat hain, Priya ko izzat nahin?
    Jo kuch bhi aap hain, hum keede-makode hain kya? Hamari koi decision nahin? Hamari jeene ka haq hi nahin?'
53. The DIG is the head of all the police in the range. There are approximately twelve ranges in the whole state of Uttar Pradesh.
54. The rejection of the *Habeas Corpus* petition in the Supreme Court was a terrible blow to Kamiyar. He paid his lawyers a vast sum of money but they completely misled him, and instead of filing the petition on his behalf (demanding that his wife be presented in court) it was incorrectly filed on *her* behalf, even when the statement said that she was in the custody of her family. The judge said that a *Habeas Corpus* petition couldn't be filed by a petitioner who was in fact not in contact with the court, and a decree of 'permission to withdraw' the case was granted. Kamiyar lost all his money, and was told that he couldn't re-submit his case. It was this frustration that caused him to climb the tower for the second time, this time demanding that the President of India intervene and order the court to accept his *Habeas Corpus* plea. Interestingly, the petition to the Supreme Court details events in Allahabad, where Kamiyar had first tried to get the legal system to intercede on their behalf, before he was forced to come to Delhi. Under Point 7 of the *Habeas Corpus* petition, it states (obviously, with alias names): '*That the petitioner's husband wanted to file a writ of Habeas Corpus at Allahabad High Court and handed over necessary documents to his advocate at Allahabad for doing the needful when abovesaid* [sic] *Hanuman Kumar came to know about the filing of Habeas Corpus at Allahabad, he* [Hanuman Kumar] *forced the parents and relatives of the petitioner's husband Kamiyar ... to direct the said advocate not to file the petition for Habeas Corpus and under pressure, threat extended by Hanuman Kumar, the parents of petitioner's husband sent an advocate from Kanpur to Allahabad. Respondent No. 7 Shri Hanuman Kumar further threatened that Kamiyar ... would be killed if he is sighted anywhere in the state of U.P.* [Uttar Pradesh].'
55. I was informed about this by the NHRC, who in fact have discretionary powers equivalent to those of the Supreme Court of India. That means that they have the power to act like a judge and treat verbal evidence (specially in the case of threats and intimidation of witnesses) as evidence admissible to the court. If a *moulvi* made this statement to them, then they had the liberty and authority to say that the marriage had been established as having taken place. The NHRC were, however, not willing to put themselves out and make such a statement.
56. Interview with Kamiyar, 27-4-1998.

57. When Kamiyar climbed the tower for the first time, the story goes, Umed Singh, Phoolan's husband was passing by in his convoy. Seeing people staring up into the sky, he enquired as to what amused them and upon hearing that it was a madman, decided to try his hand at negotiating with him to come down. It is an unlikely story, simply because Phoolan is from Bhadoi, a constituency in Uttar Pradesh, and it is just as likely that she was contacted by someone from Kamiyar's side to help and ensure his safe descent. Whatever the manner of her initial involvement, Kamiyar maintained that she helped him enormously simply by believing that he wasn't mad, and that a grave injustice had been done to the two lovers. He would say: 'She is someone who has felt how unjust our society is. She understands very well what we have been through.' Phoolan Devi was gunned down outside her official residence in Delhi in July 2001. The murder was apparently to avenge the killing of 22 high-caste Kshatriyas in Behmai.

58. Indeed, the NHRC delayed the entire issue over when enquiries could begin over Priya's whereabouts, and when she could be 'rescued' by referring to the national elections that were imminent. Repeatedly it was argued that such enquiries would be dangerous and might inflame the passions of people (even cause riots) because this was a Hindu–Muslim marriage.

59. Kamiyar described the entire O.J. Simson chase, which he had the opportunity to watch live on satellite T.V.

Conclusion

The Intimate State

This book has looked at the intersection between relations of intimacy as a basis of marriage and the protections (and obstructions) presented by the law to those who transform their new forms of intimacy into marriage in the eyes of the state. I have tried to extend Das' thesis about the state and communities 'colonising the life world of individuals' to think about the ways in which the state sets up 'intimacies' with individuals. Indeed, there can be no more powerful demonstration of this than the state legislation for self-arranged marriages through the enactment of a civil marriage law that permits inter-community marriages. Furthermore, the state is obliged to protect individuals from the wrath of their families if and when a self-arranged marriage leads to violence or threats of violence, but we have made note of the ways in which both the state (through the courts and the police) and kinship groups are oftentimes complicit in their exercise of what Chakravarti has called 'sexual governance'.

The state then, is no monolith, towering above and separate from the domestic, mundane and the everyday struggles that affect Indian families and society (indeed, there is much recent work on the anthropology of the state which bears testament to this observation about the nature of different states; notably Fuller and Harris 2000, Navaro-Yashin 2002). Sections of the Indian state have also become expert in deflecting responsibility in what I would describe as subversion-through-inadvertent-actions; the hundreds of ways in which the spirit of the law can be violated without it appearing to be the case. Love-marriage couples are thus further exposed to mortal danger, through tactics of delay, inaction as well as inappropriate inaction when they come in contact with the state and its executive organs. Take for instance a case cited in the PUDR report '*Courting Disaster*'.[1] Here, an eloping Jat girl from Haryana who surrendered before a judge is recognized as a legal adult, is recognised to have married her low-caste Dalit husband of her own 'free will', but rather than being set at liberty is sent by the judge to her maternal uncle despite her protests to the contrary, and her request for state protection. The girl (and her sister who also ran away fearing that their father would beat her for supporting her sister) were taken back to their village and were found dead the next morning with the family claiming that they had committed 'suicide' by consuming rat poison. Women in the neighbourhood alleged that they had heard the girls crying out for help in the night. The police statement claimed that the girls, 'unable to bear the ignomy and shame of what had happened to them', committed suicide. In this context, it is important that we recognise the brutal ways in which discourses of 'shame' and 'honour' in the context of love-marriages can be turned into obfuscating devices that serve to elide responsibility and conceal complicity of inappropriate decisions, police (in)action and indeed, the role of families in the deaths of their own flesh and blood.

It is all the more tragic when we consider the ways in which love-marriage couples themselves share the ambivalence of the wider society towards their marriages. As I have argued elsewhere,[2] these couples do not inhabit a separate moral universe and can often be seen to bend under the pressures of urban Indian mores. Rather than positing an alternative justification for marriage based on love and mutual attraction, antithetical to the values of caste endogamy, honour and shame, and religious separatedness, the love-marriage couples I worked with seemed to subscribe to most (if not all) of these metropolitan views and instead were keen to prove that their love was a pure, other-worldly sentiment that could disavow the allegations of lust and desire heaped upon their marital bed. It is in this light that we must recognise the courage which many couples show when they are faced with social opprobrium and are forced to declare to the state or to the police that they have married each other of their own free will.

Das reminds us that the most important feature of both tradition and modernity in contemporary India is its 'double articulation' where both emblems of 'tradition' (say, caste or religion) and 'modernity' (the bureaucracy or law) are doubly entrenched in each other (1995: 53). Implicit in the analysis of the state's 'double articulation' in society is the inevitable drawing closer of disparate constituencies; expedient alliances built temporarily and then dissolved when no longer required. The state, communities and individuals are thus involved in a constant and creative enterprise of making (and breaking) new and intimate relations.

Strathern warns us of both, the difficulties encountered in breaking kin and the newness in the relationships that emerge.

In valuing or devaluing their relationships, relatives thus become aware of the way they are connected *and* disconnected. Recombinant families just make this very visible, showing how cutting off ties leads to making others, or how household arrangements offer innumerable permutations on degrees of disconnection (2005: 26).

There are two strands we can follow from this. The first concerns the ways in which this directly applies to love-marriage individuals in India (pointedly, not 'dividuals') because as we have seen, their legal constitution and their occasional ejection from community, out into not-community, forces them to break ties they would rather maintain, and to be, in the words of dramatic Hindi films, 'dead to their families'). The second strand is to view matters from the perspective of the families themselves. These couples do *appear* to behave in exactly the same way as Strathern's Euro-American individuals because they often present their families with the threat that, as individuals they absolutely have the support of the law of the land that recognises their rights to marry and if necessary, be damned. Here we see how parents and elders can almost anticipate disconnection because of these marriages and they know that this is the very antithesis of their sort of connecting (making kin through marriage). The declaration of a couple to marry no matter what, is often viewed by their families (to borrow Strathern's words) as 'an expression of autonomy and a rejection of altruism'.

However, in the great majority of successful cases I encountered, this is not what happens. Instead, it was the love-cum-arranged marriages that seemed to come into their own, because while love-marriages often serve to represent discord, dissolution and pain, love-cum-arranged marriages are an innovation that pleases everybody by absorbing the couple within the rubric of the family and the wider community. They are interesting because they allow the expression of autonomy, but do not carry it through to its logical extreme of 'rejecting altruism'. The relative consensus that these marriages represent an 'ideal' stems from the recognition that parents would be careful and admittedly conservative in their calculations of what shocks they can absorb, and what would, even at a stretch, be imprudent. This is why some types of unions are almost always singled out as being troublesome and problematic, not because they are necessarily inherently so, but, as I have shown earlier, because there is a long history of these relationships being represented in different media as politically loaded and therefore relatively troublesome to domesticate (for instance, marriages involving Muslim boys and Hindu girls, or between high and low castes). For many other relationships, even those that start out being problematic, the families often concede that it is ultimately the happiness of their offspring that matters and so it is that extraordinary energies are expended to keep them from being ejected into not-community and to bring them within the fold. This regular occurrence of love-marriage incorporation demonstrates the ways in which the 'Indianess' of the 'Indian family' lies precisely within its double articulation of tradition (via slowly negotiated and hard-won 'arrangement') and modernity (of 'love' and loving offspring waiting patiently for arrangement). The story of love-marriage shows us that despite what communities viewed as *coercive* (rather than permissive) laws and heavy-handed state interference, it is the transformative capacity of the domestic social world and its ability to redraw its boundaries and absorb change that becomes the bedrock from which Indians can project their aspirations for the self onto the nation.

The Moral Economy of the Law and Marriage

This chapter looks at strategies in both love- and arranged-marriages in an attempt to unearth what I shall be calling provisionally, the moral economy of the law in marriage in contemporary north India. That is to say, how does actual legalisation (through a court, *nikkah* or temple registered marriage, the three most common forms of love-marriage in Delhi) help to form, mould and regulate marital relationships. Here, I define the act of legalisation (an 'act of law') as an act whose performative effect depends upon law. Put simply, how does the fact of a legal marriage (or indeed, the absence of one) impact upon love-marriage couples in their day-to-day existence. The focus then, isn't upon the process of law or the actual rituals and ceremonies of civil or religious love-marriages, but rather on its cultural logic, its meanings and effects upon the lives of the couple (both as a unit, and as separate entities with unified or divergent hopes and dreams) and upon their immediate social relations. I also draw into this discussion various agents such as kinship allies, neighbours, the police, and local women's groups who play different roles in advancing the hopes and plans of the couple as against those who oppose them and thus shape the outcome of such marital relationships. Through the interpretation of a selection of vignettes, this concluding chapter explores the ways in which people in Delhi seek to regulate both formally and informally those most slippery of subjects that concern the affairs of the heart: love, sexuality and, ultimately, marriage itself.

In a society that places such a high premium on the chastity of women, and the proper transfer of bio-moral substance through appropriately arranged marriages, I found a surprising number of cases of love affairs which held out the promise of a love-marriage. However, the reality of inappropriate liaisons, and the constant threat of family rejection or outright violence, meant that quite often the love continued but the marriage didn't follow. Indeed, in many such instances, the boy subsequently agreed to an arranged-marriage to someone else chosen by his family, while the girl was left with her honour stained.[3] What follows is a description of highly charged instances of a love affair; one from the perspective of the lover and, more briefly, the other from the perspective of the wife. What I am seeking to do here is unravel the ways in which urban Indians seek to regulate, manage and domesticate 'love' by invoking the law and indeed, a 'sense of the law'. I encountered both cases at local *Janvadi Mahilla Samiti* ('JMS') legal cells, and what I focus upon are the strategies for 'justice' that are pursued.

'Char din ki chandni, phir andheri raat'
Four Days of Moonlight, then the Darkness of Night

Geeta's mother, Kanti described her troubles to the room full of JMS women:

> The landlord was saying that I am ready to say that they have been living here as man and wife. How can those people try and deny it. I kept them here in my house. Now when Ajay took her I didn't see her for four years. Then he went and got married. Brought his bride to his parental home. He went to collect Geeta and brought her back to this *gully*. For four years she hadn't been back, for four years he had been living away from his home, but when he got married to another woman,

he brought my daughter back. He was in a bad state. He said, they have pressured me into this, they have threatened me. I shouted: 'You should have died! What sort of pressure did they put that you went and did this?' He said they told him that if he didn't get married they would kill Geeta, and her people. …They kept him under their thumb. They beat him so much that he looked like a corpse.

When Geeta was brought home, she didn't succumb quickly. For some time she struggled to save what she saw as her marriage with Ajay. One of the first things she did was to go straight to Ajay's arranged-marriage wife's home and seek out the girl's male kin. She asked them why they didn't make any enquiries about the boy before they arranged the marriage, as even a most cursory enquiry would have revealed that he was living with her. They replied: 'What reason did we have to make enquiries?' She said: 'Is there something wrong with your daughter? Has she some fatal flaw that you made her a second wife [to her].' They replied to her: 'We will see. Ours is a marriage of one-and-a-half *lakhs*. Yours is a marriage of one-and-a-half *paise*. Let's see who wins and who loses.'[4]

Ironically, this dramatic rebuff was the nub of the problem for Geeta and Ajay. They, like many love-marriage couples I worked with, had no resources and no savings. Their day-to-day financial existence was a struggle. They could just about pay the rent in the shanty housing they occupied and buy their cooking fuel and food. They often didn't have the large sums of money demanded by lawyers and court touts for legalising their unions, and certainly didn't have repositories of wealth and support when it came to dealing with the police. They lived on love and fresh air. In the formulation given by Ajay's brothers-in-law, the son's marriage of love brings nothing but shame to the parents; by bragging about their sister's marriage they are drawing attention to the brutal economic power of a dowry worth one-and-a-half *lakhs*. It is both a bribe to look after their daughter and symbolises the social recognition of the arrangement between the two families, benefiting the couple.[5]

Geeta's mother Kanti wept at her inability to make things better for her daughter. She was consoled by Pushpa, one of the JMS activists. 'Don't worry. The law hasn't gone anywhere! He was already married when he had the arranged marriage. He's got a wife, and he thinks he can marry another!' Kanti remained inconsolable: 'If only we had some *proof*. Then I could fight with it!

What can I fight with when there is no *proof*!' Pushpa was dumb-
founded: 'Did they not do an Arya Samaj marriage! They stayed
together just like that? They didn't have one of these marriages
that are common these days! They didn't borrow some *sindhur*⁶ off
someone and put it in her hair and say, look, we are married, let
us take a *photo*? They didn't have a court marriage?' The enormity
of the situation dawned on all the women in the room. While
almost none of the women approved of love-marriages, they
would happily support someone else who needed their advice or
assistance in the sort of complicated domestic matters that arose
from such unions. However, here was an instance where it appeared
as though the couple had simply cohabited without generating any
legal evidence of their marriage.

Geeta's mother's task was to try to generate some evidence
to ensure that her daughter was acknowledged in some way as
Ajay's wife. She asked the assembled women if she should try
to get Ajay to make a sworn statement on stamp paper that he
has been married and living with Geeta for the past four years,
and that he is the father of their child. Pushpa discouraged her
by saying a stamp paper affidavit wasn't worth the paper it was
written on. It had no value, even if a lawyer made a statement.
Court papers were different, *stamp* papers were different. At this
point, Geeta addressed me and I answered saying that perhaps they
could see if their marriage could be registered under the Special
Marriage Act in a court. As I understood it, the Act provided for
retrospective registration; however, it was all complicated by the
second arranged-marriage. They might have to prove first that the
second marriage was null and void before they could register their
union under the Special Marriage Act. Geeta ruefully declared that
even if this were a possible alternative, Ajay would have to consent
to this course of action, and she was doubtful he would.

A few days later Geeta told me that even now she couldn't fault
Ajay. Whatever he did, he did for his mother and father. His parents
didn't approve of Geeta because when she was little, her family had
converted to Christianity. Ajay was the eldest child. He had two
younger sisters. When talk began about arranging their marriages
the news of his marriage to Geeta spread throughout his kin and
his family's village, and the arrangements would stop short. People
heard the local gossip that the oldest child, that too a son, had
married outside his caste. When he had the arranged marriage, he

did it without Geeta even knowing it was happening. It wasn't as though he didn't want to be responsible for Geeta. He contended that he would look after both women: Geeta and his new wife.

When Ajay had first pursued Geeta, she had confronted him with the question: 'Do you want to marry me? I can't be friends with you and have my reputation ruined for nothing. Will you marry me?' Ajay had said yes, and that is how she allowed herself to fall in love with him. They didn't elope, but one day, after a quarrel with her family, he came to collect her and she declared that she was leaving. He had already rented a room in a shanty a few miles away and they went there. She says the very next day she was filled with terrible remorse. She said to Ajay, 'If you love me, you should take me before everyone [his family] and with good honour you should tell them your intentions. Instead, they went to a temple and he filled her hair with *sindhur*, thus marrying in the eyes of God. They then went to the Patiala House Sessions court where they made out an affidavit saying they were married. She says that she read later on that they could have gone to an Arya Samaj temple and they could have been legally married, but at the time, she did not know this.

Ajay's strategy was one of secrecy. He was free to go anywhere, but Geeta was confined to their new rented room. His worry was that if word got out of his marriage to Geeta it would jeopardise the arranged marriages of his sisters. He wanted his sisters to marry first and then to declare publicly his relationship to Geeta. He also felt that if Geeta had a child, then his mother would embrace Geeta as her daughter-in-law. Both these strategies were extremely familiar to me because I encountered them so frequently. Often, the only weapon on the side of the love-marriage couple was time. If they could keep their union hidden, or if they could delay arranged marriages for long enough, the parents might see that this is what the child really wanted and might eventually concede defeat, even 'arranging' the love-marriage to signal their acceptance. It would help if the loving couple didn't offend the family by ruining the chances of any other siblings having honourable arranged matches. The other strategy, of a grandchild melting stubborn hearts, is as old as the hills.

Geeta was groomed in every way so that she was an acceptable daughter-in-law to Ajay's mother. He taught her to rise early, bathe, tidy and clean the house and pray to his family deities.[7] From Geeta's point of view it appeared that they were preparing for an honourable future in his parental home. When she was unceremoniously returned to her mother's doorstep she was stunned and in shock. She says he too says he can't believe things turned out the way they did when their intentions were so different. After the initial shock, he promised Geeta that she would stay with him while his arranged marriage wife would stay with his mother. That too turned out to be a promise he couldn't keep. Geeta stayed with her mother and Ajay saw her whenever he could visit. When he did, he would cry. Geeta said,

> On the slightest discussion he would burst into tears and weep like a child. Cry like a woman. I cry less at what has happened. He cries more. Men say that women have one lethal weapon; their tears. They flow and they make men weak in their resolve. Here my man is such that he cries and makes me weak. He cries and it makes me laugh; then he goes quiet.

While Geeta sounds strong and almost stoic in dealing with this seemingly impossible situation, her mother describes the desperate time she went through after Ajay's marriage. She had returned home, he continued to visit when he could and a few months later she was pregnant. He returned to his second wife and home, and failed to show up for ages. Geeta was four months' pregnant and very subdued. One day she phoned him and told him to come and get her. He refused and they had an argument. Later, she asked some children in her *gully* to get her some tablets from the chemist and she swallowed them. Kanti noticed that she was sleeping and assumed that she was just resting. When she remained asleep in the evening, she went to wake her and discovered that Geeta wasn't responding properly. She panicked and the children began to say that Geeta-*didi* had ordered some sleeping tablets. Kanti discovered the empty packet—she had consumed the whole strip. She described what happened next:

> I telephoned Palam [where Ajay and his family now lived]. I said: *this-this* has happened. And if anything happens now you will be in trouble. That was my mistake! If I had taken her to Safdarjung [a big government hospital in Delhi], then a proper *police case* would have been made out. I took her to Palam Vihar. Over there the whole house was empty. The whole family had fled in fright. By this stage Geeta was in a

terrible way. Someone took pity and told us where they had run to. We reached the house. I went straight and caught Ajay's throat. What have you done to my daughter? Geeta was saying: I am going to stay here. I am not leaving this place. Then this is what he said: 'Go. Go die. You should have stayed there and died.' Geeta passed out. Unconscious, we took her to Palam *police chowky*. There he was called along with his mama, *papa* and in-laws. The couple were taken alone into one room.[8] When Ajay was asked anything he kept completely silent. The *police* was a *ledies* [lady]. She kept asking, 'Who is she to you?'[9] He just kept shaking and began to cry. I said: 'Are you a man?! You have loved, and look at this woman. My girl has more courage. Look at the state she is in and even then she is speaking—so why can't you speak up? After much difficulty he replied, 'Yes, I have been living with her for the past four years, and the child in her stomach, that is my child.' And then when the in-laws appeared in the room, he would begin shaking again and crying and crying. So much so that in the end, we had to admit defeat in the face of his tears. 'Let him go' I said. 'We don't want this.' The police asked us, do you want to make a case? I said, 'How will I fight a court case? I earn by washing dishes in *kothis* [big wealthy Delhi homes]. I don't have that much time to keep going again and again [to court].' So my child, I didn't make a case there either.

What is striking about Kanti's narrative is that, after Geeta swallowed the sleeping tablets, she didn't think to call a doctor or rush her to hospital, but instead saw it as an opportunity to bring to a head Ajay's failure to take responsibility for Geeta and their unborn child. Clearly Geeta supported this path of action, because Kanti describes her lucid moments when she confronted Ajay. Mother and daughter were utterly desperate to obtain a better outcome than the one presented to them by Ajay. They were willing to play with Geeta's life and that of her unborn child in the hope of pressing Ajay to demand his own rights from his parents and in-laws. When Ajay proved himself incapable of standing up to anybody, they went to the local police station with the girl now unconscious. Even here Ajay remained recalcitrant. Finally, they resigned themselves and retreated. What was the use of a police case when the boy was so incapable of taking a stand in their favour.

When her second daughter Mona decided to have a love-marriage to an unemployed youth from the *gully*, Kanti was unimpressed, but decided to get involved so that things were done properly and sufficient proofs generated in the first instance so that the boy could not turn around and pretend he hadn't married Mona.

Kanti had learnt a bitter lesson from Geeta's experience and knew not to trust the avowals of undying love she heard from Mona's boyfriend. Furthermore, there was better guarantee of the success of this relationship since the boy's mother came to convince Kanti to bless the wedding, thus signalling that they were accepting of her daughter Mona and that they would suitably arrange this love-marriage. Kanti told me in Mona's presence:

I accepted. I did her wedding. It was done thoroughly. Photographs were taken. They garlanded each other with flowers. It was done in all ways possible. The entire *gully* was invited to attend and eat. All the papers were then given to a lawyer for safe-keeping. I've been thinking that we should actually go to *parliament* to *register* the marriage...[10]

Geeta who is listening in says: 'What is the *court*? Is the *court* everything?! What can it do?' Mona is more practical. She says: 'So what? What harm is there to do it? I will do it.' Here Geeta's cynicism is understandable. She knows better than anyone else that *proofs* cannot regulate the ebb and flow of a husband's love or his resolve to remain married.

When Geeta's child was born, she knew her fate was sealed. It was a beautiful girl. She knew that her only leverage with her in-laws would have been the birth of a son. 'If it had been a boy then maybe we could have done something. They don't want to know about a girl. A girl is a girl, a boy is a boy.' She resigns herself to her fate and tells me that she has lost the will to pursue the battles her mother still finds the energy to wage.

I think to myself that if I force things, what will I achieve? For instance, if I force the matter through legal means, or force him by having him beaten up; if I force him towards me then what use is it? He will not want to be with me of his own volition. He will not want to stay with me. In his mind, that thing won't be there... that love won't remain. It will be a charade of love.[11] What use is that to anybody? I would be doing what his parents are doing to him. Forcing him to remain in their home. Keeping him there. Threatening to kill me whenever they hear that he has been to see me.

Here she tries to gain the moral ground by identifying what she believes to be the right course of action against the general advice she is being given by everyone around her. The one thing she still has is his affection and love. If she stands up to him, he will abandon her in every way possible. It is for this reason that she is unsure about suing for maintenance for her daughter. This is a path that the JMS activists are keen on, and they suggest ambitious figures that they intend to demand for Geeta's child, to be paid in a lump-sum. It would be a considerable amount of money, and many people point out to Geeta that it is important for the child to have him acknowledge her existence by supporting them financially. For Geeta's part, she still believes that Ajay will one day come and take her and her daughter away with him. To accept money from him would turn their love and the trust that evidently still exists between them into a mere financial transaction. She tells her mother that if she accepts money from him she would be turning herself into a prostitute. Kanti sees her opportunity and cannot resist the temptation to hurt: 'If it was your desire not to be a prostitute, but to be a wife, then you should have ensured that he married you first. You should have done that. Now he isn't going to marry you, is he?'

An 'act of law' could have gone some way in providing Geeta with a bit of security but it would only have been beneficial had it happened at the right time. Now, by forcing maintenance payments, she would only make things worse. Geeta's dilemma demonstrates quite dramatically the temporal interplay of changes in sentiment, in legal status and in social recognition. When she leaves home with Ajay, their commitment to each other is absolute, but they are social pariahs because they are unmarried lovers. They are also vulnerable to being prised apart as they have no legal proof of their union (which is indeed what unfortunately happens to them). When Geeta is faced with the possibility of demanding that he be legally recognised as the father of their child or suing for her daughter's rights in his wealth, she worries that whatever love he still feels for them will die because they will have replaced the love and trust in their relationship with a legal act that binds him into a relationship with his daughter. In forcing him to recognise his daughter publicly, she knows that she makes things more difficult for him and thus risks alienating him even further.

Flirt-Girl

Hema was married to Arun in February 1998. A few months later she was in the office of JMS seeking reconciliation or a divorce.

Her marriage had been arranged through a newspaper matrimonial advertisement. The boy had been described as educated to degree level, and from a wealthy Punjabi family that owned numerous Blueline buses. The girl's father's sister and her husband arranged the match and acted as *'bichauliyas'* (literally: the ones in between) for all the arrangements. Three days after the wedding Arun brought a girl home to meet his new bride. When Hema asked him who she was, he said she was *'just a friend'*. He had met her on the bus and their two families were well known to each other. He told Hema that he brought his friend over so that she wouldn't suspect anything later on. When one of the JMS members in the room asked him what he really felt for this girl, he said that if there was anything suspicious about his relationship to her, he wouldn't have brought her before his wife! 'Yes', she replied, 'but in a marriage, where is the need for a third person?'

The girl's uncle said that they had come to JMS for separation and the return of dowry. He continued: *'He had a flirt-girl.* When he brought her home he told Hema, "I can leave you anytime, but I will never leave her".' Arun and the *flirt-girl* had been living together for three years, sharing what the uncle described as *'homely relations'*. Before the marriage Hema's family got a call from the *flirt-girl* saying, 'Please don't marry your daughter to him, he is already living with me. He loves me.' The girl's family confronted the boy's family with this upsetting news. Arun's father cried and pleaded that the girl was of bad character and was trying to wreck their home. Arun's elder brother reassured them: 'Believe me, there is nothing amiss.'

The marriage went ahead and the lies tumbled out. It turned out that Arun had no degree,[12] and that far from owning buses, he was a conductor in one. In any case, Hema pleaded with Arun and her in-laws to save her marriage: 'I don't care what happened in the past. Just forget her now.' Arun flatly refused. The boy's father threatened to shoot Arun or *flirt-girl* if she ever visited the house again. While *flirt-girl* continued her daily visits to Arun, his parents put out hefty dowry demands for a car. When Hema got upset over the love affair, Arun joked with her, 'Why don't you write a letter saying I want to kill myself. I have taken my own life.' On one occasion, Arun's girlfriend was walking with Hema to the bazaar and confided in her that she ate pills everyday because they lived together [she was on the pill]. Her treatment at her in-laws deteriorated. Once, when she trimmed the edges of her hair her mother-in-law was furious and taunted her: 'Who do you think you are? Juhi Chawla?!'[13] Her husband hit her. He described what happened to everyone listening at JMS: 'I told her not to cut her hair! We have customs that prohibit it!' I asked him: 'What sort of hair does your friend have?' He couldn't hide his smile: *'Bal-kutti'* [short-hair], he replied. Kalindi,[14] a stalwart JMS activist, could bear this no more: 'You want to throw your wives under veils; but not your girlfriends. This wife of yours, she is your honour. That girlfriend is nothing?'

It was clear that Hema had no future with Arun. He loved his girlfriend and wasn't going to leave her. The girlfriend at least tried to stop Hema's parents from ruining her prospects, but they were taken up with the lies and considered Arun too excellent a match to let slip by. Hema recognised that there was nothing left for her in her marriage and one night ran away to her aunt's house. When her parents called her in-laws to say she had reached safely, they weren't interested. Clearly, this was an arranged marriage of convenience. As it was clear that Arun's family wasn't in the mood for compromise, the JMS activists set about preparing lists of the dowry that had exchanged hands so that they could set a date when Arun's family would return to Hema's family all the money and goods they had received. A few days before the appointed date, the JMS office received a call purporting to be from Hema's side, saying that they had reached a settlement with Arun's family and were going to exchange the dowry and *stridhan*[15] at a local police station. However, on the appointed Saturday, Hema's family turned up and were amazed to hear of the *fake* phone call and the trick that had been played on them by Arun's people. Arun's family were called on the phone and they said that they weren't going to give anything back. A JMS activist advised Hema's parents to file a First Information Report against Arun under Section 498 (A) of the Dowry Prohibition Act for the cognisable offence of mental and physical cruelty suffered by Hema during her brief marriage. The case was then pursued in police stations and the courts.

*

A court marriage could have changed Geeta's life, though differently, depending on when it had happened. She would not be the one suffering humiliation for having compromised her reputation by living with Ajay. She could have staked her claim, declared Ajay's second marriage illegal,[16] and her daughter could have been a legal heir to Ajay. Perhaps if she had had a court marriage, Ajay's family would not have dared to arrange a second marriage for him. They would have known that they were committing a criminal offence, although if they were powerful they might have found ways to get around even this, and there might still have been violence to contend with. Or could things have been any different after all? Arun and his *flirt-girl* hadn't had a court-marriage and yet it was their relationship that endured and caused the destruction of his arranged marriage. The one fatal flaw in Geeta's world is Ajay's vacillation and lack of resolve. This ultimately heralds her doom. What these two cases have in common is that the bond between the male partner and his parents hasn't completely broken and to some extent directs (or sanctions) his behaviour. What is also noteworthy is that Arun and his *flirt-girl*'s relationship is unique and different to all the relationships discussed in this book, because Arun rather cleverly agrees to a primary arranged marriage (which he then proceeds to ruthlessly destroy), but in so doing, he makes a play of having fulfilled his obligations to his parents and kin. Now, in all probability, he will be allowed to have a secondary marriage to *flirt-girl* and be left in peace.

In contrast, the story about Zahra and Nadim seems to indicate that legalisation of a marriage can help stave off a dissenting family and allow the couple to appeal to alternate sources of power and authority, such as the police and the law courts. The police, in the first instance, supported the couple and allowed them to remain together. Zahra was pregnant, her in-laws were happy to accept her, and it looked as though everyone had reconciled themselves to the turn of events. However, we cannot be over-optimistic about the effects of legalisation on the lives of young couples. When I revisited Nadim's family a year later, I was stunned to meet him alone and to hear that when Zahra was eight months' pregnant, she was forcibly taken at night from Nadim's home in Delhi (her brother Riaz had been accompanied by police, though the case had apparently been legally resolved already), never to be seen again. People said that Riaz and his parents had married her off elsewhere, though nobody knew any details. Nadim and his family were implicated and enmeshed in various concocted police cases filed against them by Zahra's family, which served to criminalise him and make him completely incapable of doing anything effective in terms of recovering Zahra. He was too busy trying to clear his name, stay out of jail and scrape together a living in order to pay for some legal representation. Talking to him it was clear that he was a completely broken man. Tragically, he said he had given up hope of ever seeing Zahra again, but that the only thought that sustained him was that somewhere he had a child—and his only hope was to lay eyes upon it once...

Amongst the documents that Nadim showed me was a photocopy of a signed affidavit by Zahra that pronounced in the legal language of the court that she had been kidnapped, held in captivity and raped by Nadim. It also alleged that to cover the crime the accused (Nadim) had married the applicant 'after preparing the forged documents' (of marriage). The pretext under which her brother acquired police support to 'rescue' her was a letter that she allegedly wrote from captivity in Nadim's home. The badly photocopied (some barely legible) legal documents that Nadim showed me were his own set of submissions to the court to clear his name of these very substantial and crippling criminal charges. Amongst the thick pile of papers headed with the hand scribbled title 'Documents filed in the Court alongwith [sic] list of Documents' and amongst reams of legal statements, judgements, copies of police reports and affidavits were the 'evidence' of their love. This consisted of a photo of bare-chested Nadim (partially submerged) and Zahra sitting on a rock in the middle of a stream, smiling and holding onto each other; cards from Zahra to Nadim proclaiming her love for him in English: 'Dear [Nadim], Mountain Can Fly, Rivers Can Dry, You Can Forget Me, But How Can I' and then in Urdu 'Basali hain dil main surath thumhari, kabhi kam na hogi mohobbat hamari'.[17] It is part of the intense tragedy of so many love-marriage couples who face legal entrapments through the aegis of conniving families that what was once the intimate exchange of concealed carnal knowledge between two knowing lovers, now must be exposed as the evidential grounds upon which Nadim must defend his very social existence, charged as he is with Zahra's kidnap and rape. Alfred Gell has very insightfully pointed out that love is constituted through the dual process of mutual exposure (between lovers) combined with concealment (from everybody else).[18] He says, '...(L)ove is a knowledge system, a procedure for obtaining, distributing and transforming knowledge of pre-eminent social value'. In the documentary practices for the generation of evidential 'proofs' in cases of love-marriage in Delhi we see precisely how agencies of the state bear witness to this exposure of information, transforming carnal knowledge into legal knowledge about specific individuals and their social relations and in so doing setting into play the process whereby intimacies are called to account.

Bearing in mind the tragic conclusion to Nadim and Zahra's love-marriage, a very recent news report tells us a slightly different story. Here, Additional Sessions Judge Kamini Lalu of the Delhi Court, invoked Article 21 of the Indian Constitution that guarantees the right to life and liberty to argue in strong support of a love-marriage couple remaining together despite the girl's lack of legal maturity and the various obstructions being erected by her family and the police. The case centred around a 17 year old girl who eloped with her boyfriend because of parental opposition due to a difference in caste. The couple fled Delhi for Bareilly where they got married in a Hindu temple, but the boy was arrested when they set foot back in Delhi. The Delhi judge said that she was surprised that despite the girl's statement before a magistrate that she had eloped and married the boy of her own free will, the police and the parents continued to pursue a case alleging that she had been kidnapped and raped by the man. In an unusually brave and outspoken statement, Judge Lalu said that the medical test on the girl had shown no external injury or bleeding and merely showed that there was sexual intercourse as was 'normal in a relationship between husband and wife'. Furthermore, '...The 17-year-old prosecutrix...has a right to protect her feelings from the onslaught of her parents and society. If she had run away to save herself from such an onslaught with her love, this in the view of the court is no offence'. And again, 'There is no law which prohibits a girl under 18 years from falling in love with someone. Neither is falling in love an offence under Indian Penal Code nor is desiring to marry her love'.[19] This sort of bold public statement about the legitimacy of love and love-marriages in the eyes of the law is what is sorely needed to change public perceptions of such marriages in the courts in Delhi. Judge Lalu's judicial intervention is refreshingly rare, but shows just how effective the law can be when correctly interpreted to support the rights and freedoms of individuals so enshrined by the founders of the Indian Constitution.

Before I conclude my arguments for this book, I want to discuss briefly a rather successful relationship that I encountered during my fieldwork. Now that we are familiar with the repertoire of love, elopement and arranged marriages that are crucial to understanding love-marriages in Delhi, here is an instance where a love affair is properly managed and domesticated, and the way in which this is done. In the words of Fauzia, the mother of the boy:

My son was studying in the fifth class. That's when he started it. We tried hard to stop him, saying look, it isn't good to bring disrepute to someone else's daughter. After he had already proposed to her, we learnt of it. We liked the girl anyway. She was a homely type of girl. We said to her, 'Look, if your people are ready then we are ready too.' They were of a different caste. They were Sheikhs. We were from Subzipheroze. But there was no problem with that. Our son used to roam around Block No. 12 [the area of the shanty where she lived], and visit her house. Her mother often shouted at him to leave her daughter alone. She even hit him once. We never said anything. It isn't good to besmirch the honour of a girl. Of course, she hit her daughter a lot more. She told her she would never let her marry my son. The girl told her mother that if she married, it would only be to Salim. If not, then she would not marry anyone else. Now we had heard that the girl's father liked Salim. He was our only son, he had a house, he had everything! He had a job as a mechanic. My husband and I had good habits. We would look after the girl. One day the girl's mother beat her very violently. She came running to our home. I called some of my friends and neighbours and said look, this is what has happened, what should I do? They all said, 'Don't let her stay in the house. Send her back to her parents immediately!' I took their advice. We sent her back saying, 'If you send her with happiness, then we will arrange the wedding. But not unless you agree.'

Fauzia says she had heard that the girl's father was agreeable and because the girl loved Salim she would not waver either. She decided to bide her time till they came around. At some point, they would have to concede to the marriage. She also knew that a *nikkah* without the girl's parents' consent would only lead to trouble for the marriage. The delicate balance between the two families of the loving couple would be permanently destroyed if one family declared support by openly arranging the marriage. This way, by sending the girl home, they were avoiding a scandalous elopement and were encouraging the girl's parents to engage with them in an honourable exchange.

By and by, Fauzia sent her two older daughters to talk to the girl's mother. She said she would never marry her daughter to Salim. The girl's father, however, pulled them aside and said: 'Go, I will make her ready to accept this marriage. What are your views?' Her daughters said: 'If you have your daughter's *nikkah* read today, we will take her into our home today.' So he set a date in a month's time, and the couple were happily married in the presence of elders from both families at the Nizammudin mosque. They then brought her home, and Fauzia proudly said that there was no exchange of dowry or any jewellery. They were just delighted to have a daughter-in-law and a happy son. The girl's mother still didn't accept the marriage and never visited Fauzia's house, but with the passage of time, and her daughter's frequent visits home, she seemed reconciled to events gone by. Here the advice from Fauzia's neighbours was sound: A marriage without the parents' knowledge and approval would have definitively foreclosed the immediate possibility of uniting the two families.

The cultural logic underlying the law in marriage is best seen in the ways in which love-marriage couples manage the fact of their legal union. There is an important distinction to be made between 'going legal' and 'going public', though these overlap to some extent. The 'act of law' has certain effects (tentatively safeguarding the couple), but the act of revelation about the act of law is a far more delicate affair, and it is this that all the love-marriage couples focus their energies upon.

At the start I described how couples used their legal marriages to try and force the hand of their parents, while remaining discreet so that their parents still had their reputations to save. This gave them time to negotiate and make them agree to their own choice of spouse, while simultaneously putting the pressure on because there was always the risk that the truth would out. This is why Zahra's self-elopement actually made sense, because the pregnancy meant exposure was imminent. 'Going public', however, as Geeta's story exemplifies (here without the act of law), exposes the hard edge of the moral dilemma. If you leave home without being married you risk public humiliation and abandonment. On the other hand, the *flirt-girl* and Arun needn't worry about 'going legal'. They hedged their bets on the collapse of Arun's arranged marriage, which they happily and quite actively jeopardised. Now that his parents had received their dues (in dowry and the honour stakes) through his arranged marriage, they were very likely to let him and his girlfriend marry and live, as the Hindi phrase goes, with *izzat* or honour.

Legalisation of a marriage accords a union a change in moral status, but not definitively: the same legal move can have different moral effects, depending on how it is presented (or semi-concealed) in public. It can make wives of women who would otherwise be berated as prostitutes, and turn villainous boys and *roadside-romeos* into respectable sons-in-law. It is a weapon that the couple can wield in their defence. But it is also a blunt instrument, prone to breaking ties rather than maintaining them. All the local women that Fauzia summons understand it well. This is the practical wisdom of the street. Don't cut the noses off your parents or your future in-laws by rushing into a court-marriage, *nikkah* or Arya Samaj *shadi*. If you must, then be wary of 'going public' before everyone is ready to cope with a possible backlash. In the wrong hands, or at the wrong moment, it can lead to a lifetime of pain and regret. Far better to exhaust all possibilities of reconciliation. Softly softly, catch ye monkey.

By choosing a spouse, love-marriage couples almost inevitably find themselves estranged and reluctant members of not-community. The communities they leave are not seen to be constituted of individuals but rather of interdependent parts of a complex whole. The parts are construed as religious communities, hierarchically-ranked castes, consisting in turn of kinship groups, which are ultimately formed of families. The parts are seen to negotiate status primarily through the avenue of appropriately arranged marriages. This construction makes love-marriages appear to constitute a particularly contentious rebellion against the core values of caste and community, because the careful alignment of status considerations are thrown out of gear by alliances that seem to destroy the social order. By inflecting 'secularity' into 'sexuality' (Ritu Menon's terms, 1999), love-marriage in India has historically been viewed as dangerous and subversive. This is why a large majority of people view them as being so antithetical to the very fabric of social relations.

Love-marriage couples themselves feel obliged to pretend an indifference to caste status or religious differences because these are worldly matters and the justification for their love is that it is spiritual and 'pure'. The imagery of religious devotion is central to the ways in which love-marriage couples think about and justify their love. However, the widespread illegitimacy of sexuality and desire, however configured, leaves them open to social opprobrium, and most couples try as far as possible to conceal the fact of their love-marriage through *'adjustments'* in names, personal dress and deportment, so that an image of social coherence is presented to the neighbourhood and the world.

From a formal perspective—that is, in terms of the form of a not-community of love-marriage couples—the dynamic appears to be one of the assertion of individual will and choice of marriage partner. However, in real terms—that is, in terms of the content of the relationship between not-community and the communities which create and expel them—the dynamic is less one of rebellion than it is of an engagement with the boundaries of community. This engagement shows us the ways in which groups draw and redraw (not always in the same place) their boundaries through a complex process in which they re-constitute themselves and their identities. The historical debate over Act III of 1872 saw the petitioners' arguments pushing the Keshubites further and further into not-community, such that the law which was eventually passed had been amended almost beyond recognition. However, the Brahmos' persistence in ignoring their own position as not-community and striving to 'reform Hinduism' earned them the reputation of having irreversibly shaped the modern Indian nation.

On a less grandiose scale, love-marriage couples are also dramatically redefining the parameters of 'Indian' morality and 'Indian' marriage. They do this not through open rebellion, but rather by transforming their own relationships and re-inscribing them within the terms which they hope are acceptable to their families and communities. This is how we come to understand the distinctions made by people in Delhi between a *'love-marriage'*, a *'love-cum-arranged'* marriage, and an elopement. In the *'love-cum-arranged'* marriage, the social order that has been disrupted by 'love' is seen to be restored through the arranged-marriage. An elopement on the other hand upsets the social order with the implicit declaration that 'love' could not wait for an 'arrangement'. The predetermined emphasis on parental consent by love-marriage couples is another case in point. Couples dislike the expressions of 'free consent' demanded of them by the police and the law courts because this implies a challenge to the withheld consent of their families. This is how we come to witness Durga's reluctance to *name* her marriage as a love-marriage, as well as her manipulation of the popular discourse about a woman's sexuality not being her own to dispense with as she pleases. This paradox is illustrated by the case of Zahra, the scene of whose 'violent abduction' was staged either by herself or by her own parents. As with the case of the 'dead girl' Munesh Solanki, whose parents had chosen to cremate a stranger to signify their absolute rejection of their errant offspring, violence—either real or invented—is the preferred context within which to subsume the shame and sense of honour betrayed in the act of choosing one's own spouse.

However, the constant shifting of responsibility and agency in both Durga's and Zahra's stories serves to create a space wherein compromise remains a hoped-for possibility. The rule for re-inscribing not-community into community is that the greater the ambivalence, the more space is created to allow a negotiated compromise. The characterisation of love-marriages as anti-social, 'un-Indian' unions is necessarily only half the story. What we find instead is a series of strategies by families, ethno-religious communities and the couples themselves that seek to accommodate such marriages and bring them back within the social pale through a process of re-negotiation and eventual compromise. On a theoretical level, this can be seen in a shift away from the categorisation of such marriages as not-community, through a manipulation of the boundaries of community.

In some cases, such as those of Samina and Rashmi, opposition to love-marriages need not come from their families or ethno-religious communities alone. The rise of Hindu nationalist groups in Delhi and their evident interest in the marriages taking place at Tis Hazari allows a wholesale politicisation of the domestic sexual lives of love-marriage couples. The political co-ordinates of these positions indicate that it isn't all love-marriages that get targeted, but rather inter-community marriages involving Muslims. It is the ability of such marriages to represent 'mixing' that so militates against the supremacist cause and invites their ire. The attempts to prevent such couples from availing of the legal machinery of the state is in itself a political appropriation of the law by Hindu nationalists. However, this communalism cannot wholly explain the contradictions that arise from the process of marriage in Tis Hazari. As much as couples may find their paths obstructed, they are also able to make strategic interventions to validate their love through marriage, and so counteract the authority and reach of community sanctions. The law thus retains the potential to serve as a definitive refuge by which to forestall the violent repercussions from communities that would otherwise be incumbent upon many such marriages.

Love-marriage as socially experienced is a plethora of antitheses: love and lust, marriage and abduction, legality and illegitimacy, community and not-community—all are infused in and confused by the contradiction between social strictures and individuality: the 'community seeking to colonise the life-world of the individual' and the individual resisting threats to 'selfhood' (Das 1995). What this study elucidates is the inherent necessity of flexibility in both the individual and the community in terms of the constraints both impose on each other. The processes of transgression and re-integration, typified by love-marriage phenomena, create a unique social space of moral ambivalence through which social orders transform themselves.

Whatever the outward transgressions of love-marriage couples, what is clear is that the law doesn't recognise the complexity of Indian personhood, which I have argued consists of both bounded and legally necessary individuality, and what Marriot has described as transactional 'dividuality'. The social bias against love-marriage is at odds with the permissive laws for civil and religious marriages of choice that exist in India. The procedural accommodations to 'social forms' that are made all the time in the actual praxis of law are denied in their equivalence to love-marriage couples. Thus the law as praxis constantly recognises one bundle of rights implicit in agency: that of the community demanding accountability of its individual agents. It also seems consistently to ignore a complementary bundle of rights: that of the couple or individual to make known to themselves their own efficacy or agency in contracting a legally validated marriage. Ironically, these are the very ones that are explicitly recognised in statute.

The legal practitioners in Delhi accommodate social realities which they approve of or accept, and not those which run counter to their own values. For instance, magistrates on numerous occasions in Tis Hazari refused to solemnise love-marriages without the parents of the couple making themselves present, thus ensuring that the parents were aware and able to prevent the marriage should they so desire. This same feature was sought to be introduced into the law during the debate of 1872, but was rejected by the legislative council, and rejected three-quarters of a century later again by Nehru during the 1954 legislative assembly debate on the Special Marriage Act. Despite this, in the late 1990s in the nation's capital Delhi, we find an unspoken consensus in the courts that the agency of couples is invested not partly in themselves, but only in their respective families and group. A girl having a love-marriage is 'unofficially' denied her capacity for agency (her 'efficacy') with the demand that the parents bestow this upon her in the presence of a judge. Equally, a marriage that could not be stopped prior to solemnisation is broken up by arguing that the girl's agency was appropriated by the boy, and as such, she had been 'forced' or 'pressured' into the elopement and marriage. Here, the accommodations are entirely biased towards the corporate will of the group, and against the personal rights of the love-marriage couple or the individual lover.

The predominant representation in north India is that marriage integrates a person into their community and their interests as self-agent and as agent-of-the-group are identical, (or at least mutually reinforcing), so that when they act, they do so as self-agent and agent-of-community simultaneously. The individual's ends are assumed to be advanced through the advancement of the group, and the advances of others in the group are assumed to advance the self. The social group and the individual maintain common ground when the definitions of selfhood remain compossible—when the personhood of the individual is upheld by the group and when the person remains capable of representing common group interests and values. Equally, the loss of group efficacy and agency (through, say, a loss of *izzat*) is assumed to have a bearing upon all individuals within the group. This is a scenario in which individuals and social groups mutually recognise their shared agency.

When this *status quo* is disturbed, and when the relationship between individual and group is *shown* to be antithetical, then agency becomes a contested site, and selfhood a contested arena. In some instances, the shared ground of recognition of the limits of selfhood by the individual and the social group turns into a contest for hegemony by the group and a bid for freedom by the individual. In such circumstances, the individual or couple are forced to maintain boundedness to protect themselves from the emotional and physical violence that may follow. In other cases, the couple (or the individual) is able to distance itself from the social group in order to free-up (so to speak) the margins of selfhood.

What this study of love-marriages has illustrated is that selfhood isn't only defined by the individual or the group, but by the social relations in which each individual is enmeshed. As Priya's decision to remain within her natal home and Subhash's resignation to never being united with his beloved show, the limits to selfhood aren't 'set' by social groups quite simply because they inhere in all social relationships, and consequently, in all 'persons'. As Alfred Gell reminds us, 'what persons are externally (and collectively) is a kind of enlarged replication of what they are internally' (1998: 222).

This is why love-marriage couples do not seek to build a 'couple', but rather hope to maintain a couple in a web of relationships which will ensure their future survival and guarantee their own personhood. They seek to reintegrate themselves with their families and even their communities against enormous odds. In an arranged marriage the couple is instantly embedded within a range of social relations that predetermine the transformation of their identities and their selves. Love-marriage couples on the other hand must activate kinship networks and social relationships, sometimes without the support of their families, and must find ways in which to transform and embed themselves into an unwilling community and an indifferent urban world. It isn't that the individual or the couple is subsumed within the collectivity, but that they actively negotiate their relationship with (and without) the community, and in so doing, explore the sources of their own efficacy and even their 'selves'.

Notes

1. See report on *http://www.pudr.org*
2. Mody (2002: 344)
3. A common expression used in Hindi: '*Ladki pe daag lag gayi*', translates as, the girl has been stained.
4. '*Humari shadi dedh lakh ki hai, tumhari dedh paise ki. Dekhenge, kaun jeetenge, kaun harenge.*' A lakh is 100,000 rupees. A paise is one hundredth of a rupee.

5. That is the theory anyway. To give or take dowry is a crime in India. However, its practice was so widespread during my research in Delhi that it was noteworthy only when someone made a point of saying they hadn't taken (or given) dowry. Occassionally, parents during my public interviews would praise elopements saying that the children were lifting the burden of dowry from the girls' parents, but it was difficult to tell whether these were jokes or seriously meant. On many occasions in the shanty, the narrow by-lanes between houses would be blocked by the incongruous sight of furniture arriving as dowry. It would be left out (making through passage impossible) so that everybody could see (and inspect) what was being given. Indeed, the furniture was often so big that once it was pushed into the tiny rooms there was no floor space at all, and one would often enter the room and immediately sit on the bed. A lot of the love-marriage couples didn't transact in dowry, but it is important to note that this wasn't necessarily out of ethical or moral propriety but more often than not because the parents weren't consenting to the union, so the question of dowry didn't arise. Indeed, for many women it was a source of sadness, particularly when they heard about the gift of dowry to their sisters who had more traditional marriages. Since women's rights to inheritance are still so tenuous (despite legal enactments), it is rare that the women in the *bustis* in which I worked would receive anything by way of inheritance from their father's homes once they were married. Dowry continues to act as 'a woman's share' of her natal wealth, particularly if she has brothers.

6. *Sindhur* is a red powder that some married Hindu women wear in the parting of their hair. It signifies their marital status and is believed to protect their husbands from danger.

7. Despite being Christian, Geeta seemed to adapt easily to her husband's *buniya* caste-based worship. She also married him with *sindhur* in a Hindu temple. The only person to comment on this was Kanti who seemed resigned: 'Even after accepting Jesus, she married with Hindu rites. Ok, She did what she wanted; she saw the boy [his religion] and married accordingly.'

8. Kanti indicates that the couple were on their own but it is clear from her later narrative that she was in the room too.

9. It is this police woman who uses the couplet '*Char din ki chandni; phir andhere ki raat*' (Four days of moonlight; then the darkness of night) to describe the pitiful state of affairs between Geeta and Ajay. People commonly used this phrase in connection with love-marriages and elopements, drawing attention to the transience of romantic love and its supposed miserable end.

10. Of course she meant court, but it is interesting that this sort of slippage happened frequently. Most of my informants had very limited literacy and little access to education. People would tell me in interviews that they had married in a police station (they had made a statement to the police in the context of a complaint that they were living together as man and wife), and that I should go and check as the proof of their marriage was recorded there. Or, as two women told me, after their partners had left them they realised that what they had thought was a legal court-marriage was in fact a signed statement on stamp paper drawn up by a tout or lawyer. Clearly, to the man and woman in the street, the political, the executive and the judiciary all meld into one great stamp of authority that they can barely understand, and rely upon others to faithfully interpret for them. See Das (2004) for the ways in which the bureaucratic-legal processes remain illegible to those using *and* implementing policies of the state through its myriad documentary practices.

11. She uses the term '*dikhavati pyar*'.

12. The boy and his family, pumped fresh with the indignation that follows humiliation, shouted in his defence: 'But he is educated, he is 10th standard pass!' As if that should be a consolation.

13. A famous Hindi filmstar.

14. Kalindi Deshpande, a long-term activist of JMS, and Vice-President of the All-India Democratic Women's Association.

15. *Stridhan* (literally, 'woman's wealth') is in Hindu customary practice that portion of wealth that has been gifted directly to a daughter, sister, wife or daughter-in-law. It includes gifts given at marriage, but also consists of all the wealth she may generate for herself through her lifetime. Traditionally, it included jewellery, cattle, and house goods and was distinguished from other gifts (such as dowry) by virtue of the inalienable rights women had in their *stridhan*.

16. It is illegal for a Hindu to marry more than one wife.

17. 'I have placed your image in my heart. Our love will never diminish'.

18. I am referring here to the unpublished English version of an article he wrote that was translated into French and published in *Terrain*, 1996.

19. See K. Sriharsha in *The Times of India*, 'No rape charge if minor in love elopes: Court' 30-7-07, p. 12, Mumbai.

ॐ

Bibliography

Agarwal, Bina. 1994. *A Field of One's Own: Gender and Land Rights in South Asia*. Cambridge: Cambridge University Press.

Agarwal, Purshottam. 1996. Surat, Savarkar and Draupadi: Legitimising Rape as a Political Weapon', in T. Sarkar and U. Butalia (eds), *Women and the Hindu Right*, pp. 29–57. New Delhi: Kali for Women.

Agnes, Flavia. 1996. Redefi ning the Agenda of the Women's Movement Within a Secular Framework', in T. Sarkar and U. Butalia (eds), *Women and the Hindu Right*, pp. 136–57. New Delhi: Kali for Women.

Ahearn, Laura. 2001a. *Invitations to Love: Literacy, Love Letters, and Social Change in Nepal*. Michigan: University of Michigan Press.

———2001b. Language and Agency', *Annual Review of Anthropology*, 30: 109–37.

———2004. Literacy, Power, and Agency: Love Letters and Development in Nepal', *Language and Education*, 18 (4): 305–16.

Ahmad, Aijaz. 1993. Fascism and National Culture: Reading Gramsci in the Days of Hindutva', *Social Scientist*, (238–39): 32–68.

Ahmed, Akbar S. 1992. Bombay Films: The Cinema as Metaphor for Indian Society and Politics', *Modern Asian Studies*, 26 (2): 289–320.

Ali, Daud. 2006. Courtly Love and the Aristocratic Household in Early Medieval India', in F. Orsini (ed.), *Love in South Asia: A Cultural History*, pp. 43–60. Cambridge: Cambridge University Press.

Ali, Tariq. 1985. *The Nehrus and the Gandhis: An Indian Dynasty*. London: Pan Books.

Alter, Joseph. 1996. The Celibate Wrestler: Sexual Chaos, Embodied Balance and Competitive Politics in North India', in P. Uberoi (ed.), *Social Reform, Sexuality and the State*, pp. 109–31. New Delhi: Sage Publications.

Anderson, Benedict. [1983]1991. *Imagined Communities: Reflections on the Origins and Spread of Nationalism*. London: Verso.

Anitha, S., Manisha, Vasudha, Kavitha. 1996. Interviews with Women', in T. Sarkar and U. Butalia (eds), *Women and the Hindu Right: A Collection of Essays*, pp. 329–35. New Delhi: Kali for Women.

Asad, Talal. 2003. *Formations of the Secular: Christianity, Islam, Modernity*. Stanford: Stanford University Press.

Bastavala, D. 1922. *Prince, Pylons and Patrols*. Bombay: Tata Publicity Corp.

Basu, Monmayee. 2001. *Hindu Women and Marriage Law: From Sacrament to Contract*. New Delhi: Oxford University Press.

Bauman, Gerd. 1995. Managing a Polyethnic Milieu: Kinship and Interaction in a London Suburb', *Journal of the Royal Anthropological Institute*, (N.S.) 1: 725–41.

Bauman, Gerd. 1996. *Contesting Culture: Discourses of Identity in Multi-Ethnic London*. Cambridge Studies in Social and Cultural Anthropology. Cambridge: Cambridge University Press.

Bayly, Christopher. 1991. Maine and Change in Nineteenth-Century India', in A. Diamond (ed.), *The Victorian Achievement of Sir Henry Maine: A Centennial Reappraisal*, pp. 389–97. Cambridge: Cambridge University Press.

———. 1998 [1983]   *Rulers, Townsmen and Bazaars: North Indian Society in the Age of British Expansion 1770–1870*. New Delhi: Oxford University Press.

Bayly, Susan. 1999. *Caste, Society and Politics in India from the Eighteenth Century to the Modern Age*. Cambridge: Cambridge University Press.

Bennett, Lynn. 1983. *Dangerous Wives and Sacred Sisters: Social and Symbolic Roles of High-Caste Women in Nepal*. New York: Columbia University Press.

Béteille, André 1997. Caste in Contemporary India', in Chris Fuller (ed.), *Caste Today: SOAS Studies on South Asia*. New Delhi: Oxford University Press.

———. 1991a. Individualism and Equality', *Society and Politics in India: Essays in a Comparative Perspective*, LSE Monographs on Social Anthropology, (63): 215–49. London: The Athlone Press.

———. 1991b. Individual and Person as Subjects for Sociology', in *Society and Politics in India: Essays in a Comparative Perspective*, LSE Monographs on Social Anthropology, (63): 250–75. London: The Athlone Press.

Boissevain, Jeremy. 1968. The Place of Non-Groups in the Social Sciences', *Man: The Journal of the Royal Anthropological Institute*, 3 (4): 542–56.

Bourdieu, Pierre. 1977. *Outline of a Theory of Practice*. Cambridge: Cambridge University Press.

———. 1990.   *In Other Words*. Oxford: Polity Press.

Brass, Paul. 1997. *Theft of an Idol: Text and Context in the Representation of Collective Violence*. Princeton: Princeton University Press.

Brukman, Jan. 1974. Stealing Women among the Koya of South India', in *Anthropological Quarterly*, Kidnapping and Elopement as Alternative Systems of Marriage (Special Issue), 47 (3): 304–13.

Bunsha, Dionne. 2006. 'A Serial Kidnapper and his Mission', *Frontline*, 16–29 December, 23 (25).

Butalia, Urvashi. 1998. *The Other Side of Silence: Voices from the Partition of India*. New Delhi: Viking, Penguin.

Carroll, Lucy. 1991. Daughter's Right of Inheritance in India: A Perspective on the Problem of Dowry', *Modern Asian Studies*, 25 (4): 791–809.

Chadwick, O. 1975. *The Secularisation of the European Mind in the Nineteenth Century*. Cambridge: Cambridge University Press.

Chakravarti, Uma. 1989. Whatever Happened to the Vedic Dasi? Orientalism, Nationalism and a Script for the Past', in K. Sangari and S. Vaid (eds), *Recasting Women: Essays in Colonial History*, pp. 27–87. New Delhi: Kali for Women.

Chakravarti, Uma. 1996. Wifehood, Widowhood and Adultery: Female Sexuality, Surveillance and the State in Eighteenth Century Maharashtra', in P. Uberoi (ed.), *Social Reform, Sexuality and the State: Contributions to Indian Sociology, Occasional Studies 7*, pp. 3–21. New Delhi: Sage Publications.

—1998. *Rewriting History: The Life and Times of Pandita Ramabai*. New Delhi: Kali for Women.

Chandra, Sudhir. 1998. *Enslaved Daughters: Colonialism, Law and Women's Rights*. New Delhi: Oxford University Press.

Chatterjee, Partha. 1989. The Nationalist Resolution of the Women's Qestion', in K. Sangari and S. Vaid (eds), *Recasting Women: Essays in Colonial History*, pp. 233–53. New Delhi: Kali for Women.

Chekki, D. A. 1968. Mate Selection, Age at Marriage, and Propinquity among the Lingayats of India', *Journal of Marriage and the Family*, 30 (4): 707–11.

Chowdhry, Prem. 1996. Contesting Claims and Counter-Claims: Qestions of the Inheritance and Sexuality of Widows in a Colonial State', in P. Uberoi (ed.) *Social Reform, Sexuality and the State*, pp. 65–82. London: Sage Publications.

—1997. Enforcing Cultural Codes: Gender and Violence in Northern India', *Economic and Political Weekly*, May 10: 1019–28.

Cohen, Lawrence. 1997. Semen, Irony, and the Atom Bomb', *Medical Anthropology Quarterly*, New Series, 11 (3): 301–3.

Cohn, Bernard. 1987. *An Anthropologist among the Historians and Other Essays*. New Delhi: Oxford University Press.

Concerned Citizens Tribunal–Gujarat. 2002. *Crime Against Humanity: Volume I: An Inquiry into the Carnage in Gujarat, List of Incidents and Events*. Mumbai: Anil Dharkar (Citizens for Justice and Peace).

Corwin, Lauren A. 1977. Caste, Class and the Love-Marriage: Social Change in India', *Journal of Marriage and the Family*, 39 (4): 823–31.

Das, Veena. 1995. *Critical Events: An Anthropological Perspective on Contemporary India*. New Delhi: Oxford University Press.

—1997. Masks and Faces: An Essay on Punjabi Kinship', in P. Uberoi (ed.), *Family, Kinship and Marriage in India*, pp. 198–222. New Delhi: Oxford University Press.

—2004. The Signature of the State: The Paradox of Illegibility', in V. Das and D. Poole (eds), *Anthropology in the Margins of the State*, pp. 225–52. Oxford: James Currey.

—2006. Secularism and the Argument from Nature', in David Scott and Charles Hirschkind (eds), *Powers of the Secular Modern: Talal Asad and his Interlocuters*. Stanford: Stanford University Press.

Das, Veena and Deborah Poole (eds). 2004. *Anthropology in the Margins of the State*. Oxford: James Currey.

Dalmia, Vasudha. 2006. The Spaces of Love and the Passing of the Seasons: Delhi in the Early Twentieth Century', in F. Orsini (ed.), *Love in South Asia: A Cultural History*, pp. 183–207. Cambridge: Cambridge University Press.

Datta, Pati B., S. Sarkar, T. Sarkar, S. Sen. 1990. Understanding Communal Violence: Nizamuddin Riots', *Economic and Political Weekly*, Nov. 10: 2487–95.

Derné Steve. 1995. *Culture in Action: Family Life, Emotion and Male Dominance in Banaras, India*. New York: State University of New York Press.

———. 2003. Culture, Family Structure, and Psyche in Hindu India: The Fit"and the Inconsistencies", in D. Sharma (ed.), *Childhood, Family, and Sociocultural Change in India: Reinterpreting the Inner World*. New Delhi: Oxford University Press.

Derrett, J. D. M. 1959. Sir Henry Maine and Law in India: 1858–1958', *Juridical Review*, April: 40–55.

———. 1978. Minority in the Indian Subcontinent', in *Classical and Modern Hindu Law; Vol. IV: Current Problems and the Legacy of the Past*, pp. 292–355. Leiden: E. J. Brill.

Dhanda, Amita. 1996. Insanity, Gender and the Law', in P. Uberoi (ed.), *Social Reform, Sexuality and the State: Contributions to Indian Sociology, Occasional Studies 7*, pp. 347–67. New Delhi: Sage Publications.

Dhanva, Alok. 1998. Bhagi Huin Larkiyan', in *Duniya Roz Banti Hai*, pp. 41–46. New Delhi: Rajkamal Prakashan.

Donner, Henrike. 2002. One's Own Marriage:' Love Marriages in a Calcutta Neighbourhood', *South Asia Research*, 22 (1): 79–94.

Dube, Leela. 1996. Caste and Women', in M. N. Srinivas (ed.), *Caste: Its Twentieth Century Avatar*, pp. 1–27. New Delhi: Penguin.

Dumont, Louis. 1961. Marriage in India: The Present State of the Question I: Marriage Alliances in South-East India and Ceylon', *Contributions to Indian Sociology*, (V): 75–95.

———. 1964. Marriage in India: The Present State of the Question. Postscript to Part I', *Contributions to Indian Sociology*, (VII): 77–98.

———. 1966. Marriage in India: The Present State of the Question. III: North India in Relation to South India', *Contributions to Indian Sociology*, (IX): 90–114.

———. 1998 [1970] *Homo Hierarchicus: The Caste System and Its Implications*. New Delhi: Oxford University Press.

Dwyer, Rachel. 2000. *All You Need is Money, All You Want is Love: Sex and Romance in Modern India*. London: Cassell.

Eickelman, Dale and Armando Salvatore (eds). 2004. *Public Islam and the Common Good*. Leiden: Brill.

Elwin, Verrier. 1992 [1958] *Leaves from the Jungle: Life in a Gond Village*. New Delhi: Oxford University Press.

Elwin, Verrier. 1950. *Maria Murder and Suicide*. London: Oxford University Press.

———1948. *The Muria and their Ghotul*. Bombay: Oxford University Press.

Engels, Dagmar. 1990. History and Sexuality in India: Discursive Trends', *Trends in History*, 4: 15–42.

———1996. *Beyond Purdah?: Women in Bengal 1890–1939*. New Delhi: Oxford University Press.

Forbes, Geraldine. 1979. Women and Modernity: The Issue of Child Marriage in India', *Women's Studies International Quarterly*, 2: 407–19.

Foucault, Michel. 1981. *The Will to Knowledge: The History of Sexuality: 1*. Trans. R. Hurley. London: Penguin.

Freed, Ruth S. 1971. The Legal Process in a Village in North India', *Transactions of the New York Academy of Sciences*, 2nd series, 33: 423–35.

Freitag, Sandra. 1989. *Collective Action and Community: Public Arenas and the Emergence of Communalism in North India*. Berkeley: University of California Press.

Fruzzetti, Lina M. 1982. *The Gift of a Virgin: Women, Marriage and Ritual in a Bengali Society*. Oxford: Oxford University Press.

Fuller, Chris (ed.). 1997. *Caste Today: SOAS Studies on South Asia*. New Delhi: Oxford University Press.

Fuller, Christopher, J. 1992. *The Camphor Flame: Popular Hinduism and Society in India*. New Jersey: Princeton University Press.

———1976. Kerala Christians and the Caste System', *Man: New Series*, 11 (1): 53–70.

Fuller, C. and V. Benei (eds). 2001. *The Everyday State and Society in Modern India*. London: Hurst and Company.

Fuller, Christopher and J. Harris. 2000. For an Anthropology of the Modern Indian State', in C. J. Fuller and V. Benei (eds), *The Everyday State and Society in Modern India*, pp. 1–31. New Delhi: Social Science Press.

Gell, Alfred. [1996] Love', Unpublished article.

———1996. 'Amour, Connaissance et Dissimulation', *Terrain: Revue d'ethnologie de l'Europe*, Sep. (27). Trans. Catherine Rouslin.

———1998. *Art and Agency: An Anthropological Theory*. Oxford: Clarendon Press.

Gell, Man Singh Simeran. 1993. *The Ghotul in Muria Society*. Philadelphia: Harwood Academic.

———1994. Legality and Ethnicity: Marriage among the South Asians of Bedford', *Critique of Anthropology*, 14 (4): 355–92. London: Sage Publications.

———1996. The Gatekeepers of Multiculturalism: A Response to Pnina Werbner', *Critique of Anthropology*, 16 (3): 325–35. London: Sage Publications.

Giddens, Anthony. 1992. *The Transformation of Intimacy: Sexuality, Love and Eroticism in Modern Societies*. Cambridge: Polity Press.

Gore, M. S. 1968. *Urbanisation and Family Change*. Bombay: Popular Prakashan.

Government of India. 1974. *Law Commission of India, Fifty-Ninth Report on Hindu Marriage Act, 1955 and Special Marriage Act, 1954*. New Delhi: Government of India.

Gupta, Akhil. 1995. Blurred Boundaries: The Discourse of Corruption, the Culture of Politics and the Imagined State', *American Ethnologist*, 22: 375–402.

Gupta, Charu. 2002. (Im)possible Love and Sexual Pleasure in Late-Colonial North India', *Modern Asian Studies*, 36 (1): 195–221.

Gupta, Narayani. 1986. Delhi and its Hinterland: The Nineteenth and Early Twentieth Centuries', in R. E. Frykenberg, (ed.), *Delhi Through the Ages: Essays in Urban History, Culture and Society*, pp. 250–69. New Delhi: Oxford University Press.

——1998. *Delhi between Two Empires, 1803–1931: Society, Government and Urban Growth*. Oxford: Oxford University Press.

Hansen, Thomas Blom. 1999. *The Saffron Wave: Democracy and Hindu Nationalism in Modern India*. Princeton: Princeton University Press.

Hare, Ivan. 1997. Legislating against HateThe Legal Response to Bias Crimes', *Oxford Journal of Legal Studies*, 17: 415–39.

Harlan, Lindsey. 1995. 'Abandoning Shame: Mira and the Margins of Marriage', in L. Harlan and P. Courtright (eds), *From the Margins of Hindu Marriage: Essays on Gender, Religion and Culture*, pp. 204–27. Oxford: Oxford University Press.

Harlan, Lindsey and Paul Courtright (eds). 1995. *From the Margins of Hindu Marriage: Essays on Gender, Religion and Culture*. Oxford: Oxford University Press.

Harris, Olivia (ed.). 1996. *Inside and Outside the Law: Anthropological Studies of Authority and Ambiguity*. London: Routledge.

Hashish, Shereen, A. A. 1999. Computer *Khatbas*: Databases and Marital Entrepreneurship in Modern Cairo', *Anthropology Today*, 15 (6): 7–11.

Hess, Linda. 1999. Rejecting Sita: Indian Responses to the Ideal Man's Cruel Treatment of His Ideal Wife', *Journal of the American Academy of Religion*, 67 (1): 1–32.

Hingorani, A. T. (ed.). 1966. *To the Perplexed by M. K. Gandhi*. Bombay: Pearl Publications.

Jaffrelot, Christophe. 1995. The Idea of the Hindu Race in the Writings of Hindu Nationalist Ideologues in the 1920s and 1930s: A Concept Between Two Cultures', in P. Robb (ed.), *The Concept of Race in South Asia*. Oxford: Oxford University Press.

——1996. *The Hindu Nationalist Movement and Indian Politics: 1925 to the 1990s*. London: C. Hurst and Company.

Jain, M. P. 1972. *Outlines of Indian Legal History*. Bombay: N. M. Tripathi Pvt. Ltd.

Jaiswal, Suvira. 1993. Historical Evolution of the Ram Legend', *Social Scientist*, 21 (3–4): 89–97.

Jauregui, B. and T. McGuinness. 2003. Inter-community Marriage and Social Change in Contemporary India: Hybridity, Selectivity and Transnational Flows', *South Asia; Journal of South Asian Studies*, 26 (1): 71–85.

Jayawardena, Kumari and Malthi de Alwis (eds). 1996. *Embodied Violence: Communalising Women's Sexuality in South Asia*. London: Zd Books.

Jeffery, Patricia. 1979. *Frogs in a Well*. London: Zd Press.

—1999. 'Agency, Activism and Agendas', in P. Jeffery and A. Basu (eds), *Resisting the Sacred and the Secular*, pp. 221–43. New Delhi: Kali for Women.

Jeffery, Patricia and Amrita Basu (eds). 1999. *Resisting the Sacred and the Secular: Women's Activism and Politicised Religion in South Asia*. New Delhi: Kali for Women.

Jeffery, Patricia and Roger Jeffery. 1996. *Don't Marry Me to a Plowman: Women's Everyday Lives in Rural North India*. Oxford: Westview Press.

Jha, A. 1979. *Sexual Designs in Indian Culture*. Delhi: Vikas Publishing House.

John, Mary E. and Janaki Nair (eds). 1998. *A Question of Silence: The Sexual Economies of Modern India*. New Delhi: Kali for Women.

Jones, Kenneth W. 1986. Organised Hinduism in Delhi and New Delhi', in R. E. Frykenberg (ed.), *Delhi Through the Ages: Essays in Urban History, Culture and Society*, pp. 332–50. New Delhi: Oxford University Press.

—1989 [1976] *Arya Dharm: Hindu Consciousness in Nineteenth Century Punjab*. New Delhi: Manohar.

—1990. Communalism in the Punjab: The Arya Samaj Contribution', in T. Metcalf (ed.), *Modern India: An Interpretive Anthology*, pp. 261–77. New Delhi: Sterling Publishers.

Kakar, Sudhir. 1989. *Intimate Relations: Exploring Indian Sexuality*. New Delhi: Penguin.

Kakar, Sudhir and John M. Ross. 1995. *Tales of Love, Sex and Danger*. New Delhi: Oxford University Press.

Kannan, C. T. 1963. *Intercaste and Inter-community Marriages in India*. Bombay: Allied Publishers.

Kapur, Ratna (ed.). 1996. *Feminist Terrains in Legal Domains: Inter-disciplinary Essays on Women and Law in India*. New Delhi: Kali for Women.

Karlekar, Malavika. 1996. Reflections on Kulin Polygamy: Nistarini Debi's Sekeley Katha', in P. Uberoi (ed.), *Social Reform, Sexuality and the State*. New Delhi: Sage Publications.

Kelly, John, D. 1990. Discourse about Sexuality and the End of Indenture in Fiji: The Making of Counter-Hegemonic Discourse', *History and Anthropology*, 5: 19–61.

Khilnani, Sunil. 1997. *The Idea of India*. New Delhi: Penguin.

Kidder, Robert. 1973. Courts and Confl ict in an Indian City: A Study in Legal Impact', *Journal of Commonwealth Political Studies*, 11 (2): 121–39.

Kishwar, Madhu. 1997. Yes to Sita, No to Ram: The Continuing Popularity of Sita in India', *Manushi*, 98 (Jan–Feb): 20–31.

Kolenda, Pauline. 1990. Untouchable Chuhras through their Humor: Equalising'Marital Kin through Teasing, Pretence, and Farce', in O. M. Lynch (ed.), *Divine Passions: The Social Construction of Emotions in India*, pp. 116–53. Oxford: University of California Press.

Kopf, David. 1979. *The Brahmo Samaj and the Shaping of the Modern Indian Mind*. New Jersey: Princeton University Press.

Kumar, Nita. 1988. *The Artisans of Banaras: Popular Culture and Identity, 1880–1986*. Princeton: Princeton University Press.

——1992. *Friends, Brothers and Informants: Fieldwork Memoirs of Banaras*. Berkeley: University of California Press.

Kumar, Radha. 1993. *The History of Doing: An Illustrated Account of Movements for Women's Rights and Feminism in India, 1800–1990*. New Delhi: Kali For Women.

Lewis, Oscar. 1958. *Village Life in Northern India: Studies in a Delhi Village*. New York: Vintage Books.

Lindholm, Charles. 1982. *Generosity and Jealousy: The Swat Pakhtun of Northern Pakistan*. New York: Columbia University Press.

Luhmann, Niklas. 1986. *Love as Passion: The Codification of Intimacy*. Cambridge: Polity Press.

Macfarlane, Alan. 1991. Some Contributions of Maine to History and Anthropology', in A. Diamond (ed.), *The Victorian Achievement of Sir Henry Maine: A Centennial Reappraisal*, pp. 111–42. Cambridge: Cambridge University Press.

——1986. *Marriage and Love in England: Modes of Reproduction, 1300–1840*. Oxford: Basil Blackwell.

Madan, T. N. 1993. Whither Indian Secularism', *Modern Asian Studies*, 27 (3): 667–97.

Mahmood, Tahir. 1978. *Civil Marriage Law Perspectives and Prospects*. New Delhi: Indian Law Institute.

Majeed, J. 1994. Review of in Theory: Classes, Nations, Literature by A. Ahmed', *Modern Asian Studies*, 28 (1): 217–21.

Mandelbaum, David G. 1989. Sex Roles and Gender Relations in North India', in C. M. Borden (ed.), *Contemporary Indian Tradition: Voices on Culture, Nature and the Challenge of Change*, pp. 221–37. London: Smithsonian Institute Press.

——1993. *Women's Seclusion and Men's Honour: Sex Roles in North India, Bangladesh and Pakistan*. London: University of Arizona Press.

Mani, Lata. 1989. Contentious Traditions: The Debate on *Sati* in Colonial India', in K. Sangari and S. Vaid, *Recasting Women: Essays in Colonial History*, pp. 88–126. New Delhi: Kali for Women.

Mankekar, Purnima. 1993. National Texts and Gendered Lives: An Ethnography of Television Viewers in a North Indian City', *American Ethnologist*, 20 (3): 543–63.

Marriot, McKim. 1976. Hindu Transactions: Diversity without Dualism', in B. Kapferer (ed.), *Transaction and Meaning: Directions in the Anthropology of Exchange and Symbolic Behaviour*. Philadelphia: ISHI Publications.

Marsden, Magnus. 2005. *Living Islam: Muslim Religious Experience in Pakistan's North–West Frontier*. Cambridge: Cambridge University Press.

Mayaram, Shail. 1996. Speech, Silence, and the Making of Partition Violence in Mewat', in S. Amin and D. Chakrabarty (eds), *Subaltern Studies IX: Writing on South Asian History and Society*, pp. 126–64. New Delhi: Oxford University Press.

Mazumdar, S. 1995. Women on the March: Right-Wing Mobilization in Contemporary India', *Feminist Review*, (49): 1–28.

McGregor, Ronald Stuart. 1997. *The Oxford Hindi–English Dictionary*. New Delhi: Oxford University Press.

Meisami, Scott Julie. 1987. *Medieval Persian Courtly Poetry*. Princeton: Princeton University Press.

Mendelsohn, Oliver. 1981. The Pathology of the Indian Legal System', *Modern Asian Studies*, 15 (4): 823–63.

Menon, Nivedita. 2000. Embodying the Self: Feminism, Sexual Violence and the Law', in P. Chaterjee and P. Jeganathan (eds), *Subaltern Studies XI*. Delhi: Permanent Black.

Menon, Ritu. 1999. Reproducing the Legitimate Community: Secularity, Sexuality, and the State in Postpartition India', in P. Jeffery and A. Basu (eds), *Resisting the Sacred and the Secular: Women's Activism and Politicised Religion in South Asia*, pp. 15–32. New Delhi: Kali for Women.

Menon, Ritu and Kamla Bhasin. 1998. *Borders and Boundaries: Women in India's Partition*. New Delhi: Kali for Women.

Miller, Barbara Stoler. 1977. *Love Song of the Dark Lord: Jayadeva's Gitagovinda*. New York: Columbia University Press.

Mines, Mattison. 1998. Hindus at the Edge: Self-Awareness among Adult Children of Interfaith Marriages in Chennai, South India', *International Journal of Hindu Studies*, 2 (2): 223–48.

———1992. Individuality and Achievement in South Indian Social History', *Modern Asian Studies*, 26 (1): 129–56.

———1972. Muslim Stratification in India: The Basis for Variation', *Southwestern Journal of Anthropology*, 28 (4): 333–49.

Minturn, Leigh. 1993. *Sita's Daughters: Coming out of Purdah, The Rajput Women of Khalapur Revisited*. Oxford: Oxford University Press.

Mody, Perveez. 2002. Love and the Law: Love-Marriage in Delhi', *Modern Asian Studies*, 36 (1): 223–56.

———2006. Kidnapping, Elopement and Abduction: An Ethnography of Love-Marriage in Delhi', in F. Orsini (ed.), *Love in South Asia: A Cultural History*, pp. 331–44. Cambridge: Cambridge University Press.

Mukhia, Harbans. 1999. The Celebration of Failure as Dissent in Urdu Ghazal', *Modern Asian Studies*, 33 (4): 861–81.

Nandy, Ashis. 1990. The Politics of Secularism and the Recovery of Religious Tolerance', in V. Das (ed.), *Mirrors of Violence: Communities, Riots, and Survivors in South Asia*, pp. 69–93. New Delhi: Oxford University Press.

National Human Rights Commission (NHRC), India. n. d. *The Protection of Human Rights Act 1993 with Procedural Regulations*. Delhi: NHRC

Navaro-Yashin, Yael. 2002. *Faces of the State: Secularism and Public Life in Turkey*. Princeton: Princeton University Press.

Nicholas, Ralph W. 1995. The Effectiveness of the Hindu Sacrament (*Samskara*): Caste, Marriage, and Divorce in Bengali Culture', in L. Harlan, and P. Courtright (eds), *From the Margins of Hindu Marriage: Essays on Gender, Religion and Culture*, pp. 137–59. Oxford: Oxford University Press.

Nizami. 1997. *Layla and Majnu*. Prose Adaptation by Colin Turner. New Delhi: Blue Jay Books.

O'Hanlon, Rosalind. 1991. Issues of Widowhood: Gender and Resistance in Colonial Western India', in Douglas Haynes and Gyan Prakash (eds), *Resistance and Everyday Social Relations in South Asia*, pp. 62–108. New Delhi: Oxford University Press.

Orsini, Francesca. 2002. *Hindu Public Sphere 1920–1940: Language and Literature in the Age of Nationalism*. Oxford: Oxford University Press.

Parry, Jonathan, P. 1979. *Caste and Kinship in Kangra*. London: Routledge and Kegan Paul.

———.1999. Lords of Labour: Working and Shirking in Bhilai', *Contributions to Indian Sociology*, 33 (1–2): 107–40.

———.2001. 'Ankalu's Errant Wife: Sex, Marriage and Industry in Contemporary Chhatisgarh', *Modern Asian Studies*, 35 (4): 783–820.

Pathak, Zkia and Sunder Rajan Rajeswari. 1989. Shahabano', in J. Butler and J. Scott (eds), *Feminists Theorize the Political*, pp. 257–79. New York: Routledge.

Poonacha, Veena. 1996. Redefining Gender Relations: The Imprint of the Colonial State on the Coorg/Kodava Norms of Marriage and Sexuality', in P. Uberoi (ed.), *Social Reform, Sexuality and the State*, pp. 39–64. London: Sage Publications.

Povinelli, Elizabeth. 2002. *The Cunning of Recognition: Indigenous Alterities and the Making of Australian Multiculturalism*. Durham: Duke University.

Prinjha, Suman. [1999] *With a View to Marriage: Young Hindu Gujaratis in London*. Unpublished Ph.D. dissertation, London School of Economics and Political Science.

Prior, Katherine. 1993. Making History: The State's Intervention in Urban Religious Disputes in the North-Western Provinces in the Early Nineteenth Century', *Modern Asian Studies*, 27 (1): 179–203.

Raheja, Gloria Goodwin. 1994. On the Uses of Subversion: Redefi ning Conjugality', in G. G. Raheja and A. G. Gold (eds), *Listen to the Heron's Words: Reimagining Gender and Kinship in North India*, pp. 121–48. New Delhi: Oxford University Press.

Raheja, Gloria Goodwin and Ann Grodzins Gold (eds). 1994. *Listen to the Heron's Words: Reimagining Gender and Kinship in North India*. Oxford University Press: New Delhi.

Rajadyaksha, Ashish and Paul Willemen. 1999. *Encyclopaedia of Indian Cinema*. New Delhi: Oxford University Press.

Rajagopal, Ryali. 1998. Matrimonials: A Variation of Arranged Marriages', *International Journal of Hindu Studies*, 2 (1): 107–15.

Rege, Sharmila. 1996. The Hegemonic Appropriation of Sexuality: The Case of the *Lavani* Performers of Maharashtra', in P. Uberoi (ed.), *Social Reform, Sexuality and the State: Contributions to Indian Sociology*, pp. 23–38. New Delhi: Sage Publications.

Roadarmel, Gordon C. (ed.). 1972. *A Death in Delhi: Modern Hindi Short Stories*. UNESCO Collection of Representative Works, Indian Series. Berkeley: University of California Press.

Rowe, W. L. 1960. The Marriage Network and Structural Change in a North Indian Community', *Southwestern Journal of Anthropology*, 16 (3): 299–311.

Sarkar, Tanika. 1993. Rhetoric against Age of Consent: Resisting Colonial Reason and Death of a Child-Wife', *Economic and Political Weekly*, 27 (36): 1869–78.

———. 1999. Women, Community, and Nation: A Historical Trajectory for Hindu Identity Politics', in P. Jeffery and A. Basu (eds.), *Resisting the Sacred and the Secular: Women's Activism and Politicised Religion in South Asia*, pp. 89–104. New Delhi: Kali for Women.

Sarkar, Tanika and Urvashi Butalia (eds). 1996. *Women and the Hindu Right: A Collection of Essays*. New Delhi: Kali for Women.

Satchidananda, K. (ed.). 1993. Run-Away Girls' by Alok Dhanwa. Trans. B. K. Paul and Roma Paul, *Indian Literature*, No. 153, XXVI (1): 83–87.

Scott, David and Charles Hirschkind (eds). 2006. *Powers of the Secular Modern: Talal Asad and his Interlocuters*. Stanford: Stanford University Press.

Sen, Amiya. 1980. Hindu Revivalism in Action—The Age of Consent Bill Agitation in Bengal', *The Indian Historical Review*, 7: 160–84.

Shukla, Shrilal. 1993. *Raag Darbari: A Novel*. Trans. (from Hindi) Gillian Wright. New Delhi: Penguin.

Singh, Amita Tyagi and Patricia Uberoi. 1994. Learning to 'Adjust!' Conjugal Relations in Indian Popular Fiction', *Indian Journal of Gender Studies*, 1 (1): 91–120.

Singh, K. S. (ed.). 1996. *People of India, Vol. XX, Delhi: Anthropological Survey of India*. Delhi: Manohar.

Singha, Radhika. 1993. Providential 'Circumstances: The   *Thugee* Campaign of the 1830's and Legal Innovation', *Modern Asian Studies*, 27 (1): 83–146.

Som, Reba. 1994. Jawaharlal Nehru and the Hindu Code: A Victory of Symbol over Substance?, *Modern Asian Studies*, 28 (1): 165–94.

Spear, Percival. [1943]1997. *Delhi: Its Monuments and History*. New Delhi: Oxford University Press.

——1986. Delhi: The Stop-Go' Capital: A Summation', in R. E. Frykenberg (ed.), *Delhi Through the Ages: Essays in Urban History, Culture and Society*, pp. 463–79. New Delhi: Oxford University Press.

Spencer, Jonathon. 1990. Collective Violence and Everyday Practice in Sri Lanka', *Modern Asian Studies*, 24 (3): 603–23.

Srinivas, M. N. 1952. *Religion and Society among the Coorgs of South India*. Oxford: Clarendon Press.

——1962.   *Caste in Modern India*. Bombay: Asia Publishing House.

——1966. Sanskritization', in   *Social Change in Modern India*, pp. 6–45. Berkeley: University of California Press.

——1996.   *Caste: Its Twentieth Century Avatar*. New Delhi: Penguin.

Strathern, Marilyn. 1988. *The Gender of the Gift: Problems with Women and Problems with Society in Melanesia*. London: University of California Press.

——2005.   *Kinship, Law and the Unexpected: Relatives are Always a Surprise*. Cambridge: Cambridge University Press.

——(ed.) 1987.   *Dealing with Inequality: Analysing Gender Relations in Melanesia and Beyond*. Cambridge: Cambridge University Press.

Tambiah, Stanley. 1975 [1973] From Varna to Caste through Mixed Unions', in J. Goody (ed.), *The Character of Kinship*, pp 191–229. Cambridge: Cambridge University Press.

Tarlo, Emma. 2000. Welcome to History: A Resettlement Colony in the Making', in V. Dupont, E. Tarlo and D. Vidal (eds), *Delhi: Urban Space and Human Destiny*, pp. 51–73. Delhi: Manohar.

Thadani, Giti. 1996. *Sakhiyani: Lesbian Desire in Ancient and Modern India*. London: Cassell.

Thapar, Romila. 1969. *A History of India: Volume I*. London: Pelican.

Tharu, Susie and Tejaswini Niranjana. 1996. Problems for a Contemporary Theory of Gender', in D. Chakrabarty (ed.), *Subaltern Studies IX*, pp. 231–60. New Delhi: Oxford University Press.

Therborn, Göran. 2004.   *Between Sex and Power: Family in the World, 1900–2000*. London: Routledge.

Tokita-Tanabe, Yumiko. 1999. Women and Tradition in India: Construction of Subjectivity and Control of Female Sexuality in the Ritual of First Menstruation', in M. Tanaka and M. Tachinawa (eds), *Living with Sakti:*

Gender, Sexuality and Religion in South Asia, Seri Ethnological Studies No. 50. Osaka: National Museum of Ethnology.

Trawick, Margaret. 1992. *Notes on Love in a Tamil Family*. Berkeley: University of California Press.

Uberoi, Patricia. 2006. *Freedom and Destiny: Gender, Family, and Popular Culture in India*. New Delhi: Oxford University Press.

⸻ 1998. The Diaspora Comes Home: Disciplining Desire in *DDLJ*', *Contributions to Indian Sociology*, 32 (2): 305–36.

⸻ 1997. *Family, Kinship and Marriage in India*. Oxford University Press: New Delhi.

⸻ 1996. When is a Marriage not a Marriage? Sex, Sacrament and Contract in Hindu Marriage', in P. Uberoi (ed.), *Social Reform, Sexuality and the State*, pp. 319–45. New Delhi: Sage Publications.

Uberoi, P. and A. Tyagi Singh. 2006. Learning to 'Adjust!' The Dynamics of Post-Marital Romance', in *Freedom and Destiny: Gender, Family, and Popular Culture in India*, pp. 217–47. New Delhi: Oxford University Press.

Upadhyaya, P. C. 1992. The Politics of Indian Secularism', *Modern Asian Studies*, 26 (4): 815–53.

Vanita, Ruth and Saleem Kidwai (eds). 2001. *Same-Sex Love in India: Readings from Literature and History*. Delhi: Macmillan India.

Vasudevan, Ravi. 1996. You Cannot Live in Society and Ignore It!' Nationhood and Female Modernity in *Andaz*', in P. Uberoi (ed.), *Social Reform, Sexuality and the State*, pp. 82–108. New Delhi: Sage Publications.

Veer, Peter van der. 1994. *Religious Nationalism: Hindus and Muslims in India*. Berkeley: University of California Press.

Verma, Nirmal. 1971 [1965] ' Lovers', in *Jalti Jhari*. Delhi: Rajkamal Prakashan.

Viswanathan, G. 1996. Ethnographic Politics and the Discourse of Origins', in S. Mahmood and N. Reynolds (eds), *Religious Disciplines and Structures of Modernity*, Stanford Electronic Humanities Review (SEHR), *Contested Polities*, 5 (1).

⸻ 1998. *Outside the Fold: Conversion, Modernity, and Belief*. New Jersey: Princeton University Press.

Vitebsky, Piers. 1993. *Dialogues with the Dead*. Cambridge: Cambridge University Press.

Wadley, Susan Snow. 1975. *Shakti: Power in the Conceptual Structure of Karimpur Religion*. Chicago: University of Chicago.

⸻ 1994. *Struggling with Destiny in Karimpur 1925–1984*. London: University of California Press.

Warner, Michael. 2002. *Publics and Counterpublics*. New York: Zone Books.

Washbrook, David A. 1981. Law, State and Agrarian Society in Colonial India', *Modern Asian Studies*, 15 (3): 649–721.

Werbner, Pnina. 1990. *The Migration Process: Capital, Gifts and Offerings among British Pakistanis*. Oxford: Berg.

—1995. Commentary: Critique or Caricature? A Response to Wilcken and Gell', *Critique of Anthropology*, 15 (4): 425–32.

Index